Asylum Seeking and the Global City

Asylum seeking and the global city are two major contemporary subjects of analysis to emerge both in the literature and in public and official discourses on human rights, urban socioeconomic change and national security. Based on extensive, original ethnographic research, this book examines the situation of asylum seekers in Hong Kong and offers a narrative of their experiences related to internal and external borders, the performance of border crossing and asylum politics in the context of the global city.

Hong Kong is a city with no comprehensive legislation covering refugee claims, and official and public opinion is dominated by the view that the city would be flooded with illegal economic migrants were policy changes to be implemented. This book considers why Hong Kong has become a destination for asylum seekers, how asylum seekers integrate into local and global economic markets and why the illegalization of asylum seekers plays a significant role in the processes of global city formation.

This book will be essential reading for academics and students involved in the study of migration, globalization and borders, research methods in criminology, social problems and urban sociology.

Francesco Vecchio is a postdoctoral research fellow at Charles Sturt University and collaborates with Fondazione ISMU and Hong Kong–based NGO Vision First. He develops research on mobility and borders with a focus on refugees. Vecchio completed his PhD in Criminology at Monash University and previously worked in the nonprofit sector. He completed his undergraduate studies in History at the University of Milan and obtained a Masters in Intercultural Studies from the University of Padua.

'*Asylum Seeking and the Global City* is an impressive ethnographic study of asylum seekers, their transnational networks and survival strategies in the informal economy of Hong Kong. Through his vivid and sensitive depictions of life on the margins, Francesco Vecchio provides a major analysis of the intersections of local and global forces and individual agency in irregular migration and the troubling consequences of contemporary migration control policies and practices. A must-read for all those who are interested in globalisation studies and the criminology of mobility.'

Professor Maggy Lee, Department of Sociology,
University of Hong Kong, Hong Kong

'The book *Asylum Seeking and the Global City* by Dr. Francesco Vecchio is an excellent work. The author relies on his substantial research in the field and previous experience as a NGO worker in Hong Kong to give a rich and thick description of the life of refugees and asylum seekers in that city, one of the best ethnographic accounts of life in Hong Kong. I was deeply impressed with the careful, detailed and thoughtful treatment that Dr. Vecchio gave to the rich empirical material he collected. I found particularly arresting the way in which he was able to show how the conditions and destiny of many migrants are the outcome of an almost heroic struggle between conditions outside of their control and their continuous striving to acquire a measure of power and control over their own lives and destiny. This very presence of "agency" in the migrants' lives – faced with often overarching economic and political forces – is perhaps the strongest impression with which the reader comes away from this book, where we find a wealth of empirical observation, mixed with very intelligent analysis, and a reflexive empathy for his subjects.'

Dario Melossi, Professor of Criminology,
University of Bologna, Italy

Asylum Seeking and the Global City

Francesco Vecchio

LONDON AND NEW YORK

First published 2015
by Routledge
2 Park Square, Milton Park, Abingdon, Oxfordshire OX14 4RN

and by Routledge
711 Third Avenue, New York, NY 10017

First issued in paperback 2016

Routledge is an imprint of the Taylor & Francis Group, an informa business

© 2015 Francesco Vecchio

The right of Francesco Vecchio to be identified as author of this work has been asserted by him in accordance with sections 77 and 78 of the Copyright, Designs and Patents Act 1988.

All rights reserved. No part of this book may be reprinted or reproduced or utilised in any form or by any electronic, mechanical, or other means, now known or hereafter invented, including photocopying and recording, or in any information storage or retrieval system, without permission in writing from the publishers.

British Library Cataloguing in Publication Data

A catalogue record for this book is available from the British Library

Library of Congress Cataloging-in-Publication Data

HV640.4.H85V43 2014
362.87095125—dc23
2014008547

ISBN 13: 978-1-138-68772-1 (pbk)
ISBN 13: 978-0-415-85875-5 (hbk)

Typeset in Times New Roman
by Apex CoVantage, LLC

Contents

List of tables and figures		vii
Acknowledgements		ix
Abbreviations		xi
	Introduction	1
1	The global city and asylum seeking	27
2	Global phenomena and local responses	64
3	Crossing borders into Hong Kong	103
4	Establishing life at the destination	139
5	Asylum seeker engagement with the informal economy	164
6	(Un)wanted people in the global city	194
	Index	225

Tables and figures

Tables

3.1	Entry method	104
3.2	Entry year per place of origin	105

Figures

3.1	Entry method per year	105
3.2	Facilitators of migration to Hong Kong	123

Acknowledgements

I would like to thank a small number of people for their invaluable support during the completion of this project, without whom this book would not have been feasible.

I am truly indebted to the refugee participants, who kindly shared their experiences with me and offered their time and support in allowing me into their world. Although I am prevented from naming them, I thank them sincerely. I would also like to extend my gratitude to the many people I encountered in Hong Kong, who courageously work in a very challenging field to advance the rights of those who might otherwise be denied any such rights. My thanks go to the dedicated staff and volunteers at different organizations, and in particular Vision First, Christian Action and the Vine. I would also like to thank Cosmo Beatson for the time he generously shared with me throughout the fieldwork and his contagious sense of resolve, which enormously benefited this project. In Hong Kong, I also thank Gordon Mathews and the participants in his weekly discussion group for asylum seekers and Kelley Loper for her kind assistance during the preparation of the fieldwork.

This book began as postgraduate research work. I was extremely lucky to land at Monash University, to which I owe my deepest gratitude for providing generous support and access to a rich and very diverse range of experts in the field who taught me a great deal. For their excellence as model mentors, intellectual insights and exceptional kindness, I am especially grateful to Sharon Pickering, Dharmalingam Arunachalam and Leanne Weber. My thanks also extend to Michael Janover, JaneMaree Maher, Susan Stevenson and the examiners of my thesis. At Charles Sturt University, I thank Alison Gerard for her inestimable professional assistance, and the School of Humanities and Social Sciences for generously facilitating the completion of this manuscript. I also thank Katja Franko Aas, Mary Bosworth and Sharon Pickering, editors of Routledge Studies in Criminal Justice, Borders and Citizenship, and Thomas Sutton and Heidi Lee at Routledge for their constructive feedback, gentle criticism and merciful patience.

I would also like to thank Stepworks (www.stepworks.com.hk) for creating the maps that feature at the front of this book.

x   *Acknowledgements*

This book would never have been as readable without the assistance of Julia Farrell, who provided expert and careful copyediting, for which I thank her. Finally, I thank my family for their infinite support.

Chapter 5 is partly based upon my article 'The Economy of Seeking Asylum in the Global City' (2013), *International Migration* by Wiley.

Abbreviations

CAT	Convention against Torture and Other Cruel, Inhuman or Degrading Treatment or Punishment
CIL	Customary international law
CSD	Census and Statistics Department
GDP	Gross domestic product
HKSAR	Hong Kong Special Administrative Region
ImmD	Immigration Department
ISS	International Social Service
LegCo	Legislative Council
NGO	Non-governmental organization
Refugee Convention	Convention Relating to the Status of Refugees
UK	United Kingdom
UNHCR	United Nations High Commissioner for Refugees
US	United States
USM	Unified screening mechanism

Currency converter

US$1 (United States dollar)	= HK$7.75 (Hong Kong dollar)
GB£1 (British pound)	= HK$12.92
1 euro	= HK$10.65

Source: www.xe.com (25 February 2014).

Maps

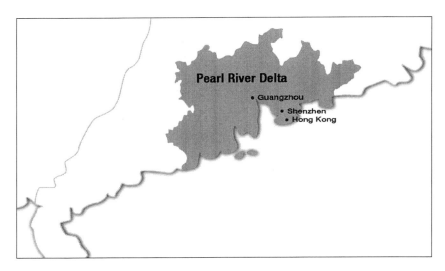

Map 1.1 China's south coast
Image courtesy of Stepworks (www.stepworks.com.hk).

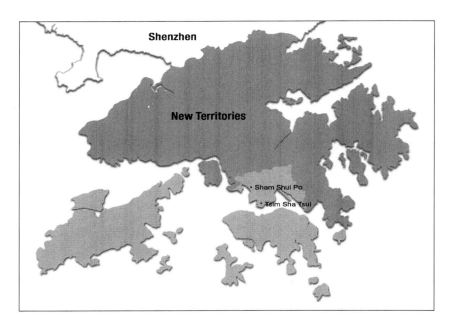

Map 1.2 Fieldwork locations in Hong Kong
Image courtesy of Stepworks (www.stepworks.com.hk).

Introduction

One day in 2006, a recently arrived South Asian man in his mid-sixties came to the offices of a Hong Kong–based non-governmental organization (NGO) that provides services for asylum seekers and introduced himself, wishing to enquire about his future options. 'I was managing a hotel in my country', he said. 'I used to welcome important people, many foreigners, even prime ministers and heads of state on official visits. And now, now I am here seeking asylum.' Tears began to wet his face. With pride, and as if to tie himself to a past that was no longer his, he gave me his business card, and not without some degree of embarrassment I gave him mine. 'Fate is sometimes cruel', he sobbed – a person spends a life forging a career, building a family, and then suddenly it can all change. I felt a deep sense of tenderness for this aging man who had lost so much. Though he feared for his life there, a few months later he decided to return to his home country. Life in Hong Kong – a wealthy global city and one of Asia's finest luxury and finance hubs – was simply too harsh for him. He had learnt that applications for asylum could remain undecided for years, and that the life he would live there would likely involve a great deal of waiting and suffering. He would be forced to live far from familiar places and loved ones, excluded from society as a dangerous social outcast, and dependent on the limited support provided by compassionate strangers.

This book began as a doctoral thesis following my pursuit of further studies intended to make sense of what I encountered as an NGO worker in Hong Kong. Through this endeavour I sought to develop my understanding of asylum seekers' lived experiences as they venture into this new society, one of the many in the Global North that are becoming increasingly less welcoming towards travellers who seek a safe haven. During my time in Hong Kong, I noticed that, whether or not by design, public policies and practices appeared to remove asylum seekers from most of the population's sight by confining them to specific, immiserating socioeconomic and political spaces. They were being constructed as undesirable guests inhabiting a sort of intangible 'natural area' – a largely ignored segment of society within an urban context that was both the outcome and the foundation of extensive and far-reaching social transformation, in ways partly reminiscent of Robert E. Park's scholarly heirloom (see Deegan 2011). In a classic study on the city, Park and colleagues suggested that distinctive, natural areas develop where people share similar individualities as a result of being subject to

2   *Introduction*

analogous pressures (Park et al. 1925). In Hong Kong, I observed how asylum seekers seemed to be viewed in public and official accounts as 'other', walled in by indifference, prejudice and disapproval, for they are seen as too numerous in number, illegal and criminal and contributing nothing but problems to society (see Lai and Tjhung 2013).[1] Examining asylum seekers' day-to-day social interactions and economic and political marginalization, in order to fully appreciate the source and nature of their alleged deviance and hence to develop an analytical perspective that escapes narrow characterizations of asylum seekers, became the aim of this study.

Asylum seekers are often the least welcome group in wealthy societies. Frequently depicted as 'illegals' demanding assistance or welfare and committing crimes, asylum seekers are said to lie and cheat the institution of asylum for their own profit (cf. Bohmer and Shuman 2008; Bloch and Schuster 2002). Asylum seeking, at least in the form in which it is conceived in this book, is a relatively new phenomenon in Hong Kong. Travellers from countries in Africa and South Asia seeking international protection first arrived almost unnoticed in the early 2000s, when churches and NGOs, I was told, were approached by impoverished foreigners requesting assistance. Since that time, they have been living in urban areas where they are able to interact with the local resident population. As they come from a range of culturally diverse countries, they include people from all walks of life, who frequently have very little in common, and often face considerable difficulties in securing a livelihood. Public perception and government policies alike largely represent this group as morally reprehensible, illegal economic migrants bent on abusing asylum mechanisms in order to work illegally in the city. In part due to previous experiences of refugee influxes which are still etched into the city's psyche, like the arrival of Chinese refugees fleeing communism and Vietnamese 'boat people' between the 1970s and 1990s, current arrivals are tarred with the same unsympathetic brush, which defines asylum seekers according to neat, homogeneous categories (Vecchio and Beatson 2013) – a process mirrored in many countries around the globe (Coutin 2005; Webber 2012; Muus 1997).

It is against this background that this book explores the experiences of asylum seekers and the extent to which these experiences are impacted by both structural and individual agency factors. In this analysis, I define structural factors as the institutional and societal frameworks that organize and shape people's decision making, social relations and survival strategies. Agency denotes the capacity of people to reason and negotiate their environment in the pursuit of an objective (Bakewell 2010). The analysis presented here in part draws on Jacobsen's (2006) livelihoods approach to the study of urban refugee populations, which incorporates an understanding of context, refugees' assets and strategies and the outcomes of their migration. The intent is to examine the empirical data I collected in Hong Kong to offer an in-depth and more critical understanding of the links between the experiences of asylum seekers and the dynamics and processes underlying their mobility and livelihood, which are by no means disconnected from the broader society.

Understanding asylum seeking in the global city

To understand refugee experiences and the challenges refugees face in host urban environments – where the term 'refugee' is used by Jacobsen (2006) to refer to recognized refugees, asylum seekers, migrants enjoying some form of temporary protection and those whose refugee status has been denied but have yet to depart the city, a use of terminology that I borrow, although, for reasons that will be explained later in this chapter, I utilize interchangeably with the preferable term 'asylum seeker' – Jacobsen argues that it is of utmost importance to consider both the actions of refugees and the underlying social, political and economic context within which these actions take place. Put another way, refugees' experience of adaptation, suffering and the bargains they must strike daily, within and beyond their country of arrival, is influenced by the opportunity structure that is inherent to their host society. Conversely, this structure is often impacted by the arrival and survival strategies of refugees whose agency contributes to shape not only immigration policies, and the treatment and control of refugees, but also the spaces of economic engagement available to them in local communities – engagement that can have positive outcomes for the cities in which they live (Jacobsen 2006; Campbell 2006). Their contribution, however, largely escapes public attention and recognition and is often seen as reason to suggest that the journey of these refugees might be motivated by reasons other than the need to flee persecution. Forced migration scholarship has advanced the view that in countries of the Global North the understanding of who refugees are has become a tangible representation of the politics and policy context underpinning the reception of refugees (Zetter 1991, 2007). Popular attitudes and policy towards refugees may shift quickly towards either acceptance or denial according to the types of people arriving and public and official representations of them (Ramakers 1997; Ludwig 2013). In many countries, the label of 'refugee' is consequently split into a range of other migrant categories which are adopted to limit access to the rights and entitlements reserved for 'genuine' refugees – a status that is increasingly difficult for asylum seekers to obtain when facing complicated entry regulations and unrealistically narrow asylum thresholds purportedly aimed at protecting host countries from the so-called threat posed by undeserving, opportunistic characters (Zetter 2007; Bohmer and Shuman 2008). Concerns over the abuse of the asylum system (or 'asylum abuse') have multiplied in the media, political debates and populist rhetoric around the globe, with asylum seekers being treated as at best unworthy, and at worst terrorists and criminals, often as a result of the agency they demonstrate in engaging with irregular border crossing or taking active steps to secure a livelihood (Pickering 2001; Kaye 1998; Dal Lago 2009). While this phenomenon will be given further consideration in later chapters, it is worth noting here that asylum seekers generally face increasingly harsh living conditions pending a determination on their claim. International legal frameworks make overtures of humanitarian protection and specific legal, economic and social rights to people who seek refugee status. However, across the globe refugee protection is increasingly limited to insufficient, conditional assistance and restrictive conditions of stay.

4   *Introduction*

Moreover, as asylum seekers in Hong Kong are not afforded legal status and work rights, their opportunity structure is severely impacted, and livelihoods can only be pursued within certain limited local and transnational socioeconomic spaces. It is a key contention of this book that while asylum seekers in Hong Kong are effectively forced to live in conditions of protracted socioeconomic insecurity, it is precisely these living conditions that enable them to generate largely positive outcomes for the host society. On the one hand, the rights and protection awarded to those crossing international borders in search of a safe haven are diluted to shape them as illegal economic migrants and criminals (cf. Schuster 2011; Oelgemöller 2011; Gerard 2014). On the other, the widespread assumption that the institution of asylum is under siege by undeserving claimants largely defines asylum seeker agency, and yet this very agency provides Hong Kong with a formidable mechanism of social and labour control.

My research sought to shed light on the knowledge and expectations of asylum seekers in relation to Hong Kong, the degree of choice available to them in travelling to Hong Kong and how they secured a livelihood once in the city. The aim is to provide a critical understanding of asylum seeker decision making, the assets and strategies they employ (which are commonly perceived as asylum abuse), and hence to explore the reasons for the arrival of asylum seekers in Hong Kong and their supposed propensity to break the law by engaging in income-generating activities. The objective is thus to situate the lived experiences of asylum seekers within their socioeconomic context and to include within the analysis both micro-level and macro-level factors. Based on a thorough analysis of the ethnographic data, I claim that asylum seekers in Hong Kong have become useful personae non gratae: while they are officially and publicly labelled as unwelcome, their presence – albeit under conditions of rigidly controlled illegality – is valuable in economic terms. The current state of asylum in Hong Kong, I argue, is revealing of certain changes evident in several spheres that structure and organize contemporary labour markets (cf. Wallerstein 1979; Sassen 1988, 2001). At the same time, these conditions are illustrative of how some of the transformations inherent to globalized patterns of mobility and socioeconomic change are shaped by asylum seekers, who must negotiate the uncomfortable social, political and economic spaces created by the host society whose hostility towards previous refugee influxes continues to be revived by new arrivals. On one level, this book reveals how the condition of asylum seekers in Hong Kong is closely intertwined with the complexity, interconnectedness and rapid change that increasingly defines the lives of global citizens. On the other, it explains how the government's complicated entry and asylum procedures can result in a de facto regulative mechanism that facilitates specific patterns of refugee economic engagement. In this scenario, asylum seekers become an integral part of the production of socioeconomic and political outcomes related to global and local processes of neoliberal economic restructuring. This largely occurs via a process comparable to what some migration scholars have termed 'differential inclusion' – the construction of a sociopolitical and legal context that contains the agency of certain migrant populations within an 'elusive borderzone between inclusion and exclusion, between inside and outside' (Mazzadra 2011: 131; Calavita 2003). In particular, asylum seekers emerge as agents who furnish the local economy with the knowledge, networks and labour needed for small businesses and local residents affected by globalizing change to create and connect with new income opportunities, both within and beyond Hong Kong's boundaries.

The stories presented in this book condense within a few chapters rich documentary evidence that is highly revealing of the livelihoods of asylum seekers in a context – that of the global city – that has come to be seen as a key strategic site for understanding the forces that organize and remodel our societies. In this book, I introduce the reader to the context and everyday practices that underlie asylum seekers' precarious and insecure status, and thus their striving to procure an income at the lower echelons of society in economic sectors where their agency appears to support both the income-generating capacity of specific strata of local residents and Hong Kong's global competitiveness. Michele Acuto (2011) argues that the global city is an entrepreneurial entity, a city marked by obvious, albeit contested, socioeconomic transformation where the less affluent and professionally qualified residents contribute to urban world-class development to an extent comparable to that of the more visible global elites who control much of the world's economy. In this vein, McEwan et al. (2005: 928) contend that research into low-end ethnic activities and migrant networks can uncover 'forms of agency that are usually ignored in traditional economic narratives of global cities'. Such agency is part of the complex, multi-level agency that cities demonstrate 'in the global' realm – an area of urban analysis that warrants further research (Acuto and Steele 2013).

At the core of this analysis lies the understanding that asylum seeker livelihoods are dependent upon the degree of choice they can exercise within a context of diminished opportunities. The negotiation of these opportunities increases their reliance upon assets and strategies that raise the likelihood of their being depicted as opportunistic abusers of asylum mechanisms, in turn legitimizing the multifaceted exclusionary practices at play in Hong Kong. At the same time, asylum seekers' confinement within specific socioeconomic and legal spaces funnels their agency towards the production of specific economic outcomes, which are revealing of the human costs of both the global city and government policies aimed at or insensitive to the experiences of those who are the most vulnerable to the socioeconomic transformation inherent to a rapidly globalizing world.

Framing vulnerability: Shaping the boundaries of refugee behaviour

A rich body of literature examines asylum seeking and irregular migration in relation to the control mechanisms that wealthier states devise to stem and regulate migrant populations under conditions of increased globalization (cf. Aas and

6 *Introduction*

Bosworth 2013; Weber and Pickering 2011; Pickering 2005). Very rarely, however, is asylum seeking analyzed with regard to capitalism and the global city. An urban livelihoods perspective dictates that the analysis of border politics and policies in host countries, the way these policies are implemented and the regulative function of local institutions and public perceptions illuminates whether and how asylum seekers adjust to institutional and societal frameworks in shaping their survival strategies (Jacobsen 2006). For Jacobsen, this macro-level context defines the vulnerability of asylum seekers. In this book, this vulnerability is largely understood in relation to the challenges asylum seekers face when inserted into neoliberal globalized processes that encourage the transnational movement of capital, products and people. In this vein, asylum seekers are conceived of as sharing with other migrants many of the problems travellers typically face when seeking to enter and live in new countries.

As is the case for other migrants, asylum seekers' chances of securing adequate jobs are dependent upon the specific economic structure of the city in which they live. In global cities, the local socioeconomic structure is said to be tailored to support the functions that these cities fulfil in the global economy, which generate social inequality, polarization and diverse migratory patterns at the two ends of the spectrum of income distribution (Mollenkopf and Castells 1991; Sassen 2001). According to leading scholar Saskia Sassen (2001), who has popularized the idea of the global city, while these agglomerations of power and inequality increasingly require specialized and highly skilled people to run the complex matrix of global business operations, casualized and informal labour patterns have also grown this context in order to build and service an urban environment that is conducive to global city status. Certain sectors of the job market in these two streams require migrant labour power; and while only some migrants are allowed to transfer their skills internationally, 'others have to fill unskilled jobs in spite of their skills' (Knowles and Harper 2009: 10). Asylum seekers arguably fall within the latter category. A more critical understanding of their experiences cannot but consider the surge of global economic forces and neoliberal institutional structures which frame the global city's supposed tendency to generate demand for labour in the expanding urban low-grade and underpaid economy.

In this view, noteworthy is that an apparent tension has materialized in the span of a few decades between the requirement for porous borders in global cities in order to retain or build their command-centre functions and political and public understandings of this porosity. Several scholars argue that a structural shift seems to have occurred which has led to a significant hyperactivity on the part of governments in richer countries in seeking to enforce a more punitive culture of control based on the logic of deterrence and the prioritization of 'immigration crime' (Bosworth and Guild 2008; Guild 2009; McCulloch and Pickering 2012). Often proclaiming their actions to be guided by popular arguments such as the need to contain public expenditure or to protect national security or human rights principles, richer states have extended their coercive powers to effectively immobilize and illegalize certain migrant categories. The most noticeable consequence of this

Introduction 7

has been that those who cannot but engage in ever more expensive and dangerous journeys in the absence of legal alternatives have found themselves facing an array of risk factors which increase their vulnerability while also effectively shaping their agency (Weber and Pickering 2011; Collyer 2005).

The illegalization of migration

Migrant vulnerability is increasingly enforced via inflexible asylum and immigration policies which subtly manipulate the agency of refugees. Some scholars contend that the purpose of such elaborate legal and border frameworks is to deter unwanted arrivals and at the same time force those who successfully engage in border crossing to 'voluntarily' leave their new host society (Hassan 2000; Webber 2011). For example, rejected asylum seekers who have not yet been deported may face greater difficulties in ensuring their survival when the services to which they had been previously entitled are suddenly cut following a decision on their asylum case (Johansen 2013). Powerful instruments have also been enacted at the state level with the explicit intention of criminalizing or preventing asylum seekers from claiming refugee status, thus turning asylum seekers into illegal migrants when their claim cannot be either effectively substantiated or processed in the preferred country of refuge (Schuster 2011; Dauvergne 2008). Other scholars note that the purpose of fortified borders and restrictive mobility regimes may not be confined to preventing the arrival of asylum seekers or expediting their expulsion. Rather, restrictive border controls are also aimed at amplifying the 'deportability' of migrants via processes that figuratively imprint on their bodies their 'otherness' in terms of legal status, racial identity and exploitability (De Genova 2002; Calavita 2005). In other words, the condition of 'deportability' plays a significant role in demarcating internal social and political boundaries (Nevins 2002; Dauvergne 2008). It denotes the deportable migrant as a distinct identity, whose individuality trespasses their humanity to become a social category of its own. As often happens with other categories of migrant from whom society demands diligent subordination (Ladegaard 2013), a high degree of objectification is involved in a process that transforms migrant subjects into 'non-persons', leaving them to live a life at the margins of society (Dal Lago 2009). Denied legal status and racially profiled, these people find themselves 'stuck' in a sort of 'second state of immobility' (Haugen 2012) where their 'liminal legality' (Menjivar 2006) entails a great deal of ambiguity, uncertainty, desperation and physical destitution (Núñez and Heyman 2007).

Labour exploitation

[T]he disciplinary operation of an apparatus for the everyday production of migrant 'illegality' is never simply intended to achieve the putative goal of deportation. It is deportability, and not deportation per se, that has historically rendered undocumented migrant labor a distinctly disposable commodity.

(De Genova 2002: 438)

8   *Introduction*

A number of writers have pointed out that the process by which certain migrant populations are illegalized entails inclusion as well as exclusion (Calavita 2005; De Genova 2011). That is, migrants lacking regular immigration status can find restricted spaces within society where they may carry on with their lives in line with the specific needs of the host society. For example, analyzing the impacts of the globalized economy, Cohen (2006) argues that contemporary social categories group individuals in countries of the Global North according to their level of social wage and the degree of protection they receive from law and order agencies. There are three such groupings: citizens, who enjoy a wide array of rights and full participation in society; denizens, who are the privileged aliens who often hold multiple citizenships but have a limited or no right to vote; and those known as helots, referring to a group of people who in ancient times toiled for the Spartans and had no (or few) rights. According to Cohen, it is within this third group that refugees, asylum seekers and low-income and illegal migrants have come to be grouped together. Their categorization as such is the outcome of a new form of social stratification at the bottom of which individuals find themselves in highly vulnerable situations. These individuals become the key means of ensuring labour flexibility in advanced, service-based economies and at the same time are an easy target for public resentment towards increasing numbers of migrants who are reshaping the social and economic fabric of the host society (Cohen 2006; Basso 2010).

In this context, precarious legal status intersects with socioeconomic structural factors to constrain migrant choices. Further, as emerges from the narratives of asylum seekers presented in this book, refugee legal status is 'sticky' (Landolt and Goldring 2010). While migrants are at times able to shift their status (Schuster 2005), their chances of climbing the social ladder are severely limited by the time they have spent in subordinate positions as 'illegals', and thus by the constraints and hardship they face when lacking regular immigration status. Such stressors may be related to the social networks and skills they acquire in the host society, but also to the far-reaching and persistent effects of their labelling by the broader society (Melossi 2003; Pellegrino 2012). In other words, illegalized migrants are forced to form or access social networks within certain spaces, where they find themselves embedded in particular contexts and can develop certain forms of human capital (Engbersen and van der Leun 2001). Most of these spaces can be seen as characterized by what McKay et al. (2011) term 'exploitative solidarity', which can lead to the criminalization of the migrants involved. As Melossi (2013: 286) elegantly asserts, 'The problem is of course that the condition of being without documents places the foreign citizen within a set of conditions and constrictions that increase all the risk factors for criminal behaviour enormously'. The modern helots have effectively become a cheap, exploitable and expendable workforce. Asylum seekers – who should be exempted by international law from being defined as illegal migrants – become the most vulnerable to exploitation, as they are simultaneously deprived of kinship support and subjected to numerous restrictions which force them to seek livelihoods in the informal, underground

Introduction 9

economy under highly precarious conditions (Jacobsen 2002, 2006). Moreover, this survival strategy reinforces their criminalization and the negative public perceptions of their purported deviancy (Squire 2009).

Despite the alleged aim of existing asylum mechanisms of ensuring protection for those whose personal circumstances force them to seek safety overseas, asylum seekers' untenured status in Hong Kong appears to engender unequal power relations which impact upon their lived experiences. While economic explanations seem relevant, noteworthy is that they may only partly reveal asylum seekers' socio-legal exclusion. Migration and matters related to national identity, illegality, terrorism and national security are generally merged in richer societies, with the aim of representing certain forms of migration as a risk that necessitates urgent restrictive measures to ensure the safety of citizens (Bigo 2002, 2011). Some scholars have pointed out that in pressing for more restrictive approaches to migration, states have further fuelled exclusionary narratives, which in turn have set the scene for more enforcement enhancement (Cornelius et al. 1994). This process has created what Squire (2009) calls a 'self-fulfilling circle', which enables states to govern and articulate citizenship through immigration control (Bosworth and Guild 2008). Immigration control is in fact one of the defining features of the modern sovereign state (Weber 2007) and as such is an important means to constitute territorial order in terms of both governance and national belonging (Sassen 1996; Squire 2009). Although Hong Kong is not a sovereign state but a Special Administrative Region (HKSAR) of the People's Republic of China, under the 'one country, two systems policy' it enjoys relatively broad administrative independence in relation to immigration policy.[2] Further, geopolitical priorities and identity discourses intersect with the needs of this global city (Smart 2003) to shape the vulnerability and livelihoods of both the lawfully resident population and those in contrast to whom the ideal citizen (or urban resident) is defined.

Framing agency: Social capital

The research presented in this book relies upon and contributes to a burgeoning current of analysis in migration and forced migration studies, which investigates the sociability of refugee and migrant populations as an essential determinant of their migration outcomes (Castles 2003; Korac 2009; Khosravi 2010). Asylum seekers and refugees emerge in the contemporary literature as agentic subjects, in contrast to the passive, powerless individuals pushed beyond familiar borders who have no say in their migration depicted by earlier studies and popular stereotypes (cf. Stein 1986). For example, several scholars have recently shed much needed light on the refugee journey by providing close-up accounts of asylum seeker decision making, expectations and reasons for travelling long distances to specific destinations, and the resources they utilize to survive (Zimmermann 2009a, 2009b; Barsky 2000; Gilbert and Koser 2006; Agier 2008). Significant in these findings is that refugees regard even their asylum screening interview as an

10 *Introduction*

opportunity to demonstrate their agency (Ludwig 2013). While screening interviews can be a cause for frustration when asylum seekers find that their interviewers are unable or unwilling to understand their story (Bohmer and Shuman 2008), the very act of sitting in an interview room, attempting to convince the other side to grant them refugee status, testifies to their courage and efforts at exerting control over their own life and destiny.

One key contention of this book is that spaces of immiseration and social exclusion are forced upon asylum seekers in Hong Kong, who are consequently compelled to exert their agency in ways that necessarily amplify perceptions of both their deviancy and the burden they pose for the city, thereby supporting the rationale for the illegalization of asylum seekers (cf. Weber and Bowling 2008). Limited by negative representations of their motivation for seeking asylum, their needs homogenized, asylum seekers are exposed to practices, networks and risks that increase their vulnerability. However, not every asylum seeker ends up living in poverty in Hong Kong. When they suffer destitution and frustration as a consequence of the uncertainties related to living in liminal spaces of non-belonging, this condition is in part a result of their own rational decision making. The narratives and stories of the refugee participants presented in this book emphasize their capacity to read their surroundings, frame their choices and evaluate the consequences of their actions, in accordance with their assets and skills and the amount and quality of information they possess. What emerges most powerfully is that the people whose lives might as well be said to be 'wasted' (Bauman 2004) are not only able to secure a livelihood, but also strive ambitiously to take advantage of the very structural conditions said to oppress them. The stories offered in this book of South Asian asylum seekers providing important liaison functions between local retailers and foreign tourists in Hong Kong; of African participants shipping containers of cheap Chinese-manufactured goods to their countries; and of those who struggle in difficult and dangerous jobs, at times earning sufficient trust and money to develop their own business opportunities or move up the labour hierarchy to supervise other underprivileged workers, all demonstrate the adaptive capacity of these people. These narratives illustrate the everyday experiences and survival strategies of refugees in Hong Kong, and why, how and which income-generating activities are adopted to negotiate their environment. Collectively, they provide an account of the emotions, strengths, weaknesses and desires of the people who chose to speak with me, who acted as agentic individuals in ways similar to those adopted by people working in urban centres all over the world. Seminal research in this field reveals how Somali refugees in Nairobi successfully devise transnational trading strategies in order to negotiate from below the constraints they face due to their untenured legal status (Campbell 2006). In a similar fashion, Mathews (2011) has identified the ingenious activities adopted by refugees and other migrants in such contexts, highlighting processes of 'low-end globalization' which bring together international traders, co-ethnic asylum seekers, travellers on short visas and local residents in connecting business networks between Hong Kong and the Global South.

Introduction 11

Critically, social capital emerges in the literature and this research as an asset that empowers the dynamics that drive both exclusion and profit seeking. Since the mid-1980s, much of the literature on international migration has linked migratory movements to social capital, by analyzing the interpersonal ties on which would-be migrants, immigrants and non-immigrants rely for migration and employment (Boyd 1989; Kloosterman et al. 1998; Poros 2001). Social networks convey the information and material resources necessary to meet the challenges related to mobility. In his research on wartime migration in Afghanistan, Harpviken (2009) demonstrates how the interpersonal connections that form migrants' social networks clearly impact on how different people cope with the same external factors. Koser and Pinkerton (2002) extensively document how people who need to flee their country, but whose mobility is hindered by restrictive visa regimes, may seek the help of third parties to successfully cross international borders. The likelihood of capture at the border for those engaging in irregular border crossing is indeed dependent largely on the human and social capital that would-be irregular migrants bring with them. The more the migrant relies on people who have previously followed the same migratory route, the better will be their chances of eluding border controls (Singer and Massey 1998). From a different angle, Jacobsen (2002, 2006) explains that social capital is a resource upon which refugees rely extensively in pursuing their livelihoods. Refugees are often unable to access the kinds of resources available to local citizens, such as housing, health care, education and jobs. However, they may employ their own resources, accessible through networks that may not be readily available to locals, such as transnational relations and ethnic ties, or through the formation of ad hoc networks instrumental in accessing material and emotional support (Banki 2006).

Jacobsen (2006) also rightly stresses that refugees have differing levels of access to resources. Moreover, social capital may not always lead to positive results. For example, social relationships with deviant others in conditions of duress can result in the transmission of deviant values which affects individual agency (Agnew 1992). Martinez and Slack (2013) write that when irregular migrants are denied legitimate opportunities to improve their livelihoods they may be exposed to new networks, norms and values which increase their likelihood of being exposed to exploitation and policing (Melossi 2013). Refugees' reliance on some networks may lead them to land in countries about which they know little and where they have no relatives who can support them (Koser 1997; Collyer 2005). The degree and reliability of information they can obtain impact their assets and strategies, hence making all the difference between a successful migration trajectory and one that leads to despair and suffering upon their arrival.

In relation to this context, we could argue that, barred from working and lacking regular immigration status, asylum seekers in Hong Kong are thrown to the economic wolves. However, their destinies do not appear to be dependent only upon conditions that are largely outside their control. Rather, in this book I map the endless oscillation between asylum seekers' insecurities and frustrations, on

12 *Introduction*

the one hand, and their continuous efforts to attain a measure of power over their destiny, on the other. It is against this backdrop that structural and agency factors are examined in this book, to understand the social implications of overarching economic and political processes that engender the vulnerability of underprivileged travellers, and how these travellers manage their socio-legal exclusion to exploit which resources and why. In turn, this analysis explains their involvement in specific economic sectors and the outcomes of their 'exploitation'.

Documenting life on the margins

Scholars from many disciplinary backgrounds engage in research into refugee populations (Harrell-Bond 1988). While their foci and settings may differ, there are some common issues related to how one defines the people under study, what method is best suited to their analysis, and the ethics of conducting research with vulnerable populations. In this section, I explore the reasons why I utilize the term 'asylum seeker', as briefly set out earlier in this chapter, and the reasons for and difficulties experienced in engaging in a largely ethnographic work. I then conclude with a discussion of the ethical considerations that guided my approach in this research.

Asylum seekers and refugees

International refugee law defines a refugee as a person who seeks refuge in a foreign country because his or her life is endangered by war, generalized violence and/or persecution on account of race, religion, nationality, political opinion or membership in a particular social group (Gibney 2004; United Nations High Commissioner for Refugees [UNHCR] 1996). An asylum seeker is defined as a person whose claim for refugee protection is yet to be definitively evaluated. A refugee livelihood framework tends to popularize a 'common sense' usage of the term 'refugee' which goes beyond the previous technical definition to include persons facing equally vulnerable situations (Jacobsen and Landau 2003; Landau 2004). This redefinition is aimed particularly at lending a more human face to the experiences of those who are controlled by elaborate bureaucratic structures (cf. Harrell-Bond et al. 1992; Harrell-Bond and Voutira 2007; Zetter 2007). In this analysis, I take this latter definition of refugee and elaborate on it to use it interchangeably with the preferred term 'asylum seeker' – unless legal implications are specifically considered, in which case they are made explicit. This choice is closely tied to the circumstances that led to the conception of this research project. In this book, I intend to explore the process of asylum seeking and the agency demonstrated by those who access screening mechanisms in Hong Kong. I acknowledge that the term asylum seeker has acquired a rather negative connotation in contemporary public discourses (Zetter 2007; Kaye 1998). Nonetheless, the term refugee largely bears equally negative implications (Pickering 2001; Okojie 1992). These two terms are comparable when both labels come to collectively describe a group seen as a 'problem', and especially a 'deviant' one (Pickering 2001). The refugee label, though, seems to enjoy a higher moral standing in the community of those seeking asylum in Hong Kong, as the term refugee is often associated with its legal definition, thereby equating the refugee to a 'genuine' refugee, as we will see in Chapter 2. Moreover, I have opted to use this term as a beginning point, for it allows for simplification of a rather confusing situation consequential to the peculiar approach of the Hong Kong Government to asylum seeking.

Despite being part of the People's Republic of China, and China being a signatory to the 1951 Convention Relating to the Status of Refugees (the Refugee Convention), Hong Kong has firmly resisted the extension of this instrument to the territory (Loper 2010). Since 1992, the city has nonetheless been party to the 1984 Convention against Torture and Other Cruel, Inhuman or Degrading Treatment or Punishment (CAT), and a two-track asylum screening system is currently available to people seeking a safe haven (Ramsden and Marsh 2013). On the one hand, the UNHCR is allowed to perform refugee screening in the city. On the other, the Hong Kong Government assesses claims under Article 3 of the CAT, which prohibits the *refoulement*, or removal of a person to a country where they would face torture or other inhumane treatment. Terms like asylum seeker, refugee, torture claimant and torture victim are therefore widely used in media and public discourse, at times without a clear basis in any international legal instrument. Moreover, protection can be sought via either or both of the previous mechanisms, meaning that the previous categories often overlap. To complicate matters further, recent judgments handed down by the Hong Kong Court of Final Appeal[3] have resulted in the government announcing the implementation of a unified screening mechanism (USM), soon to replace the two-track screening system (Legislative Council [LegCo] 2013; Ngo 2013). The government has since begun to use the term '*non-refoulement* claimant' to refer to 'persons not having the right to enter and remain in Hong Kong (e.g. illegal immigrants and overstayers)' who apply for protection under CAT, Article 3 of the Hong Kong Bill of Rights – which gives effect to Article 7 of the *International Covenant on Civil and Political Rights*, which the Hong Kong Court of Final Appeal has recently recognized as an additional tool available to people seeking asylum[4] – and Article 33 of the Refugee Convention (LegCo 2013: 2), all of which will form the new basis for scrutinizing claims for protection under the USM. The term *non-refoulement* claimant, I believe, highlights the pleas of people who do not wish to be returned to their country of origin, in a context in which the Hong Kong Government presently does not grant leave to stay to those very few claimants who are recognized to be either refugees or torture victims. Recognized refugees are expected to be resettled by the UNHCR in other countries, and no clear procedures are said to be in place concerning people who merit the status of torture victim (Ip 2010). Moreover, the procedures involved in the CAT and UNHCR mechanisms may take several years, and recognition rates are notoriously very low. Chapter 2 details how those who seek asylum struggle for recognition in this context.

14 *Introduction*

Indeed, very few of my participants were recognized as refugees or torture victims. The most common experience I recorded in Hong Kong was that of seeking asylum rather than obtaining it. Moreover, when this status is obtained, very few legal and practical differences apply. Recognized refugees and successful torture claimants still have no right to remain in Hong Kong and thus continue to experience the same challenges they faced prior to their applications being approved. It is apparent that successful claimants endure a precarious life in no ways different from that of other asylum seekers who yet search for the opportunity to normalize their life – a need that goes far beyond seeking *non-refoulement* (cf. Zimmermann 2009a). The data presented in this book emphasize how asylum entails a lengthy search for stability, which the term 'asylum seeker', in my view, most powerfully conveys, while also highlighting the vulnerability of people who face complicated and restrictive regulations.

Pursuing the insider angle from the outside

In line with similar previous studies, a non-probability sampling technique was used in this research, including quotas for key explanatory variables and various starting points from which I obtained snowball samples (Bloch 2004, 2007; Harrell-Bond and Voutira 2007). Furthermore, in the time I was in Hong Kong I committed to a largely ethnographic effort to gain in-depth understanding of two phenomena: the populations that are generally referred to as 'hidden' in that they seek to minimize their visibility (Harrell-Bond and Voutira 2007); and economic activities that by their very nature are often concealed from strangers, the analysis of which therefore requires negotiation of the social boundaries that often separate the researcher from their study subjects, particularly when they come from different environments (Madden 2010). In this context, ethnography offers a valuable scientific tool for generating 'thick' accounts of the links and associations which often escape public attention but which may explain a great deal about supposedly deviant behaviours. Ocejo (2013: 17) emphasizes how spending time on developing close connections with research subjects and an insider understanding has the potential to reveal the back areas which 'reflect deeper meanings beyond their public display'. It is precisely in this way that I attempted to overcome the difficulties that frequently emerge when sampling techniques cannot rely on quantitative 'data sets' to count refugees and their composition, and thereby strengthen the credibility and representativeness of the research findings (cf. Jacobsen and Landau 2003). It is important to note that I collected a considerable volume of information concerning the numbers of asylum seekers in Hong Kong. However, this was drawn from official, aggregated statistics, which account for neither asylum seekers lodging multiple claims nor those who are in the territory before or after a claim is made and are subsequently rejected. Further, the data upon which it would have been possible to develop a quantitatively representative sample – that is, data collected by the government-contracted service provider for asylum seekers, the Hong Kong branch of the International Social Service (ISS) – were covered by professional secrecy (cf. May 2001). So

Introduction 15

in 2010 and 2011 I immersed myself within a core group of 75 asylum seekers, who accepted me into their lives and soon began to share with me their environment, challenges and networks, including contact with their friends, employers, business partners and the lawyers and humanitarian workers with whom they interacted. This approach was followed in order to be geographically inclusive while also selective about the nationality and gender of my participants and was dictated by practical and conjectural reasons alike. On the one side, I attempted to narrow the sample while still allowing for a wide variety of experiences to be captured. My attention was drawn particularly to asylum seekers from sub-Saharan Africa, Sri Lanka and Bangladesh as they collectively appeared to display the complexity of current patterns of mobility and livelihood among all asylum seekers. At the same time, noting that the dynamics of finding work and of border crossing are gendered (Landolt and Goldring 2010; Gerard and Pickering 2012), and that in Hong Kong public understandings largely refer to male populations when associating deviancy with asylum seeking, a choice was made to focus on male asylum seekers. On the other side, the longer I was in Hong Kong, the more asylum seekers I was able to find in clustered social communities geographically spread throughout the territory. While these communities were not isolated from each other, the patterns of economic engagement that I recorded within them differed, and this appeared to have less to do with nationality than with gender and the specific networks upon which the asylum seekers relied in their geographical contexts.

Ethnography is not without its challenges, and indeed the reliability of its findings is largely dependent upon the researcher's capacity to gain acceptance among the research subjects and then perceive their viewpoint on matters, which may not be immediately apparent from an outsider's perspective (Madden 2010). Mathews (2011) describes how his research fieldwork was facilitated by his being a white person in a vibrant multiethnic environment, in which his position as a professor earned him the trust of his research subjects, which in turn elicited their participation. In a similar fashion, I negotiated the social distance between myself and the refugee population on the basis that I, too, was a foreigner in Hong Kong – an outsider to both the population under study and the local community. Of course, the degree of insight I was able to gain into these refugee communities was limited as I could not read all of the complexities and dynamics of human behaviour that are recognized through the use of a shared language. However, being an outsider offered some advantages, especially given the nature of my research and Hong Kong's social environment. Had I been Chinese I would probably have been taken for an undercover police officer when questioning people about their illegal businesses (cf. Mathews 2011). Conversely, were I of African or South Asian descent I would likely have gained insight into that particular ethnic group – although possibly I may have been distrusted by factions within the same group, depending on their legal status and social network – but I would have jeopardized my chances of gaining much insight into other ethnic groups. Indeed, I quickly realized that the different ethnic groups, even when they share the same experiences and environments, often do not trust each other. The competitive markets in which

16 Introduction

they operate certainly do not foster harmonious inter-ethnic or co-national bonds, although conflict of any sort rarely emerged as a significant factor shaping the asylum seekers' experiences.

I drew largely on my previous experience as an NGO worker in Hong Kong to gain access to the refugee population. Initially, I introduced myself as a university researcher, but I found that trust and information were elicited more quickly when I added that I had experience working with charity groups assisting refugees in Hong Kong. I was then often overwhelmed by questions from the participants about my thoughts on government policy, support services and the potential benefits of my research for refugees. I found this interaction to be an effective icebreaker, encouraging the participants' interest in the research. My work was also facilitated by the help of long-time asylum seekers I had previously known and who provided me with invaluable starting points for snowball participation. My principal concern in this regard was to ensure that I had access to a variety of refugee situations in which refugees in Hong Kong commonly find themselves. I therefore put considerable effort into forming trustful connections with the asylum seekers, while a significant amount of time was spent walking around the Kowloon peninsula and the New Territories seeking to meet potential interviewees, often introduced to me by their friends. These were the people who opened their homes, showed me their neighbourhoods and introduced me to their landlords, employers and acquaintances. On several occasions, a number of asylum seekers took turns to accompany me on visits to dilapidated shacks and illegal dwellings where impoverished asylum seekers lived. At other times, I walked through the same dwellings, randomly speaking with passers-by to ask whether they were, or knew people who might be, interested in sharing their stories. These encounters normally began as a one-on-one conversation but would then develop into a large group conversation, with many men gathering around to join in (cf. Gardner 2010). While this approach could appear to be a violation of confidentiality in interview proceedings, for these men this was normal behaviour, and these encounters elicited their participation and enabled greater insight. Their thirst to obtain information, such as the latest updates concerning asylum, and a glimpse of hope about their future in Hong Kong drew these men to such gatherings.

Offering people cash for their participation on occasion also significantly improved my chances of accessing and recruiting new participants while also making the participants feel more comfortable about the research. Quite surprisingly, the refugees felt that they would not endanger themselves by sharing their stories with me. Any assistance I provided was seen as evidence that I was not a government agent trying to find out whether they were working illegally. In their experience, government agents extort information by means of force; they do not pay for it. Moreover, while these small contributions of money greatly assisted me to 'break the ice', they highlighted the desperate need for cash, as participants were always in need of money to pay their rent and bills. The literature on refugees generally notes that vulnerable research participants may choose to lie at times because of shame, fear of being exposed or the expectation that they will be rewarded for their participation (Harrell-Bond and Voutira 2007; Wengraf 2001). I cannot deny that this ever happened in my research. In one case, I believe a Bangladeshi interpreter summarized or even altered the participants' answers. Insofar as most of the participants had limited schooling, the interviews were compromised to some extent as the first interpreter I engaged directed the focus onto their need for help rather than their motives and circumstances for engaging in migration and work-related activities. As a result, participants told me stories that they thought I wanted to hear, possibly in the hope of benefiting from the research, financially or otherwise. While this was certainly a shortcoming, which later prompted me to find another interpreter, this episode illustrated the participants' needs and use of the research as a way to improve their condition, which can essentially be seen as a survival strategy – which the research aimed to identify. More generally, however, the fact that someone was going to the trouble to visit them, and learn about their lives, was favourably regarded among the asylum seekers I met. It made them feel respected and valued – something they rarely experienced in Hong Kong. One of the research objectives was to explore the participants' living conditions and how current laws affect their livelihood. This was achievable as the great majority of participants were extremely welcoming and understanding. As I discovered, the ease of doing research with this marginalized group of 'voiceless' individuals came primarily from their determination to candidly share their problems, thoughts and dreams.

Finally, my methodological approach made use of what Vrecer (2010) defines as 'participant organisation' – engagement with the community organizations with which one volunteers to gain access to the research population. In my case, I did not volunteer my time to any particular organization – more asylum seekers were to be found in remote areas – but I maintained close links with such organizations so that I could refer to them any person who was in need of their services. For example, on one occasion I met an African asylum seeker who had just arrived in Hong Kong, had no place to sleep and whose visa was expiring that same day. He told me his story and showed me the pictures and documents he had saved in his email account as evidence to support his refugee claim. He showed me physical evidence of his having been tortured, despite my insisting that I believed his story regardless. By mobilizing the refugee support network that I had come to know, we were able to find him a guest house initially and a more comfortable room later, as well as legal advice. Step by step I walked him through the process, and I learnt a great deal in doing so. He still emails me every now and then, addressing me very respectfully even though he is twice my age.

Ethical research with asylum seekers

A few comments are due concerning the ethics of approaching refugee populations for research purposes. Researchers engaged with vulnerable populations are understood in the literature as having an obligation to both satisfy the demands of the academy, in terms of rigour and theoretical advancement, and ensure that the

18   *Introduction*

knowledge they generate is used to protect the people they study (Jacobsen and Landau 2003). This ethical approach is what Jacobsen and Landau call the 'dual imperative' of refugee research, which has become an essential requirement for research into refugees. However, this approach is problematic at times. Several scholars have highlighted the difficulty facing researchers in terms of striking a balance between their role as academics and their responsibility as advocates (Koser et al. 2004).

My research methods and findings were never altered so as to present only those views that do not undermine the rights and appropriate representation of the asylum seekers (cf. Koser et al. 2004; Mackenzie et al. 2007). However, the possibility that the research could be used to increase the vulnerability of asylum seekers in Hong Kong has kept me awake some nights. While I took measures to ensure I would not raise unsolicited attention or improperly manage information that could lead to participants being discovered by the authorities (cf. Vearey 2009), I frequently worried about one situation that Koser et al. (2004: 61) describe in the following terms:

> I am doing some work at the moment on human smuggling and asylum seekers. What the work has found is that perhaps 75 percent of asylum seekers arriving in the UK [United Kingdom] today are smuggled there . . . They need to work straight away to start paying money back to lenders. . . . But where does that leave us, as researchers? Do I really want to go to the Home Office in the UK and say: 'I can prove that actually most of these asylum seekers are criminals and are breaking the law'. I side with advocates, but most asylum seekers in the UK are breaking the law, because they have no other option.

The problem concerns how to produce rigorous research in the face of the difficulty of predicting how research findings will be used. This issue was raised by a number of non-refugee key informants during the course of my fieldwork in Hong Kong. In particular, they expressed concern over how and whether this study could benefit refugees given that a key feature of my research was to examine their involvement in informal or illegal activities in the local economy. In the view of these informants, this amounted to telling the authorities that asylum seekers do break the law by working illegally, which could reinforce public opinion that they are deviant illegal migrants who abuse asylum mechanisms.

Some scholars claim that the adoption of a sound research methodology should reduce the risks that such research will be misused to support ineffective or harmful strategies (Landau and Jacobsen 2005; Mackenzie et al. 2007). While this may be a cogent argument, in my view the failure to improve our knowledge in order to deal with identified problems, for fear of the possible consequences, may worsen the hardships facing asylum seekers. Their prospects of improving their lives appear to be obstructed by the persistence of enduring exploitation and the risk of repatriation upon the (unfair) dismissal of their asylum claims. Furthermore, this asylum 'problem' is now largely a matter of great public concern in Hong Kong. The institution of asylum, and thus the rule of law in which Hong Kong takes pride (Mathews et al. 2008), appears to be severely compromised by the mechanisms of border politics which effectively inflict certain levels of violence on asylum seekers. As Krasmann (2007) says, once a punitive culture of control attains broad public support, it may expand beyond certain categories of people identified as undesirable and dangerous to include others deemed to be equally risky. The risk of being smeared and labelled as a dangerous outcast is indeed not limited to asylum seekers only, and Chapter 1 details how the marginalized local poor also appear to be subjected to similar performances of state power.

An outline of the book

This book is composed of six chapters in addition to this introduction. The first two chapters examine the vulnerability of asylum seekers in Hong Kong, with Chapter 1 analyzing Hong Kong from a global perspective and in its local and historical context. In Chapter 1, the aim is to explore the relationship between the transformations and dynamics of change that globalization engenders in terms of class polarization and the division of labour, on the one hand, and the governance of this change which shapes the vulnerability of local and foreign residents alike, on the other. Chapter 2 reveals the politics that structure refugee agency. Drawing extensively on asylum seekers' narratives, it reveals how the inception of internal borders purportedly erected to deter and differentiate unwanted people creates specific spaces of belonging and non-belonging which underlie various forms of harm for asylum seekers.

Chapter 3 examines the vulnerability and the agency involved in border crossing in order to explain the reasons why Hong Kong has become a preferred destination for asylum seekers on a new global geopolitical map of safe places with high standards of living. In order to provide critical knowledge of public and official perceptions that asylum seekers travel to Hong Kong to find jobs, the knowledge that asylum seekers possess about Hong Kong prior to their departure from their country of origin, the level of choice they exert in relation to selecting a destination, the involvement of third parties in their migration and the reasons why the journey is increasingly shaped by illegality are all analyzed. In this chapter, the livelihood framework is complemented by an understanding that the global city and asylum seeking create the transnational linkages that influence migratory patterns and border control measures. If asylum seekers endure difficult and dangerous journeys to reach sanctuary, their confrontation with borders continues upon their arrival as they face policies and public opinion that demonstrate the prevalence and impact of fluid, portable borders (Weber 2006). Chapter 4 expands on the concepts introduced in the previous chapters and examines the discrepancy between asylum seekers' expectations of a safe and productive life at the destination and the reality of social and institutional structures which effectively punish them for displaying levels of agency that contradict the dominant image of a genuine refugee.

Chapter 5 explores asylum seeker agency and the impact of asylum seekers' legal status on their ability to generate income. It provides an analytical framework within which it is suggested that asylum seekers deliver significant economic

20 *Introduction*

benefits to Hong Kong via the flexible and cheap labour they (informally) provide to specific sectors of the economy. At the same time, they provide reliable transnational linkages that create trading opportunities which potentially advance the status of Hong Kong as a global city. It is posited that asylum policies are pivotal to enabling limited refugee agency in those spaces in which asylum seekers are likely to increase economic opportunities for the local resident population. Finally, Chapter 6 analyzes the outcomes of asylum seekers' survival strategies and suggests that local and global circumstances appear to have affected the networks and various informal markets that impact on asylum seekers' experiences. Conclusions are drawn about the current structure of asylum in Hong Kong, as the chapter raises questions concerning its ethics and rationale and suggests that the livelihoods of asylum seekers in this city are exemplary of both the most appalling and the most positive consequences of the global economy, the renationalization of politics (Sassen 1996) and the use of asylum as a mechanism of migration control.

Notes

1 See online comments available at: http://visionfirstnow.org/2013/05/09/the-compound-under-a-tree/.
2 The former British colony was returned to the People's Republic of China in 1997, but the Joint Declaration originally signed by the British and Chinese governments maintained that the territory would enjoy a 50-year period of administrative independence post-1997.
3 See *Ubamaka Edward Wilson v. Secretary for Security* (FACV 15/2011) and *C v. Director of Immigration* (FACV 18–20/2011).
4 See *Ubamaka Edward Wilson v. Secretary for Security*.

References

Aas, K. F. and Bosworth, M. (2013) (Eds.) *The Borders of Punishment: Migration, Citizenship, and Social Exclusion*, Oxford: Oxford University Press.
Acuto, M. (2011) 'Finding the Global City: An Analytical Journey through the "Invisible College"', *Urban Studies*, 48(14): 2953–2973.
Acuto, M. and Steele, W. (2013) (Eds.) *Global City Challenges: Debating a Concept, Improving the Practice*, Houndmills: Palgrave Macmillan.
Agier, M. (2008) *On the Margins of the World: The Refugee Experience Today*, Cambridge: Polity Press.
Agnew, R. (1992) 'Foundation for a General Strain Theory of Crime and Delinquency', *Criminology*, 30(1): 47–87.
Bakewell, O. (2010) 'Some Reflections on Structure and Agency in Migration Theory', *Journal of Ethnic and Migration Studies*, 36(10): 1689–1708.
Banki, S. (2006) 'Burmese Refugees in Tokyo: Livelihoods in the Urban Environment', *Journal of Refugee Studies*, 19(3): 328–344.
Barsky, R. F. (2000) *Arguing and Justifying: Assessing the Convention Refugees' Choice of Moment, Motive and Host Country*, Aldershot: Ashgate.
Basso, P. (2010) (Ed.) *Razzismo di Stato: Stati Uniti, Europa, Italia*, Milano: FrancoAngeli.
Bauman, Z. (2004) *Wasted Lives: Modernity and Its Outcasts*, Oxford: Polity Press.

Introduction 21

Bigo, D. (2002) 'Security and Immigration: Toward a Critique of the Governmentality of Unease', *Alternatives*, 27: 63–92.

Bigo, D. (2011) 'Freedom and Speed in Enlarged Borderzones', in V. Squire (Ed.) *The Contested Politics of Mobility: Borderzones and Irregularity*, Abingdon: Routledge: 31–50.

Bloch, A. (2004) 'Survey Research with Refugees: A Methodological Perspective', *Policy Studies*, 25(2): 139–151.

Bloch, A. (2007) 'Methodological Challenges for National and Multi-sited Comparative Survey Research', *Journal of Refugee Studies*, 20(2): 230–247.

Block, A. and Schuster, L. (2002) 'Asylum and Welfare: Contemporary Debates', *Critical Social Policy*, 22(3): 393–414.

Bohmer, C. and Shuman, A. (2008) *Rejecting Refugees: Political Asylum in the 21st Century*, Abingdon: Routledge.

Bosworth, M. and Guild, M. (2008) 'Governing through Migration Control', *British Journal of Criminology*, 48(6): 703–719.

Boyd, M. (1989) 'Family and Personal Networks in Migration', *International Migration Review*, 23(3): 638–670.

Calavita, K. (2003) 'A "Reserve Army of Delinquents": The Criminalization and Economic Punishment of Immigrants in Spain', *Punishment & Society*, 5(4): 399–413.

Calavita, K. (2005) *Immigrants at the Margins: Law, Race and Exclusion in Southern Europe*, Cambridge: Cambridge University Press.

Campbell, E. H. (2006) 'Urban Refugees in Nairobi: Problems of Protection, Mechanisms of Survival, and Possibilities for Integration', *Journal of Refugee Studies*, 19(3): 396–413.

Castles, S. (2003) 'Towards a Sociology of Forced Migration and Social Transformation', *Sociology*, 37(1): 13–34.

Cohen, R. (2006) *Migration and Its Enemies: Global Capital, Migrant Labour and the Nation-State*, Aldershot: Ashgate.

Collyer, M. (2005) 'When Do Social Networks Fail to Explain Migration? Accounting for the Movement of Algerian Asylum-Seekers to the UK', *Journal of Ethnic and Migration Studies*, 31(4): 699–718.

Cornelius, W. A., Martin, P. L. and Hollifield, J. F. (1994) (Eds.) *Controlling Immigration: A Global Perspective*, Stanford: Stanford University Press.

Coutin, S. B. (2005) 'Contesting Criminality: Illegal Immigration and the Spatialisation of Legality', *Theoretical Criminology*, 9(1): 5–33.

Dal Lago, A. (2009) *Non-persone: L'esclusione dei Migranti in Una Società Globale*, Milano: Feltrinelli.

Dauvergne, C. (2008) *Making People Illegal: What Globalization Means for Migration and Law*, Cambridge: Cambridge University Press.

Deegan, M. J. (2011) 'The Chicago School of Ethnography', in P. Atkinson, A. Coffey, S. Delamont, J. Lofland and L. Lofland, *Handbook of Ethnography*, London: Sage Publications: 11–25.

De Genova, N. (2011) 'Alien Powers: Deportable Labour and the Spectacle of Security', in V. Squire (Ed.) *The Contested Politics of Mobility: Borderzones and Irregularity*, Abingdon: Routledge: 91–115.

De Genova, N. P. (2002) 'Migrant "Illegality" and Deportability in Everyday Life', *Annual Review of Anthropology*, 31: 419–447.

Engbersen, G. and van der Leun, J. (2001) 'The Social Construction of Illegality and Criminality', *European Journal on Criminal Policy and Research*, 9(1): 51–70.

22 Introduction

Gardner, A. M. (2010) *City of Strangers: Gulf Migration and the Indian Community in Bahrain*, New York: Cornell University Press.

Gerard, A. (2014) *The Securitization of Migration and Refugee Women*, Abingdon: Routledge.

Gerard, A. and Pickering, S. (2012) 'The Crime and Punishment of Somali Women's Extra-Legal Arrival in Malta', *British Journal of Criminology*, 52: 514–533.

Gibney, M. J. (2004) *The Ethics and Politics of Asylum: Liberal Democracy and the Response to Refugees*, Cambridge: Cambridge University Press.

Gilbert, A. and Koser, K. (2006) 'Coming to the UK: What Do Asylum-Seekers Know about the UK before Arrival?', *Journal of Ethnic and Migration Studies*, 32(7): 1209–1225.

Guild, E. (2009) *Security and Migration in the 21st Century*, Cambridge: Polity Press.

Harpviken, K. B. (2009) *Social Networks and Migration in Wartime Afghanistan*, Houndmills: Palgrave Macmillan.

Harrell-Bond, B. (1988) 'The Sociology of Involuntary Migration: An Introduction', *Current Sociology*, 36(1): 1–6.

Harrell-Bond, B. and Voutira, E. (2007) 'In Search of "Invisible" Actors: Barriers to Access in Refugee Research', *Journal of Refugee Studies*, 20(2): 281–298.

Harrell-Bond, B., Voutira, E. and Leopold, M. (1992) 'Counting the Refugees: Gifts, Givers, Patrons and Clients', *Journal of Refugee Studies*, 3/4: 205–225.

Hassan, L. (2000) 'Deterrence Measures and the Prevention of Asylum in the United Kingdom and United States', *Journal of Refugee Studies*, 13(2): 184–204.

Haugen, H. Ø. (2012) 'Nigerians in China: A Second State of immobility', *International Migration*, 50(2): 65–80.

Ip, C. (2010) 'Protected in HK but Denied Right to Work', *South China Morning Post*, 28 November. Viewed 29 November 2010: www.unhcr.org/cgi-bin/texis/vtx/refdaily?pass=463ef21123&id=4cf3531e5

Jacobsen, K. (2002) 'Livelihoods in Conflict: The Pursuit of Livelihoods by Refugees and the Impact on the Human Security of Host Communities', *International Migration*, 40(5): 95–121.

Jacobsen, K. (2006) 'Refugees and Asylum Seekers in Urban Areas: A Livelihoods Perspective', *Journal of Refugee Studies*, 19(3): 273–286.

Jacobsen, K. and Landau, L. B. (2003) *The Dual Imperative in Refugee Research: Some Methodological and Ethical Considerations in Social Science Research on Forced Migration*, Rosemarie Rogers Working Paper No. 19, The Inter-University Committee on International Migration. Viewed 1 June 2009: http://web.mit.edu/cis/www/migration/pubs/rrwp/19_jacobsen.html.

Johansen, N. B. (2013) 'Governing the Funnel of Expulsion: Agamben, the Dynamics of Force, and Minimalist Biopolitics', in K. F. Aas and M. Bosworth (Eds.) *The Borders of Punishment: Migration, Citizenship, and Social Exclusion*, Oxford: Oxford University Press: 257–272.

Kaye, R. (1998) 'Redefining the Refugee: The UK Media Portrayal of Asylum Seekers', in Koser, K. and Lutz, H. (Eds.) *The New Migration in Europe: Social Constructions and Social Realities*, Houndmills: Macmillan Press: 163–182.

Khosravi, S. (2010) *'Illegal Traveller': An Auto-Ethnography of Borders*, Houndmills: Palgrave Macmillan.

Kloosterman, R., van der Leun, J. and Rath, J. (1998) 'Across the Border: Immigrants, Economic Opportunities, Social Capital, and Informal Business Activities', *Journal of Ethnic and Migration Studies*, 24(2): 249–268.

Introduction 23

Knowles, C. and Harper D. (2009) *Hong Kong: Migrant Lives, Landscapes, and Journeys*, Chicago: The University of Chicago Press.

Korac, M. (2009) *Remaking Home: Reconstructing Life, Place and Identity in Rome and Amsterdam*, New York: Berghahn Books.

Koser, K. (1997) 'Social Networks and the Asylum Cycle: The Case of Iranians in the Netherlands', *International Migration Review*, 31(3): 591–611.

Koser, K. and Pinkerton, C. (2002) *The Social Networks of Asylum Seekers and the Dissemination of Information about Countries of Asylum*, London: Home Office. Viewed 1 June 2009: www.homeoffice.gov.uk/rds/pdfs2/socialnetwork.pdf

Koser, K., Werbner, P. and Ang, I. (2004) 'Cultural Research and Refugee Studies', *Social Analysis*, 48(3): 59–65.

Krasmann, S. (2007) 'The Enemy on the Border: Critique of a Programme in Favour of a Preventive State', *Punishment & Society*, 9(3): 301–318.

Ladegaard, H. J. (2013) 'Demonising the Cultural Other: Legitimising Dehumanisation of Foreign Domestic Helpers in the Hong Kong Press', *Discourse, Context and Media*, 2: 131–140.

Lai, S. and Tjhung, M. (2013) 'Hong Kong's Refugee Shame', *Timeout*, 19 June–2 July: 16–22. Viewed 20 July 2013: http://visionfirstnow.org/uploads/Time-Out-Refugee-Shame-feature-Jun20131.pdf

Landau, L. B. (2004) *Urban Refugees Study Guide*, Oxford: Forced Migration Online. Viewed 1 August 2009: www.forcedmigration.org/guides/fmo024/fmo024.pdf

Landau, L. B. and Jacobsen, K. (2005) 'The Value of Transparency, Replicability and Representativeness', *Forced Migration Review*, 22: 46.

Landolt, P. and Goldring, L. (2010) *The Long Term Impacts of Non-Citizenship on Work: Precarious Legal Status and the Institutional Production of a Migrant Working Poor*. Viewed 15 August 2012: www.yorku.ca/raps1/events/pdf/Landolt_Goldring.pdf

Legislative Council (LegCo) (2013) *Panel on Security of the Legislative Council Screening of Non-refoulement Claims*, LC Paper No. CB(2)1465/12–13(01), 2 July. Viewer 1 September 2013: http://visionfirstnow.org/uploads/Legco-Screening-of-Non-refoulement-claims.pdf

Loper, K. (2010) 'Human Rights, Non-refoulement and the Protection of Refugees in Hong Kong', *International Journal of Refugee Law*, 22(3): 404–439.

Ludwig, B. (2013) ' "Wiping the Refugee Dust from My Feet": Advantages and Burdens of Refugee Status and the Refugee Label', *International Migration*.

Mackenzie, C., McDowell, C. and Pittaway, E. (2007) 'Beyond "Do No Harm": The Challenges of Constructing Ethical Relationships in Refugee Research', *Journal of Refugee Research*, 20(2): 299–319.

Madden, R. (2010) *Being Ethnographic: A Guide to the Theory and Practice of Ethnography*, London: Sage.

Martinez, D. and Slack, J. (2013) 'What Part of "Illegal" Don't You Understand? The Social Consequences of Criminalizing Unauthorized Mexican Migrants in the United States', *Social & Legal Studies*, 22(4): 535–551.

Mathews, G. (2011) *Ghetto at the Center of the World: Chungking Mansions, Hong Kong*, Chicago: The University of Chicago Press.

Mathews, G., Ma, E. K-w. and Lui, T-l. (2008) *Hong Kong, China: Learning to Belong to a Nation*, Abingdon: Routledge.

May, T. (2001) *Social Research: Issues, Methods and Process*, third edition, Maidenhead: Open University Press.

24 Introduction

Mazzadra, S. (2011) 'The Gaze of Autonomy: Capitalism, Migration and Social Struggles', in V. Squire (Ed.) *The Contested Politics of Mobility: Borderzones and Irregularity*, Abingdon: Routledge: 121–142.

McCulloch, J. and Pickering, S. (2012) (Eds.) *Borders and Crime: Pre-Crime, Mobility and Serious Harm in an Age of Globalization*, Houndmills: Palgrave Macmillan.

McEwan, C., Pollard, J. and Henry, N. (2005) 'The "Global" in the City Economy: Multicultural Economic Development in Birmingham', *International Journal of Urban and Regional Research*, 29(4): 916–933.

McKay, S., Markova, E. and Paraskevopoulou, A. (2011) *Undocumented Workers' Transitions: Legal Status, Migration, and Work in Europe*, Abingdon: Routledge.

Melossi, D. (2003) ' "In a Peaceful Life": Migration and the Crime of Modernity in Europe/Italy', *Punishment & Society*, 5(4): 371–397.

Melossi, D. (2013) 'People on the Move: From the Countryside to the Factory/Prison', in K. F. Aas and M. Bosworth (Eds.) *The Borders of Punishment: Migration, Citizenship, and Social Exclusion*, Oxford: Oxford University Press: 273–290.

Menjivar, C. (2006) 'Liminal Legality: Salvadoran and Guatemalan Immigrants' Lives in the United States', *American Journal of Sociology*, 111(4): 999–1037.

Mollenkopf, J. H. and Castells, M. (1991) (Eds.) *Dual City: Restructuring New York*, New York: Russell Sage Foundation.

Muus, P. (1997) (Ed.) *Exclusion and Inclusion of Refugees in Contemporary Europe*, Utrecht: ERCOMER.

Nevins, J. (2002) *Operation Gatekeeper: The Rise of the Illegal Alien and the Making of the U.S.-Mexico Boundary*, New York: Routledge.

Ngo, J. (2013) 'No Information for NGOs on New Hong Kong System for Asylum Seekers', *South China Morning Post*, 3 November. Viewed 3 November 2013: www.scmp.com/news/hong-kong/article/1346216/no-information-ngos-new-hong-kong-system-asylum-seekers

Núñez, G. G. and Heyman, J. McC. (2007) 'Entrapment Processes and Immigrant Communities in a Time of Heightened Border Vigilance', *Human Organization*: 66(4): 354–65.

Ocejo, R. E. (2013) (Ed.) *Ethnography and the City: Readings on Doing Urban Fieldwork*, New York: Routledge.

Oelgemöller, C. (2011) ' "Transit" and "Suspension": Migration Management or the Metamorphosis of Asylum Seekers into Illegal Immigrants', *Journal of Ethnic and Migration Studies*, 37(3): 407–424.

Okojie, P. (1992) 'The March of the Invaders: Racism and Refugee Policies in Europe', *Race Relations Abstracts*, 17(1): 5–29.

Park, R., Burgess, E. W. and McKenzie R. D. (1925) *The City*, Chicago: University of Chicago Press.

Pellegrino, V. (2012) 'La Clandestinità come Progetto Trans-nazionale: Un Caso di Studio sulle Migrazioni Marocchine in Emilia (Nord Italia)', *Mondi Migranti*, 2: 205–226.

Pickering, S. (2001) 'Common Sense and Original Deviancy: News Discourses and Asylum Seekers in Australia', *Journal of Refugee Studies*, 14(2): 169–186.

Pickering, S. (2005) *Refugees and State Crime*, Sydney: The Federation Press.

Poros, M. V. (2001) 'The Role of Migrant Networks in Linking Local Labour Markets: The Case of Asian Indian Migration to New York and London', *Global Networks*, 1(3): 243–259.

Ramakers, J. (1997) 'The Challenges of Refugee Protection in Belgium', in P. Muus (Ed.) *Exclusion and Inclusion of Refugees in Contemporary Europe*, Utrecht: ERCOMER: 96–116.

Ramsden, M. and Marsh, L. (2013) 'The "Right to Work" of Refugees in Hong Kong: Ma v Director of Immigration', *International Journal of Refugee Law*, 25(3): 574–596.

Sassen, S. (1988) *The Mobility of Labor and Capital: A Study in International Investment and Labor Flow*, Cambridge: Cambridge University Press.

Sassen, S. (1996) *Losing Control? Sovereignty in an Age of Globalization*, New York: Columbia University Press.

Sassen, S. (2001) *The Global City: New York, London, Tokyo*, second edition, Princeton: Princeton University Press.

Schuster, L. (2005) 'The Continuing Mobility of Migrants in Italy: Shifting between Places and Statuses', *Journal of Ethnic and Migration Studies*, 31(4): 757–774.

Schuster, L. (2011) 'Turning Refugees into "Illegal Migrants": Afghan Asylum Seekers in Europe', *Ethnic and Racial Studies*, 34(8): 1392–1407.

Singer, A. and Massey, D. S. (1998) 'The Social Process of Undocumented Border Crossing among Mexican Migrants', *International Migration Review*, 32(3): 561–592.

Smart, A. (2003) 'Sharp Edges, Fuzzy Categories and Transborder Networks: Managing and Housing New Arrivals in Hong Kong', *Ethnic and Relation Studies*, 26(2): 218–233.

Squire, V. (2009) *The Exclusionary Politics of Asylum*, Houndmills: Palgrave Macmillan.

Stein, B. N. (1986) 'The Experience of Being a Refugee: Insights from the Research Literature', in C. Williams and J. Westermeyer (Eds.) *Refugee Mental Health in Resettlement Countries*, Washington, DC: Hemisphere Publications: 5–23.

United Nations High Commissioner for Refugees (UNHCR) (1996) *Convention and Protocol Relating to the Status of Refugees*, Geneva: UNHCR.

Vearey, J. (2009) *The Responsibility to Protect and the Need to Affect Change: Undocumented Migrants, Research Ethics and Methodology*, Migration Methods and Field Notes, 8, Johannesburg: Forced Migration Studies Programme, University of Witwatersrand.

Vecchio, F. and Beatson, C. (2013) 'Resisting Government Labelling and Engaging the Community: The "March For Protection" in Hong Kong', *Oxford Monitor of Forced Migration*, 3(1): 24–29.

Vrecer, N. (2010) 'Living in Limbo: Integration of Forced Migrants from Bosnia and Herzegovina in Slovenia', *Journal of Refugee Studies*, 23(4): 484–502.

Wallerstein, I. (1979) *The Capitalist World-Economy*, Cambridge: Cambridge University Press.

Webber, F. (2011) 'How Voluntary Are Voluntary Returns?', *Race & Class*, 52(4) 98–107.

Webber, F. (2012) 'Borderline Justice', *Race & Class*, 54(2): 39–54.

Weber, L. (2006) 'The Shifting Frontiers of Migration Control', in S. Pickering and L. Weber (Eds.) *Borders, Mobility and Technologies of Control*, Dordrecht: Springer: 21–44.

Weber, L. (2007) 'Policing the Virtual Border: Punitive Preemption in Australian Offshore Migration Control', *Social Justice*, 34(2): 77–93.

Weber, L. and Bowling, B. (2008) 'Valiant Beggars and Global Vagabonds: Select, Eject, Immobilize', *Theoretical Criminology*, 12(3): 355–375.

Weber, L. and Pickering, S. (2011) *Globalization and Borders: Death and the Global Frontier*, Houndmills: Palgrave Macmillan.

Wengraf, T. (2001) *Qualitative Research Interviewing*, London: Sage Publications.

Zetter, R. (1991) 'Labelling Refugees: Forming and Transforming a Bureaucratic Identity', *Journal of Refugee Studies*, 4(1): 39–62.

26 *Introduction*

Zetter, R. (2007) 'More Labels, Fewer Refugees: Remaking the Refugee Label in an Era of Globalization', *Journal of Refugee Studies*: 20(2): 172–192.

Zimmermann, S. (2009a) 'Irregular Secondary Movements to Europe: Seeking Asylum beyond Refuge', *Journal of Refugee Studies*, 22(1): 74–96.

Zimmermann, S. (2009b) 'Why Seek Asylum? The Role of Integration and Financial Support', *International Migration*, 48(1): 199–231.

1 The global city and asylum seeking

The Introduction identified Jacobsen's (2006) livelihood framework as a useful theoretical tool to advance critical understandings of how urban refugee populations manage their lives against a backdrop of policies, laws and social norms that impact refugee agency to produce specific outcomes. In this chapter, I develop this framework by including perspectives from the global city paradigm, which offers an equally constructive tool to gain in-depth understanding of the vulnerability of asylum seekers, and hence their agency and the outcomes of their migration, in the context of Hong Kong.

The Introduction explained that the aim of this research was to provide attentive descriptions and analyses of the lived experiences of the asylum seekers who arrive in this global city so as to comprehend the deviancy that official and public views generally attribute to people alleged to travel to Hong Kong for the purpose of exploiting asylum mechanisms and unlawfully engaging in economic activities. Under this proposition, the vulnerability of asylum seekers is generated by a conceptualization of asylum that is evinced by the socioeconomic role that asylum seekers play in this city, one that is strongly intertwined with the notion of asylum abuse. The purpose of this chapter is therefore to frame asylum by a set of findings from the literature the relevance of which may at first appear tenuous. Nonetheless, refugee mobility and experiences appear to be largely defined by global economic forces and neoliberal institutional structures that define the global city's tendency to generate demand for labour in the expanding urban low-grade and underpaid economy. As noted in the Introduction, part of this economy is reliant on (irregular) migrant workers (Sassen 2001), and asylum seekers constitute a labour reserve prepared to engage with the economic activities typical of the new urban economy. This is not to say that no differences exist between asylum seekers and labour migrants, but in the context of Hong Kong, the two categories largely overlap, often not because of any rational choice on the part of asylum seekers, but because the boundaries that usually divide the two groups are blurred in this city.

An analysis of this specific context is thus believed to provide meaningful perspectives to situate the experiences of asylum seekers and critically evaluate the claims of asylum abuse. Such claims are in fact a constant thread that knits together the many arguments presented in the chapters that follow, for these

28   *The global city and asylum seeking*

claims impact the background that determines the availability, mix and extent of the resources asylum seekers can access; the strategies they use to access them; and the goals they can feasibly achieve. In this light, this chapter reveals that the notion of asylum abuse is rooted in dynamics that extend beyond the fear that asylum seekers lie for their own benefit. Instead, this notion appears to be based in socioeconomic and political processes that are strictly interwoven with Hong Kong's emergence as a renowned global city.

The chapter is divided into three sections, each dealing with interrelated aspects primarily intended to investigate the socioeconomic transformation that has occurred in Hong Kong in terms of social polarization and the division of labour. In particular, the opportunity structure affecting asylum seekers is discussed in light of global economic restructuring and local governance, which determine the spaces within which local residents can generate income. Hong Kong is thus analyzed in connection to its local and historical context, including previous compelling migratory inflows which have shaped the overall development of policies around perceptions of refugees. In this regard, the interconnectedness and at times contradictory relation between the 'global' and the several levels of the 'local' are found here to be critical in defining current experiences of asylum in Hong Kong.

Accounting for the opportunity structure: The global city

When the British declared sovereignty over Hong Kong in 1841, the 'fragrant harbour' – as it was then translated into English – consisted of a few sparsely populated fishing villages. Today, after 156 years of colonial rule, and almost two decades of socialist control brought about by the transfer of sovereignty from the UK to the People's Republic of China in 1997, Hong Kong has grown to occupy the role of a global metropolis, connected to other privileged cities and pivotal to the growth of the global economy (Meyer 2000; Chu 2008). As part of a powerful and interdependent network of global cities operating at a vast geographical scale that comprises leading financial centres such as New York, London and Tokyo (Friedmann 1986; Sassen 2001), Hong Kong has become a key location for the regional and international coordination, exchange and consumption of capital and highly specialized services, at the gateway to China's interior and bustling economy (Meyer 2000). However, Hong Kong not only functions as a centre and meeting place for high-level financial activities and an intermediary between the second-largest national economy and the globalized world. It is also a site of structural social transformation, much of which appears to be consistent with descriptions of the 'global city' in terms of social inequality, consumption patterns and the casualization of labour (Sassen 1998, 2001).

Globalization scholars generally note that, since the 1970s, the world has changed as capital was released from its national constraints and capitalism progressively advanced to reach virtually every nation in the world. We live in a time in which highly mobile capital and financial markets appear to have assumed dominance over industrial and agricultural production (Coleman and Sajed 2013). At the same time, economic neoliberal principles based on the postulation that economic growth and human well-being are better enhanced via the liberalization of the economy have become predominant in the corridors of power of both national governments and the supranational institutions that regulate global trade and finance (Harvey 2005). This change, according to several scholars, has resulted in the rescaling of the strategic territories that articulate the global economy (Brenner 1999; Sassen 2001). Simply put, the state's capacity to control the economy has weakened, and a clearly observable tendency has emerged of the general retreat of the nation-state from economic governance. This development has created new opportunities for other scales to emerge, and global cities have become one site that has benefited from this worldwide shift (Sassen 2001, 2005). Global cities are complex constructs, the major defining feature of which is that they possess the specialized producer services that corporate firms need in order to control and articulate their increasingly dispersed global operations. In other words, in an era of 'time and space compression' (Harvey 2005; Falk 1999), whereby capital moves faster and distances are increasingly of less importance due to innovations in information and transportation technologies (Castells 2000), corporate operations are more complex and divided across multiple sites. Further, given the intensive and increasing global competition, corporations no longer control every process of the production chain. Rather, they outsource many of their functions, including those that are contracted to firms that specialize in accounting, finance, legal and other services, which tend to cluster in particular cities due to both the nature of their business dealings and the ease of networking with their counterparts around the globe (Sassen 2001; Venables 2001).

Global cities have thus become vital as nodal intersections in the articulation and control of global economic flows. Yet this function – while contested by some scholars (Smith 2013) – is performed by people and requires appropriate infrastructures to operate. In effect, the abstractness of capital mobility finds its counterpart in the materiality of the city (Acuto 2011). Ever more numerous are the office towers located in city centres, which provide the space for the economic activities of our time. Likewise, increasingly numerous are the hotels and serviced apartments that compete for prime locations in urban areas. State-of-the-art airports, railways and digital highways are built in record time and are continuously renovated and expanded to accommodate the growing demand for transnational services. Noteworthy is that the changing urban landscape of the global city is not aimed solely at building an environment purposefully supportive of the global economy. Rather, it is also intended to market an image of the city that is strictly intertwined with its material (re)development (Zukin 1992). Just as corporations compete with each other to minimize operational costs and gain larger market shares, so do global cities compete with each other to retain and enhance their centrality in the new complex and integrated global system (Ancien 2011; Robinson 2002). Luxurious lifestyles in cosmopolitan and dynamic environments possessed of all comforts and amenities supposedly nurture an appearance of vitality conducive to human resources, foreign investments and tourism. Ever higher buildings reshape the skyline and the hierarchical geography of successful cities, while the organization of mega-events and sparkly fireworks displays instil confidence in

30 *The global city and asylum seeking*

the city. In this view, global cities become sites of new cultural forms of spending which underscore both the homogenization and universalization of consumption patterns now based on affluence, emulation and materialism (Levine 2007). Critically, one key contention of the global city paradigm is that the rise of these new forms of consumption produces a chain of dynamics which engender vast and growing polarization in the occupational, income and spatial distribution between classes (Sassen 2001).

To draw a parallel with Hong Kong, there is no doubt that the former British colony has developed to resemble a global city. Central to Hong Kong's economic structures are the processes that reshape capital and power relations in terms of financial markets, producer services and telecommunication technologies (Meyer 2000; Jao 1997; Chiu and Lui 2009). The impressive boom in financial activities that occurred following World War II has been extensively documented (Jao 1997; Schenk 2001).The socio-spatial dynamics of urban economic change have also been analyzed, emphasizing a link between wealth disparities and urban spatial segregation (Forrest et al. 2004; Lee et al. 2007). In this light, some scholars highlight that Hong Kong is an ideal place for examining social dynamics in an era of globalization, as the city has 'undergone the critical transformation postulated in the global city literature in the most striking manner' (Chiu and Lui 2009: 82). Indeed, the transformation that has taken place in Hong Kong has as much to do with the large-scale financial activities and the 'glittering lights' of much of the recent urban redevelopment as it does with an apparent divide between the haves and have-nots, and the related inequality to which an increasingly demanding class of well-off professionals contributes.

Framing the 'dual' city

The labour requirements of corporations have been argued to give rise in global cities to a workforce possessed of high levels of training and specialization (Friedmann 1986; Sassen 2001). Citing population census micro-data, Chiu and Lui (2009) find that the number of managers and professionals in Hong Kong has grown by 40.3 per cent and 81 per cent, respectively, in a relatively short span of time, from 1991 to 2001 – an increase that brought the two categories to account for about 15 per cent of the employed population, which rose to 20 per cent in 2012 (Hong Kong Government 2013a). A similar upward trend is evinced in the number of transnational elites who have taken residence in the city (Chiu and Lui 2009). Hong Kong's emergence as a leading financial centre has indeed changed the social strata and the composition of the labour force, and Findlay et al. (1996) and Li et al. (1998) note that this has occurred at a time when the size of the expatriate community has grown despite the return of Hong Kong to China and the departure of numbers of British nationals previously employed in the colonial government. According to Findlay et al. (1996), the rise and diversification of the 'expat' community suggests that the employment opportunities for highly skilled foreign-born individuals have flourished within the new economy of an expanding global city. Partly confirming this trend, the Hong Kong Immigration Department

The global city and asylum seeking   31

(ImmD) has stated that 28,625 non-Chinese professionals from nearly 100 countries were admitted into Hong Kong for employment in 2012 (ImmD 2013), adding to the 30,557 and 22,280 professionals admitted for the same reason in 2011 and 2010, respectively (ImmD 2011, 2012).

Although the size of this population is a small fraction of a population of 7.1 million people, the expansion of a well-educated and presumably highly paid class of individuals favoured by substantial gains in real income and wealth has to a large extent mirrored changes in consumer behaviour (Chan 2000). Luxury items, stylish brands, foreign cuisine and costly apartments in brand new high-rise buildings, conveniently located a short distance from the financial heart of the city, have in recent years come to symbolize the new vision of a 'good life'. All over the territory, modern shopping malls have popped up like crystal mushrooms to offer the latest styles in fashion design and interior decor, presenting to the local resident population and visitors alike an image of the city as the ultimate Asian shopping paradise (McDonogh and Wong 2005). At the same time, elegant apartment towers featuring swimming pools, gyms and high-tech gadgets, often named in hard-to-pronounce but romantic, exotic-sounding European languages, have come to challenge the usual space-poor, noisy, crowded surroundings of the city by evoking idealized representations of a vibrant, exciting experience in sophisticated milieus.

Additionally, Hong Kong boasts a capacity of 1000 daily flights networking the city with over 180 destinations worldwide, generating a passenger turnout of 56 million in 2012.[1] Hong Kong's service sector generates over 90 per cent of the territory's gross domestic product (GDP) (Lung 2012), while tourism has skyrocketed in terms of occupational opportunities in recent decades (Lee et al. 2007) and has become one of the city's four pillar industries, together with financial services, trading and logistics and professional and producer services (Census and Statistics Department [CSD] 2013). Adding to the global dimension of this city, the Hong Kong International Airport and the harbour located at the end of the Pearl River Delta are among the world's busiest cargo and containerized manufactured products gateways, offering multiple linkages between China and the world. As global cities assume different roles in the global economy, the fortunes of Hong Kong pivot around its gateway function, which has earned the city a privileged position on a par with New York and London for high-connectivity capacity (Chubarov and Brooker 2013). It is this connectivity that is of outmost importance in attracting large cohorts of tourists and professionals to Hong Kong (cf. Beaverstock et al. 2000; Iredale 2000). Infrastructure and new construction sites open regularly across town, and gentrification has become an inevitable part of life in a place where extensive urban development is impossible for the territory's limited size and the tendency is to replace residential property every 50 years, or increasingly sooner to suit new trends and redevelopers' desires for profit (Ley and Teo 2013).

In terms of occupation, the global city paradigm contends that the existence of these high-income lifestyles has fed the expansion of an array of elementary occupations in low-grade and labour-intensive sectors, poorly paid but necessary

32   *The global city and asylum seeking*

for the construction and maintenance of residential and commercial buildings, hotels and restaurants, and for the day-to-day caretaking of household activities. Importantly, this change has occurred at a time when manufacturing has receded from the major urban centres of advanced economies. Over the past three decades, a substantial volume of scholarship has highlighted the link between capitalism and the spatial redistribution of the international division of labour, highlighting how the production processes previously concentrated in the industrial areas of those cities where consumption was highest are now scattered all over the world to benefit from cheaper labour (Friedmann and Wolff 1982; Cohen 1987). In turn, a massive shift in employment has been observed in many global cities, resulting in a visible polarization of labour and income structures (Mollenkopf and Castells 1991). As Acuto (2011) has recently stressed, the global city does not necessarily entail only positive qualities as epitomized in the luxury on display in major shopping malls. Rather, 'being "global" entails both pay-offs and high prices. . . . Global cities are equally sites of opportunities and relegation, ridden by social inequality as much as open to mobility, characterised by billionaire elites and wretched ghettos, whose "right to the city" is often systematically denied' (Acuto 2011: 2961).

In this view, Chiu and Lui (2009) have analyzed Hong Kong in relation to the claim that the deregulation of the global economy and the concentration in core cities of people with administrative and executive qualifications have caused the expansion of low-grade personal service work. They found that both the top and bottom levels of the labour market have grown, and the number of people employed in elementary occupations in particular has risen to outnumber the growth in all other major occupational categories, although in relative terms their increase marked a modest 26 per cent from 1991 to 2001. Based on a rare comparison of polarizing tendencies in major Asian cities, Tai (2006, 2010) similarly argues that Hong Kong's occupational structure appears to be impacted by a dual inflow of immigrants who have swollen the size of the resident groups that make a living on the lower echelons of the occupational ladder.[2] If technological advancement and the new international division of labour have enabled the transferability of skills across borders, the same developments have notably helped create both the 'necessity and the desire' for people in the developing countries at the periphery of the world to migrate to core, advanced economies in search of work (Wills et al. 2009: 2). Large influxes of immigrant populations have thus contributed to an impression of social polarization, as their job opportunities lie at the lower end of the occupation ladder, thus escalating income inequalities. For example, Massey (2007) finds staggering contrasts between wealth and poverty in London, while Willis et al. (2009) similarly assert that growing numbers of both unemployed and 'working poor' face no option but to take up jobs generally regarded as the '3Ds' – dangerous, demeaning and dirty. This is particularly true for migrant populations, whose opportunities are further diminished by the lack of access to state benefits, generally reserved for ordinary citizens. While the evidence of increased polarization between groups at the top and bottom of society is contradictory (cf. Hamnett 1994), these studies attest to the growth in the relative size of low-wage labour markets and the lessened chances to move up the occupational ladder for certain strata of both local and migrant populations.

According to the global city literature, economic restructuring tends to cluster workers at the top and bottom ends of the labour market as the middle-income occupations in manufacturing disappear and employees are forced to seek jobs in those sectors now distinctive of the global city. While the highest qualified and trained workers in manufacturing can trade their skills for better wages at the top levels of the new occupational hierarchy, the trend identified by Sassen and colleagues, and hypothesized as a general phenomenon, is that lower skilled, middle-income earners in manufacturing can only end up in the expanding low-wage, labour-intensive sectors, where intense competition is coupled with a general downgrading of the tasks performed, which in turn causes a downgrading effect over the value of the workers themselves, now more vulnerable to exploitation (Sassen 1998, 2001). The service economy is argued to be shaped around new personnel requirements because employers must keep operating costs down in a new phase of capitalism in which subcontracting, part-time work and the casualization of employment relations emerge as the paradigmatic forms of employment (Wills et al. 2009). Cianconi (2011) rightly argues that flexibility was once perceived as a means to advance human freedom. Under the present economic conditions, however, it mostly entails precarization. While this condition seems to affect all echelons of the occupational structure, the low-wage sectors are the most affected, as large cohorts of workers are hard pressed to accept jobs not only on less favourable terms, but also in which wages are often insufficient to make ends meet. Friedmann (1986: 77) calls this shift in employment an 'evolution of jobs'. Especially in labour-intensive sectors, the general trend is for small businesses and micro-enterprises employing low-skilled workers to offer increasingly occasional and lower paid work, often under 'sweatshop conditions' and with little or no benefits (Sassen 2001; Gordon and Harloe 1991). Of particular importance is that, as workers have moved away from manufacturing, the political power of trade unions in organizing production has diminished, resulting in pay and working conditions being controlled by purely economic market forces to a great extent (Hjarnø 2003). This development has meant that a large 'informal' economy has emerged. A wide array of micro-manufacturing and service jobs previously performed legally are now undertaken in violation of the public regulatory framework, as employers have sought better profit margins both by avoiding government regulations related to minimum wage, safety and overtime conditions, and by ensuring more flexibility in relation to working hours and the dismissal of employees (Champion 1994; Sassen 1991).

Hong Kong appears to have followed this trend in the past few decades. The extent to which urban change has caused the social and economic shifts postulated in the global city literature is, however, a matter of contention. The main arguments of this 'polarization debate' are briefly discussed subsequently for they shed light on how the current labour market structure affects the possibilities for certain local residents to attain an income, and this, I argue, shapes the vulnerability of asylum seekers.

34 *The global city and asylum seeking*

The polarization debate in Hong Kong

A number of studies have analyzed Hong Kong in relation to the social polarization claim (Lee et al. 2007). However, to a large extent the results have been ambivalent. For example, Chiu and Lui (2009) indicate that polarization in the occupational structure of the Hong Kong labour market is an observable phenomenon in both absolute and relative terms. They nonetheless contend that the evidence of income polarization is less clear, as even when there is a widening income gap between the lowest and highest income groups, there is still a net real income growth for all groups, although at the lower level this seems to be marginal and therefore to have only a limited influence on improving livelihoods. In terms of occupation, Lee and Wong (2004, in Lee et al. 2007) draw similar conclusions when observing an expansion of professional jobs and low-wage service work, alongside a reduction in traditional average-wage jobs and white-collar occupations in manufacturing and other sectors of the industrial economy. Lee et al. (2007), instead, assert that when a more detailed occupational segmentation is applied against the generally accepted three-way segmentation of the labour market, the disappearing 'middle' of the labour force described by Chiu and Lui (2009) is not so apparent. At the heart of this argument in fact is that no precise classification of skills and social groups is included in the original global city literature (Tai 2006). For example, Lee et al. (2007) found that there are a large number of mid-level service jobs, namely associate professional jobs, which can hardly be seen to fit into the low-wage sectors. In their view, while globalization destroys many manufacturing jobs, it also creates plenty of professional ones, suggesting a process of professionalization rather than polarization (cf. Hamnett 1994). This finding is supported by other scholars, who assert that, depending on whether categories such as clerks and service and shop sales workers are considered middle- or low-income occupations, either polarization or professionalization may be identified as predominant (Borel-Saladin and Crankshaw 2009). In a similar way, Tai (2010: 745) suggests that 'under the umbrella of social polarisation, scholars use their own variables to tell different stories of social polarisation in their own cities'. He found that when a more detailed occupational segmentation is applied to the Hong Kong labour market, the evidence indicates rather accentuated professionalization tendencies. However, when immigration data is inserted into the picture, a dual foreign labour market becomes evident.

Importantly for the purpose of this study, this debate appears to have largely overlooked the role played by irregular migrant populations in urban labour markets – a deficiency that the present research aims to partly fill. Studies on social polarization in Hong Kong, and elsewhere, have been mostly based on official statistics as the primary source of information, thereby accounting for the formal occupational structures, housing and patterns of spatial segregation, as well as household income disparities. However, little attention has been paid to the growth of informal economic activities and their supposed capacity to generate demand for cheaper workers, many of whom are irregular migrants (Samers 2002). Noteworthy in this regard is that Friedmann (1997: 24) describes these

The global city and asylum seeking   35

people as 'non-persons' (also Dal Lago 2009), or large, floating populations invisible on official maps and not monitored by the state when their official residence continues to be elsewhere.

Sassen (2001) explains that social polarization is the outcome of the structural conditions that foster informalization in the economy, which facilitates the absorption of a growing migrant workforce. Part of this workforce lacks regular immigration status and hence is more exploitable by employers seeking to keep costs down to ensure the viability of their business. Indeed, the growth of employment demand in certain service sectors is rarely met entirely within the local labour market. This occurs because economic growth, coupled by a pervasive culture that idealizes the achievement of individual success through the attainment of increasingly higher levels of education, has contributed to reducing the value of certain menial tasks. These jobs have become less attractive to local populations but are being undertaken by a less sophisticated foreign workforce attracted by the relatively better living conditions and wages available in 'rich' countries (Chiswick 2001; Sassen 1999; Wills et al. 2009). Moreover, the rising number of unregulated workers at the bottom of the salary distribution scale generally causes a visible expansion of a sort of parallel society that caters for these workers' consumption needs and limited earnings (Sassen 2001). Workers in labour-intensive, small-scale subcontracting and low-wage sectors cannot afford the luxury goods on offer in global cities. They need to rely on low-cost producers and retail shops where returns are marginal and small profits are possible only by employing cheaper labour. This development is particularly visible in the 'ethnic economy', where many jobs lie at the fringes of legality and employers can take advantage of their co-nationals who lack regular immigration status (Grzymala-Kazlowska 2005). As De Genova (2002) reminds us, the long struggle between capital and labour power is effectively resolved by the commodification of the latter when either rigid conditions of stay or an untenured legal status is imposed on people who are then forced to accept and perform any work.

Equally important for this study is the argument that Lee et al. (2007) set forth concerning the coexistence of professionalization and growing income inequality in Hong Kong. These authors explain that the shift from industrial to post-industrial labour structures has made it extremely difficult for workers employed in low-end jobs to escape poor working conditions when they lack both the educational credentials and working experience that are valued in a knowledge-based economy. To briefly summarize the events that explain the surge of what Lee et al. (2007) call the 'low-income-poverty' trap, Hong Kong experienced a phase of rapid industrialization in the 1950s and 1960s. However, when China opened up to foreign capital in the early 1980s, Hong Kong manufacturing firms seized the opportunity to reduce costs and retain international competitiveness by moving their factories across the border (Chiu and Lui 2009; Law and Lee 2013). Over 80 per cent of the labour force in manufacturing was forced out of work within just 15 years, which created a large pool of unemployed blue-collar workers who had to find work in other sectors of the economy. According to Zhao et al. (2004), the sudden presence of this mass of about half a million people in

36 *The global city and asylum seeking*

search of work triggered a decrease in the real income of the working class and produced a downgrading effect on wages at the lower end of the social hierarchy, as their skills and education levels could hardly be competitive except in the lower skilled occupations. Additionally, the rising hardship experienced by low-income families forced women to enter the labour market, especially when their husbands became unemployed. This further pushed down wage levels in low-paid service jobs, 'reinforcing the bondage of the low-income-poverty cycle' and reducing opportunities to escape poverty (Lee et al. 2007: 27). Thus, a large army of 'working poor', occasionally employed and often enduring long periods of unemployment, was created by economic restructuring. Professionalization augmented social inequalities because the professional and semi-professional labour markets began to recruit entrants from university graduates at a time when the capacity of workers in low-grade service sectors to retain their jobs was also impacted. Indeed, the global city can require ever more qualified workers even in low-wage jobs at the bottom of the occupational hierarchy (Law and Lee 2013).

Law and Lee have recently argued that one important legacy of British colonialism is the presence of over 60,000 South Asians in Hong Kong, some of whom have been in the territory for generations while others have arrived more recently (CSD 2012). The colonial policy to recruit military forces from the Indian subcontinent allowed South Asians to develop their niche in security-related jobs (O'Connor 2012). However, many of these jobs were lost when a large mass of blue-collar workers entered the security services and competition impelled workers to professionalize their skills. Law and Lee note that professionalization does not occur solely in middle-income jobs, but also affects low-wage personal services work when increasing emphasis is placed on service quality. Even at the lower end of the occupational structure, workers can be required to look and act professionally, for which they need to obtain qualifications, language skills and licences, the cost of which is to be borne by the prospective employees. In practice, a lack of knowledge and skills prevents certain labour workers from entering the professional and semi-professional sectors, or even retaining their low-waged jobs. Simultaneously, the lowly paid casual jobs these people occupy hinder the acquisition of the skills without which upward mobility is generally impossible (Lee et al. 2007).

Working in poverty in Hong Kong

In 2011, an Oxfam report found that in Hong Kong 534,100 people in 144,400 families with children aged 15 and under fell below the poverty line that year, living in a state of high food insecurity (Oxfam 2011). Low-income families were said to turn to food banks for help, and many lined up at banks to cash precious, though palliative, handouts donated by the government to Hong Kong's permanent residents as a remedy for the previous year's excessive budget revenues (Tam 2011). During the time I spent in Hong Kong meeting with and studying refugee populations, I often observed disturbing scenes of poverty-stricken individuals struggling to make ends meet. For example, in the early hours of the morning,

The global city and asylum seeking 37

I witnessed elderly men quietly sitting at McDonald's with no meal before them, blankly gazing into the distance, yet checking nearby tables for leftovers.

Poverty, arguably one powerful indicator of social inequality, is structural in Hong Kong. While Hong Kong's per-capita GDP is one of the highest in the world – standing at HK$285,403, with an unemployment rate of 3.3 per cent in 2012 (Hong Kong Government 2013b) – the poverty line that the Hong Kong Government set in 2013 at half the median household income, or HK$3600 per month for one person, indicates that about 1.3 million people live in poverty – roughly one in seven persons (Ngo 2013). Saunders et al. (2013) reveal that Hong Kong's Gini coefficient, the most common measurement tool to identify inequality in the income and wealth distribution between classes, was over 0.4 in 2010, similar to that recorded in only the United States (US), Singapore and Qatar. This record has in fact been a permanent feature of Hong Kong since 2001, when income inequality surged to its worst in over 40 years and marked the widest gap between rich and poor among all of the developed nations (Zhao et al. 2004). In this regard, Zhao et al. note that only the top 30 per cent of Hong Kong households enjoy a continual increase in income share, in the face of heavy declines experienced at the bottom. In effect, the lower the income group in Hong Kong, the greater is the reduction in its share, meaning that while the very rich benefit greatly from economic restructuring, the disadvantaged and the poor generally benefit the least. Further, it has been identified that over 40 per cent of the Hong Kong population faces severe levels of multiple deprivation of essential items in their daily life. Importantly, these levels of deprivation are twice as high for foreign-born residents than for native residents in Hong Kong (Saunders et al. 2013).

This section has highlighted that, while global cities are sites of extreme mobility and openings, the dynamics that lead to the rise of demand for workers at the top of the labour market engender vulnerability for those whose skills allow employment only in the vast, though peripheral labour markets of the global city. These people are consigned to jobs that are precarious, lowly paid and often degrading. Social polarization may yet be statistically unproven. However, numbers of Hong Kong people pursue a living in poverty, evincing an obviously splintered society in which asylum seekers constitute just one group among the most deprived. By focusing on these asylum seekers' livelihoods, this research will illustrate how their experiences are shaped within this context of diminished opportunities and growing exploitation. Hong Kong then emerges as a distinctive, stratified complex of nuanced parts each reliant on the others for profits and labour, where groups of disadvantaged residents make a living by exploiting the labour and resources of those beneath them: the asylum seekers – who are not immediately discernible in census data and labour statistics for being institutionally excluded from making meaningful social contact with the mainstream society (see Chapter 2). In this view, globalization creates oppressive structural conditions entailing relegation and immiseration for large strata of the Hong Kong population. Nonetheless, this very structure is shaped by apparent heightened mobility at the Hong Kong border for employment, tourism and, arguably, asylum (see Chapter 3). Asylum seekers become the means for certain strata of local residents to negotiate their

38 *The global city and asylum seeking*

social conditions. Residents of South Asian and other immigrant backgrounds in particular, who lack skills or whose skills are not valued, can raise their living conditions by making use of the agency of the asylum seekers, and by doing so raise their capacity to generate income while possibly lowering the impact of the low-income-poverty trap (see Chapters 4 and 5).

Accounting for governance in economic restructuring

In this section, the focus is placed on the production of the structure that was introduced earlier, in relation to state agency addressing the forces of globalization. Staggering is that the economic restructuring of this global city, and importantly its social consequences, is not just the result of exogenous forces and purely market dynamics. The economic forces of neoliberal globalization are mediated by governments that support the expansion of market economies. To this extent, inequality appears largely based on an entrepreneurial mentality that is transmitted to the weaker strata of society. The discussion below is aimed at evincing this argument, to base the analyses presented in this and subsequent chapters and in turn to reveal the areas in the literature to which this research can contribute empirical insight.

Governing economic restructuring

Earlier in this chapter, it was stated that the materiality of urban redevelopment is not only valuable for the city to explicate its 'command and control' functions. It is also aimed at branding the city in an ever more competitive race for human resources, tourism and inward investment (Zukin 1992). Over the past two decades, global city research has emphasized the role of governance in either enabling or constraining global capital mobility (Hill and Kim 2000). In particular, models based on state-centred developmental capitalism have been said to play a key role in the rise or demise of global cities in Asia (Hill and Kim 2000; Short and Kim 1999; Tai 2006). According to several scholars, however, the importance of state and urban politics and policies has been somewhat downplayed in the original formulation of the global city paradigm (Ancien 2011). For the scope of this study, it is important to note that state intervention in economic and social planning has led to the formation of labour market and polarization patterns that are at times very different from those hypothesized by global city theorists (Tai 2006, 2010). Moreover, Burgers and Musterd (2002) note that different cities adapt to global change in different ways, depending on their characteristics and historical background, including the political environment, which Yeoh (2005) claims constitutes a critical variable in post-colonial contexts. Global cities may indeed assume a specific symbolic meaning for governments aiming to affirm national identity.

While this national identity argument, in the context of Hong Kong, will be given attention in the last section of this chapter, it is worth noting here that, as Parnreiter (2013) states, the lack of analysis of the politics surrounding the global

The global city and asylum seeking   39

city is a well-recognized assessment. Chiu and Lui (2009), for instance, structure their impressive analysis in *Hong Kong: Becoming a Chinese Global City* around the notion that local political, social and geographical factors have greatly influenced the development of this city. Above all, the political stalemate in which the government is said to have entered after Hong Kong was returned to China, due to the departure of the British business elites and the emergence of new economic powers which exert significant pressure on the political establishment, has been a major factor affecting the present and future role of this city in the global economy. Importantly, Hong Kong's labour, immigration and social policies have been devised and framed within this context, which have shaped the poverty underlying asylum seekers' engagement with the informal economy.

Two arguments to emerge in the global city literature deserve clarification before proceeding to analyze the role of the Hong Kong Government in exacerbating social polarization. One argument refers to the above-mentioned claim that the state mediates the effects of neoliberal globalization. In this vein, Hamnett (1994, 1996b) posits that 'Sassen is wrong' to generalize the polarizing effects of economic restructuring because the presence in some European cities of strong welfare programmes has meant that global economic pressures have not resulted in the expansion of low-wage service economies; rather, in these contexts globalization has generated a large number of unemployed and a state-dependent population. This line is shared by Wills et al. (2009), who develop their theoretical framework on how 'global cities work' based on their understanding of London as a city with large numbers of unemployed citizens living on paltry state benefits who would rather be unemployed than work in extremely low-wage jobs. Thus, large inflows of migrants travel to wealthier societies to fill vacancies in sectors in which locals are unwilling to work. In Hong Kong, where the government has traditionally attributed little importance to extensive forms of social protection, Lee et al. (2007) argue that some of those who were displaced by deindustrialization contributed to growing unemployment rates and consequently helped push down wages in certain service sectors. In the view of both Lee et al. and Wills et al., the existence of a lowly paid and labour-intensive service sector is not questioned. However, Lee et al. contend that wage levels have been affected not only by processes of economic restructuring based on a 'demand-side' model that explains labour casualization and economic informalization as subsequent to the rise of high-end consumption patterns, but also by a large labour supply of unemployed workers – an army of people the presence of which seems to have generated fear among those in employment that they might lose their jobs were they to complain about deteriorating wages and working conditions.

Strictly related to this argument is the debate that has sprouted around the role that low-skilled immigration plays in expanding the informal economy, and indeed if an extremely low-wage service sector has manifested and if so, why. The existence of declining wages and conditions of work is central to explanations of much recent global mobility (cf. Wills et al. 2009). However, there is disagreement in the literature about the impact of push and pull factors on the demand-supply equation, in particular on whether the downgrade pressure on

40   *The global city and asylum seeking*

wages and the growth of informal relations of work are the result or the driving force of large-scale migration. Friedmann (1986: 73), for example, suggests that 'because the "modern" sector is incapable of absorbing more than a small fraction of this human mass, a large "informal" sector of microscopic survival activities has evolved'. Importantly, Hamnett (1996a: 1428) contends that the economic processes described by Sassen, ending in the production of a sweatshop economy and increasing social polarization in key US cities, 'may be the product of both the nature of the welfare state and a high level of immigration from low-wage countries'. It is in this light that Hong Kong is analyzed subsequently. In so doing, the role of welfare politics is analyzed, while immigration, and its significance for the overall development of Hong Kong and its asylum policy, is examined in the last section of this chapter, in relation to both the processes of global city and identity formation. It is also hoped that the research findings presented in this book will enable an empirical appraisal of whether and how the informal economy is impacted by low-skilled (irregular) immigration.

Constructing the vulnerability of the disadvantaged in Hong Kong

In their final remarks on 'dual' New York, Castells and Mollenkopf (1991: 413) conclude that social polarization

> seem[s] to be linked to the emerging occupational structure in the dominant global cities of the new information-based economy. However, the reproduction of such inequality in the spheres of collective consumption and public policy is not structurally determined. Occupational polarization and income inequality become translated into a widespread urban dualism . . . only when public policy mirrors the naked logic of the market.

Additionally, it has been argued that the disempowerment of labour unions has impacted the emergence of an extremely low-paid area within the service sector, which has come to be characterized by informal relations of production and higher employability of irregular migrants (Hjarnø 2003). According to Hjarnø (2003: 128), when a situation of 'underdeveloped democracy in the labour market' exists, namely when there is a lack of mutual collaboration between employers and employees, an extensive informal economy is likely to develop depending on the resources that the state employs to prevent unlawful employment and the severity of the punishment imposed on employers who disregard the public regulatory framework. Both these arguments are in my understanding applicable to the present circumstances affecting the condition of the Hong Kong residents at the lower echelons of the labour and income structures, and thereby the vulnerability of asylum seekers in Hong Kong.

One reason Zhao et al. (2004) identify to explain growing income inequality in Hong Kong is the Hong Kong Government's role in promoting a 'business-friendly' economy, privileging economic growth over social justice. These authors argue that the privatization of public services in the 1990s in the absence of strong

The global city and asylum seeking   41

labour unions impacted negatively on real wages in the low-skilled sectors, as fierce competition among private and privatized services impelled service providers to reduce operating costs. This led to fewer benefits, more short-term and subcontracting work and harsher living conditions for a large number of 'non-core' workers (Zhao et al. 2004). Goodstadt (2013) similarly argues that during the Asian financial crisis in 1997–98 the government began to act as if it were a business enterprise facing recession. It downsized its structure and outsourced many of the services it previously controlled to firms that were compelled to offer the best service at the lowest price in order to survive. Many civil servants were laid off, which elongated the ranks of those seeking jobs in the private labour market, augmenting precarization across the entire service sector. Indeed, Lee and Wong (2004, in Lee et al. 2007) found that the number of part-time workers almost doubled between 1994 and 2002. These authors also identified that in the construction industry many employers increasingly resorted to subcontracting, turning their casual workers into self-employed labourers so as to increase operational flexibility and circumvent labour protection laws.

Scholars generally agree that the Hong Kong Government has maintained a largely indifferent stance before the human suffering caused by economic restructuring and public service privatization (cf. Zhao et al. 2004; Goodstadt 2013). The Hong Kong Government is a bureaucratic administration, backed by a partly elected legislature and influenced by powerful business elites who have traditionally lobbied for low taxation and low wages (Chan 1998; Wong and Yuen 2012). Moreover, it generally submits to the neoliberal principles underlying free-market competition as the engine of economic growth and sees the latter as the sine qua non condition for improving the human condition (cf. Harvey 2005). Under this economic principle, allocations of resources to social welfare are generally as sparse as possible (Zhao et al. 2004). Especially during the Asian financial crisis, the understanding that Hong Kong was vulnerable to market volatility sparked in government officials the idea that a balanced budget was to be rigorously maintained to face any eventualities. Put simply, the government sided with the richest classes, and the degree of protection that the low-skilled worker and poorer classes enjoyed diminished. Goodstadt (2013) posits that this historic moment gave rise to Hong Kong's 'new poor', parts of which include the elderly, the disabled and families on the verge of falling into extreme poverty in case of illness or dismissal from precarious employment; others are the residents compelled to perform low-wage jobs or devise new income strategies when faced with the limited welfare they can receive from the government, in line with its passive stance towards addressing income inequality (Zhao et al. 2004).

In this regard, Chan (2011) importantly argues that a component of this 'passive' stance has been the government's active pursuit of a policy of minimizing welfare expenditure at a time when the number of unemployed seeking welfare benefits to cope with economic restructuring had risen. In Chan's view, the government resorted to utilizing 'workfare' to exert control over the people eligible to receive assistance while de facto reaffirming and strongly enhancing its free-market values. A 'siege mentality' had indeed developed in the 1990s around

42 *The global city and asylum seeking*

the (false) idea that the government was in no position to bear the costs that expanding welfare provisions would likely generate to account for the increased numbers of unemployed (Goodstadt 2013). Goodstadt speaks of widespread 'paranoia' in the administration and business elites that was fuelled by anxieties and fears around the risk of Hong Kong developing into a welfare state. Moreover, the notion that higher levels of welfare provision were unaffordable strengthened the assumption that the poor were undeserving of state benefits, as they came to be considered solely responsible for their impoverished condition, which in turn justified minimal welfare spending and the preservation of Hong Kong's 'residual welfare system'. Thus, an expansion of social services was deemed not only unsustainable, but also undesirable. An argument was made in government quarters that if assistance were to be disbursed to acceptable levels, more people would try to access these benefits, which would encourage people to give up their jobs and expand the ranks of an unemployed, state-dependent population (cf. Hamnett 1994). Obviously, if this were to occur, economic growth would have been impacted and taxes raised, and the interests of the most powerful necessarily upset (Goodstadt 2013).

This welfare scenario cannot but bring to mind a clear analogy with the treatment presently reserved for the asylum seekers in most developed countries, and certainly in Hong Kong. As will be argued in the following chapter, asylum seekers are afforded only very minimal assistance through the ISS, to prevent their destitution. This assistance, however, is only disbursed in a form that would not attract excessive numbers of travellers to Hong Kong to seek these benefits. In the case of welfare assistance for both the local and the asylum seeker population, fear that benefits might be abused apparently legitimizes the government's retrenchment from its social (and legal) responsibilities, and in the particular case raised by Chan, this occurs when the pursuit of a specific model of growth leaves little consideration for (if not the production of) the plight of the weaker. Indeed, fear and abuse become tools to which the government can resort to advance specific political objectives. This understanding is based on Wacquant's (2009) insightful analysis of the US government's use of the 1996 welfare reform as a clear exercise in state crafting.

In 1996, poverty was 'normalized' in the US by presenting it as an inevitable consequence of the present times, and the burden of assistance was cleverly shifted from state coffers to the poor's empty wallets when economic changes and government efforts to reshape market relations required 'poverty-level wage' labour (Wacquant 2009: 98). The poor would receive only minimal financial assistance as a temporary measure on which it would be very difficult to survive. At the same time, in Hong Kong a series of training programs and welfare contractual obligations were introduced to supposedly change the poor's behaviour and enhance their work motivation. In such contexts, as argued by Wacquant, poverty becomes a matter of the individual responsibility of each poor person, while 'oppressive' workfare measures fashion a 'threatening social atmosphere that discourages needy citizens from seeking public benefits' (Chan 2011: 29). In turn, Hong Kong's well-established tradition of 'self-reliance' is strengthened

The global city and asylum seeking   43

(Chan 1998) and the market arguably provided with the 'new service proletariat of the dualizing metropolis' (Wacquant 2009: 101) – namely, a large pool of cheap workers who feel they are compelled to find jobs in the peripheral niches of an increasingly segmented labour market. Unemployment is no longer a major problem in Hong Kong; however, the problems facing the poor have worsened (Wong 2012; Lee et al. 2007).

When in late 2013 over a million people were said to be living in poverty in Hong Kong, Chief Secretary Carry Lam was reported as saying that the government would tackle the problem. However, in what can be seen as a summary of the previous argument, Lam claimed that such an effort had to be made in consideration of the fact that poverty could never be completely eradicated and public funds needed to be prudently distributed (Ngo 2013). Indeed, in Hong Kong poverty is confronted via economic growth and governed through fear and stigma. The latter elevates labour as a familiar and civic duty while excluding potential welfare claimants. Fear legitimizes political objectives apparently related to economic restructuring. A clear ethic of work based on the idealization of entrepreneurship and suspicion about welfare abuse begins to take shape; this line is examined in the remainder of this section in relation to asylum seekers, who clearly emerge in this book as the occupants of the last echelon of a socioeconomic ladder that hinges on labour exploitation in a market-driven economy.

Building opportunities at the lower end of the labour hierarchy

In his study on the onset of new poverty in Hong Kong, Goodstadt (2013: 35) asserts the link between privatization, subcontracting and the growth of informal relations of production and employment. He illustrates that when the government began to privatize public services on the assumption that the public sector needed to operate at more reasonable costs, 'evidence emerged of widespread abuse of contract workers, together with extensive disregard of labour legislation and outright fraud by government contractors'. Importantly, Goodstadt states that the government pledged to intervene but contractors remained free to breach the regulatory framework a number of times before being blacklisted by the government. In this context of apparent lax enforcement of the law, Law and Lee (2013) assert that subcontractors in construction are widely known to make use of South Asian irregular migrants (at times asylum seekers) to fill jobs for which the wages and conditions are the least appealing to the local and even the Chinese migrant population. In light of such an assertion, the aim of this section is to elucidate some of the aspects of a seemingly sized economy thriving on informality and to speculate on government attitudes which, if I am allowed this metaphor, appear to lean firmly towards the carrot rather than the stick.

First, it is important to note that a 'dual' economy seems to have flourished in Hong Kong, whereby the first economic level relates to the financial services mostly concentrated in Central – the pulsing heart of the city, as the name of the district suggests – and the second refers to the less-studied informal sector, which is conveniently less publicized in the Tourism Board brochures, but which

44 *The global city and asylum seeking*

thrives on a bustling of activities in several districts, at times in close proximity to the city's financial nodes. Despite the fact that a substantial volume of literature points to the interdependency of formality and informality in the economy, and the difficulty of clearly delineating between the two (Castells and Portes 1989; Munck 2002; Chen 2006; Sassen 1991), in Hong Kong the connection between formality and informality is often unclear and summarily forgotten. Concerns have been raised in public and official debates over the legitimacy of the lower-end economic activities taking place in the city and the immigration status of the people who perform them.[3] This manifestation of public censure can, however, be taken as a confirmation that the informal economy exists and is perhaps expanding in Hong Kong.

The kinds of informality with which this section is concerned are limited to specific activities, for this book will demonstrate that the spaces of economic informalization in which I most often found asylum seekers working are those that Sassen (2001) describes as broadly rotating around the formation of an ethnic economy, often confined to the least privileged urban geographies. Here, some low-income residents are forced to devise survival strategies within an economic environment in which their choice of earning opportunities is severely impacted by the Hong Kong Government's support of neoliberal economic restructuring. Some of these residents are of South Asian background. Others emigrated from China. Often they own small and micro-businesses that survive on cheaper sources of labour while offering affordable services to the lower-waged classes in the global city. More importantly, these are the entrepreneurs who have been driven to seeking an income on the margins of mainstream society, but who appreciate the profit to be made by capturing the flows that contribute to the transformation of the city. As noted earlier in this chapter, global cities are sites of inequality as well as opportunities (Acuto 2011). These opportunities are not limited to the global elites. Global economic forces and institutional structures influence labour market dynamics similar to the way in which urban socioeconomic, political and cultural spaces are shaped by those who struggle at the bottom of society (Benton-Short et al. 2005), especially when limited welfare imposes self-reliance. In this context, globalization creates the structural conditions that foster practices of economic informalization but in so doing also enables the burgeoning of myriad social and economic activities which low-income urban residents initiate and from which they benefit (Sassen 2001). Then, rather than being solely places of polarization and exclusion (or rather precisely because of this), global cities become 'sites of exchange' in which the poor and immigrant populations are not merely at the mercy of global processes of capital accumulation but rather participate in the life of societies and shape them by, for instance, revitalizing desolate urban areas or posing new challenges to existing labour regulatory frameworks (Kloosterman et al. 1999; Smith and Guarnizo 1998).

This research identified several local entrepreneurs who were generating income by engaging in the recycling of the electrical and electronic waste that is generated in consumerist societies (Grossman 2006) or targeting low-end demand for inexpensive clothing and food, including ethnically specific food, and mobile phones, watches and high-tech products. Small, immigrant-owned businesses were often meeting the local and increasingly more transnational demand for cheaper services, which rely on a ready supply of networks as well as co-ethnic migrants willing to work hard for a small salary. Such services and other related economic activities occur within what is generally defined as the informal economy.

The informal economy encompasses a set of activities that are normally legitimate, but which are either unregulated by or defy the public regulatory framework, such as through tax evasion or the use of unrecorded payments and the employment of labour in breach of immigration regulations (Chen 2006; Castells and Portes 1989). Critically, several scholars argue that informality does not occur because entrepreneurs are unwilling to abide by the law, but because they may be lacking either the resources to do so or the knowledge of the law (Kloosterman et al. 1998). In the former case, entrepreneurs may occasionally or consistently resort to informality as a survival strategy (Castells and Portes 1989). While this argument is considered in Chapter 5, it is noteworthy here that regulatory changes such as restrictive labour laws which raise the cost of hiring and dismissing workers, costs saving considerations, flexibility, and importantly the perception of law enforcement are all major considerations that entrepreneurs must take into account when pondering the risk of 'going informal' (Godfrey 2011). Informality is indeed the 'quintessential response of the small firms minimizing cost, risk, inconvenience and paperwork' (Ojo et al. 2013: 591). In this regard, entrepreneurs of immigrant background who lack high levels of human and financial capital, and are either prevented from entering or unable to generate sufficient income in declining manufacturing and other mainstream service industries, may devise alternative strategies of income generation, depending on the host society's opportunity structure and the social capital available to them (Kloosterman et al. 1999). In this vein, several employers of South Asian background interviewed for this research revealed that they had previously earned wages in construction work, while others had been denied semi-professional jobs as their skills were not recognized locally. By contrast, they were attracted by the idea of becoming their own boss and being able to avoid confrontations with their employers about unpaid wages and excessive workloads (cf. Ojo et al. 2013). These entrepreneurs created their own business in 'niche' ethnic markets where, however, the ease of entry for other entrepreneurs similarly seeking income-generating opportunities impose stringent competition. Driven to offer quality services at affordable prices, business owners engage in undercutting and evade regulatory systems to ensure the survival of their business (Jordan and Travers 1998). Asylum seekers are not permitted to work in Hong Kong. However, this research will demonstrate that they are employed, or their services as self-employed individuals are sought, because they provide this local resident population with opportunities to generate new or expand their income opportunities.

Informality is not limited to ethnic businesses. For example, Godfrey (2011) asserts that service producer firms can turn to informality when state regulations encumber competitiveness and the necessary speed of transactions appropriate to the time. We can argue it is for this reason that governments often employ

46 *The global city and asylum seeking*

what migration scholars call a 'benevolent ambiguity' (Chiswick 2001; Davila and Pagan 1997; Hillman and Weiss 1999), or a sort of '*de facto* but not *de jure* amnesty', towards the exploitation of workers where the presence of this labour is regarded as vital to economic performance (Chiswick 2001: 81). Of course some employers and workers are arrested and prosecuted. In Hong Kong, the ImmD has stated that 37,428 operations against illegal employment were carried out between the end of 2009 and 2012, resulting in 12,729 'illegal workers' and 1644 employers being arrested, although only 483 of these workers and 358 employers were sentenced (ImmD 2013). Nonetheless, scholars argue that government officials can tolerate informality when the lack of tax revenues removes the capacity, and thus the need, to provide welfare services (Godfrey 2011). In Hong Kong, it could be argued that, while workfare compels numbers of residents affected by the polarizing consequences of economic restructuring to seek out new income-generating strategies, informality is tolerated as an unintended but necessary outcome because the government's pursuit of a free-market mentality rooted in low taxation propels entrepreneurship at a level of the social hierarchy which undercuts the need to disburse welfare benefits.

Evidence of the existence of an ostensibly large informal economy is provided, for instance, in the literature on the history of Hong Kong's post-war housing. Smart (1989, 2001) posits that a large number of illegal dwellings continue to be tolerated by the authorities and traded illegally to meet demand from low-income families for cheaper rents. Smart also suggests that recent arrivals and low-income earners now inhabit the most squalid squatter areas, which has resulted in increasing moral divisions and public stigma being attached to those living in these dwellings (Smart 2001: 37). The literature on Hong Kong's industrial development similarly reveals how one of its key features has been the influx of large numbers of 'illegal refugees' from mainland China and the creation of numerous small local firms that have employed them (Cheng and Gereffi 1994). The roots of this global city are indeed laid on its historical past as an entrepôt and an export-oriented economy for low-cost manufacturing products, the production and commercialization of which relied on extensive networks of small and informal producers (Glasmeier 1994; Chiu and Lui 2009).

Two considerations can be made following the previous arguments. On one side, informalization seems to be structurally based in Hong Kong, as is poverty. Indeed, several scholars argue that informal labour markets are not necessarily growing in or typical of global cities but rather can be viewed as a long-standing characteristic of existing patterns of economic organization in many countries (Quassoli 1999; Reyneri 1998). This is certainly a cogent argument in relation to Hong Kong, especially in view of what Cheng and Gereffi (1994: 201) claim to be this city's traditional adherence to a '*laissez-fair* economy'. However, global economic restructuring has given rise to the emergence of new and more extensive inequalities which have apparently impacted the morale of the least privileged classes (Goodstadt 2013), who now exhibit a new form of anti-rich sentiment (Ley and Teo 2013).

On the other side, the light industrial items that were previously produced in Hong Kong, such as clothing and watches, are now manufactured in China. If

The global city and asylum seeking 47

this is true for the clothing and high-tech brands, the production of which is out-sourced by corporate power, China also produces the inexpensive goods that are increasingly traded in developing countries as a valid alternative to expensive First World products (Mathews et al. 2012). A number of people in Hong Kong make a living by buying and selling these relatively cheap and affordable items, often informally. According to dated estimates, in the early 1990s the informal economy accounted for 13 per cent of Hong Kong's GDP (Kuchta-Helbling 2000). In more recent times, most of the businesses surveyed by Mathews (2011) in his fieldwork in Hong Kong operated informally. Further, it has been claimed that over 20 per cent of the mobile phones now in Africa have been purchased in and shipped informally from Hong Kong (Mathews 2011). In one of the major sectors in which asylum seekers are employed – recycling – hundreds of thousands of tonnes of steel and copper scrap and electrical and electronic waste are exported annually to China to be processed (Kojima and Yoshida 2005). Critically, Kojima and Yoshida (2005: 55) argue that electrical and electronic waste is banned in China, but that these shipments find their way through Hong Kong often because Hong Kong's custom inspection is 'considerably more lenient'. As Chapter 5 will illustrate, some of my research participants are engaged in recycling waste that is either imported from overseas or generated in Hong Kong, a city in which con-sumerism produces over 70,000 tonnes of computers and electrical and electronic equipment yearly.[4] Some of these items are reused and recycled formally; others propel a micro-economy based on waste in which asylum seekers are key players.

Reading Hong Kong's immigration and asylum 'problem'

The unique cultural and geopolitical position of Hong Kong is a critical factor to be taken into account when seeking to understand the vulnerability of both the local resident and the refugee populations. Hong Kong is a Chinese city but is clearly distinct from mainland China. It retains power over its immigration pol-icy, and under the 'one country, two systems' arrangement, it responds to grow-ing global and regional mobility by applying a clearly polarized approach. On one side, Hong Kong welcomes and actively engages in a global headhunt for professional talent of the kind needed to support its economic and technological advancement. On the other, the entry of foreign workers in menial jobs is strictly regulated, and barriers are applied in many ways to ensure that their stay, when-ever necessary, remains temporary.[5]

The focus of Hong Kong's immigration policies is summarized well by the for-mer director of immigration, Peh Yun-lu, who stated that to 'boost Hong Kong's competitiveness in today's globalised world and secure its role as a prominent cos-mopolitan city and a global financial, trade, tourist and logistics centre, we spare no efforts in implementing policies that help attract talent, professionals and capi-tal from other parts of the world' (ImmD 2008: 7). By contrast, foreign low-skilled workers are regulated by the Supplementary Labour Scheme to relieve shortages of labour on a limited scale. Consistent numbers of foreigners are recruited at low wages in domestic work to relieve local and expatriate educated, married women of their domestic duties and allow them to contribute to the economy (Hewison

48 *The global city and asylum seeking*

2004; Skeldon 1995). This 'immigration management' approach is applied to Chinese mobility also. In effect, while Hong Kong has become a Chinese city, the border dividing the former colony from China – instead of disappearing – has preserved and to some extent enhanced the function of regulating the influx of Chinese mainlanders (Zhao et al. 2004). Several schemes cater for the entry of investors, talent and professionals from China, which have attracted over 65,000 professionals since such programmes were first implemented a decade ago (ImmD 2013). The immigration of other migrant Chinese is instead capped at a quota of 150 people per day, mostly to allow entry to mainland Chinese spouses and non-adult children of Hong Kong residents, who are often former immigrants themselves now settled in the territory (Newendorp 2008; Siu 1996).

In this section, I further investigate the opportunity structure of the local residents most likely to engage in some sort of economic activity with the asylum seekers in Hong Kong by focusing on the literature that explores recent regular and irregular Chinese migration to Hong Kong. This inflow is the most visible and quantitatively important and arguably accounts for most of the migratory movements at the lower end of the income hierarchy. Moreover, studies into this flow deserve attention for they contribute towards evincing the surge of the condition of 'deportability' that has been attached to certain migrant categories, as identified in the Introduction (De Genova 2002). An argument is made that a parallel is self-evident between what Goodstadt (2013) calls a 'siege mentality' developed in official quarters around the conviction that welfare benefits would be abused by excessive numbers of unemployed were they enticed to apply for state benefits and the idea that a 'floodgate' would open were not Hong Kong authorities operating restrictive immigration controls aimed at discouraging excessive numbers of incompatible 'others' from exploiting Hong Kong's economic development. In other words, a distinct 'control culture' (Law and Lee 2006) has emerged in Hong Kong at a time when specific economic conditions and statecrafting needs have necessitated the delineation of categories of people perceived as extraneous to the prevailing conventional values and norms shaping Hong Kong society (cf. Yeoh 2005; Ku 2004). Along these lines, this section offers valuable insight into the government's use of migration and its overall impact on Hong Kong's social structures (cf. Hamnett 1994, 1996a). At the same time, the subsequent discussion underscores how the present vulnerability of certain strata of the local resident population has been influenced by global economic restructuring and workfare in addition to the policies and discourses around identity which emerged in relation to Chinese mobility and Hong Kong's colonial past. Contemporary practices and attitudes towards recent inflows of asylum seekers have been shaped against this context.

Chinese immigration and the floodgate scenario

In Hong Kong, migration has long determined the structural development of the former colony (Lam and Liu 1998). Prior to 1949, Hong Kong was tightly integrated into the Chinese economy and society, and even after China became a communist country, people continued to move across the border, reinforcing a wide range of socioeconomic networks (Lam and Liu 1998; Smart and Smart 1998). As Shipp (1995: 13) has rightly acknowledged, 'the only true resource of Hong Kong, after Victoria Harbour, has always been its people'. Each wave of Chinese immigrants from the mainland has boosted population levels, capital and knowledge and provided the labour supply that Hong Kong needed in order to develop into a labour-intensive manufacturing economy. A huge increase in population in Hong Kong due to returnees and refugees escaping the communist regime in China, however, created a shortage of housing, food and clothes, which forced the government to implement restrictive border controls (Lam and Liu 1998; Law and Lee 2006). Yet border controls did not stop the movement, and most Chinese immigration in the post-war period took place illegally (Lam and Liu 1998). Siu (1996) quantifies the number of arrivals as 400,000 in the 1950s, 120,000 in the 1960s, more than half a million in the 1970s and another half a million in the 1980s and 1990s combined. At one point in time, up to 750 people a day are argued to have made their way into Hong Kong, half of whom evaded detection and blended into society (Siu 1996).

While labour-intensive industrialization in Hong Kong created a shortage of workers that was filled by these 'illegal refugees' (Cheng and Gereffi 1994), in an era of deindustrialization not all migrants are considered valuable for receiving countries. Some commentators contend that immigration from China was tolerated only insofar as it met demand for unskilled workers during times of industrial expansion (Law and Lee 2006; Smart 2003). Until the mid-1970s, although Hong Kong was enforcing border controls, illegal immigration was largely permitted to allow family reunions and to provide local employers with a readily available cheap workforce. Hong Kong's lax application of immigration controls, allowing those who were able to avoid detection to settle in the territory, resembled 'that of countries which do not officially admit that they take worker migrants, but do so in practice' (Destexhe 1995, in Law and Lee 2006: 220). However, when economic restructuring led to labour market structural transformation that valued brain power over menial skills, mainland immigrants came to be seen as a burden rather than an asset. Exclusionary policies were implemented to deter further arrivals (Law and Lee 2006; Smart 2003). As stressed by Law and Lee (2006: 235), 'the Hong Kong state has a long tradition of using economic conditions as the most important premise for policy-making, not merely in relation to immigration control, but to nearly all aspects of public policy-making'. While humanitarian values seldom occupy a significant role in the Hong Kong Government's policies, 'economic prosperity is regarded as the cornerstone of the state's legitimacy' (Law and Lee 2006: 235). According to this view, once economic advancement came to be pursued through the attainment of higher levels of education and professionalization, unskilled migrants were constructed in public debates and the media alike as a threat to economic prosperity.

Restrictive policies are generally said to stigmatize migrant populations, which come to be seen as an unwanted, potentially dangerous social class (Bigo 2002, 2011; Dal Lago 2009). This produces social targets, which in the case of the Chinese mainlanders has meant being subjected to stricter regulatory mechanisms,

50 *The global city and asylum seeking*

social discrimination and exclusion from social welfare systems such as public housing and financial assistance (Law and Lee 2006; Smart 2003). If, on the one hand, these measures were (supposedly) aimed at deterring arrivals, on the other, the consequences for the regular and irregular immigrants in Hong Kong were enormous (Smart 2003). As the threat these people posed for Hong Kong was exaggerated, prejudice against them spread rapidly, and mainlanders came to be described as incompatible with Hong Kong people (Ku 2001; Smart 2003). In relation to the right of abode issue, for example, the government made clear its view on the type of population that Hong Kong did not need to support its prosperity. When in January 1999 the Hong Kong Court of Final Appeal decided that the government's scheme to prevent 1.67 million Chinese who were related to Hong Kong residents from acquiring the right of abode was unconstitutional according to Article 24 of the Basic Law (Hong Kong's mini-constitution), the government asked the Standing Committee of the National People's Congress to reinterpret the article to restrict that right (Smart 2003). The Hong Kong Government justified this extreme measure by speaking in terms of a 'flood' of people who would ravage the city's resources and jeopardize its development (Ku 2001; Smart 2003).

In this climate, the fear of opening the floodgates to overwhelming waves of 'new immigrants' reinforced discrimination, rooted in the notions of 'otherness' and inferiority that distinguished Chinese immigrants from the skilled, well-educated Hong Kong people (Law and Lee 2006). Despite large segments of the population being related to previous inflows of immigrants, as more resident people came to identify themselves with Hong Kong, they also became more eager to protect their lifestyle and thus turned hostile to further arrivals (Siu 2009). Importantly, mainlanders in Hong Kong are often still subjected to discrimination and marginalization (Newendorp 2008). Lawfully resident Chinese immigrants constitute a major proportion of Hong Kong's impoverished population. Because of their lack of local knowledge or locally recognized qualifications, and sometimes because of language barriers, they often earn less than the average Hong Kong employee (Law and Lee 2006). In addition, prejudice seems to play a significant role in forcing immigrants from the mainland to get jobs in the lower-skilled sectors, for lower wages. The result is that their levels of education and their being labelled as culturally unable to integrate into Hong Kong society make it all too difficult for these people to compete in a knowledge-based economy (Lee et al. 2007). In this regard, a clear pattern of downward mobility for new arrivals has been noted (Newendorp 2008), which exacerbates income inequality and occupational polarization (Chiu and Lui 2004), although Zhao et al. (2004) contend that the relatively small number of new arrivals compared to the total number of poor people in Hong Kong suggests that income inequality is not the result of large-scale immigration (cf. Hamnett 1996a).

Forcing the politics of identity onto South Asian residents

The origin of the formation of a Hong Kong identity is generally located in the late 1960s, in connection to the 1967 leftist riots (Mathews et al. 2008), when the colonial government realized that it needed to create a civil society and an 'ideal citizen' who would identify with Hong Kong (Law and Lee 2013). Negative representations of poverty and backward cultural conditions were attached to Hong Kong's unwieldy neighbour. Deindustrialization and the emergence of Hong Kong as a post-industrial city reinforced and indeed enhanced this process of identity formation, which was based in the government's attempt to 'de-Sinicize' the colony in times of political turmoil (Lee and Law 2013). If the social status of the more recent Chinese arrivals was affected, immigrants of South Asian background were also singled out as a distinct social category of people constructed in negative terms.

South Asians have resided in Hong Kong since 1841 and have contributed significantly to the economic and cultural well-being of the territory (White 1994). For example, among the earliest policemen under British rule were Indian Sikhs (Pluss 2005) and Pakistanis (Law and Lee 2013). The prestigious University of Hong Kong was founded with the financial assistance of a well-known Indian Parsi businessman, and Hong Kong's famous Star Ferry was founded by a South Asian 'self-made' entrepreneur (White 1994). Ironically, the border fencing which today prevents many South Asian and other asylum seekers from easily travelling to Hong Kong was built by South Asian engineers to regulate the flow of people between China and Hong Kong. Law and Lee (2013) note that, prior to the development of a local Hong Kong identity, ethnic relationships among South Asian and Chinese residents were relatively harmonious. However, following government attempts to de-Sinicize Hong Kong, a sense of superiority developed among Hong Kong's people, based on the colony's economic attainments, which were counterpoised against the relative poverty of the regional periphery. This sense of superiority influenced the way South Asians inhabiting the lower ranks of the social and income ladder began to be viewed by mainstream society. Moreover, after the handover, the government's attempt to re-Sinicize Hong Kong resulted in the implementation of policies that de facto forced numbers of South Asian residents into a state of relegation, such as policies aimed at valuing the use of the mother tongue in secondary school teaching, which caused ethnic minority children of low-income families to be placed in low-quality schools (Law and Lee 2013). While several studies have examined the exclusion faced by these ethnic minorities in the education system (Heung 2006; Bhowmik and Kennedy 2012), others have revealed the vulnerability of Pakistani, Indian and Nepali residents in relation to unemployment and prejudice in the labour market (Ku et al. 2006). Some research has also raised concerns about the risk of creating an underclass posed by such inequality and marginalization in the context of the government's ostensible indifference towards the livelihoods of the most disadvantaged (Ashencaen Crabtree and Wong 2012; Law and Lee 2013).

Six thousand 'illegal refugees' today in Hong Kong

Research into the contribution and consequences of the Chinese migratory influx in relation to economic, social and political structural transformation in Hong Kong is important for two reasons. On the one hand, it confirms the role of government agency and local factors in determining processes of global economic

52   *The global city and asylum seeking*

restructuring (cf. Hamnett 1994, 1996a; Ancien 2011). In the case of Hong Kong, it is noteworthy that the existence of strong social and cultural ties between the Hong Kong and Chinese populations, as well as the political transformation that took place in China after World War II, appears to have shaped the development of immigration policies and attitudes towards foreign nationals and those residents perceived to be foreign. Under this proposition, Tai (2006) argues that governments in Asia have played a central role in promoting economic growth by adopting strategies that manage the migratory pressures exerted at their borders. It is obvious that new forms of urban social stratification are the result of the interplay of globalization and local policy, whereby welfare and immigration policies can directly or indirectly shape and remodel labour markets and public perceptions of diversity and otherness. In this view, more light can also be shed on the changes that occurred when Hong Kong factories moved to China in the 1980s, as the absence of a strong union movement left industrial firms free to plan economic restructuring and production strategies without the need to negotiate with workers (cf. Hjarnø 2003). Chiu et al. (1997) have argued that the unions that had close links to political parties played an important role in keeping the numbers of foreign workers at a level lower than that demanded by business associations. While the government did not intervene to stop the relocation of Hong Kong factories across the border, pressure was exercised on its immigration policy, which impacted on economic restructuring to the extent that Chiu et al. have questioned whether a larger intake of cheaper factory workers would have slowed the economic transformation that occurred in Hong Kong at the time; we could as well ponder whether the fate of asylum seekers would be different today. It is claimed that now labour shortages are plaguing some of Hong Kong's vital service sectors. Plans to introduce foreign workers are nonetheless hampered by unions and lawmakers concerned about the loss of local jobs (Lee and Siu 2013).

Beyond evincing the role played by institutional regimes as gatekeepers, a second related reason why research into Chinese immigration to Hong Kong is important is that these studies have indirectly shown how the notion of 'refugee', as it has developed in Hong Kong over the past 60 years, is at best ambivalent. For example, Law and Lee (2006) affirm that, despite their poor circumstances and living conditions in Hong Kong, Chinese immigrants have rarely demanded improvements from the authorities. This is because most fled from China's communist regime and had no other viable place to which to escape. Previous reports have indicated that in the 1950s, 52.3 per cent of the 'new immigrants' left China for political reasons, and another 8.5 per cent for a combination of political and economic reasons (Hambro 1955, in Law and Lee 2006). The colonial government, however, labelled them 'refugees' without properly recognizing the rights that this status legally and morally implies. A report from the Commission on Labour released in the wake of the Asian economic crisis in Hong Kong states that

> the ingress of over 700,000 *refugees* from mainland China since 1949 has had a marked effect on the labour situation in the Colony, the chief characteristic of which is an excess of unskilled labour. Previously the ebb and flow of

The global city and asylum seeking 53

the working population was closely aligned to the economic opportunities in Hong Kong and China. The *refugees*, however, have shown no desire to return to the mainland, even though Hong Kong is unable to offer to all the prospect of earning a reasonable living.[6] (Commission on Labour 1997, in Smart 2003: 222)

Other than providing a rationale for restrictive border controls, this passage indicates how current perceptions of asylum are likely to have been shaped by past experiences, such that issues related to immigration; cross-border political, social and economic divisions; illegality; and asylum have converged to flatten the distinctions among them, thus obscuring the legal status of refugees.

This perception has also been influenced by the influx of over 200,000 Vietnamese refugees who flocked to Hong Kong in the 1980s and 1990s, which raised concerns over the economic sustainability of accepting such large numbers of migrants (Davis 1991). Thomas (2000) demonstrates that after the international community retracted much of its support for the resettlement of these refugees, Hong Kong's public opinion turned very much against new arrivals. They came to be viewed as a threat to society and, consequently, were identified as migrants seeking to escape poverty rather than political persecution. It is no coincidence that, while insisting that the UNHCR repay the city for the money it spent over 20 years on caring for Vietnamese refugees,[7] the Hong Kong Government has ever since refused the extension of the Refugee Convention to the territory (Loper 2010).

Today there are about 6000 asylum seekers in Hong Kong.[8] Despite their limited number, this historical connotation of the 'refugee', together with hegemonic discourses on Hong Kong identity and the need to maintain tight control over unwanted migration, has contributed towards the harsh conditions currently faced by this population. Chapter 2 will evince the anxiety and exclusionary rhetoric surrounding asylum seeking, and thus the mechanism underlying their exclusion. Widespread is the feeling in official and public discourse that numerous people, of the 'wrong kind', are travelling to tiny and overpopulated Hong Kong; that the territory's borders are under siege by hordes of paupers escaping severe economic conditions in chaotic and dangerous countries of the Global South; and that growing demographic imbalances between the North and South mean that larger numbers of desperate and ambitious migrants will try, via any means possible, to gain access to their land of opportunity (cf. Martin 1993). Anticipating the argument presented in the next chapter, it is noteworthy to mention here the outraged reaction of much of the Hong Kong media when a court ruling in March 2009 found that a group of Pakistani asylum seekers were not breaking the law by working in street markets. Several newspapers depicted asylum seekers as 'illegal immigrants [who] know how to use international convention[s] to protect themselves' (McKenzie 2009: 25). The spectre of a refugee 'flood' or 'invasion' was raised as black and brownish faces were deemed to be gathering en masse on Chinese shores, waiting for a chance to cross into Hong Kong. Brian Barbour, an advocate for refugees formerly based in Hong Kong, explains the situation by stressing the

54 *The global city and asylum seeking*

anomalous interchangeable use by local people of the words 'asylum seekers' and 'illegal immigrants' (McKenzie 2009).

This attitude towards refugees in effect has emerged globally as a consequence of an enormous confusion over issues of migration and asylum, which the media has often exacerbated by using watery metaphors such as 'waves' and 'floods' to describe the unstoppable arrival of this movement of people (Mountz 2010; Crisp 2007). This has resulted in the perceived need to erect giant protecting walls along borders and in representations that reduce the individuality of migrants to mere numbers and statistics. Stereotyped perceptions of asylum have been encouraged, which have made it easy for host populations to control the gates and ignore the plight of refugees at their doorsteps (Crisp 2007). Asylum seekers in Hong Kong are branded as outsiders, and as has been the case for other classes of disadvantaged local residents, they are made extraneous to the social and cultural fabric of the host society, and deviant for standing outside its norms. They are labelled 'illegals', which amplifies their deviancy via the symbolic function of grouping together individuals as undeserving for being in a particular space without state authorization (cf. Nevins 2002; Dal Lago 2009). In so doing, they become a problem, one whose socioeconomic impact this research is set out to investigate.

Conclusion

The global city is a site of enormous pressures and transformation, where forces operating at global and local levels combine to shape urban institutional and socioeconomic conditions. Hong Kong is a truly modern city. It is one of the most vertical and densely populated cities in the world, and its skyline is impressive whether one ventures along the harbour sides dividing Hong Kong Island from Kowloon or gazes upon its architectural wonders from the summits of the most popular tourist attractions. Yet, in many ways, the social inequalities Sassen (2001) references to describe the global city are present, and widening, in Hong Kong. While globalization undoubtedly brings economic prosperity to global cities, global capital production and capital accumulation equally result in serious 'harm', often overlooked in public discourses as some people are (culpably) left behind.

The Hong Kong Government has spared no efforts in recent years in promoting economic advancement, even at the expense of the most vulnerable. On the one hand, the government's neoliberal approach to the economy has boosted Hong Kong's global city status. On the other, economic restructuring has been supported by control mechanisms implemented by the government aimed at addressing population and migration management. This approach has widened social inequality and impacted the local resident and migrant populations alike. Further, many low-skilled workers have been unable to keep up with changes that have drastically reduced their chances of upward mobility and the kinds of occupations they can compete for in a knowledge-intensive society. If growing inequality is linked to the changing occupational structure in Hong Kong, a segmented labour market appears nonetheless to be fertile ground for individual entrepreneurship, one that is reliant on this very same inequality. Subcontractor

The global city and asylum seeking   55

and often family-based entrepreneurs are afforded ever cheaper indentures and profit margins. However, they apparently manage increased flexibility by shifting the burden of neoliberalism onto the lower social classes. When the government's retrenchment from supplying adequate welfare services contributes to generating incentives for workers in low-end businesses to become self-reliant, informal relations of production seem to be (re)produced, and asylum seekers have become involved in this process.

It is interesting in this regard that while some studies emphasize how the poor and the informal economy are a problem for city officials who would rather relocate them to the edges of the city to make room for redevelopment and please the sensibility of the wealthiest and powerful (Beckett and Hebert 2008; Müller 2013), in Hong Kong the informalization of the economy does not necessarily appear to be a negative phenomenon requiring state intervention. Rather, it represents an opportunity, as those whose contribution to society is limited to jobs typical of the new proletariat or self-employment in small-scale activities may weather their condition by weaving the urban and transnational circuits that open the spaces of globalization. This is a key contention of my research. Within a livelihood framework, the vulnerability and agency of the asylum seekers in Hong Kong are structured by a background of labour casualization and policies that render this population particularly attractive to deal with, especially for employers who are incapable of providing better conditions of work. Harvey (1990) and other scholars have argued extensively that this type of migrant is now the archetype of the new worker in an era of postmodernism (Wills et al. 2009; Calavita 2005). It is valuable to repeat here, however, that the blurring of boundaries between asylum seekers and irregular migrants does not mean that all asylum seekers engage in informal economic activities or that all irregular migrants are asylum seekers. Yet the following chapters will demonstrate that all asylum seekers are made irregular migrants in Hong Kong, as their presence in the territory is necessarily characterized by a period of 'illegality' in light of the manner in which they cross the border or because they overstay their visa pending a decision on their case. Moreover, while asylum seekers are said to be motivated in their quest for asylum principally by the need to escape life-threatening events, which force them to seek refuge abroad, irregular migrants are generally associated with a voluntary, economic imperative for migration (Koser 2007). Nonetheless, the two drives of migration are not mutually exclusive. However, a distinction between the two forms of movement is often utilized by the Hong Kong Government to reaffirm its policy not to grant asylum and accede to the Refugee Convention. This highlights the need for an analysis of the reasons why asylum seekers are situated within structures that appear to encourage their agency while accidentally, or rather intentionally, organizing the outcome of their migration. Considering the experiences of other underprivileged populations in Hong Kong, a more than legitimate doubt arises as to the real intention of the government in pursuing its current asylum policy.

It is perhaps in this view that the significance of this chapter extends beyond developing a framework in which to situate the experience of the asylum seekers. With the remainder of this book, this chapter offers insight into the social and

56 *The global city and asylum seeking*

political consequences of this global city. The experiences of the asylum seekers that are narrated hereafter will reveal much about cities extending their geoeconomic reach and functioning to become global. At the same time, they will ground the evidence in the contentious notion of social polarization and the role of local institutional structures in crafting unequal yet thriving urban settings.

Notes

1 www.hongkongairport.com/eng/business/about-the-airport/welcome.html.
2 A dual inflow of migrant workers is actively pursued by the Hong Kong Government. On one side, a number of schemes have been implemented to attract global elites to advance the economic interests of the city. On the other, foreign domestic helpers are increasingly recruited at low wages to serve the needs of local households. There were 312,395 foreign domestic helpers in Hong Kong in 2012, of whom 50 per cent were from the Philippines and 48 per cent from Indonesia (ImmD 2013), while the number of households is 2.3 million (CSD 2012).
3 For example, see comments that appeared in the media warning readers that 'South Asian and African political refugees are flocking into Hong Kong to make money' (Tao 2009: 1). A concerned reader wrote to an English-language newspaper that 'these unemployed refugees take illegal jobs, make money and [do] not pay taxes' (*The Standard* 2009). In a similar expression of fear and confusion around the status and actions of these new arrivals, the Honourable Starry Lee requested in the LegCo that the government report on the recent upward trend of South Asians and Africans entering Hong Kong illegally and 'seeking political asylum as a "cover" . . . to stay in Hong Kong' and temporarily work (LegCo 2009).
4 www.wastereduction.gov.hk/en/workplace/weee_intro.htm.
5 For example, while skilled and well-off foreigners are permitted to request permanent residency after seven years of continuous residence, foreign domestic helpers are excluded from this opportunity and cannot easily change their line of work. A series of judicial review applications have challenged government policies in this area. One such case of a domestic helper who had worked in Hong Kong for over 25 years drew intense public attention, with various quarters debating the question of the right of abode for foreign domestic helpers. The Court of Appeal decided that refusing permanent residency to foreign helpers was not unconstitutional, as their presence in Hong Kong was, as quoted by the *South China Morning Post*, 'not different from that of refugees and prisoners in kind, but only in degree' (Chiu and Lau 2012).
6 Emphasis added, to highlight the ambiguous use of the word 'refugee'.
7 See LegCo meeting (A10/11–24) Honourable Abraham Shek to Secretary for Security, 13 April 2011, in which the government is asked to inform the council on the steps undertaken to recover the HK$1162 million spent on assisting 'the Vietnamese migrants'.
8 This number is difficult to statistically quantify because asylum seekers use multiple mechanisms of *non-refoulement* protection available in the former colony. In 2012, there were 4892 outstanding CAT cases (ImmD 2013), while, according to the UNHCR, in mid-2013 there were 1332 asylum seekers and 94 recognized refugees in Hong Kong (see country profiles, www.unhcr.org).

References

Acuto, M. (2011) 'Finding the Global City: An Analytical Journey through the "Invisible College" ', *Urban Studies*, 48(14): 2953–2973.
Ancien, D. (2011) 'Global City Theory and New Urban Politics Twenty Years On: The Case for a Geohistorical Materialist Approach to the (New) Urban Politics of Global Cities', *Urban Studies*, 48(12): 2473–2493.

Ashencaen Crabtree, S. and Wong, H. (2012) '"Ah Cha"! The Racial Discrimination of Pakistani Minority Communities in Hong Kong: An Analysis of Multiple, Intersecting Oppressions', *British Journal of Social Work*, 43(5): 945–963.

Beaverstock, J. V., Smith, R., Taylor, P. J., Walker, D. and Lorimer, H. (2000) 'Globalization and World Cities: Some Measures and Methodologies', *Applied Geography*, 20(1): 43–63.

Beckett, K. and Hebert, S. (2008) 'Dealing with Disorder: Social Control in the Post-industrial City', *Theoretical Criminology*, 12(1): 5–30.

Benton-Short, L., Price, M. D. and Friedman, S. (2005) 'Globalization from Below: The Ranking of Global Immigrant Cities', *International Journal of Urban and Regional Research*, 29(4): 945–959.

Bhowmik, M. K. and Kennedy, K. J. (2012) 'Equitable Educational Provision for Hong Kong's Ethnic Minority Students: Issues and Priorities', *Educational Research Journal*, 27(1–2): 27–49.

Bigo, D. (2002) 'Security and Immigration: Toward a Critique of the Governmentality of Unease', *Alternatives*, 27: 63–92.

Bigo, D. (2011) 'Freedom and Speed in Enlarged Borderzones', in V. Squire (Ed.) *The Contested Politics of Mobility: Borderzones and Irregularity*, Abingdon: Routledge: 31–50.

Borel-Saladin, J. and Crankshaw, O. (2009) 'Social Polarisation or Professionalisation? Another Look at Theory and Evidence on Deindustrialisation and the Rise of the Service Sector', *Urban Studies*, 46(3): 645–664.

Brenner, N. (1999) 'Globalisation as Reterritorialisation: The Re-scaling of Urban Governance in the European Union', *Urban Studies*, 28(1): 39–78.

Burgers, J. and Musterd, S. (2002) 'Understanding Urban Inequality: A Model Based on Existing Theories and an Empirical Illustration', *International Journal of Urban and Regional Research*, 26(2): 403–413.

Calavita, K. (2005) *Immigrants at the Margins: Law, Race and Exclusion in Southern Europe*, Cambridge: Cambridge University Press.

Castells, M. (2000) *The Rise of the Network Society: The Information Age*, Oxford: Blackwell.

Castells, M. and Mollenkopf, J. H. (1991) 'Conclusion: Is New York a Dual City?', in J. H. Mollenkopf and M. Castells (Eds.) *Dual City: Restructuring New York*, New York: Russell Sage Foundation: 399–418.

Castells, M. and Portes, A. (1989) 'World Underneath: The Origins, Dynamics, and Effects of the Informal Economy', in A. Portes, M. Castells and L. A. Benton (Eds.) *The Informal Economy: Studies in Advanced and Less Developed Countries*, Baltimore: The John Hopkins University Press.

Census and Statistics Department (CSD) (2012) *2011 Population Census: Summary Results*, Hong Kong: Viewed 10 May 2014: www.census2011.gov.hk/pdf/summary-results.pdf

Census and Statistics Department (CSD) (2013, April) *Hong Kong Monthly Digest of Statistics: The Four Key Industries and Other Selected Industries in the Hong Kong Economy*, Hong Kong, Author. Viewed 1 February 2014: www.statistics.gov.hk/pub/B71304FC2013XXXXB0100.pdf

Champion, A. G. (1994) 'International Migration and Demographic Change in the Developed World', *Urban Studies*, 31(4–5): 653–678.

Chan, A. H. N. (2000) 'Middle-Class Formation and Consumption in Hong Kong', in B. H. Chua (Ed.) *Consumption in Asia: Lifestyles and Identities*, London: Routledge: 98–134.

58 The global city and asylum seeking

Chan, C-K. (1998) 'Welfare Policies and the Construction of Welfare Relations in a Residual Welfare State: The Case of Hong Kong', *Social Policy & Administration*, 32(3): 278–291.

Chan, C. K. (2011) 'Hong Kong: Workfare in the World's Freest Economy', *International Journal of Social Welfare*, 20: 22–32.

Chen, M. A. (2006) "Rethinking the Informal Economy: Linkages with the Formal Economy and the Formal Regulatory Environment', in B. Guha-Khansnobis, R. Kanbur and E. Ostrom (Eds.) *Linking the Formal and Informal Economy*, Oxford: Oxford University Press: 93–120.

Cheng, L-L. and Gereffi, G. (1994) 'The Informal Economy in East Asia Development', *International Journal of Urban and Regional Research*, 18(2): 194–219.

Chiswick, B. R. (2001) 'The Economics of Illegal Migration for the Host Economy', in M. A. B. Siddique (Ed.) *International Migration into the 21st Century: Essays in Honour of Reginald Appleyard*, Cheltenham: Edward Elgar: 74–85.

Chiu, A. and Lau S. (2012) 'Court Overturns Maid Abode Ruling', *South China Morning Post*, 29 March. Viewed 29 March 2012: http://www.scmp.com/article/996923/court-overturns-maid-abode-ruling

Chiu, S. and Lui, T-L. (2009) *Hong Kong: Becoming a Chinese Global City*, Abingdon: Routledge.

Chiu, S. W. K., Ho, K. C. and Lui, T-L. (1997) *City-States in the Global Economy: Industrial Restructuring in Hong Kong and Singapore*, Boulder: Westview Press.

Chiu, S. W. K. and Lui, T-L. (2004) 'Testing the Global City-Social Polarization Thesis: Hong Kong since the 1990s', *Urban Studies*, 41(10): 1863–1888.

Chu, Y. W. (2008) 'Deconstructing the Global City: Unravelling the Linkages that Underlie Hong Kong's World City Status', *Urban Studies*, 45(8): 1625–1646.

Chubarov, I. and Brooker, D. (2013) 'Multiple Pathways to Global City Formation: A Functional Approach and Review of Recent Evidence in China', *Cities*, 35:181–189.

Cianconi, P. (2011) *Addio ai Confini del Mondo: Per Orientarsi nel Caos Postmoderno*, Milano: FrancoAngeli.

Cohen, R. (1987) *The New Helots: Migrants in the International Division of Labour*, Aldershot: Avebury.

Coleman, W. D. and Sajed, A. (2013) *Fifty Key Thinkers on Globalization*, Abingdon: Routledge.

Crisp, J. (2007) 'Vital Distinction', *Refugees*, 148: 4–14.

Dal Lago, A. (2009) *Non-persone: L'esclusione dei Migranti in Una Società Globale*, Milano: Feltrinelli.

Davila, A. and Pagan, J. A. (1997) 'The Effect of Selective INS Monitoring Strategies on the Industrial Employment Choice and Earnings of Recent Immigrants', *Economic Inquiry*, 35(1): 138–150.

Davis, L. (1991) *Hong Kong and the Asylum-Seekers from Vietnam*, New York: St. Martin's Press.

De Genova, N. P. (2002) 'Migrant "Illegality" and Deportability in Everyday Life', *Annual Review of Anthropology*, 31: 419–447.

Falk, R. (1999) *Predatory Globalization: A Critique*, London: Polity Press.

Findlay, A. M., Li, F. L. N., Jowett, A. J. and Skeldon, R. (1996) 'Skilled International Migration and the Global City: A Study of Expatriates in Hong Kong', *Transactions of the Institute of British Geographers*, 21(1): 49–61.

Forrest, R., La Grange, A. and Yip, N. M. (2004) 'Hong Kong as a Global City? Social Distance and Spatial Differentiation, *Urban Studies*, 41(1): 207–227.

The global city and asylum seeking 59

Friedmann, J. (1986) 'The World City Hypothesis', *Development and Change*, 17(1): 69–83.

Friedmann, J. (1997) *World City Futures: The Role of Urban and Regional Policies in the Asia-Pacific Region*, Hong Kong: Hong Kong Institute of Asia-Pacific Studies, The Chinese University of Hong Kong.

Friedmann, J. and Wolff, G. (1982) 'World City Formation: An Agenda for Research and Action', *International Journal of Urban and Regional Research*, 15(1): 269–283.

Glasmeier, A. K. (1994) 'Flexibility and Adjustment: The Hong Kong Watch Industry and Global Change', *Growth and Change*, 25: 223–246.

Godfrey, P. C. (2011) 'Toward a Theory of the Informal Economy', *The Academy of Management Annals*, 5(1): 231–277.

Goodstadt, L. F. (2013) *Poverty in the Midst of Affluence: How Hong Kong Mismanaged Its Prosperity*, Hong Kong: Hong Kong University Press.

Gordon, I. and Harloe, M. (1991) 'A Dual to New York? London in the 1980s', in J. H. Mollenkopf and M. Castells (Eds.) *Dual City: Restructuring New York*, New York: Russell Sage Foundation: 377–395.

Grossman, E. (2006) *High Tech Trash: Digital Devices, Hidden Toxics, and Human Health*, Washington, DC: Island Press.

Grzymala-Kazlowska, A. (2005) 'From Ethnic Cooperation to In-Group Competition: Undocumented Polish Workers in Brussels', *Journal of Ethnic and Migration Studies*, 31(4): 675–697.

Hamnett, C. (1994) 'Social Polarization in Global Cities: Theory and Evidence', *Urban Studies*, 31(3): 401–425.

Hamnett, C. (1996a) 'Social Polarization, Economic Restructuring and Welfare State Regimes', *Urban Studies*, 33(8): 1407–1430.

Hamnett, C. (1996b) 'Why Sassen is Wrong: A Response to Burgers', *Urban Studies*, 33(1): 107–110.

Harvey, D. (1990) *The Condition of Post-modernity: An Enquiry into the Origins of Cultural Change*, Cambridge: Blackwell.

Harvey, D. (2005) *A Brief History of Neoliberalism*, Oxford: Oxford University Press.

Heung, V. (2006) 'Recognizing the Emotional and Behavioral Needs of Ethnic Minority Students in Hong Kong', *Preventing School Failure*, 50(2): 29–36.

Hewison, K. (2004) 'Thai Migrant Workers in Hong Kong', *Journal of Contemporary Asia*, 34(3): 318–335.

Hill, R. C. and Kim, J. W. (2000) 'Global Cities and Developmental States: New York, Tokyo and Seoul, *Urban Studies*, 37(12): 2167–2195.

Hillman, A. L. and Weiss, A. (1999) 'A Theory of Permissible Illegal Migration', *European Journal of Political Economy*, 15(4): 585–604.

Hjarnø, J. (2003) *Illegal Immigrants and Developments in Employment in the Labour Markets of the EU*, Aldershot: Ashgate.

Hong Kong Government (2013a, July) 'Hong Kong: The Facts. Population'. Viewed 1 February 2014: www.gov.hk/en/about/abouthk/factsheets/docs/population.pdf

Hong Kong Government (2013b, August) 'Hong Kong: The Facts. Statistics'. Viewed 1 February 2014: www.gov.hk/en/about/abouthk/factsheets/docs/statistics.pdf

Immigration Department (ImmD) (2008) *Annual Report 2007–2008*, Hong Kong: Author.

Immigration Department (ImmD) (2011) Annual Report 2009–2010, Hong Kong: Author. Viewed 1 February 2014: www.immd.gov.hk/publications/a_report_09–10/eng/ch1/index.htm

Immigration Department (ImmD) (2012) *Annual Report 2011*, Hong Kong: Author. Viewed 1 February 2014: www.immd.gov.hk/publications/a_report_2011/en/ch1/index.html

60 *The global city and asylum seeking*

Immigration Department (ImmD) (2013) *Annual Report 2012*, Hong Kong: Author. Viewed 1 February 2014: www.immd.gov.hk/publications/a_report_2012/en/foreword/vision.htm

Iredale, R. (2000) 'Migration Policies for the Highly Skilled in the Asia-Pacific Region', *International Migration Review*, 34(3): 882–906.

Jacobsen, K. (2006) 'Refugees and Asylum Seekers in Urban Areas: A Livelihoods Perspective', *Journal of Refugee Studies*, 19(3): 273–286.

Jao, Y. C. (1997) *Hong Kong as an International Financial Centre: Evolution, Prospects and Policies*, Hong Kong: City University of Hong Kong.

Jordan, B. and Travers, A. (1998) 'The Informal Economy: A Case Study of Unrestrained Competition', *Social Policy & Administration*, 32(3): 292–306.

Kloosterman, R., van der Leun, J. and Rath, J. (1998) 'Across the Border: Immigrants, Economic Opportunities, Social Capital, and Informal Business Activities', *Journal of Ethnic and Migration Studies*, 24(2): 249–268.

Kloosterman, R., van der Leun, J. and Rath, J. (1999) 'Mixed Embeddedness: (In)formal Economic Activities and Immigrant Businesses in the Netherlands', *International Journal of Urban and Regional Research*, 23(2): 252–266.

Kojima, M. and Yoshida, A. (2005) 'Hong Kong: The Transit-port for Recyclable Wastes & Secondhand Goods', in Kojima, M. (Ed.) *International Trade of Recyclable Resources in Asia, Institute of Developing Economies*. Viewed 25 June 2013: http://d-arch.ide.go.jp/idedp/SPT/SPT002900_007.pdf

Koser, K. (2007) *International Migration: A Very Short Introduction*, Oxford: Oxford University Press.

Ku, A. S. (2001) 'Hegemonic Construction, Negotiation and Displacement: The Struggle over Right of Abode in Hong Kong', *International Journal of Cultural Studies*, 4(3): 259–278.

Ku, A. S. (2004) 'Immigration Policies, Discourses, and the Politics of Local Belonging in Hong Kong (1950–1980)', *Modern China*, 30(3): 326–360.

Ku, H-b., Chan, K-w. and Sandhu, K. K. (2006) *A Research Report on the Employment of South Asian Ethnic Minority Groups in Hong Kong*, Hong Kong: Department of Applied Social Sciences, The Hong Kong Polytechnic University.

Kuchta-Helbling, C. (2000) *Background Paper – Barriers to Participation: The Informal Sector in Emerging Democracies, The World Movement for Democracy Second Global Assembly: Confronting Challenges to Democracy in the 21st Century*. Viewed 1 July 2013: www.rrojasdatabank.info/informalEnglish.pdf

Lam, K. C. and Liu, P. W. (1998) *Immigration and the Economy of Hong Kong*, Hong Kong: City University Press.

Law, K. Y. and Lee, K. M. (2006) 'Citizenship, Economy and Social Exclusion of Mainland Chinese Immigrations to Hong Kong', *Journal of Contemporary Asia*, 36(2): 217–242.

Law, K. Y. and Lee, K. M. (2013) 'Socio-political Embeddings of South Asian Ethnic Minorities' Economic Situations in Hong Kong', *Journal of Contemporary China*, 22(84): 984–1005.

Lee, A. and Siu, P. (2013) 'Unionists Voice Support for Government's Labour Import Policy', *South China Morning Post*, 25 October. Viewed 25 October 2013: www.scmp.com/news/hong-kong/article/1339071/unionists-voice-support-governments-labour-import-policy

Lee, K. M., Wong, H. and Law, K. Y. (2007) 'Social Polarisation and Poverty in the Global City: The Case of Hong Kong, *China Report*, 43(1): 1–30.

The global city and asylum seeking 61

Legislative Council (LegCo) (2009) *Asylum Seekers*, LCQ19, 1 April 2009. Viewed 1 June 2009: www.info.gov.hk/gia/general/200904/01/P200904010219.htm

Levine, M. (2007) 'Challenging the Culture of Affluence: Schools, Parents, and the Psychological Health of Children', *Independent School*, 67(1): 28–36.

Ley, D. and Teo, S. Y. (2013) 'Gentrification in Hong Kong? Epistemology vs. Ontology', *International Journal of Urban and Regional Research*.

Li, F. L. N., Findlay, A. M. and Jones, H. (1998) 'A Cultural Economy Perspective on Service Sector Migration in the Global City: The Case of Hong Kong', *International Migration*, 36(2): 131–155.

Loper, K. (2010) 'Human Rights, Non-refoulement and the Protection of Refugees in Hong Kong', *International Journal of Refugee Law*, 22(3): 404–439.

Lung, A. K. L. (2012) 'Hong Kong and the Knowledge-based Economy: Developments and Prospects', *Asian Education and Development Studies*, 1(3): 294–300.

Martin, P. (1993) 'The Migration Issue', in R. King (Ed.) *The New Geography of European Migrations*, London: Belhaven Press: 1–16.

Massey, D. (2007) *World City*, Cambridge: Polity Press.

Mathews, G. (2011) *Ghetto at the Center of the World: Chungking Mansions, Hong Kong*, Chicago: The University of Chicago Press.

Mathews, G., Ma, E. K-w. and Lui, T-l. (2008) *Hong Kong, China: Learning to Belong to a Nation*, Abingdon: Routledge.

Mathews, G., Ribeiro, G. L. and Alba Vega, C. (Eds.) (2012) *Globalization from Below: The World's Other Economy*, Abingdon: Routledge.

McDonogh, G. and Wong, C. (2005) *Global Hong Kong*, New York: Routledge.

McKenzie, H. (2009) 'No Direction Home, *Timeout*, 10–23 June: 23–26.

Meyer, D. R. (2000) *Hong Kong as a Global Metropolis*, Cambridge: Cambridge University Press.

Mollenkopf, J. H. and Castells, M. (Eds.) (1991) *Dual City: Restructuring New York*, New York: Russell Sage Foundation.

Mountz, A. (2010) *Seeking Asylum: Human Smuggling and Bureaucracy at the Border*, Minneapolis: University of Minnesota Press.

Müller, M. M. (2013) 'Penal Statecraft in the Latin American City: Assessing Mexico City's Punitive Urban Democracy', *Social & Legal Studies*, 22(4): 441–463.

Munck, R. (2002) *Globalisation and Labour: The New Great Transformation*, London: Zed Books.

Nevins, J. (2002) *Operation Gatekeeper: The Rise of the Illegal Alien and the Making of the U.S.-Mexico Boundary*, New York: Routledge.

Newendorp, N. D. (2008) *Uneasy Reunions: Immigration, Citizenship and Family Life in Post-1997 Hong Kong*, Stanford: Stanford University Press.

Ngo, J. (2013) 'Carrie Lam Faces Critics on Government's Approach towards Poverty', *South China Morning Post*, 30 October. Viewed 30 October 2013: www.scmp.com/news/hong-kong/article/1343064/carrie-lam-faces-critics-governments-approach-towards-poverty.

O'Connor, P. (2012) *Islam in Hong Kong: Muslims and Everyday Life in China's World City*, Hong Kong: Hong Kong University Press.

Ojo, S., Nwankwo, S. and Gbadamosi, A. (2013) 'Ethnic Entrepreneurship: The Myths of Informal and Illegal Enterprises in the UK', *Entrepreneurship & Regional Development: An International Journal*, 25(7–8): 587–611.

Oxfam (2011) *Survey on the Impact of Soaring Food Prices on Poor Families in Hong Kong*. Viewed 13 January 2012: www.oxfam.org.hk/filemgr/1630/FoodSurveyReport Aug2011_revised.pdf

62 The global city and asylum seeking

Parnreiter, C. (2013) 'The Global City Tradition', in M. Acuto and W. Steele (Eds.) *Global City Challenges: Debating a Concept, Improving the Practice*, Houndmills: Palgrave Macmillan: 15–32.

Pluss, C. (2005) 'Constructing Globalized Ethnicity: Migrants from India in Hong Kong', *International Sociology*, 20(2): 201–224.

Quassoli, F. (1999) 'Migrants in the Italian Underground Economy', *International Journal of Urban and Regional Research*, 23(2): 212–231.

Reyneri, E. (1998) 'The Role of the Underground Economy in Irregular Migration to Italy: Cause or Effect?', *Journal of Ethnic and Migration Studies*, 24(2): 313–332.

Robinson, J. (2002) 'Global and World Cities: A View from off the Map', *International Journal of Urban and Regional Research*, 26(3): 531–554.

Samers, M. (2002) 'Immigration and the Global City Hypothesis: Towards an Alternative Research Agenda', *International Journal of Urban and Regional Research*, 26(2): 389–402.

Sassen, S. (1991) 'The Informal Economy', in J. H. Mollenkopf and M. Castells (Eds.) *Dual City: Restructuring New York*, New York: Russell Sage Foundation: 79–102.

Sassen, S. (1998) *Globalization and Its Discontents: Essays on the New Mobility of People and Money*, New York: New Press.

Sassen, S. (1999) *Guests and Aliens*, New York: New Press.

Sassen, S. (2001) *The Global City: New York, London, Tokyo*, second edition, Princeton: Princeton University Press.

Sassen, S. (2005) 'The Global City: Introducing a Concept', *Brown Journal of World Affairs*, 11(2): 27–43.

Saunders, P., Wong, H. and Wong, W. P. (2013) 'Deprivation and Poverty in Hong Kong', *Social Policy & Administration*.

Schenk, C. R. (2001) *Hong Kong as an International Financial Centre: Emergence and Development, 1945–1965*, New York: Routledge.

Shipp, S. (1995) *Hong Kong, China: A Political History of the British Crown Colony's Transfer to Chinese Rule*, London: McFarland and Company.

Short, J. R. and Kim, Y. H. (1999) *Globalization and the City*, Harlow: Longman.

Siu, H. F. (2009) 'Hong Kongers and New Immigrants', *Hong Kong Journal*, 14. Viewed 18 November 2009: www.hkjournal.org/archive/2009_summer/4.htm

Siu, Y. M. (1996) 'Population and Immigration: With a Special Account on Chinese Immigrants', in M. K. Nyaw and S. M. Li (Eds.) *The Other Hong Kong Report 1996*, Hong Kong: The Chinese University Press: 327–347.

Skeldon, R. (1995) 'Immigration and Emigration: Current Trends, Dilemmas and Policies', in D. H. McMillen and M. Si-Wai (Eds.) *The Other Hong Kong Report 1994*, Hong Kong: The Chinese University Press: 165–186.

Smart, A. (1989) 'Forgotten Obstacles, Neglected Forces: Explaining the Origin of Hong Kong Public Housing', *Environment and Planning D: Society and Space*, 7(2): 179–196.

Smart, A. (2001) 'Unruly Places: Urban Governance and the Persistence of Illegality in Hong Kong's Urban Squatter Areas', *American Anthropologist*, 103(1): 30–44.

Smart, A. (2003) 'Sharp Edges, Fuzzy Categories and Transborder Networks: Managing and Housing New Arrivals in Hong Kong', *Ethnic and Relation Studies*, 26(2): 218–233.

Smart, A. and Smart, J. (1998) 'Transnational Social Networks and Negotiated Identities in Interaction between Hong Kong and China', in M. P. Smith and L. E. Guarnizo (Eds.) *Transnationalism from Below*, London: Transaction Publishers: 103–129.

Smith, M. P. and Guarnizo, L. E. (1998) (Eds.) *Transnationalism from Below*, London: Transaction Publishers.

Smith, R. G. (2013) 'Beyond the Global City Concept and the Myth of "Command and Control"', *International Journal of Urban and Regional Research*.

The Standard (2009) 'Refugees in the Making?', 7 May. Viewed 7 May 2009: www.the standard.com.hk/news_detail.asp?pp_cat=20&art_id=81778&sid=23748096&con_type=1&d_str=20090507&sear_year=2009

Tai, P. F. (2006) 'Social Polarisation: Comparing Singapore, Hong Kong and Taipei', *Urban Studies*, 43(10): 1737–1756.

Tai, P. F. (2010) 'Beyond "Social Polarization"? A Test for Asian World Cities in Developmental States', *International Journal of Urban and Regional Research*, 34(4): 743–761.

Tam, M. (2011) 'Elderly Quick to Stake their Claims to HK$6,000', *South China Morning Post*, 29 August. Viewed 29 August 2011: www.scmp.com/article/977462/elderly-quick-stake-their-claims-hk6000

Tao, F. T. (2009) '亞非政治難民爆湧港搶食潮' [South Asian and African political refugees flock into Hong Kong to make money], *Sing Tao Daily*, 11 April, p. 1.

Thomas, J. (2000) *Ethnocide: A Cultural Narrative of Refugee Detention in Hong Kong*, Aldershot: Ashgate.

Venables, A. J. (2001) 'Geography and International Inequalities: The Impact of New Technologies', *Journal of Industry, Competition and Trade*, 1–2: 135–159.

Wacquant, L. (2009) *Punishing the Poor: The Neoliberal Government of Social Insecurity*, Durham: Duke University Press.

White, B. S. (1994) *Turbans and Traders: Hong Kong's Indian Communities*, Hong Kong: Oxford University Press.

Wills, J., Datta, K., Evans, Y., Herbert, J., May, J. and McIlwaine, C. (2009) *Global Cities at Work: New Migrant Divisions of Labour*, London: Pluto Press.

Wong, H. (2012) 'Changes in Social Policy in Hong Kong since 1997: Old Wine in New Bottles?', in W-m. Lam, P. L-t. Lui and W. Wong (Eds.) *Contemporary Hong Kong Government and Politics*, second edition, Hong Kong: Hong Kong University Press: 277–296.

Wong, W. and Yuen, R. (2012) 'Economic Policy', in W-m. Lam, P. L-t. Lui and W. Wong (Eds.) *Contemporary Hong Kong Government and Politics*, second edition, Hong Kong: Hong Kong University Press: 251–275.

Yeoh, B. S. A. (2005) 'The Global Cultural City? Spatial Imagineering and Politics in the (Multi)cultural Marketplaces of South-east Asia', *Urban Studies*, 42(5–6): 945–958.

Zhao, X., Zhang, L. and Sit, T. O. K. (2004) 'Income Inequalities under Economic Restructuring in Hong Kong', *Asian Survey*, 44(3): 442–473.

Zukin, S. (1992) 'The City as a Landscape of Power: London and New York as Global Financial Capitals', in L. Budd and S. Whimster (Eds.) *Global Finance and Urban Living: A Study of Metropolitan Change*, Abingdon: Routledge: 195–233.

2 Global phenomena and local responses

In the previous chapter, Hong Kong emerged as a city marked by inequality, both social and economic. Two worlds seem to coexist in the same narrow city space, where wealth is considered the principal yet unspoken marker of personal success and the peripheral experiences of disadvantaged groups remain largely unseen, even when occasionally reflected on the front page of a newspaper. Predictably, asylum seekers live in the least privileged of these two realities. Caged in what some of the participants called an 'open-air prison', surrounded by walls as invisible as they are unbreakable, they see their much-longed-for opportunities for personal advancement clipped like the wings of birds the farmer does not want to fly too high.

This chapter seeks to develop understandings of the vulnerability of asylum seekers. While the previous chapter explored the socioeconomic and political structure which impacts asylum seekers' vulnerability by crafting the spaces where they develop local networks and generate an income, this chapter illustrates how this vulnerability is effectively shaped. This chapter explores the structural forces and processes underlying the contours of the contemporary condition of asylum seekers in Hong Kong. I pay particular attention to the laws and administrative and social contexts that construct the barriers and exclusion that asylum seekers must confront to procure a livelihood. First, I highlight the significance of this analysis for the arguments made in this book. Referring to the narratives of asylum seeker participants, the first section reveals how these people perceive the policies that produce their vulnerability and explores the socio-legal mechanisms by which this group of individuals is homogenized as a foreign 'other'. It is argued that, in Hong Kong, legal status operates as a clear marker of inclusion and exclusion. Asylum seekers' experiences of the restrictions imposed on them by law, policy and prevailing social norms powerfully highlight the spaces that confine them. The rationale that motivates these people to engage in informal economic activities is explained in light of the data presented in this chapter.

Second, I explore the vulnerability of asylum seekers by examining the asylum mechanisms in place in Hong Kong, as viewed by asylum seekers. On the one hand, the prevailing attitudes towards asylum seekers evident within public and official discourses are analyzed vis-à-vis increased concern over the number of people purportedly abusing the asylum system and calls for more restrictive policies to ensure order in the city. On the other hand, the evidence cited to support such claims

Global phenomena and local responses 65

is examined against asylum seeker experiences of these screening mechanisms in Hong Kong. This informs understanding of why and how asylum seekers are shaped into distinctive social characters within clearly defined spaces of movement. The aim is to offer a narrow, although critically important, snapshot of the daily liminal life into which asylum seekers are forced in Hong Kong, so as to understand the various forms of their (deportable) vulnerability, and thus to empirically ground further analysis of asylum seeking and economic engagement in this global city.

The 'deportability' of undesirable asylum seekers

Divided by borders

Several commentators have argued that the geographical borders between nations are today no longer simply neutral lines of separation. While borders are political constructions that demarcate two or more areas, emphasis is increasingly placed on the laws, institutions and especially the values and cultures that either unite or divide populations, depending on which side of the border they inhabit. In other words, borders delineate practices of belonging and non-belonging. They distinguish norms and exceptions and define communities and citizens. By so doing, they become tools of exclusion (Rajaram and Grundy-Warr 2007).

From this perspective, border controls no longer take place exclusively at the sites and spaces traditionally designed for this function (Mountz 2010; Araujo 2011). Rather, they have shifted spatially and temporally to affect migrants at all stages of their journey (Weber 2006). Additionally, the border is increasingly personalized, distinguishing people according to the capital and skills that rich societies arbitrarily associate with certain foreign travellers (Neumayer 2006; Cohen 2006). It is within this spectrum of belonging and non-belonging that a potent and pervasive discourse distinguishing 'us' from 'them' is constructed (Dauvergne 2008; Dal Lago 2009).

In Hong Kong, the foreigner is often portrayed as an unfamiliar body that might threaten social stability, especially when they come from, or are perceived to come from, less developed countries (Ku 2001; Newendorp 2008). In this chapter, I argue that a widely expressed fear about the arrival of people 'extraneous' to Hong Kong has emerged in response to perceptions of the heightened insecurity that this movement might generate, particularly given that the government has seemingly been unable to effectively seal the territory's porous borders. As posited in the previous chapter, similar developments occurred during the period of mass arrivals of Vietnamese boat people (Thomas 2000; Loper 2010) and especially during times of economic restructuring aimed at halting the influx of low-skilled mainland Chinese (Law and Lee 2006; Smart 2003). As is discussed in detail subsequently, in 2009, concomitant with the suspension of the CAT screening mechanism[1] and rising numbers of arrivals of asylum seekers, new control mechanisms were introduced. With the support of the media, representations of deviant asylum seekers driven by personal economic interest were strengthened.

Dal Lago (2009) argues that the result of such a process is typically the conflation of asylum seekers with the figure of the illegal migrant, socially constructed as a real threat. Asylum came to prominence within Hong Kong's public discourse

66 *Global phenomena and local responses*

and debate when it was perceived to be a problem – that is, when it was claimed that waves of undesirable migrants were arriving in the territory to abuse asylum and work illegally. Importantly, it is contended here that restrictive policies aimed at building defensive barricades around the city not only made it difficult for migrants from specific countries to legally travel to the territory (see Chapter 3), but also affected the social inclusion and livelihood of the people who did manage to cross the border and seek asylum in Hong Kong (see Chapters 4 and 5). Those people who are unable to secure legal status in destination countries have been said to live as 'outsiders within', at the margins of mainstream society (Da Lomba 2010; Calavita 2005). Often, they are caught within an 'entrapment process' (Núñez and Heyman 2007) that starves them into living a life of forced deprivation, coupled with a loss of dignity and self-worth. De Genova (2011: 102–103) speaks of this condition in terms of a 'border spectacle', by means of which migrants' illegality is rendered spectacularly visible in order to transform them into an anonymous, inferior 'phantasmagorical ubiquity'. For their supposed deviancy, migrants are thus depicted as a menace, which heightens perceptions of their otherness and portrays them as 'enemies', in turn justifying the use of extraordinary measures to exclude them (Krasmann 2007). As external border control is often ineffective in stopping or removing unwanted people, the categorization of undesirables into enemy types facilitates their marginalization and hence the condition of indefinite precariousness (De Genova 2011) in which their agency then becomes embedded (Engbersen and van der Leun 2001). In the HKSAR, greater awareness of asylum issues has in effect meant that policies aimed at controlling or deterring the number of arrivals did not result solely in the portrayal of some types of travellers as potential threats to the growth of the city's social and economic prosperity, but also marginalized and excluded asylum seekers already living within its geographical borders. Based on interviews I conducted in Hong Kong with the people who have been subjected to such policies, it appears that the impacts of these policies weigh heavily on the immigrant body, particularly by forming their 'deportability' (cf. De Genova 2002), or specific social, political and especially economic spaces to which asylum seekers become institutionally confined.

The importance of legal status, or lack thereof, as a figurative border that impacts on the lived experiences of asylum seekers in Hong Kong was very clearly highlighted by several of the participants in this study. Many were frustrated by their present circumstances. In particular, they felt that their opportunities to make a living, or to feel 'like a human being' in the wording of some, were considerably limited. The narratives of the participants speak powerfully of the brutality of the border and asylum seekers' feelings as shaped by their environment. One West African interviewee named Erick, who had been waiting for two years for his asylum claim to be processed, fervently argued:

> You are here and you don't know your future. You live day by day. . . . People don't consider you; they don't give you any chance to improve your life. You may have some gift to use in society, but there are so many regulations and laws that don't allow you to move forward. I was telling you, even to find a place to stay, a home, a decent place, you have to struggle to pay deposit, and

Global phenomena and local responses   67

considering the money you get from social welfare and that you can't work – sometimes I think of going back home, because it is better to face the difficult situation at home. Here it is the same difficult situation. At home people have real guns, but here also they have other types of guns, shooting at you, because you are like a target. Every day they shoot you. It is the same death you live every day. (African participant, 18)[2]

For several participants, the greatest impact of their situation was the feeling that their life had stopped in Hong Kong. The lack of economic rights in particular, such as the right to lawfully engage in income-generating activities, and the policies governing the services available to asylum seekers, like those offered by the government-contracted NGO, the ISS, were perceived as drastically reducing the spaces within which asylum seekers can manoeuvre to exercise their decision making and pursue a livelihood. For instance, a young man from an East African country described the difficult time he faced in Hong Kong, stressing that his friends and he were wasting their time there. 'We are mentally dead', he said, 'because we can't work, we can't have education, but we have ambitions, we have dreams, and we have different talents and skills. But we are in a trap' (African participant, 27).

Echoing the previous comments, other interviewees described how they felt 'useless', as the skills they had brought to Hong Kong, ranging from doctoral qualifications to craftsmanship, had gone to waste. One South Asian participant vehemently expressed that he felt uneasy and unwelcome in Hong Kong. He added that he was not happy 'because my family doesn't live with me and there is not enough to live with. It is mental torture' (Bangladeshi participant, 37). Likewise, in a meeting with a co-national participant, one young Bangladeshi interpreter, who often helped with translation, reflected on his friend's and his own condition, summing up the views expressed by many of the asylum seeker participants. In his opinion, the 'government is torturing us because we can eat, sleep and live; but there are still problems, such as a lot of tension. Every day we need to think of how to buy some things that we need, but there is no money. . . . You need something but you can't get it. We have dreams, we see them, but we can't reach them' (Bangladeshi participant, 38). A friend of his, who lived in squatter housing in the New Territories, similarly commented: 'I can live . . . but everything is useless. . . . Happiness is not just eating and sleeping, because these are not the only needs that a person has' (Bangladeshi participant, 43).

Interestingly, Zimmermann (2009a, 2009b) argues extensively for the irrelevance of the conceptual separation between the safety concerns and socioeconomic interests of refugees, upon which policy-makers and public opinion often insist. In her analysis of Somali refugees in the UK, she stresses that her participants had ambitions, desires and hopes that were not only related to safety, as safety was not the only thing they had lost when they fled their country. As she claims, refugees seek durable solutions aimed at achieving a normal life. Indeed, what drives asylum seekers to leave their homes is not only the universal human drive for self-preservation, but also the need to find a place where they

68 *Global phenomena and local responses*

can reconstruct themselves and their lives (Zimmermann 2009a). The participants in Robinson and Segrott's (2002: 52) research shared the opinion that 'the prospect of living on welfare benefits was sometimes seen as inevitable in the period immediately upon arrival in the UK but was generally viewed as highly undesirable in the long term'. These comments suggest that asylum seekers expect to earn a living, in part as a way to regain a sense of self-respect lost during flight. The data captured from my interviews similarly showed that asylum seekers hope to assume a productive role in society and thereby to improve their well-being and social and economic status. As one participant argued: 'I have safety, but I don't have a good life, because a good life is when you work on your own' (African participant, 24).

Powerfully apparent from the interviews was the idea of asylum seekers suffering mental torment, including frustration, melancholy and boredom, in enduring a life of economic hardship and immiseration. In this regard, several participants stressed that they had been transformed into beggars by their life in Hong Kong, marked by routine activities that involved minimal spending. At the same time, they constantly needed to ask for help from sympathetic people and charities. As a Sri Lankan interviewee emotionally argued, the extraordinarily long periods of waiting he had to endure over seven years in Hong Kong, and the circumstances which he felt left him without a chance to direct his future, risked causing unnecessary suffering to his children also: 'If we are here for long, it will be very bad for my family. By bad I mean that even my children's future will be to ask help, help, help – like me now, I ask help. I don't want my children to beg for help. I'm a beggar now, but we are not like this' (Sri Lankan participant, 16). Harrell-Bond (2002) emphasizes that refugee agency can be seriously harmed by governments and other agencies wrongly, yet intentionally, assuming that all refugees are the same, stereotyped as sharing the same values and needs (Zetter 1991, 2007). The psycho-social well-being of refugees, especially their self-esteem, is affected as a result, increasing their vulnerability due to a state of prolonged liminality (Vrecer 2010).

In Hong Kong, several participants referred to their situation as 'hell' or sometimes as a 'prison' enclosed by invisible yet oppressive walls. When asked to explain how their life was impacted by their tenuous legal status and lack of economic rights, several interviewees added that in addition to feeling like beggars they felt humiliated. Their mental health suffered. A number of participants shared the view that life in Hong Kong was 'like jail, [because] we have freedom but not happiness' (Sri Lankan participant, 84g), with one commenting that 'whether I stay in Hong Kong or go back to Bangladesh my life is already destroyed' (Bangladeshi participant, 58). Others, especially recent arrivals, expressed the opinion that mental health was the first thing that would be at risk when placed in an environment that deprived them of the opportunity to continue either or both education and the work they had previously undertaken in their country of origin. A Sri Lankan participant expressed the view that '[i]f my body gets addicted to this [laziness], I get crazy. I have never been like this before and that's why I don't want to be like this. The mind is free and I don't want to think of my past. That's

Global phenomena and local responses 69

a big problem. I try to make a new life soon. I don't want to stop my life now' (Sri Lankan participant, 72).

From the previous discussion, it can be argued that the asylum seekers interviewed experienced their exclusion in terms of an inability to exert their agency in ways they desired. The impact of a legally defined social border was thus powerfully evident. The participants were often distressed and 'unhappy', citing their dissatisfaction with being unable to control their life and future. On the one hand, the financial problems related to scarce government support and the lack of lawful opportunities to engage in either the formal economy or education were found to greatly impact decision making and livelihoods. On the other, their social and economic marginalization threatened to damage their mental health. They affirmed that they could not simply sit and wait for someone to care for them. A young West African participant, who had just arrived in Hong Kong, conveyed this point in describing his reaction when he learnt from fellow asylum seekers about the sort of future he was likely to endure in the city:

> It would be difficult for me to stay two, three, five years in this situation, because in my country I was an orphan since I was six. My mother was a farmer and I farmed too. I know that life is a struggle and I can take care of myself. I farmed and worked for other people too. I have never been free during holidays. I always worked in my village and made some money. With that money I could pay school fees and my room. I have never been idle like this, waiting for something – it is the situation in Hong Kong that obliges me to stay like this. Also what ISS give us is not our food. It is also the same food; so shall I eat the same food for five years? . . . I'm young now but I cannot work, so when shall I work? When I'm old? I don't know – I can't control my life. In Hong Kong [it] is like this. (African participant, 13)

This chapter presents the argument that the hardships endured by asylum seekers that shape their vulnerability in Hong Kong are the outcome of policies aimed at both homogenizing asylum seeker experiences and needs and punishing migrants who bypass legitimate border controls and thereby defy law and order. Weber and Pickering (2011) very neatly describe the routine production of harm, ending in actual or social death, which the complex institution of border control generates for illegalized travellers. Such harms are often associated with the state's goals of deterring arrivals and reasserting sovereignty and national identity (Melossi 2003) – and this is especially evident in the current period when Hong Kong is grappling with the problems related to becoming a global city on Chinese soil (cf. Law and Lee 2006, 2013). It is noteworthy that, as participant Erick identified, the suffocating border that several asylum seekers in the present study experienced also impacted their conviction to argue their asylum case. A number of participants claimed that they would have gladly left Hong Kong had their home country been in a state to provide them with safety. They said that they felt unwelcome in the territory, which contributed to their anxiety about their future, indirectly persuading them to accept the temporary nature of their stay in Hong Kong and

70 *Global phenomena and local responses*

thus impeding their integration. It is in this context that the comments set out subsequently must be understood. For instance, some interviewees explained that they thought they would have better opportunities elsewhere, and that they were hoping to leave Hong Kong in order to seek them out. An outspoken West African asylum seeker, commenting on his present circumstances, stated that he was just waiting for the situation at home to improve. 'My life now is not good', he said, 'I only know that my life will be the same like now, and I have to accept it, until the time comes that I can leave' (African participant, 10). Another interviewee similarly affirmed: 'I think I can make my life better if I leave. . . . In some time I will go, because I know what I'm looking for, and Hong Kong cannot provide that' (African participant, 09). In this view, some asylum seekers negotiated the structural constraints in Hong Kong by devising strategies that would allow them to leave the territory. This 'voluntary' departure from Hong Kong arguably exempted the government from providing asylum seekers with effective protection, while also offering the authorities a justification for branding asylum seekers as illegal economic migrants.

While forcing asylum seekers through legal measures to endure economic and emotional hardship via their marginalization, paradoxically the same government policy appears to have crafted spaces in which refugee agency is to some extent tolerated. In their analysis, Weber and Pickering (2011: 97) acknowledge that '[a]gainst this spectre of abject marginalization it is important to recognize that illegalized migrants still seek to participate in social and economic life within the limits of their politico-juridical status.' The analysis in the following chapters reveals how asylum seekers have acquired an important role in Hong Kong society, namely in the economic realm, as a direct result of the punishment they have endured as illegal migrants. Indeed, their active involvement in specific social and economic contexts is understandable given the legal, psychological and social marginalization evidenced in this chapter.

Further light can be shed on how these asylum seekers were impacted by structural forces that compelled their agency within carefully defined boundaries by looking at the legal arguments and the language applied to their migration in Hong Kong.

The legal environment in Hong Kong

An 'illegal immigrant' or 'overstayer' is a person who crosses the border into Hong Kong or remains in the territory without the legal permission of the authorities. Conversely, an 'asylum seeker' is either one of the previously mentioned persons who lodges an application for asylum with the local UNHCR office. In addition, asylum may be sought when illegal immigrants and overstayers lodge an application under Article 3 of the CAT.[3] It is therefore apparent that the legal status of the asylum seeker, who is treated no differently from any other arrival in Hong Kong, does largely overlap with that of an illegal immigrant. Beyond affecting the status of an asylum seeker in theory, this also has practical consequences for the persons concerned. On this point, refugee advocates often

Global phenomena and local responses 71

highlight the difficulty of working to promote the rights of this vulnerable group of people precisely because the words 'asylum seeker' and 'illegal immigrant' are now understood by the majority of people to be synonymous (McKenzie 2009). The boundary normally dividing the two categories is at best blurred, if seen to be existent at all, in official and public debates alike. Consequently, even the motivation leading prospective asylum seekers to enter the territory can be easily misinterpreted.

In the following pages, what is generally termed the 'asylum–migration nexus' (Castles 2007; Crisp 2008) is examined in the context of Hong Kong: first, in view of the laws and the mounting politicization of asylum issues; and second, in light of the frequent media reports that, particularly in 2009, have depicted the continuous arrival of non-Chinese asylum seekers/illegal immigrants as a threat to the orderly operation of society. This exercise is important to advance the arguments that asylum policies are constructed in ways that create internal boundaries within which asylum seekers must adapt their livelihoods, but which also lead to hardship and despair. At the same time, it presents the context against which examples of refugee experiences of exclusion are discussed in the final section of this chapter.

Hong Kong–based human rights lawyer Mark Daly (2009: 15) argues that, since the provisions introduced to deal with the Vietnamese refugees were effectively removed from the Immigration Ordinance (Cap115) in 1998, 'there was and is a complete lack of legislation, regulation and/or coherent overall policy to deal with asylum seekers, refugees and now a growing number of Convention Against Torture (CAT) claimants'. This state of affairs has led to a number of legal challenges by recognized refugees and asylum seekers. Judicial reviews have been heard at several levels of the Hong Kong court system, with the most important decided at the Court of Final Appeal – the highest court in Hong Kong. A number of cases have reviewed issues of detention, prosecution, legal rights and procedural fairness. As an example, three such judicial reviews launched to legally challenge government policies on asylum seekers are briefly examined here to explore the legal framework that contributes to the vulnerability of asylum seekers. The first two cases were that of *C v Director of Immigration*[4] and *MA v Director of Immigration*,[5] in which it was argued that the principle of *non-refoulement* exists in customary international law (CIL) and that recognized refugees should be given the right to work pending their resettlement. In the third case, conversely, it was argued that welfare support should be provided for the most vulnerable asylum seekers while their claims remain undecided. If the significance of these cases lies in the impact they have had on the life of asylum seekers in Hong Kong, they also show the arguments put by Hong Kong courts and the public administration in relation to commonly held notions around asylum and its control.

In *C v Director of Immigration*, six asylum seekers, who had their application for refugee status rejected by the UNHCR, argued that Hong Kong had an obligation not to *refoule* refugees under both Hong Kong law and the CIL. Further, they claimed that, rather than the UNHCR, the government was responsible for

72 *Global phenomena and local responses*

screening asylum applications. The Court of Appeal dismissed the review. The judgement recognized that the notion of *non-refoulement* had developed into the CIL, but an argument was made that there was no obligation on the Hong Kong Government to set up an internal system. The court upheld the argument that it is the UNHCR's mandate to protect refugees, and that it is an acceptable practice for the director of immigration to refer to this agency any person seeking asylum in Hong Kong. This case was later granted leave to be heard at the Court of Final Appeal,[6] and the previous judgement was reversed in March 2013. An argument was made that, because of the serious harm potentially caused by an error in screening procedures, it is not sufficient for the government to rely on UNHCR refugee status determination to decide whether to return a rejected asylum claimant to his or her country of origin. Instead, the government must make its own determination on asylum cases, ensuring the highest standards of fairness. Yet the court did not decide on the CIL and maintained that 'nothing in this judgment calls into question the Government's policy not to grant asylum' or that it had any obligation to 'facilitate the assimilation and naturalization of refugees'.[7]

In the other judicial review application, four mandated refugees and one screened-in torture claimant, to date the first of four torture claimants ever to be recognized in Hong Kong, argued that they should be given the right to work because they had been waiting in Hong Kong for periods of between six and nine years, with no durable solution in sight. The UNHCR was said to be still processing their resettlement, while the Hong Kong Government was said to have 'zero published guidelines or information available to successful torture claimants' (Ip 2010). Indeed, while being recognized as a torture victim in Hong Kong is extremely rare, the ImmD apparently has no policy on how to proceed with people who are found to be torture victims, other than agreeing to not return them to the country where they faced or may face torture. The five claimants argued that the ImmD's blanket policies had forced them to remain stranded in Hong Kong for prolonged periods of time, dependent on the mercy of friends and charities to survive at a subsistence level, even when there was little prospect for them to be resettled in the foreseeable future. They argued that the lack of appropriate policies infringed the injunction against cruel, inhuman or degrading treatment and the right to employment and gravely compromised their right to a private life.

While the judgement acknowledged that the claimants had been stranded, the review was nonetheless dismissed. The court posited:

> As the courts, including this Court, have noted on various occasions, in the light of Hong Kong's small geographical size, huge population, substantial daily intake of immigrants from the Mainland, and relatively high per capita income and living standards, and given Hong Kong's local living and job market conditions, almost inevitably Hong Kong has to adopt very restrictive and tough immigration policies and practices.[8]

While stressing the difficult position of Hong Kong, the judgement further pointed to the necessary discretional power of the director of immigration in seeking to

Global phenomena and local responses 73

balance the structural forces likely to drive large flows of people towards the territory:

> When deciding whether the decision of the Director, whether at the policy level or at the individual decision level, is rational or reasonable in the public law sense, the court is bound to have substantial regard to the overall immigration picture as a general justification for the Director's policy or exercise of discretion concerned. . . . In particular, I have already extracted from the evidence the concerns over the 'strong pulling force' in attracting a large number of illegal immigrants to Hong Kong by any or any apparent relaxation in the employment policy of the Director. . . . The Director is entitled to think that any sign, however tenuous, of potential relaxation in the Government's attitude towards illegal immigrants would likely be interpreted, with or without attempts on the part of 'human smugglers' to talk up their hopes and expectations, as 'a ray of hope' for illegal immigrants.[9]

The two judicial review applications and the arguments presented in each case reveal that, in the first place, not only are comprehensive legislation and policies in relation to asylum lacking in Hong Kong, but also existing measures appear irrational at best, although for what may be interpreted in official quarters as a valid reason. Noteworthy is that the individuality of the claimants is often effectively denied in the name of the collective interest. Similar to what occurs in many other developed countries, the floodgates controlling the ebb and flow of migration are efficiently mastered when both the individuality of the migrant is reduced to mere numbers and statistics and their movement is strictly controlled to deter further arrivals. On this account, the government's desire to firmly maintain the legal right to decide whether to remove a person from or allow them to stay in the territory, and under what conditions, even when an application for asylum is made and substantiated, should be understood in light of its strong deterrent effect and, in turn, its capacity to appease popular anxieties concerning an imminent invasion. Indeed, exclusionary measures crafted around incoherent asylum policies and legislation certainly impact asylum seekers in Hong Kong, who are continually reminded of their precarious status. This reinforces the city's image as an inhospitable destination for people wishing to seek asylum. In this regard, the following letter from the director of immigration, addressed to the previously mentioned claimants in response to their request for the right to work, explicates the tough stance of the government:

> The Administration has a firm policy of not granting asylum and does not have any obligation to admit individuals seeking refugee status under the Convention. Claims for refugee status which are lodged in Hong Kong are dealt with by the UNHCR. For those accepted as having refugee status by the UNHCR, removal actions against them may, upon the exercise of the Director of Immigration's discretion on a case by case basis, be temporarily withheld pending arrangements for their resettlement elsewhere in the

74 *Global phenomena and local responses*

world by the UNHCR. Albeit these persons have been so recognized by the UNHCR, the Administration owes no obligation to them arising from their refugee status.[10]

The government's refusal to sign the Refugee Convention and set out relevant procedures concerning substantiated claims remains unchanged. Asylum seekers and torture victims are consequently made to endure emotional and economic hardship as a result of their illegal status for the likely deterrent effect their punishment is believed to produce on those hoping for a better life in Hong Kong.

For the purposes of this analysis, it is evident that a strong link has been established between asylum seekers and illegal migrants in Hong Kong. Discourses of asylum appear to promote the view that meeting the needs of asylum seekers would increase the number of illegal migrant arrivals, who would themselves look to become asylum seekers in order to enjoy such treatment, thereby conflating the two categories of migrant. If there remains here some semblance of differentiation between refugees and illegal migrants, interestingly this distinction appears blurred by the rationale supporting the assistance mechanism that provides social services to asylum seekers. In 2006, the government set up an in-kind support system for asylum seekers as a result of judicial litigation[11] in which it was claimed that asylum seekers should be given support while waiting for screening procedures to be completed (Daly 2009).[12] The Social Welfare Department was then instructed to contract NGO ISS to administer the mechanism. However, the system had to include assistance in a form 'considered sufficient to prevent a person from becoming destitute while at the same time not creating a magnet effect which can have serious implications on the sustainability of our current support system'.[13]

From this perspective, it is apparent that this system is underpinned by a belief that the number of asylum seekers would increase disproportionately were they to be provided with a significant, or even adequate, amount of assistance. The siege or floodgates scenario that is cyclically raised in Hong Kong to justify the government's lack of political will in considering the plight of the least fortunate explains its restrictive policies (cf. Goodstadt 2013). In other words, the conviction that a large number of arrivals would abuse the system and take advantage of the generous benefits reserved for a limited number of people, were control measures to be loosened, has proved to be resistant. Such interpretation has had serious consequences – as will be demonstrated subsequently – for public opinion and asylum seekers alike.

The depiction of asylum seekers as bogus claimants

In recent years, Hong Kong has experienced a significant upward trend in the number of people seeking asylum from countries in South Asia and Africa, despite the absence of reception processes for refugees in the territory. Since the introduction of more restrictive border control measures, this influx has stabilized and partly decreased. There were 670 asylum seekers in 2004 and 1097 in 2005 who requested protection at the UNHCR. In 2006, there were 2407 pending cases with the UNHCR, and 2282 new applications were lodged in 2007. Thereafter, a slow but perceptible decrease brought the number of new asylum claims to 1265 and 1272 in 2008 and 2009, respectively, to fall further in 2010 and 2011.[14] As of January 2012, there were 597 asylum seekers and 152 recognized refugees in Hong Kong.[15] On the other hand, between 1992 and 2004, 44 CAT claims were received by the Hong Kong Government, whereas over the four years from 2005 to 2008, the number of CAT claims rose to 186, 541, 1583 and 2198, respectively. In the first 8 months of 2009, 2132 CAT claims were lodged, representing a clear upward trend in contrast with the UNHCR figures.[16] These trends can be seen to relate to concomitant events that apparently impacted on asylum seeker decision making. First, CAT screening procedures were suspended for about a year in 2009, in response to a court ruling that the screening mechanism was not meeting the high standards of fairness it was supposed to maintain (Loper 2010). An enhanced mechanism allowing publicly funded legal representation was then launched on 24 December 2009, with the aim of processing 400 cases within the first 12 months (LegCo 2010, 2011). Second, on 14 November 2009, the Immigration (Amendment) Ordinance was enacted, which specified that it is a criminal offence for illegal immigrants and persons pending removal to take up unlawful employment in Hong Kong. The number of non-ethnic Chinese illegal migrants intercepted at sea dropped significantly thereafter. Torture claims also decreased in number. In 2010, a total of 1809 torture claims were received, a 45 per cent downturn on the 3286 claims lodged in 2009. In addition, between 14 November 2009 and 31 December 2010, 1536 torture claimants withdrew their claims and voluntarily repatriated (ImmD 2011).

Media and official commentary has asserted that the previous figures are indicative of asylum abuse. Further, as about 90 per cent of the claims were lodged by applicants upon their arrest or when facing repatriation, an argument was made in government quarters that claimants were resorting to asylum 'in order to prolong their stay' because 'about half of the claimants are illegal immigrants ("IIs") and the other half overstayers' (LegCo 2011). While it is likely that some people have thus been 'abusing' asylum, I equally infer that asylum seekers have been quickly and coherently constructed as a problem in public discourses, not only in terms of their numbers but also their motivation and moral standing, which may be commonly perceived as contrary to the accepted rationale for seeking asylum and Hong Kong society's traditional focus on orderly compliance with the rule of law. Indeed, asylum seekers have been transformed into suspicious and bogus claimants through the juxtaposition of matters of security, legality and asylum, and thus construed as a real threat (cf. Mountz 2010; Dal Lago 2009).

In response to two successive court rulings in March 2009[17] – one of which found that a group of Pakistani asylum seekers was not breaking the law by working in street markets and the other that four asylum seekers had been unlawfully detained by the ImmD, who were then afforded damages (Tsui 2009a, 2009b) – numerous media articles reported an alarming increase in the number of boats caught illegally bringing asylum seekers to Hong Kong. News reports at the time

76 *Global phenomena and local responses*

reminded readers that 'illegal migrants who claimed asylum status immediately on being arrested could now work for up to 18 months while their applications were processed' (Lo 2009). It was argued that loopholes in the legislation were being exploited by illegal migrants and the smugglers who were bringing them to the territory. A senior police inspector was quoted as saying: 'Snakeheads [smugglers] on the mainland may have been spreading rumours that non-Chinese illegal immigrants will be offered asylum during their detention' (Li and Tsang 2009). Another officer, referring to the discovery of a new passageway used by people smugglers, similarly argued that '[i]t is very dangerous for Hong Kong that people can slip into the city and then leave again without detection. . . . This raises the spectre that they can come here, commit crimes and leave with impunity' (Crawford 2009).

Asylum and the increasing number of detections at sea came to be defined in relation to the potential risk of receiving a flood of arrivals, reinforced by rumours that in South Asia and Africa prospective asylum seekers were being told that they could work in Hong Kong. The image of little boats slipping through the tight mesh of legal controls, flouting law and order, made the situation appear critical and reinforced the association between asylum seeking and deviant behaviour. In the Chinese-language press, in particular, photos and reports at times depicted the small boats used by smugglers and numbers of handcuffed illegal migrants being escorted along mountain trails by military-uniformed police officers. These photos and reports were accompanied by headlines (translated) such as '13 Pakistanis crowded in a small sampan, 16-year-old smuggler brings in fake asylum seekers' (*Headlines Daily* 2009), or 'Lost and without food "they surrender", 17 smuggled South Asians arrested' (*Ming Pao* 2009a).

The impact of such press coverage on public opinion is difficult to assess. Nonetheless, refugee advocates in Hong Kong largely appear to share the views expressed in the media. From an examination of media articles and interviews conducted with human rights lawyers and charity workers, it emerged that asylum seekers were widely suspected of being bogus until proved otherwise. On 15 May 2009, the *South China Morning Post* reported the opinion of a human rights lawyer that the government should not delay legislation on assessing asylum seekers because '[t]he delay has fuelled the perception in some quarters in India, Pakistan and Nepal that Hong Kong was a place where you could work.' The same human rights lawyer was then quoted as saying that, had proper legislation been put in place, 'they [the Hong Kong Government could] then control and manage the system and wipe out abusers from the genuine asylum seekers' (Lo and Nip 2009).

Another respected lawyer who represents asylum seekers, referring to the alleged increase in the number of asylum seekers involved in drug dealing, was quoted as commenting that '[i]f it is the case that some individuals are drug dealing it will only justify even more inappropriate policing in Hong Kong. . . . This will not help at all and will just harden prejudices against genuine refugees and claimants here' (Carney 2011). While this commentator rightly linked rising law enforcement to worsening public perceptions, stressing that there was a sense

Global phenomena and local responses 77

among the police that all asylum seekers were bogus claimants, he nonetheless seemed to share the opinion that some asylum seekers are in Hong Kong to work or commit crimes. Indeed, as one concerned citizen put it, 'Either claimants are genuine and their lives at risk, so they require support and protection, or they are merely economic migrants whose claims should be quickly disposed of and dealt with accordingly' (*South China Morning Post* 2010). In practice, clear indicators of asylum abuse have been highlighted to defend the legal process that was hoped would be established to deal with successful claims. However, this has led to the assumption that certain claims are bogus a priori and need to be disposed of quickly. As one charity worker explained in the *South China Morning Post*, the rationale behind this assumption is that, '[i]n all honesty, the majority of genuine cases would not dare to work illegally for fear of jeopardising their only hope of getting resettled in a third country and starting afresh' (Bernal 2010).

This process of homogenization of refugee experiences appears so ingrained in Hong Kong that, even after the Immigration Ordinance was amended in 2009 to rectify that asylum seekers could not work in the city, a police officer commented in relation to the arrival of another boatload of eight men seeking political asylum that '[w]e do not rule out the possibility that they just want to find work in Hong Kong. . . . Initial investigation showed the illegal immigrants do not know about the new law' (Lam and Tsang 2009). The Chinese media reported this story in similar terms (*Ming Pao* 2009b).

This study found that, importantly, discourses surrounding genuine and abusive asylum seekers shaped the participants' perceptions of themselves. From the interviews, it emerged that there was a fracture within the asylum seeker community. On the one hand, there were people who claimed that they deserved international protection. On the other, there were those who were said to take advantage of the asylum mechanisms in order to unlawfully prolong their stay in the territory and work illegally. Interestingly, only a very few interviewees admitted that their case was not genuine, while many questioned the genuineness of other asylum seekers, even though they only appeared to have a superficial understanding of their stories. For example, echoing the aforementioned comment by Bernal (2010), one West African interviewee stressed that '[s]ome people do business because not all asylum seekers are the same. There are real asylum seekers and those who are more like economic migrants. . . . Most of the people who are genuine don't want to risk [working] because it is illegal, and when you are found doing it, it might jeopardize your case' (African participant, 02). While this participant believed that lodging an application for asylum is incompatible with certain behaviours that he deemed might jeopardize one's protection, he nevertheless revealed that '[o]nce I was tempted to do something, because my wife calls me all the time and speaks about the children – they need money, and I feel I want to work.' This participant explained that he was frustrated by his current situation and felt that he needed to work. However, as he spoke it became apparent that he was applying preconceived notions about categories of asylum to his fellow asylum seekers who faced similar circumstances. Indeed, it was clear that several of the participants interviewed had been exposed to an interpretation of asylum and illegality

78 *Global phenomena and local responses*

since arriving in Hong Kong that they had come to make their own. The participants who were not involved in illegal economic activities stated that their decision not to do so was based on a fear of the likely negative consequences for their asylum case. Conversely, the people who were working were viewed as 'fake', as they evidently did not fear being returned to the country where they claimed to have faced, or they would face, persecution.

A Sri Lankan participant, for example, argued that within his group of co-nationals there were clear indicators of genuineness, whereas Sinhalese could go home and their only reason for seeking asylum was to try their luck and perhaps be resettled to another country. Another Sri Lankan interviewee echoed this view in saying that perhaps only 10 per cent of the asylum seekers from his country had serious problems at home. According to him, while the rest had come to Hong Kong to work, he believed that he was 'the real asylum seeker; and I have every proof' (Sri Lankan participant, 14). One South Asian participant explained that he had taken practical steps to fight what he believed was plaguing the asylum system in Hong Kong: 'I sent a letter giving suggestions to Immigration, saying there were categories who they needed to give refugee status [to]' (Pakistani participant, 34). According to this man, abuse was rampant, driven by story fabrication for the purpose of staying longer in the territory to work. He believed that hundreds of his co-nationals were entering Hong Kong illegally in the belief that they could manipulate the asylum mechanisms. 'They need to change the system or it won't stop. Out of 6000 people, maybe one person is a real case', he said. Clearly, this interviewee believed that his case was genuine, but that because of the false claims of others clogging the system, he was forced to endure a long, exhausting waiting period that drove him and his family into poverty. Interestingly, his case was later refused by both the UNHCR and Hong Kong's ImmD, and he blamed illegal economic migrants who were making the job of UNHCR and immigration officers difficult, rather than the incompetency of the authorities or the possibility that his personal circumstances did not warrant such a claim.

This analysis does not explore the factors that forced the participants to flee their country of origin. Therefore, the fact that some of them could indeed safely return to their country is not denied here. Nevertheless, as will be discussed in the following chapters, this research found that the friction between asylum seekers' desire to engage in a fulfilling life and the structural constraints that limit their agency was negotiated differently by asylum seekers facing different circumstances, both in Hong Kong and in their country of origin. Rather than an indication of asylum abuse, the agency displayed by some of the asylum seekers must be understood against the backdrop of policy and discourse aimed at marginalizing this group, at a time when their claim was being morally demoted for its deviant, economically motivated intent. In practice, loopholes in legislation were blamed on asylum seekers who reportedly exploited them for profit. In turn, the burden of proof resting on asylum seekers to substantiate their claims became more difficult to fulfil. If several participants clearly had in mind a neat line of demarcation separating genuine refugees from others, this line, beyond being marked by refugee agency, was also strongly tied to the notion of status, representing either the higher moral standing of recognized refugees in the eyes of the public or the equivalent perceived social attainments of the asylum seeker in the country of origin. As a young African interviewee emotionally described when referring to the difficult circumstances he was experiencing in Hong Kong: 'Sometimes people ask you if you have gone to university – this is life in Hong Kong, because you are not a refugee, but an asylum seeker' (African participant, 18). For this participant, marginalization, if not open discrimination, powerfully impacted his self-esteem, thus drawing a social border between areas of belonging and non-belonging. He felt that he was looked down upon and that his motivation for coming to Hong Kong was viewed with suspicion because his claim was still pending and he did not manifestly show his bona fides through recognized parameters of personal success. In other words, not only are there genuine and fake asylum seekers, but in his experience this distinction carries little meaning when asylum seekers are inserted into social contexts that supposedly assign legitimacy only to the claims of people whose refugee status is confirmed by the competent authority. However, the number of recognized refugees in Hong Kong is normally very low compared to the number of applications. In 2011, Yeung wrote in *China Daily* that the prospects for a positive UNHCR outcome were as likely as winning the lottery. In effect, during my interviews with lawyers and charity workers in Hong Kong I was told that this rate is no higher than 3–5 per cent, despite the UNHCR claiming to recognize over 10 per cent of asylum claimants in Hong Kong (Man 2013). Moreover, to date only four torture victims have ever been recognized in the territory, out of over 12,400 applications. These numbers most likely influence public opinion by conveniently supporting official conceptions that asylum seekers are bogus claimants.

Based on the previous findings, it is plausible to argue that if the legal status of asylum seekers in Hong Kong largely overlaps with that of illegal migrants, their social status reflects the degrading symbolism and terminology now commonly applied to certain types of migration (Nevins 2002). The marginalization of asylum seekers described by the participants in this chapter came to be exacerbated by official and media reports that characterized illegal immigrant groups as extraneous to Hong Kong. It was assumed that their origin and illegality essentially determined the characteristics of those deemed to belong to that group. Of particular significance here is that the inferiorization and homogenization of asylum seekers – processes presented as legitimate – were reinforced by the mechanisms purportedly aimed at safeguarding the institution of asylum.

Screening mechanisms of exclusion

In his auto-ethnography of the border, Khosravi (2010) masterfully describes the dynamics of exclusion faced by many border crossers who seek help from the UNHCR. UNHCR offices are sparsely located in troubled areas and neighbouring countries across the globe. However, the institution of asylum is most often inaccessible for the abstractness of the laws and conventions and the evident procedural arbitrariness that underlies the UNHCR's and governments' screening

80 *Global phenomena and local responses*

mechanisms (Bohmer and Shuman 2008; Amit 2011; Jubany 2011). For the large majority of the interviewees in Hong Kong, this inaccessibility negatively impacted their lives. Comments such as those cited subsequently highlight the powerful constraints they experienced. Such comments were not uncommon.

> [I was rejected. I was given] the same reasons they give anyone: that your story is not consistent, and things like that – I just feel that they are now selecting people, like people from Somalia. But they are not the only ones. . . . It is not that I'm not happy because they closed my case, I'm not happy because they really messed with my life. They kept me here waiting for four years, optimistically. I was really optimistic and I waited for four years; I didn't do anything. And one day they call and say they are sorry but they have closed my case. If they had closed my case in just one year, it would have been fine. I would have thought of something else, like going to another country, or maybe take the risk and go back to my country, but after five years where can I go? At that time I just freshly finished my studies; I was really nice. But now it is very difficult. . . . Now we stay here and we do bad things. We didn't used to drink and now we drink – it's just messing with your life. That's why I'm not happy. And the way they handled my case. If it wasn't a good case, why keeping [*sic*] me here for four years. They could have just sent me a letter after one year or six months. I would have understood. I would have said: 'OK, time for me to look for another way.' I am a man, I need to fight, you know?! But after five years of suffering, you can't. (African participant, 06)
>
> There are many people that have no case at all, but get the status of refugees. Others that should need protection are instead rejected. I have been here for so long that I have seen so many things. I now know how the UNHCR work. They accept or reject people according to their credibility, but they are not credible themselves. They should know who is fake and who is not. This is their job. But they know how to process cases! – you just need to go out and talk to people and you would know who is fake and who is not. Just need to go and speak a few times. Listen to them and put yourself in their shoes; then you know. No need to ask for so many documents; just talk. The UNHCR decide on people's life. They send people from the law school to screen people instead of taking the process onto a more humanitarian level. . . . I thought they would understand my case because it is plain and clear, and they would protect me in the way I felt I had to be protected. Up until now I don't know what is going to happen to me. I don't know. I'm in a political world. I am disappointed, of course. . . . And the guys [UNHCR officers] always changed. Even the guy that gave me the result was not the person who interviewed me. But, really, I can't be happy with some of the questions I was asked; even the reasons for rejecting my case were not relevant to me. . . . I really can't go back to my country now. That is the problem. There is no light at the end of the tunnel. I want to leave Hong Kong if I can't be really protected here, but go where, and how? It is a dilemma. . . . I'm just sitting and waiting, honestly. (African participant, 02)

Global phenomena and local responses 81

Similar to the findings of research conducted on refugee screening procedures in other countries (Cohen 2001; Crawley 1999, 2010), many asylum seekers in Hong Kong spoke of the difficulties they faced resulting from the long periods they had to wait for their claim to be decided, the traumatic loss of control over their lives while awaiting a decision on their refugee status and the inadequate ways in which screening procedures were carried out. An argument is made here that, while the structure of asylum in Hong Kong impacts the vulnerability of asylum seekers, public and official understandings of abuse of the asylum system have largely been based on conditions of marginalization produced by that same system. In other words, if the opinion is widespread that large numbers of opportunistic individuals are benefiting from laws and conventions intended to protect a select few, the experiences of some asylum seekers indicate that they become abusers because they are constructed in that way by the mechanisms set up to protect them.

Indeed, mirroring the low UNHCR acceptance rate in the territory, very few participants in this study were recognized as refugees. However, rather than this being indicative of abuse, as many commentators claim,[18] several asylum seekers argued that they had been rejected due to the procedural unfairness inherent to the system. On the one hand, they argued that only asylum seekers from a select few countries had a fair chance of being recognized as refugees (cf. Bohmer and Shuman 2013). On the other, the border that asylum seekers personify in this context, illustrated by the documents they need to provide and the identity to which they are expected to conform in order to be positively assessed for refugee status, presented as an insurmountable obstacle for many claimants, not because their fear of persecution was unfounded, or so they believed, but because of procedural quibbles often aimed at challenging the credibility of claimants (Bohmer and Shuman 2008; Khosravi 2010). As Bohmer and Shuman rightly identify, an asylum seeker's future is often dependent on a few hours of interviewing, yet they often lack the intellectual or practical tools needed to meet the standards required by the body assessing their claim. Many of the participants in this research revealed how they often felt uneasy with the manner of questioning in these assessment interviews, as well as the number of interviews they had, the documents they were asked to provide to substantiate their claim and the interviewers themselves. Further, many had no legal representation to help them extract and articulate their stories. As a result, some people were afraid or reluctant to share the truth with people they barely knew, with the result that their cases were jeopardized. An African interviewee explained his experience with the interviewer in the following terms: 'He asked me to tell him my history, but I was afraid to tell him everything, because maybe they could give my information to other people, so I couldn't trust him' (African participant, 32). A Sri Lankan participant similarly argued that his fear was necessarily related to past negative experiences with authorities in his country, and, despite being assured of confidentiality, his worries persisted: 'I was a bit scared to tell my problem to people I didn't know. They could arrest me and put me in jail. In my country this is what they do, so I thought maybe here was the same' (Sri Lankan participant, 16).

82   *Global phenomena and local responses*

As it emerged, several participants had been rejected or knew of friends whose claims had been turned down because their story lacked consistency (Herlihy et al. 2002). The participants' accounts revealed how claimants were generally required to relay their stories in great detail, at times to the extent that it was easy to make mistakes, such as confusing one date for another – a problem that was exacerbated given that trust had not previously been established between speaker and listener. In addition, the intrinsic categories and assumptions that UNHCR and ImmD officers applied to validate a story often did not conform to the reality of a situation (Bohmer and Shuman 2013). A Pakistani interviewee, for instance, argued: 'The officer questioned me so many times, saying, "You tell me this story, but were not there any police?" His mind was that the police in my country are like the police in Hong Kong. I said no. The police there are helpless' (Pakistani participant, 34). Moreover, sometimes during these interviews what officers regarded as important did not always align with the stories the applicants wanted to share or the information they believed they should provide. Applicants also expected that the interviewers would believe them and understand their story (Bohmer and Shuman 2008). However, this expectation relied on a degree of empathy and competency[19] on the part of the authorities that is often lacking (Crawley 2010). A significant volume of research in other countries has revealed how the asylum seeker is often perceived as a suspect rather than a potential victim by screening officers, who weigh his or her story against political considerations on the asylum seeker's country of origin (Coutin 2001) and against preconceived assumptions about the predisposition of asylum seekers to lie about their real motivations for taking their migratory journey (Jubany 2011; Fassin 2013). A South Asian interviewee, for example, said that he was extremely disappointed because he had repeatedly explained his problems but was not believed. Consequently, he had been left in the dark concerning his case for over four years, only to be occasionally called in for further interviews to retell stories already narrated. He stressed that he had been asked questions that he thought were not relevant. He said he was questioned about his future – a line of questioning he felt was aimed at proving him to be an economic migrant. He also demanded that the UNHCR explain procedures he did not understand. In this regard, he explained one interaction with a UNHCR official: ' "When I came I had problems, but now, four years later, why do you still interview me?" The officer was laughing – then he asked me what my dream is. I said that I also have dreams. Even in Hong Kong we are allowed to have dreams of a better life' (Sri Lankan participant, 84g). Years later, I was told by this participant of his intention to leave Hong Kong, as he had grown increasingly restless and displeased about his treatment at the hands of the UN refugee agency.

If the burden of proof on asylum seekers is particularly rigorous and screening procedures difficult to understand, a few other points surfaced in the participants' narratives that indicate an inaccurate impression of asylum seekers abusing the system. First, because of the sorts of difficulties described previously, a number of interviewees explained that they had either stopped pursuing their UNHCR case or had not applied for asylum under the Refugee Convention, relying instead

Global phenomena and local responses 83

on the CAT. On this point, many participants considered the UNHCR to be 'useless'. I argue that it is in this context that the decrease in UNHCR applications should be understood, at a time when CAT applications increased significantly, in 2009, as discussed earlier. For instance, an African participant explained that he would not recommend that people in his situation approach the UNHCR when there are other options for seeking protection. In a similar fashion, Bangladeshi nationals revealed that they followed their friends' advice when deciding whether to access asylum and through which mechanism. Several of them, discouraged by long periods of waiting, gave up on their claim, stating: 'Sometimes I would go to the UNHCR and wait for a long time for an interview that maybe was five minutes long. I went there so many times for nothing that later I decided not to go anymore' (Bangladeshi participant, 62). Others explained that they came to know about the UNHCR late during their stay in Hong Kong, one commenting: 'When I knew about the UNHCR many people told me that it was not useful. I had already the torture claim and there was no need to go to the UNHCR' (Bangladeshi participant, 42). If the previous comments demonstrate the naivety of some participants in trusting their friends' word or in their approach to the issue of asylum, they also indicate that in the views of some asylum seekers the UNHCR does not always represent the institution of asylum. Indeed, many participants could barely explain the meaning of asylum. Protection was therefore often accessed via alternative means. Some participants in particular appeared to think that accessing either the Refugee Convention or the CAT was roughly equal in terms of safety. Indeed, short-term practical needs related to getting out of detention appeared to prevail in influencing decision making.

A few participants said that they had not requested help from the UNHCR because a torture claim was all they believed was needed to ensure their release from detention. Asylum seekers who do not enjoy the right of abode in Hong Kong are subject to arrest when they are found not in possession of the documents required to remain in the territory. However, their removal, and possible prosecution for their mode of entry, is suspended under a CAT claim. In this case, asylum seekers are generally provided with a recognizance, colloquially known as an 'Immigration paper', and are released from detention and permitted to reside in Hong Kong pending the determination of their case (Sampson et al. 2011).[20] Several participants believed that this was the main benefit of the CAT system, as it ensured an informal, temporary permit to stay.

Second, and importantly when compared to the rationale underlying asylum and the provision of services to asylum seekers, a number of participants argued that they had lodged an application for asylum with the UNHCR but were later forced to stop pursuing their claim because they could not afford to pay for the transportation to go to the UNHCR office once a month as required. Money to cover the costs of transportation to attend interviews at the UNHCR and ImmD is supposedly provided through the ISS support system. However, many participants said that, by the time they gave up their case, they had not received any such financial assistance. Moreover, individual case assessments could take months before services were provided and, as is discussed subsequently, not all of the

84   *Global phenomena and local responses*

participants received the same services. A Bangladeshi interviewee, for instance, affirmed: 'I went there three times. At that time I had some money and I could afford to go. After that I didn't have money for transportation and I missed the interview. Then I didn't go again' (Bangladeshi participant, 64). Similarly, one of his co-nationals said: 'I applied at the same time I applied for torture [a CAT claim], but at that time ISS didn't give me transportation money, so I didn't go to the UNHCR anymore' (Bangladeshi participant, 67). Moreover, if money was an important issue limiting people's ability to seek asylum, some participants also argued that travelling to the UNHCR offices was risky if they had overstayed their visa and were living far from the offices, as they might be picked up on the streets by the authorities. Recent reports in fact show that Hong Kong authorities perform three times more identity checks and searches on the streets than police in New York and London (Boehler 2013).

One common issue to emerge from the interviews was the lack of information about the meaning of asylum and the content of the two conventions. Moreover, the participants often relied, quite naively, on the practical, short-term benefits of asylum mechanisms, rather than seeking more permanent solutions to their problems. This is understandable considering that their previous knowledge of asylum was limited, and that the two mechanisms are certainly not publicized and asylum seekers might only hear of them once they gained access to charity groups whose remit covers refugee well-being and rights. It is significant that when I asked the participants whether they had applied for asylum or knew about the UNHCR, sometimes they responded by saying that they had never heard of the UN agency, even among those who had been residing in Hong Kong for some time and had applied for the CAT. For instance, a very young and inexperienced Bangladeshi interviewee, who had arrived in Hong Kong a year earlier and whose CAT claim was at the final stages, described how he was afraid of being returned to his country. He argued that he could not go back home and was desperate to find alternatives. The following brief conversation exemplifies the lack of knowledge of the UNHCR among asylum seekers, indirectly suggesting that the low UNHCR success rates may not tell the whole truth about asylum in Hong Kong:

> I really cannot go back to my country because if I go I will be killed. My family only had some property and they sold everything to send me out. If I'm returned now, they can't send me out again.
> *Did you go to the UNHCR?*
> What is it? (Bangladeshi participant, 57)

Finally, the assumption that the institution of asylum is being abused has largely been based on the fact that the great majority of CAT applications are lodged a long time after the asylum seeker has arrived in the city and/or upon their arrest. In this regard, the narratives of the participants indicate that, while some certainly applied late and only after being detained, such an act could hardly be taken as evidence of abuse. The great majority of the interviewees explained their late access to the CAT mechanism by arguing that either they had no knowledge of such a mechanism and therefore preferred not to sign papers they did not understand or they feared detention. In effect, and as I observed during the fieldwork, in order to lodge an application under Article 3 of the CAT, an applicant was normally taken into custody as part of the procedures undertaken to verify their identity and method of entry. Furthermore, a number of participants stated that, even if they knew of the system and were very much in need of it, they took their time in deciding whether to access it; rather than surrendering themselves, they waited to be arrested on the streets. One young Bangladeshi participant, for example, explained that he had lodged an application only once he had been arrested by the police: 'I knew that if police catch you, then you can get the Immigration paper. But I didn't want to get arrested because I didn't want to go to jail. I had the UNHCR paper' (Bangladeshi participant, 62). Similarly, an African participant questioned the rationale underpinning the asylum system: 'I wondered why I needed to go to prison in order to get assistance' (African participant, 02). On this point, many of the interviewees said that they had no previous experience of detention, and that they had never even been to a police station. The idea of being detained involved images of policing that were strongly linked to police in their country of origin, and when they shared their experiences of detention with their fellow asylum seekers, reactions were often mixed. In general, these participants knew that the time they would spend in detention would most likely not be too long, probably only a few weeks. Also, Hong Kong police and immigration facilities certainly do not resemble those in their countries. However, it was the uncertainty related to leaving their fate in the hands of police and immigration officers while being constrained behind walls that impacted their decision making. For example, a Bangladeshi man explained his rather adventurous encounter with the authorities. He said that he wanted to be arrested in order to apply for asylum and receive ISS assistance, but at the same time, he did not want to surrender himself because he was afraid that his application would be turned down, or worse, that he would be deported. As per his account, he arrived in Hong Kong in 2006. At that time, he saw that many of his friends in the territory had immigration papers, so he asked how he could obtain such papers for himself. He tried to surrender himself on two occasions, but he was turned away by the police as they were too busy to deal with him. Unable to gather the courage to walk into a police station a third time, he tried to be arrested by walking very close to police officers on the streets. In this way, he tried his 'luck' numerous times, and it was an exceptional three years before he was arrested. He said to me that since he had lodged his claim he was relieved of most of his previous daily worries about food and accommodation, and that he was 'happy' (Bangladeshi participant, 38).

Other participants stated that they did not lodge a CAT application until they received notice that the UNHCR had closed their case. In this regard, an African participant convincingly explained: 'I applied for [the] CAT not long ago because it is not long ago that the UNHCR rejected me. . . . I came here for the UNHCR so I wanted to wait for it. I didn't know anything about [the] CAT and I didn't come for it' (African participant, 06). From the interviews, it was also evident that misinformation about the CAT mechanism clearly prevented a number of

86 Global phenomena and local responses

participants from claiming in due time that they would be subjected to torture or inhuman treatment if returned to their country of origin. While a few participants had no idea of the existence of the CAT, importantly, some argued that they believed that lodging concomitant applications under the two systems was not ideal. One African interviewee said that he had considered accessing the CAT screening mechanism, but that the advice he received from his fellow asylum seekers suggested he should not because 'if you applied for the UNHCR and for [the] CAT at the same time, you may not have any chance with the UNHCR. . . . But when I was arrested I saw a lawyer and I was advised to apply for [the] CAT' (African participant, 17).

The following chapters discuss the significance of social networks in enabling information sharing within and beyond the refugee community in Hong Kong. Important decisions regarding one's protection and livelihood are made on the basis of examples set out by one's fellow asylum seekers. However, especially among those living in rural areas, far from the city where information can circulate more easily through the work of charity groups, the average level of knowledge of asylum was low, as summarized in the following comment: 'I know that with the torture claim I can stay here, I can live here. I know only this' (Bangladeshi participant, 42). Furthermore, this knowledge appeared to be acquired predominantly while in detention. As a South Asian participant explained: 'There are many Bangladeshis in detention and they told me that if I wanted to stay in Hong Kong I needed to apply for CAT' (Bangladeshi participant, 68). Many other interviewees similarly commented that they had come to know about the torture claim only following their arrest. From this perspective, it can be said that the lack of reliable information about asylum certainly impacted on asylum seekers' decision making and consequently contributed to their representation as abusers of the system. Furthermore, the concept of asylum, and related procedures, was mostly incomprehensible to a large number of participants, to the extent that some were not even sure whether they had a case open or of the reasons supporting their case. One interviewee said that he had applied while in detention: 'But I don't know. I never had interviews. . . . I don't know whether they accepted the application or not. Maybe I don't have a torture claim, or maybe I have it' (African participant, 07).

It is not my intention to argue here that no one abuses the asylum regime in Hong Kong. As this research did not explore the reasons for people fleeing their country of origin, no evidence was collected to sustain such a claim. However, it is apparent from this research that the purported evidence of widespread abuse is not as solid as is suggested when analyzed in light of refugees' experiences of asylum mechanisms. In addition, it is clear that the evidence for such abuse may indeed be shaped by structural factors that impact on the decision making of people who consequently act as if they were abusers. If the UNHCR's low recognition rates and the late access to CAT procedures have been said to demonstrate that Hong Kong is vulnerable to opportunistic individuals seeking asylum for economic benefit, this study does not support this interpretation. Instead, the story of the asylum seeker as abuser appears to be supported by empirically questionable

Global phenomena and local responses 87

evidence which distorts refugee agency. The dominant representation portrays the individual migrant as the sole responsible agent for a system that is in fact weighted towards rejecting refugees (Bohmer and Shuman 2008; Jubany 2011) and seems to increasingly turn asylum applicants into morally despicable people for seeking international protection accessible through mechanisms that are not well understood. It is via this process that asylum seekers are being depicted as 'illegal migrants' (Schuster 2011), thus their being routinely and lawfully punished to endure conditions of marginalization and immiseration.

In the next section, the precariousness and marginalization facing asylum seekers in Hong Kong are examined. This will inform understanding of the effect of asylum policies which contribute to the creation of a population deprived of its basic rights. It will be argued that the insufficiency of the provisions on which asylum seekers are expected to live in the HKSAR appears strongly linked to their involvement in informal income-generating activities.

Daily experiences of exclusion

Ager and Strang (2004, 2008) have formulated 10 domains that constitute a productive framework with which to examine the structural barriers to refugees' achievements and the degree of refugee integration into the receiving society. These domains include areas of activity in the public arena, such as employment, education, housing and health; the legal status and rights of refugees, which are said to be a prerequisite to social cohesion; the factors affecting refugee agency, such as language and cultural knowledge; and, finally, the social ties that connect all of the domains. Based on my research, it is clear that refugees in Hong Kong have limited legal rights. Ager and Strang's framework is therefore used here to examine the effects of this lack of rights across the domains upon which refugee integration is dependent. While facilitators and social ties are examined in greater detail in the following chapters, what Ager and Strang (2008: 170) call 'markers and means' – housing, employment, health and education – are here analyzed in terms of their impact on well-being. However, because education and health did not emerge as particularly relevant in the refugee narratives,[21] and lawful employment is not allowed, I introduce to the previous framework two related sub-categories – food and money – to better mirror how inclusion and exclusion played out in relation to the lack of financial resources resulting from the absence of economic rights.

Pending the determination of their claim, asylum seekers whose identity has been confirmed by the local authorities are generally entitled to a form of basic assistance. Such services consist mainly of accommodation, either in a limited number of shelters and flats rented by the ISS, inclusive of basic furniture, bedding and cooking utensils, or in rooms self-arranged by asylum seekers, for which a rental allowance of about HK$1000[22] is paid to the landlord upon presentation of a copy of the lease. Additionally, several bags of foodstuffs are provided every 10 days, to be collected from designated grocery stores; toiletries are provided on a monthly basis; and a basic transportation allowance is provided to enable

88 *Global phenomena and local responses*

asylum seekers to report to Immigration and the UNHCR. At times, a transportation allowance is also available to enable asylum seekers to attend medical appointments, carry out religious worship and meet legal representatives. If the system appears to adequately cover the needs of the majority of asylum seekers, in reality, while rental allowance and food were provided to most of the people interviewed for this study, the provision of the other services was highly discretionary and based on case-by-case assessments.

Housing

According to a large number of interviewees, the services provided, and the form they took, were not covering all of their basic needs. First, during the fieldwork I identified that only a very small number of asylum seekers lived in shelters or ISS-provided flats – indeed, only one shelter (for minors) was identified together with a handful of flats temporarily allocated to a few families. All of the people interviewed for this study lived in self-arranged accommodation obtained at market rental prices. Very few said that they found rooms for HK$1000 per month or less that included utilities such as water and electricity. A significant majority of the participants and their friends stated that their rent was over HK$1200, at times reaching HK$2200 per person. Rooms for HK$1000 were found only in squatter houses in the New Territories, sometimes built of wooden walls and iron sheets, or in old buildings in Kowloon, where privately owned apartments were partitioned into tiny rectangular rooms at times barely large enough for a mattress, many with a shared toilet and no kitchen. These forms of accommodation are apparently common in low-income districts, although mostly unheard of among well-off people living in the city.[23] Ever more expensive rental and restrictive government social policies force many of the poor in Hong Kong to live in such conditions (Chua 2011; Goodstadt 2013). Financially excluded from renting more expensive and safer places, asylum seekers shared the same housing setting with the local poor, although their legal status, skin colour and very often non-existent Cantonese language skills greatly hindered their ability to manage their circumstances.

As an example, one African participant insisted that he had a hard time finding a room because foreigners were discriminated against. Angrily, though resigned to the tough reality, he revealed that '[s]ometimes you just knock on the door of an agency and they ask you to leave without even listening to you' (African participant, 01). He added that his skin colour appeared to agitate local Chinese people, especially if they did not speak English and were not familiar with dealing with foreigners from certain countries. Another participant stressed that he had been trying for over two months to get a place for himself but was discouraged by local people's lack of understanding and empathy. He said that cheap rooms were available only at small property agencies, but in these places 'agents don't speak English, so there is a problem' (African participant, 15). As a result, this participant had to rely on the Chinese wife of a fellow African friend, who could spare only a few hours a week to assist him.

Global phenomena and local responses   89

Several participants emphasized that they received no help from the ISS in seeking to secure a place for themselves. In particular, while grateful for the minimal government support they did receive, some participants blamed the system for throwing them into the fray. The attitude of ISS case workers was specifically censured for circumstances that asylum seekers believed could have been easily avoided had they been given practical tools to compete in the market. For example, one African participant claimed that he was told by the ISS that he needed to look for a room by himself, and only when he found one would he be paid HK$1000 per month as rent allowance. He said that he was told that he had to rely on friends for help, but he was new to the city and knew no-one who could help him. Another participant similarly explained: 'The problem is that if you ask them [the ISS] to go with you and talk to the agent, they say no. They say you have to talk to the agents by yourself' (African participant, 26). Still, another interviewee said that rental prices were too high, 'but when I go to [the] ISS to tell them I need more money, they say, "find another house"' (African participant, 30). In this regard, very few participants felt that they had been helped by the ISS in any practical way to deal with local agents and landlords. In addition, bureaucratic difficulties often hampered their efforts. As a couple of young, newly arrived African participants sadly recounted, they were sleeping rough outside in the cold winter months despite having found a room. The problem was that the ISS procedures did not match market requirements. '[The landlord] said the room was HK$2200', one participant said, 'He said no deposit was required, but he wanted one month's rent in advance and then we could get the keys. But [the] ISS said they would pay only after we were in the room and they visited us' (African participant, 74).

Rooms for HK$1000 were rare, so asylum seekers seized them whenever possible. The condition of such properties was often crumbling and/or overcrowded. On one occasion, I was brought to a house where six asylum seekers shared three rooms, each paying HK$1000. The landlord was living in a newly refurbished house next to the one rented to the Bangladeshi tenants, and the latter house was in an advanced state of neglect despite the visible efforts of the residents to maintain a semblance of decorum. Other than the three rooms, their home included a simple kitchen located outdoors, partitioned by waist-high walls blackened by layers of oil, next to the toilet, and an impracticable shower hidden by broken plastic curtains. A long path from the main road led to the legally questionable dwelling, situated behind factory walls and along an open-air sewage. No wonder the tenants described it 'as a small and dirty place in the jungle' (Bangladeshi participant, 52).

Additionally, even when such places were secured, worries concerning living arrangements did not end, challenging the mental well-being and decision making of asylum seekers. 'My room is HK$1000 including electricity and water, but when the electricity is high, the landlord complains and asks [for] money', a Bangladeshi interviewee protested with me, 'I just tell him to go to [the] ISS to complain, and if he continues to bother me I call the police' (Bangladeshi participant, 68). This man's tough stance against the landlord was explicable in the

90 *Global phenomena and local responses*

context of experiencing months of abuse from him. 'He is a greedy man', he continued, 'Sometimes I cook [on an electric stove] and he comes to my room and turns off the electricity. The other day I went out at night and when I returned I found the door was open; he was there! I really want to move, but it is very expensive to find another place.'

Left on their own to manage their place in society, these asylum seeker participants were forced by their circumstances to engage with landlords through difficult intercultural relations, often without a positive result. If a few participants said that they found understanding people, who turned a blind eye to money owed to them, many others stated that their landlords had little sympathy for their situation. In a few cases, they were said to be taking advantage of their tenants, for example, by altering the electricity meter or bills, increasing rent with little notice and even locking tenants out of their room if utilities were not paid or the room needed to be quickly vacated. An African participant revealed that his landlady often increased the rent with only a few days' notice, forcing him into dire need of cash to satisfy her requests. Another interviewee similarly highlighted the difficulty of talking to local Chinese, as he desperately sought the means to meet his landlord's demands: 'The landlord only speaks Chinese, so when you see him and you want to explain something he just says, "rent, rent, rent". At midnight he comes and knocks on the door and asks for money and money' (African participant, 28). The experiences narrated about accommodation revealed a common feeling of fatigue and stress among the participants caused by the many difficulties they faced with high rent, landlords' pressing demands and their inability to discuss their rights and duties with their landlord. In this regard, a father of two explained that it was not easy to live in a state of rejection in Hong Kong: 'It is very difficult. It is a problem. . . . The aircon in my room is not working but the landlord doesn't want to change it – so many things the owner doesn't want to change. . . . It is not only me. Many people are facing these problems' (African participant, 26).

In self-arranged housing, furniture and cooking utensils were generally not provided, adding to the difficulties. An African asylum seeker who arrived in Hong Kong a couple of months before our meeting observed that, while he was able to find a room to share with a fellow co-national, for many weeks they had been unable to afford any furniture and appliances other than a rice cooker. As a consequence, they slept on the floor and cooked all at once the perishable food received every 10 days from the ISS-contracted grocery stores. Paradoxically, they continued this practice even when provided with a refrigerator by a local charity. They explained that, while the fridge was new, they lacked an extension cord and adaptor to plug it in. Apparently the ISS told them that this was not something they could provide. A charity similarly turned down their request because they had no cords or adaptors available, and their fellow asylum seekers could not spare any – yet the cost to buy these two items would have amounted to less than HK$80.

Another problem said to be gravely affecting refugee vulnerability related to the money that a considerable majority of the participants had to pay as a deposit to their landlords, generally in the form of one or two months' rent plus half a month's rent for agency fees, in case their services were used. This was regarded as one of the greatest obstacles to securing accommodation, as the ISS generally refused to help with this matter. For example, a Bangladeshi interviewee emotionally argued that he had to rely on meagre family finances sent from his country of origin, while another participant, who was unable to rely on funds from overseas, described how he had been sleeping with different friends each night for over eight months. Sadly, a Sri Lankan participant added that he felt compelled to pawn his wife's jewellery to pay over HK$5000 of rent, deposit and agency fees, to provide his family with a place to live. Powerless before the landlord, with immense regret he lost his family treasures when the room was later vacated and the deposit forfeited.

Food

Food was the second issue that contributed significantly towards the participants' marginalization. Many expressed their concern about a system that limited their choices in regard to food. They stressed that they preferred supermarket coupons over collecting food on specific days at designated shops, as coupons meant they were free to shop for the items they wanted rather than being presented with a limited selection of food from which they were asked to choose. Other than the importance of choice, what really mattered was the dignity of people who could not afford to shop in supermarkets but were forced to go to specific stores on appointment, gather food alongside other asylum seekers and often walk long distances carrying heavy plastic bags that attracted people's attention. As one participant persuasively argued, in the present form the collection system does not provide all of the foodstuffs and services that one would reasonably think are necessary, while harming the mental well-being of asylum seekers. He said:

> It is very stressful. . . . I have to walk all the way. . . . Then you arrive there and everyone is fighting and pushing and rushing – And then I have to walk back with two bags of food. If it was possible to have vouchers, you would just buy what you want. Like water – [the] ISS don't give you water. For me it is so inconvenient. Also, sometimes you take food home and you see the meat or something else is not fresh or it is expired. Most of the times I check the items before I take them home, but sometimes you don't have time, and there are so many people there. Many times I have a list of 10 items [to collect]; I go home and I see only seven; I go back to the shop and they tell you they can't do anything about that. So – it is very stressful. (African participant, 08)

From the previous comments, and from observations I made during the fieldwork, it emerged that several participants believed that a greater degree of choice around food would improve their living standards and probably their standing in society as they would feel less discriminated against. Furthermore, several participants

92 *Global phenomena and local responses*

said that the food they were given was not food they were used to eating. A few people mentioned that they needed spices and vegetables that some stores had on the shelves, but which were not included in the list of items from which asylum seekers could select their rations. These ingredients were necessary to cook their traditional dishes. In this regard, it is noteworthy that the migration of some participants to Hong Kong involved radical and unexpected lifestyle changes. This seemed to impact their perception and memories of their country of origin, reviving a collective sense of belonging to a distant home. As the asylum seekers explained, food is naturally the easiest aspect of one's culture to claim and reproduce, thus accounting for their persistent dislike of local Hong Kong cuisine. Further, in some circumstances national pride appeared to surge, probably in response to what was perceived to be the demeaning treatment or impoverishment experienced in Hong Kong. As Italian novelist and philosopher Luigi Pirandello (1993) masterfully reveals in *The Late Mattia Pascal*, human beings are multi-identitied (Sen 2006), and people can assume one identity or another to escape the 'gaze' of the mainstream of society. In this sense, some asylum seeker participants sought to lift their dignity, by either claiming a new identity or reshaping an old one, in order to overcome the homogenizing categories that force deprivation and exclusion and cast asylum seekers as worthless individuals. When questioned about Hong Kong society, these participants resented their circumstances and, as if to protect themselves, tended to praise all the more highly the culture and traditions, including the food habits, of their home country. Partly confirming such observations, it was found that sharing food is a practice that asylum seekers believed distanced their culture from that of Hong Kong people. Food was thus seen as an important social event. When I visited asylum seekers in their homes, I was often invited over for lunch or dinner to taste their local dishes. However, special ingredients not provided by the ISS were frequently lacking.

The quality and quantity of food that asylum seekers received from the ISS were also said to be largely unsatisfactory. When questioned about the services and food items they received, the African and South Asian interviewees alike argued along the lines of the following comment: 'We have to say thank you because it is something given to us, but I feel our food is different. Also, [the] ISS give us two chickens for 10 days. It is not enough. We have to buy some food by ourselves, but how to buy?'(Sri Lankan participant, 16). Another participant explained that in shops the food was cheaper than the price of the items that they were collecting. Also, 'sometimes food finishes before 10 days, but you have to wait or you go to friends to get food' (Sri Lankan participant, 21). One interviewee I met in the New Territories summarized his neighbours' views in saying that the shop where he was supposed to collect food at times served items whose use-by date had expired. Therefore, he and other asylum seekers asked the ISS whether they could collect food from another shop, farther from where they lived, but this meant they could have to pay for transportation, which the ISS was not providing. Gas cylinders to cook were also not provided, while utensils and electrical appliances were not easily available from charities. On this point, a Sri Lankan participant explained that his refrigerator had been broken for a long time,

Global phenomena and local responses 93

but although a replacement had been long promised to him, he was still forced to throw away the food he could not refrigerate. He commented: 'If I had money I would buy it' (Sri Lankan participant, 16).

Money

Lack of money was a factor shaping the experiences of a significant majority of the people interviewed for this study. Beyond the in-kind assistance provided for rent and food mentioned previously, the ISS did not provide asylum seekers with any sort of financial support, other than a very limited transportation allowance to report to Immigration and the UNHCR, via the cheapest route available. Yet asylum seekers lamented that money was necessary to ensure their basic needs, such as clothing, cooking utensils and appliances; to pay their transportation costs, rent and bills; and to top up their mobile phone credit. Research has demonstrated that mobile phones are key to expanding networks and obtaining information among refugees attempting to adapt to a new life in exile (Glazebrook 2004). In Hong Kong, the ImmD, the UNHCR, local charities and the ISS rely on this instrument to keep in touch with the highly mobile population of their concern. However, requests made by asylum seekers to include in their monthly provision a minimum amount to charge the credit on their mobile phones have been repeatedly turned down, apparently because such support would contradict the principle of providing only limited in-kind assistance.[24]

For example, one interviewee argued that 'when your clothes are dirty you can't even take them to the laundry because you have no money to pay. Also, to have a phone number you need to pay money, and if [the] ISS, Immigration or [the] UNHCR call you and you have no money, you can't receive the call' (African participant, 29). Indeed, whether a call is made or received, charges apply in Hong Kong. Additionally, at one point a South Asian participant explained that his daughter had been sick for a few days. At the hospital, he was told of dietary changes that he would need to implement to help his daughter get well. Yet this meant that he needed money he did not have. He was told to replace the usual baby formula with soy milk–based formula, the cheapest can of which was HK$350; however, the ISS told him any item priced over HK$250 would not be provided. Another South Asian interviewee laconically observed that the items he was given did not cover his monthly needs. He said he would receive only one razor per month, therefore forcing him to buy replacements himself. Eggs, bread and vegetables were also bought at the market because, as he said, '[t]his [what he received] is hurting our dignity. I was quite happy with my business in my country. And now – this is a downgrading for me' (Pakistani participant, 34). Another participant similarly argued: 'I bought these boxes of tissues because no one provides them. . . . And now I'm tired of taking money from my country, from my brother and relatives' (Bangladeshi participant, 36). When a participant spoke of his relationship with his fellow church members, amusingly he narrated their astonished disbelief at how he managed his living in Hong Kong: 'When I go to church and I meet some Chinese, they ask me what I am doing here and I say "nothing". They are surprised. Then

94 *Global phenomena and local responses*

they ask how I can survive here – I tell them I just have HK$100 from the church. They don't believe it is possible. I told them of [the] ISS and they still think about money, how I can live without money' (Sri Lankan participant, 12).

The factors underpinning asylum seekers' engagement in informal economic activities and the various strategies they adopt to cope with their circumstances can be found most convincingly in these narratives of exclusion. As I was told: 'Sometimes we have to go out and try to do something' (African participant, 26) because 'everything is expensive. [The] ISS is not doing enough. So we struggle to make our own business, or anything, to make money and complete the rent' (African participant, 09). From this perspective, the marginalization that these asylum seekers endured in the several domains pertaining to migrant inclusion (Ager and Strang 2008) appears consequential to the prolonged legal limbo facing asylum seekers and the many limitations imposed on their well-being by the in-kind support system supposedly there to provide for them. In other words, while it is not denied that many asylum seekers travel to Hong Kong with the intention of working – a fact that does not necessarily conflict with a genuine asylum application (Zimmermann 2009a) – the adoption of specific livelihoods is related to and a result of the dire circumstances they face.

Conclusion

This chapter has analyzed the socioeconomic and political vulnerability of asylum seekers and advanced the idea that in the domains in which non-nationals with precarious immigration status face restrictions, asylum seekers in Hong Kong are bound by subsistence living conditions (cf. Stewart 2005; Healey 2006; Da Lomba 2010; Block 2000). Their agency and identity is consequently shaped by and against this background. De Genova (2002), Khosravi (2010) and other commentators are referring to such circumstances when they argue that unauthorized migrants and refugees often exist in liminal, deportable conditions (Núñez and Heyman 2007). The identity of asylum seekers is shaped as they are stripped of their individuality to conveniently fit state-defined categories of migrant values, needs, deviancy and motivation (Zetter 1991; Melossi 2003). This study demonstrates that the asylum seeker participants, during periods of supposedly high migratory pressure, were routinely constructed as abusers of the asylum system, and that this process was very much supported by the failure of asylum screening mechanisms to recognize them as genuine refugees in the majority of cases (Bohmer and Shuman 2008). As a result, the participants described how they were regularly subjected to prejudice and, as per Stewart (2005: 509), to levels 'of innuendo or violence unthinkable to ordinary citizens'.

In reality, the marginalization of asylum seekers as social and legal outcasts emerges in this chapter as the consequence of processes that can be seen as organized deviance perpetrated by the state (Pickering 2005; Grewcock 2009), or new forms of racism (Basso 2010), in ways partly similar to the processes by which the Hong Kong Government previously confined the local poor and other immigrant populations to specific socioeconomic spaces within society (see Chapter 1).

Global phenomena and local responses 95

However, while lawfully resident populations can access and compete for jobs in the formal and informal labour markets, asylum seekers are constrained by the borders dividing citizens and non-citizens – especially when the latter are deemed poor, uneducated and racially different or inferior. These borders become permanently inscribed on the immigrant body (Dauvergne 2004; Weber 2006). Calavita (2003, 2005) and De Genova (2002) have clearly demonstrated, in this regard, that policies aimed at controlling or deterring the number of migrants entering the state do not always achieve their stated objectives. Rather, they create the conditions that define the levels of social and economic inclusion of foreigners in the country of destination. Furthermore, these policies are often crafted in such a way that the marginalization of certain categories of immigrants has the consequence of abetting specific state interests while at the same time consigning this population to the underground or informal economy (Jacobsen 2006).

In Hong Kong, this process seems to be underway. While the analysis of the involvement of asylum seekers in informal economic activities will be the focus of the following chapters, here it can be said that the institutionalized irregularity and hardship the participants have endured in the HKSAR have forced them into a state of constant mental and financial insecurity. I argue that this facilitates conditions of flexibility and exploitation in the workplace that the new economic structure of the global city is said to demand (Sassen 2001; Cohen 2006). According to many of the participants, economic engagement with society is important for creating opportunities to improve one's livelihood and well-being. Their involvement in such activities, however, has spawned a process of criminalization that has added to their vulnerability, thus fracturing the refugee community.

A notable finding in this regard has been that the in-kind support system designed to meet the basic needs of vulnerable asylum seekers in Hong Kong has encouraged their marginalization. Relief models for assisting refugees have often been found to be detrimental to the real needs of refugees and host societies alike. Citing Harrell-Bond and Elliot's work on ex-Yugoslavian refugees, Vrecer (2010) argues that the provision of services to refugees whose full participation in society is impeded by the host government hampers long-term integration and creates unnecessary tension between refugees, service providers and the state. This can result in the most vulnerable being overlooked as it is wrongly assumed that all people have the same needs, leading to a waste of valuable resources. Most importantly in the case of Hong Kong, this appears to severely constrain the spaces of manoeuvring for the participants precisely because their stay must remain temporary. At the same time, however, the system does allow for some, albeit limited opportunities. While the participants maintained that they were thankful for the minimal aid they received, the limited scope and insufficient provision of the in-kind assistance forced them into a state of discontent, as in many cases their lives had taken a turn for the worse. These circumstances drove the participants to find alternative means of survival.

This feeling of being poorly tolerated, if not 'unwanted', in Hong Kong was perceived and explained as a barrier to normality, which angered many of the participants. However, while some intended to participate in mainstream society

96 Global phenomena and local responses

to address this problem, the more they felt marginalized, noting how hard the path to protection and integration would be, the more processes of strategic, deliberate differentiation seemed to occur. At times this involved reclaiming their pride and 'otherness' by demeaning the local culture, which produced no significant result other than to emphasize the border that made them a foreign body within the host society. For instance, based on the interviews with refugee workers, it emerged that these workers attached very little meaning to the variety of food items provided and to whether the participants knew how to cook. When single male asylum seekers were asked about their cooking arrangements, many of them were at a loss, one observing, 'In my country men don't cook' (African participant, 32). While this was often interpreted as signifying an overly demanding population, it also reflects the processes of forced adaptation faced by these asylum seekers, only briefly viewed in the narratives of some participants in this chapter but examined further in the following.

This chapter has explored the socioeconomic and political structure that compels and in part defines refugee agency in Hong Kong. Particularly important has been the analysis of allegations that asylum seekers abuse asylum mechanisms in order to work illegally in the territory, as this has a direct impact upon policy and public views. Given its significance for the purposes of this study, this point is considered further in the next chapter, in which the motivation of asylum seekers to seek protection specifically in Hong Kong and the structural and agency factors that facilitate or hinder their arrival in the former British colony are analyzed.

Notes

1 An administrative screening mechanism within the ImmD was set up in 2004, as per the Court of Final Appeal's decision in *Secretary for Security v Sakthevel Prabakar*, FACV16/2003, 8 June 2004. The screening mechanism was then suspended for about a year following the result of *FB v Director of Immigration*, HCAL51/2007, 5 December 2008, in which screening procedures were challenged for failing to meet the high standards of fairness set out in the Prabakar case. Changes were later introduced, and screenings recommenced in December 2009.
2 Throughout this book, participants' names have been changed, while the number following participants' nationality/group refers to a number I assigned to each participant in the research.
3 It is important to note that, as per the Court of Appeal's decision in *CH v Director of Immigration*, CACV59/2010, 18 April 2011, policies formulated by the director of immigration can require people seeking protection in the territory under Article 3 of the CAT to pursue their claim only after their permitted period of stay has expired.
4 *C v Director of Immigration*, CACV132/2008, 21 July 2011. See also *CCPL Rights Bulletin*, 2(2), September 2011, available at: www.law.hku.hk/ccpl/Docs/Vol2-Issue2%20 Sept%202011.pdf; and Loper (2010).
5 *MA v Director of Immigration*, HCAL10/2010, 6 January 2011. See also Ramsden and Marsh (2013) for a detailed discussion of the legal argument put forward during the hearings.
6 *C v Director of Immigration*, FACV18/2011, 25 March 2013.
7 Ibid., para 49, 5.
8 Ibid., para 97.
9 Ibid., para 98, 105.

10 Ibid., para 116.
11 A number of similar cases culminating in the establishment of a support system initiated with *D v Director of Social Welfare*, HCAL163/2005 (Daly 2009).
12 Before that time, no government assistance was provided to people seeking asylum in Hong Kong. Very limited assistance was provided by the UNHCR to a few of the most vulnerable asylum seekers, but due to budget constraints the UNHCR stopped providing financial assistance to asylum seekers in May 2006 (*Bc Magazine* 2007).
13 *Brief on the Provision of Humanitarian Assistance to Asylum Seekers and Torture Claimants*, Social Welfare Department, unpublished document provided to the author on 24 May 2010.
14 UNHCR Statistical Yearbook in the years 2005–10, available at: www.unhcr.org.
15 UNHCR, Hong Kong Snapshot Statistics, available at: www.unhcr.org/cgi-bin/texis/vtx/page?page=49e488026&submit=GO.
16 From a global perspective, these numbers of arrivals are in reality comparatively low. For example, Germany and France are the developed countries that received the highest numbers of asylum applications in 2012, with 64,500 and 55,100 claims received respectively (UNHCR 2013).
17 *Waseem Abbas and Others v Secretary for Justice*, HCAL8/2009, 2 March 2009; and *A v Director of Immigration*, HCAL100/2006, 3 March 2009.
18 See, for example, LegCo, LC Paper No. CB(2)3077/05–06, 25 September 2006, in which it is argued that the low UNHCR success rate reflects the low number of asylum seekers who genuinely need protection. Available at: www.legco.gov.hk/yr05–06/english/panels/ws/minutes/sews0718.pdf.
19 A recent court judgement in Hong Kong quashed the immigration director's determination and adjudicator's decision to reject a Pakistani torture claimant due to procedural improprieties, including the failure to make sufficient inquiry into the applicant's country conditions. Further, the judgement highlighted how the decision to reject the applicant's claim before objectively unambiguous evidence was 'unqualified' and 'unreasonable'. See *AM v Director of Immigration and William Lam*, HCAL102/2012, 20 November 2013.
20 Practice says that 'If a person who enters Hong Kong without adherence to proper procedures is an asylum seeker or a torture claimant, this, of itself, will not result in a prosecution' (*Waseem Abbas v Secretary for Justice*, HCAL8/2009, 2 March 2009: 8). However, a person can be detained pending removal. Previously a person could be detained indefinitely, although the power to detain was to be used specifically for the purpose of removal. On this basis, a number of asylum seekers successfully challenged their detention (*A v Director of Immigration*, CACV 314/2007, 18 July 2008), arguing that their removal was not foreseeable in the near future and their detention was ergo unlawful. Now an asylum seeker can expect to be detained for a period of between a few hours and three months (Vision First 2013), after which time asylum seekers are required to generally enter into recognizance under s36(1) of the Immigration Ordinance. Annex ID334A (7/2007), generally provided to recognizance holders, explains that this paper does not give the holder permission to stay in Hong Kong and the person is still liable to be detained if he or she fails to comply with any of the requirements such as reporting to Immigration, maintaining good behaviour and attending interviews. In addition, the paper holder is forbidden from taking up any employment unlawfully.
21 Free education opportunities were not available unless asylum seekers were underage. Other opportunities could be pursued if the asylum seekers were able to secure a private donor, which was a rather difficult task and thus not very often pursued. Health care, instead, is generally available on an emergency basis. Indeed, several asylum seekers commended the professionalism of local hospitals, although at times they had to go through long periods of waiting (cf. Goodstadt 2013).
22 Housing allowance was raised to HK$1200 in 2011.

98 *Global phenomena and local responses*

23 Subdivided flats in old buildings cyclically come to the public's attention whenever accidents occur that raise concerns over the safety of certain blocks due to the illegal practice of dividing flats into small rooms that have no fire escape routes. The collapse of a building in To Kwa Wan in January 2010 and a fire that erupted in one such flat in another building in the same district in early 2011, both causing loss of lives, instigated government plans for a crackdown on illegal structures. This has led to rising rents and in some cases demolitions (Ng 2011), both of which have impacted asylum seekers.
24 This point was raised in a Refugee Forum organized with social services providers, held in Hong Kong on 15 September 2010.

References

Ager, A. and Strang, A. (2004) *Indicators of Integration*, Home Office Development and Practice Report, 28. Viewed 14 May 2009: www.homeoffice.gov.uk/rds/pdfs04/dpr28.pdf

Ager, A. and Strang, A. (2008) 'Understanding Integration: A Conceptual Framework', *Journal of Refugee Studies*, 21(2): 167–191.

Amit, R. (2011) 'No Refuge: Flawed Status Determination and the Failures of South Africa's Refugee System to Provide Protection', *International Journal of Refugee Law*, 23(3): 458–488.

Araujo, S. G. (2011) 'Reinventing Europe's Borders: Delocalization and Externalization of EU Migration Control through the Involvement of Third Countries', in M. Baumann, A. Lorenz and K. Rosenow (Eds.) *Crossing and Controlling Borders: Immigration Policies and Their Impact on Migrants' Journeys*, Leverkusen: Budrich UniPress: 21–44.

Basso, P. (2010) (Ed.) *Razzismo di Stato: Stati Uniti, Europa, Italia*, Milano: FrancoAngeli.

Bc Magazine (2007) 'Seeking Safety: Refugees in Limbo', 231, 3 May. Viewed 3 May 2007: www.bcmagazine.net/hk.bcmagazine.issues/bcmagazine_webissue231/03seeking safety.html

Bernal, J. K. (2010) 'Begging for Basic Rights', *South China Morning Post*, 13 November. Viewed 13 November 2010: www.scmp.com/article/730254/begging-basic-rights

Bloch, A. (2000) 'Refugee Settlement in Britain: The Impact of Policy on Participation', *Journal of Ethnic and Migration Studies*, 26(1): 75–88.

Boehler, P. (2013) 'Hong Kong Police Stop-and-Search Tactics Questioned after 1.6m Spot Checks Last Year', *South China Morning Post*, 24 November. Viewed 24 November 2013: www.scmp.com/news/hong-kong/article/1364087/police-tactics-queried-after-16m-spot-checks-last-year

Bohmer, C. and Shuman, A. (2008) *Rejecting Refugees: Political Asylum in the 21st Century*, Abingdon: Routledge.

Bohmer, C. and Shuman, A. (2013) *Narrating Atrocity: Obstacles to Proving Credibility in Asylum Claims*, Working Paper 7, Refugee Law Initiative. Viewed 9 October 2013: http://sas-space.sas.ac.uk/4851/1/RLI_Working_Paper_No._7.pdf

Calavita, K. (2003) 'A "Reserve Army of Delinquents": The Criminalization and Economic Punishment of Immigrants in Spain', *Punishment & Society*, 5(4): 399–413.

Calavita, K. (2005) *Immigrants at the Margins: Law, Race and Exclusion in Southern Europe*, Cambridge: Cambridge University Press.

Carney, J. (2011) 'Asylum Seekers Recruited as Drug Dealers', *South China Morning Post*, 8 May. Viewed 8 May 2011: www.scmp.com/article/967149/asylum-seekers-recruited-drug-dealers

Castles, S. (2007) 'The Migration-Asylum Nexus and Regional Approaches', in S. Kneebone and F. Rawlings-Sanaei (Eds.) *New Regionalism and Asylum Seekers*, New York: Berghahn Books: 25–42.

Global phenomena and local responses 99

Chua, H-W. (2011) 'Social Shortfall', *South China Morning Post*, 22 November. Viewed 22 November 2011: www.scmp.com/article/985584/social-shortfall

Cohen, J. (2001) 'Questions of Credibility: Omissions, Discrepancies and Errors of Recall in the Testimony of Asylum Seekers', *International Journal of Refugee Law*, 13: 293–309.

Cohen, R. (2006) *Migration and Its Enemies: Global Capital, Migrant Labour and the Nation-State*, Aldershot: Ashgate.

Coutin, S. B. (2001) 'The Oppressed, the Suspect, and the Citizen: Subjectivity in Competing Accounts of Political Violence', *Law & Social Inquiry*, 26(1): 63–94.

Crawford, B. (2009) 'Fishing Village Is Conduit for Illegal Migrants', *South China Morning Post*, 18 October. Viewed 18 October 2009: www.scmp.com/article/695779/fishing-village-conduit-illegal-migrants

Crawley, H. (1999) *Breaking Down the Barriers: A Report on the Conduct of Asylum Interviews at Ports*, London: Immigration Law Practitioners' Association.

Crawley, H. (2010) ' "No One Gives You a Chance to Say What You Are Thinking": Finding Space for Children's Agency in the UK Asylum System', *Area*, 42(2): 162–169.

Crisp, J. (2007) 'Vital Distinction', *Refugees*, 148: 4–14.

Crisp, J. (2008) Beyond the Nexus: UNHCR's Evolving Perspective on Refugee Protection and International Migration, Research Paper No. 155, Geneva: UNHCR.

Dal Lago, A. (2009) *Non-persone: L'esclusione dei Migranti in Una Società Globale*, Milano: Feltrinelli.

Da Lomba, S. (2010) 'Legal Status and Refugee Integration: A UK Perspective,' *Journal of Refugee Studies*, 23(4): 415–436.

Daly, M. (2009) 'Refugee Law in Hong Kong: Building the Legal Infrastructure', *Hong Kong Lawyer*, 9: 14–30.

Dauvergne, C. (2004) 'Sovereignty, Migration, and the Rule of Law in Global Times', *The Modern Law Review*, 67(4): 588–615.

Dauvergne, C. (2008) *Making People Illegal: What Globalization Means for Migration and Law*, Cambridge: Cambridge University Press.

De Genova, N. P. (2002) 'Migrant "Illegality" and Deportability in Everyday Life', *Annual Review of Anthropology*, 31: 419–447.

De Genova, N. (2011) 'Alien Powers: Deportable Labour and the Spectacle of Security', in V. Squire (Ed.) *The Contested Politics of Mobility: Borderzones and Irregularity*, Abingdon: Routledge: 91–115.

Engbersen, G. and van der Leun, J. (2001) 'The Social Construction of Illegality and Criminality', *European Journal on Criminal Policy and Research*, 9(1): 51–70.

Fassin, D. (2013) 'The Precarious Truth of Asylum', *Public Culture*, 25(1): 39–63.

Glazebrook, D. (2004) 'Becoming Mobile after Detention', *Social Analysis*, 48(3): 40–58.

Goodstadt, L. F. (2013) *Poverty in the Midst of Affluence: How Hong Kong Mismanaged Its Prosperity*, Hong Kong: Hong Kong University Press.

Grewcock, M. (2009) *Border Crimes: Australia's War on Illicit Migrants*, Sydney: Institute of Criminology Press.

Harrell-Bond, B. (2002) 'Can Humanitarian Work with Refugees be Humane?', *Human Rights Quarterly*, 24(1): 51–85.

Headlines Daily (2009) '13巴漢擠在小舢舨 16歲蛇頭偷運假難民' [13 Pakistanis crowded in a small sampan, 16-year-old smuggler brings in fake asylum seekers], 10 October. Viewed 15 October 2009: http://news.stheadline.com/dailynews/content_hk/2009/10/10/90782.asp

Healey, R. L. (2006) 'Asylum-Seekers and Refugees: A Structuration Theory Analysis of Their Experiences in the UK', *Population, Space and Place*, 12: 257–271.

100   *Global phenomena and local responses*

Herlihy, J., Scragg, P. and Turner, S. (2002) 'Discrepancies in Autobiographical Memories – Implications for the Assessment of Asylum Seekers: Repeated Interview Study', *British Medical Journal*, 321: 324–327.

Immigration Department (ImmD) (2011) *Immigration Department Year-End Briefing 2010*, 13 January. Viewed 20 August 2011: www.immd.gov.hk/en/press/press-releases/20110113.html

Ip, C. (2010) 'Protected in HK but Denied Right to Work', *South China Morning Post*, 28 November. Viewed 28 November 2010: www.scmp.com/article/732147/protected-hk-denied-right-work

Jacobsen, K. (2006) 'Refugees and Asylum Seekers in Urban Areas: A Livelihoods Perspective', *Journal of Refugee Studies*, 19(3): 273–286.

Jubany, O. (2011) 'Constructing Truths in a Culture of Disbelief: Understanding Asylum Screening from Within', *International Sociology*, 26(1): 74–94.

Khosravi, S. (2010) *'Illegal Traveller': An Auto-Ethnography of Borders*, Houndmills: Palgrave Macmillan.

Krasmann, S. (2007) 'The Enemy on the Border: Critique of a Programme in Favour of a Preventive State', *Punishment & Society*, 9(3): 301–318.

Ku, A. S. (2001) 'Hegemonic Construction, Negotiation and Displacement: The Struggle over Right of Abode in Hong Kong', *International Journal of Cultural Studies*, 4(3): 259–278.

Lam, A. and Tsang, P. (2009) 'Eight IIs, Snakehead Caught Off Sai Kung', *South China Morning Post*, 30 November.

Law, K. Y. and Lee, K. M. (2006) 'Citizenship, Economy and Social Exclusion of Mainland Chinese Immigrations to Hong Kong', *Journal of Contemporary Asia*, 36(2): 217–242.

Law, K. Y. and Lee, K. M. (2013) 'Socio-political Embeddings of South Asian Ethnic Minorities' Economic Situations in Hong Kong', *Journal of Contemporary China*, 22(84): 984–1005.

Legislative Council (LegCo) (2010) *Letter to LegCo Secretariat*, LC Paper No. CB(2)348/10–11(01), 18 November, Hong Kong. Viewed 10 May 2013: www.legco.gov.hk/yr10-11/english/panels/se/papers/se1019cb2-348-1-e.pdf

Legislative Council (LegCo) (2011) *Background Brief Prepared by the Legislative Council Secretariat for the Meeting on 12 April 2011, Torture Claim Screening Mechanism*, LC Paper No. CB(2)1454/10–11(4), 7 April, Hong Kong: Legislative Council, Panel on Security.

Li, N. and Tsang, P. (2009) '2 Snakeheads and 9 Illegal Immigrants Caught in Sea Chase', *South China Morning Post*, 24 July. Viewed 24 July 2009: www.scmp.com/article/687753/2-snakeheads-and-9-illegal-immigrants-caught-sea-chase

Lo, C. (2009) 'Ruling Blamed for Influx of Asylum Seekers', *South China Morning Post*, 14 May. Viewed 14 May 2009: www.scmp.com/article/680185/ruling-blamed-influx-asylum-seekers

Lo, C. and Nip. A. (2009) 'Introduce Law on Asylum Seekers, Rights Lawyer Says', *South China Morning Post*, 15 May. Viewed 15 May 2009: www.scmp.com/article/680363/introduce-law-asylum-seekers-rights-lawyer-says

Loper, K. (2010) 'Human Rights, Non-refoulement and the Protection of Refugees in Hong Kong', *International Journal of Refugee Law*, 22(3): 404–439.

Man, J. (2013) 'Hong Kong: No Friend to Asylum Seekers', *The Atlantic*, 18 March. Viewed 18 March 2013: www.theatlantic.com/china/archive/2013/03/hong-kong-no-friend-to-asylum-seekers/274107/

McKenzie, H. (2009) 'No Direction Home', *Timeout*, 10–23 June: 23–26.

Global phenomena and local responses   101

Melossi, D. (2003) ' "In a Peaceful Life": Migration and the Crime of Modernity in Europe/ Italy', *Punishment & Society*, 5(4): 371–397.

Ming Pao (2009a) '迷路斷糧「自首」 17南亞蛇客被捕' [Lost and without food 'they surrender', 17 smuggled South Asians arrested], 10 August. Viewed 12 August 2009: http://life.mingpao.com/cfm/dailynews3b.cfm?File=20090810/nalgo/gou1.txt

Ming Pao (2009b) '修例後首截南亞人蛇 8人被棄荒島稱不知新例' [First South Asian illegal immigrants caught after the amendment. 8 abandoned on a desert island don't know of new legislation], 30 November. Viewed 30 November 2009: http://life.ming pao.com/cfm/dailynews3b.cfm?File=20091130/nalgg/gga1.txt

Mountz, A. (2010) *Seeking Asylum: Human Smuggling and Bureaucracy at the Border*, Minneapolis: University of Minnesota Press.

Neumayer, E. (2006) 'Unequal Access to Foreign Spaces: How States Use Visa Restrictions to Regulate Mobility in a Globalized World', *Transactions of the Institute of British Geographers*, 31(1): 72–84.

Nevins, J. (2002) *Operation Gatekeeper: The Rise of the Illegal Alien and the Making of the U.S.-Mexico Boundary*, New York: Routledge.

Newendorp, N. D. (2008) *Uneasy Reunions: Immigration, Citizenship and Family Life in Post-1997 Hong Kong*, Stanford: Stanford University Press.

Ng, K-C. (2011) 'Crackdown on Illegal Signs and Building Works', *South China Morning Post*, 14 January. Viewed 14 January 2011: www.scmp.com/article/735613/ crackdown-illegal-signs-and-building-works

Núñez, G. G. and Heyman, J. McC. (2007) 'Entrapment Processes and Immigrant Communities in a Time of Heightened Border Vigilance', *Human Organization*, 66(4): 354–365.

Pickering, S. (2005) *Refugees and State Crime*, Sydney: The Federation Press.

Pirandello, L. (1993) *Il Fu Mattia Pascal*, Milano: Garzanti.

Rajaram, P. K. and Grundy-Warr, C. (2007) 'Introduction', in P. K. Rajaram and C. Grundy-Warr (Eds.) *Borderscapes: Hidden Geographies and Politics at Territory's Edge*, Minneapolis: University of Minnesota Press: ix–xl.

Ramsden, M. and Marsh, L. (2013) 'The "Right to Work" of Refugees in Hong Kong: Ma v Director of Immigration', *International Journal of Refugee Law*, 25(3): 574–596.

Robinson, V. and Segrott, J. (2002) *Understanding the Decision-Making of Asylum Seekers*, Research Study No. 243, London: Home Office. Viewed 13 May 2009: www. homeoffice.gov.uk/rds/pdfs2/hors243.pdf

Sampson, R., Mitchell, G. and Bowring, L. (2011) *There Are Alternatives: A Handbook for Preventing Unnecessary Immigration Detention*, Melbourne: The International Detention Coalition.

Sassen, S. (2001) *The Global City: New York, London, Tokyo*, second edition, Princeton: Princeton University Press.

Schuster, L. (2011) 'Turning Refugees into "Illegal Migrants": Afghan Asylum Seekers in Europe', *Ethnic and Racial Studies*, 34(8): 1392–1407.

Sen, A. (2006) *Identity and Violence: The Illusion of Destiny*, New York: W. W. Norton and Company.

Smart, A. (2003) 'Sharp Edges, Fuzzy Categories and Transborder Networks: Managing and Housing New Arrivals in Hong Kong', *Ethnic and Relation Studies*, 26(2): 218–233.

South China Morning Post (2010) 'Loopholes mean genuine asylum seekers suffer', Letter to the Editor, 28 November. Viewed 28 November 2010: www.scmp.com/ article/731851/loopholes-mean-genuine-asylum-seekers-suffer

102 *Global phenomena and local responses*

Stewart, E. (2005) 'Exploring the Vulnerability of Asylum Seekers in the UK', *Population, Space and Place*, 11: 499–512.

Thomas, J. (2000) *Ethnocide: A Cultural Narrative of Refugee Detention in Hong Kong*, Aldershot: Ashgate.

Tsui, Y. (2009a) 'Asylum Seekers Allowed to Work', *South China Morning Post*, 3 March. Viewed 3 March 2009: www.scmp.com/article/671869/asylum-seekers-allowed-work

Tsui, Y. (2009b) 'Asylum Seekers Who Filed Torture Claims Get Damages for Time in Jail', *South China Morning Post*, 4 March. Viewed 4 March 2009: www.scmp.com/article/671949/asylum-seekers-who-filed-torture-claims-get-damages-time-jail

United Nations High Commissioner for Refugees (UNHCR) (2013) *UNHCR Global Trends 2012*, Geneva: Author. Viewed 25 January 2014: http://unhcr.org/globaltrends june2013/UNHCR%20GLOBAL%20TRENDS%202012_V05.pdf

Vision First (2013) *Hong Kong Needs Welfare Services for New Arrivals*. Viewed 1 January 2014: http://visionfirstnow.org/2013/12/13/hong-kong-needs-welfare-services-for-new-arrivals/

Vrecer, N. (2010) 'Living in Limbo: Integration of Forced Migrants from Bosnia and Herzegovina in Slovenia', *Journal of Refugee Studies*, 23(4): 484–502.

Weber, L. (2006) 'The Shifting Frontiers of Migration Control', in S. Pickering and L. Weber (Eds.) *Borders, Mobility and Technologies of Control*, Dordrecht: Springer: 21–44.

Weber, L. and Pickering, S. (2011) *Globalization and Borders: Death and the Global Frontier*, Houndmills: Palgrave Macmillan.

Yeung, M. (2011) 'Nowhere to Call Home', *China Daily*, 23 August. Viewed 23 August 2011: www.chinadaily.com.cn/hkedition/2011-08/23/content_13167556.htm

Zetter, R. (1991) 'Labelling Refugees: Forming and Transforming a Bureaucratic Identity', *Journal of Refugee Studies*, 4(1): 39–62.

Zetter, R. (2007) 'More Labels, Fewer Refugees: Remaking the Refugee Label in an Era of Globalization', *Journal of Refugee Studies*: 20(2): 172–192.

Zimmermann, S. (2009a) 'Irregular Secondary Movements to Europe: Seeking Asylum Beyond Refuge', *Journal of Refugee Studies*, 22(1): 74–96.

Zimmermann, S. (2009b) 'Why Seek Asylum? The Role of Integration and Financial Support', *International Migration*, 48(1): 199–231.

3 Crossing borders into Hong Kong

A livelihoods approach towards developing an understanding of refugee conditions upon arrival in the country of refuge cannot refrain from focusing on the experiences of refugees with border crossing. In effect, it was noted in Chapter 2 that the internal border, constructed to socially and legally marginalize certain categories of migrant, is born of those lines that nation-states draw on cartographic maps to separate and order political territories. In a context of worldwide 'securitization of migration', whereby migration has come to constitute a risk to the liberal world that must be countered by stringent border controls and new technologies of surveillance (Guild 2009; Huysmans 2000; Pickering and Weber 2006), the experience of asylum seeking is increasingly shaped by discourses of deterrence and choice, which build on those lines and erect ever higher walls that exacerbate the vulnerability of asylum seekers (Weber and Pickering 2011).

The aim of this chapter, therefore, is to contribute to understandings of asylum seeker vulnerability, by focusing on the social and legal processes on which their movement is dependent, in relation to the networks they form and utilize and the structural and agency factors that determine their final or contingent country of refuge. It is understood that as legal entry into the developed countries that have traditionally received the highest numbers of asylum applications is now extremely difficult for some categories of traveller, a number of undeterred asylum seekers are forced to take ever more dangerous and costly journeys, which often involve unauthorized border crossing (Koser 2000; Webber 2004). As a consequence, increasing numbers of people are being turned into 'illegal' migrants even before they arrive at their destination (Oelgemöller 2011; Gerard 2014), while some are ending up in alternative and transit regions peripheral to their planned destination country (Akcapar 2009). Hong Kong, in this view, has become a viable alternative destination for seeking asylum, and, I argue, this city's 'global' status affects new, contingent asylum routes.

Each of the three sections in this chapter deals with intertwined aspects of the processes that determine arrival in Hong Kong – the routes and methods of travel that are used to enter the territory; the networks that have an impact on migrant decision making; and asylum seeker expectations of economic and safety concerns. Drawing upon the descriptive, evocative stories collected during my fieldwork, an analysis of the participants' narratives is offered that highlights the

104 Crossing borders into Hong Kong

dynamics and reasons underlying the rise of Hong Kong as a significant destination in a new global geopolitical map of countries with high standards of living that are seen as safe for asylum seekers fleeing persecution and poverty. This analysis reveals that an image of Hong Kong is being circulated in developing countries as one of the fastest-growing economies peripheral to coveted destinations. However, this appears to have reduced the legal opportunities to enter Hong Kong for nationals of countries that tend to produce the largest numbers of asylum seekers, thereby aligning the city more closely to those countries for which it is seen as an alternative destination. Asylum seeker vulnerability is necessarily affected.

Refugee routes and strategies of border crossing

The HKSAR is situated on China's south coast, enclosed by the Pearl River Delta and South China Sea (see Map 1.1). It is positioned at close proximity to the former Portuguese colony of Macao and two of the most populated and recently developed megalopolises in the region, the cities of Guangzhou and Shenzhen. The main ports of entry to Hong Kong are the Hong Kong International Airport, which is one of the world's largest passenger terminals and a prime transfer hub for many airlines connecting destinations in the Asia-Pacific region, Europe and North America; the ferry terminals in Kowloon and Hong Kong Island, which connect Hong Kong to Macao and industrial areas in the Pearl River Delta; and the border-crossing land posts of Lo Wu and Lok Ma Chau, which join Hong Kong to Shenzhen via two of the most heavily used immigration control points.

Many of my asylum seeker participants entered Hong Kong using one of the previously mentioned entry points. A considerable number, however, entered via alternative means, including the use of small speedboats to cross a narrow strip of sea between Shenzhen and the remote shores of the New Territories. The manner in which the asylum seekers entered the territory appears largely dependent on the geographies of their origin countries and the arrangements made concerning their itinerary – that is, whether the last segment of their journey was organized in China or elsewhere. It also seems to be closely related to the year in which their journey took place. The data presented in Table 3.1 shows that arrival through China involves higher numbers of unauthorized entries than via the airport. Of the 75 participants in the target group, 35 arrived in Hong Kong without proper authorization – including authorized entry in possession of forged or unlawfully

Table 3.1 Entry method

	Airport	Land/sea	Total
Authorized	26	14	40
Unauthorized	12	23	35
Total	38	37	75

Crossing borders into Hong Kong 105

obtained travel documents. Of these 35 unauthorized entrants, 23 entered from China by land or sea, and 12 landed at the Hong Kong International Airport.

For the time frame considered, the interviewees are more or less distributed equally per year of arrival, with the majority arriving between 2005 and 2007 and in the years 2009 and 2010. More recently, a clear tendency towards unauthorized entry has been observed in Hong Kong among asylum seekers originating from countries for which a tougher visa regime has impacted patterns of migratory movement (see Figure 3.1). In addition, the data indicate that the majority of arrivals from these countries, Bangladesh in particular, were mainly concentrated in the years prior to 2007, at a time when a more liberal visa regime provided a larger number of asylum seekers with easier access to the territory[1] (see Table 3.2). The same can be observed for people from Africa, who arrived in Hong Kong throughout the previously mentioned period but who reflect considerable differences across years among the nationalities involved. For example, new arrivals from the Democratic Republic of the Congo and Ghana were hardly met during the fieldwork, despite their arrival numbers previously being large. Although official statistics could not be retrieved, the majority of African interviewees who arrived legally in 2009 and 2010 appeared to be Guineans, Togolese and Ugandans, whose passports did not need a visa or for whom a visa was said to be easily obtainable. There was a significant spike in the number of unauthorized entrants to Hong Kong in 2010, which was partly evident in the high number of Somali interviewees who had landed very recently at the time of the interviews.

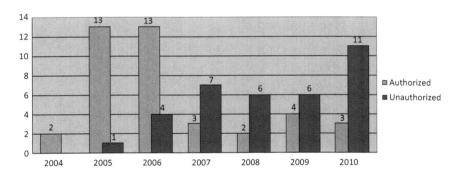

Figure 3.1 Entry method per year

Table 3.2 Entry year per place of origin

	2004	2005	2006	2007	2008	2009	2010
Africa		5	3	4	2	6	13
Sri Lanka	2	5	3	3	2	1	1
Bangladesh		4	11	3	4	3	

106 *Crossing borders into Hong Kong*

While these data are not quantitatively noteworthy, as they draw from a small number of interviewees, they do offer some insight into the changing nature of border crossing into Hong Kong. Furthermore, the data seem to support previous research that indicates that the stringent border controls in Western countries affect migrants' decision making, leading to a growth in illicit operations (Koser 2000; Andreas 2000). Migrant journeys appear increasingly dependent on ever more complex itineraries which often require interspersed journeys and experienced agents, who take on some of the traditional functions previously held by relatives and friends in conveying information and facilitating entry to particular countries (Koser 1997; Koser and Pinkerton 2002). As is demonstrated throughout this book, these data appear to confirm the existence of a symbiotic relationship between receiving states and the vast industry of migration (Mountz 2010). The latter finds its raison d'être in the need of the state to control and limit the arrival of certain people, while the former effectively deprives the migrants who manage to enter of the opportunity to integrate into society, by justifying their legal exclusion on the basis of their alleged propensity to utilize criminal networks to gain entry into Hong Kong. In this regard, the data reinforce the findings of studies such as Bodomo's (2011) on the occurrence of racial profiling at entry points in Hong Kong, which is based on the belief that people from certain groups are more likely to break the law. Further, in a sort of shrewd operation that shifts onto migrants the matrix of risk that certain travellers allegedly pose to destination societies, the increased exposure to harm that migrants face as a result of border control mechanisms that 'pre-empt' their 'illegality' is empirically evinced, revealing the risks and costs that asylum seekers incur (Weber and Pickering 2011).

The participants narrated a wide variety of experiences regarding their landing in the former British colony. Indeed, arrival was often circumstantial. In many cases, Hong Kong was not the final destination chosen upon departure, but it became so at a later stage, either voluntarily or for reasons beyond the asylum seekers' control. In addition, a range of stories were collected concerning irregular border crossing. Some routes involved unauthorized or undocumented entry, while others included the use of unlawfully obtained travel documents. Clear patterns of arrival are nonetheless visible when methods and dynamics of entry are divided according to entry point.

Entry at the airport

About half of the participants arrived at the Hong Kong International Airport. Of them, the majority entered the territory either without a visa or holding business permits generally granted for periods of stay of between 7 and 30 days. A sizeable number of participants from Bangladesh, for instance, who arrived between 2005 and the end of 2006 said that they had 14-day visa-free entry and arrived in groups of between 2 and 20 individuals, together with the person who planned their journey or guided them to Hong Kong. It was not unusual for some of these arrivals to be returned to Bangladesh at the entry point. In particular, one participant reported

Crossing borders into Hong Kong 107

that he was allowed to enter Hong Kong only on his second attempt, while another admitted that he resorted to unauthorized entry by boat when his previous legal attempt failed. The Sri Lankan asylum seekers made similar arrangements for their journey to Hong Kong, before visa requirements came to be applied to this nationality group. I was often told that the choice of Hong Kong as a destination was made because entry was visa free. For example, one interviewee argued that because he wanted to escape the oppressive grip that the Tamil Tigers had exercised on him since his youth but 'did not know how to travel' (Sri Lankan participant, 33), he managed to find an agent who later explained that of the countries that allow departure at short notice, Hong Kong would be the easiest into which to gain entry. He explained that he could not stay in his country 'and to go to other countries was too expensive. . . . The agent said he had been many times in Hong Kong', so they chose to travel there.

When travellers had a visa or their passport allowed them visa-free entry, Hong Kong was an easy destination to reach provided that they were informed about it. Nonetheless, the participants confirmed that upon landing they had to demonstrate to customs agents that they had money with them, to validate their reason for travelling and to lower the perceived risk that they would overstay. As Hong Kong and China are business destinations for increasing numbers of traders from developing countries (Mathews 2011; Yang 2012), the availability of appropriate financial resources was also a requirement for some categories of traveller. One informant, for instance, argued that, 'as I had a business visa, I had to dress accordingly. I wore a suit and I showed Immigration that I had cash with me' (African participant, 02). An inability to provide a guarantee of one's financial resources would most likely result in a refused entry. Weber and Gelsthorpe (2000) have examined the decision making of immigration officers in determining whether travellers pose a threat to society, and thus the use of technologies of risk management that sort individuals into risk class categories, according to the real or presumed danger the traveller embodies (van Munster 2009; Bigo 2002). Based on previous statistical trends, travellers' likelihood of offending or seeking asylum becomes strictly associated with their nationality and certain other of their characteristics (Dauvergne 2008; Guild 2009), leading to profiling, control and suspicion. In Hong Kong, 'misunderstandings' often arise at the airport, with travellers of certain ethnic origins complaining that they are being racially singled out and subjected to levels of security checks not normally applied to other travellers (Bodomo 2011). Khosravi (2010: 76) rightly argues that the 'border exposes me [the traveller] to a gaze that does not *see* me as an individual but *reads* me as a type. . . . The gaze is a hierarchically interwoven complex of gender, racial and class factors'. Indeed, while entry is determined by one's passport, officials profile certain categories of traveller based on assumed values and societal norms.

In this sense, the journey of several participants was affected by the heightened risk they faced of being returned home. They were forced to seek creative means of gaining access to the territory by circumventing the barriers to their entry. While some resorted to assuming a particular role, as required by the Hong Kong authorities or instructed by their agent, other participants, less aware of

108   *Crossing borders into Hong Kong*

their circumstances, were forced to rely on their 'good luck', which often made them travel longer distances while risking never being able to apply for asylum. To illustrate, one inexperienced participant from an East African country, who had recently arrived in Hong Kong and had just learnt how to apply for asylum, said that when he entered Hong Kong he was asked to provide evidence that he had the means to support himself during his stay. Having less than US$50 in his possession, he was granted entry, but instead of being permitted to stay in the territory, he was escorted to board a bus to China, where he had a one-month valid visa. He later arrived in Guangzhou where he fortuitously met a fellow countryman who suggested he return to Hong Kong if his intention was to seek asylum. To facilitate his return, this man offered to buy him a one-way plane ticket to Africa, departing from Hong Kong, to allow the participant to re-enter the HKSAR.

Hong Kong was not always the preferred destination for those who arrived at the airport. Rather, sometimes arrival in the territory was due to unforeseen circumstances that occurred along the journey. On this point, it is apparent that increased worldwide securitization of migration interplays significantly with Hong Kong's status as a global city. Data on passenger flows at the airport are important indicators of how global cities are positioned in the world, and Hong Kong is one of those cities that link different economic zones (Smith and Timberlake 2002). In 2012, some 48.62 million people visited Hong Kong, representing a 15.9 per cent increase on 2011. Of this number, 11.56 million people travelled through the airport (ImmD 2013). It has been reported that the airport is planning to increase the total passenger throughput by 2030 to 97 million, growing at a compound annual growth rate of 3.2 per cent from the over 50 million in 2011.[2] It is plausible to argue that the greater are the numbers of people who transit relatively freely through Hong Kong en route to other destinations, the more likely it will be that some of these travellers will be forced to remain in a less desirable destination when problems occur along the way. In other words, as Hong Kong strengthens its role as a regional hub for airborne travellers, the rising use of technologies of control in certain countries (Pickering and Weber 2006) may cause travellers to seek asylum in transit cities, where larger numbers of international passengers are found and even expedited by the local authorities.

A couple of examples sketched subsequently validate the previous argument by exposing the increasing complexity of asylum seekers' itineraries as a result of the securitization of migration.

> Masur travelled from Africa to India in order to travel on to Europe. But once in India he realized that some other fellow countrymen had been caught and returned from Europe, indicating that that route was no longer safe. Plans to travel to North America via Shanghai were then made by the agent who helped organize his journey. For this, Masur had to go to another South Asian country, apply for a Chinese visa and then fly to Shanghai. The ticket included a transit of a few hours in Hong Kong. A problem arose, however, when he went through passport control in Shanghai, and he was sent back to the airport of departure. However, once in Hong Kong he was held by immigration

Crossing borders into Hong Kong 109

authorities. Masur was questioned about why he had been returned and, rather than allowing him to board his next flight, his ticket and passport were withheld, 'because they needed to find out why I was sent to Hong Kong'. (African participant, 70)

In another case, Kumar, an interviewee from North Africa, travelled visa free to Thailand with the intention of joining his friends in Japan. To quote from my fieldwork notes:

> In Thailand Kumar contacted someone who would provide him with a passport that would not require a visa for Japan, and whose rightful owner resembled him to an acceptable extent. As he said, Thailand is a place in which thousands of people from many countries make preparations for the last leg of their travel, whether in Asia, North America or Europe. Some of these people are found and arrested by the authorities, but others, generally Caucasian-looking, manage to stay in the country without great difficulty. When the flight ticket and a Greek passport were ready, Kumar left for a neighbouring country to embark on a flight to Japan. However, Japanese customs denied him entry and sent him back to where he departed, where he was detained and forced to pay US$800 to facilitate his release. After returning to Thailand, Kumar started his search for another passport, and, mindful of the previous experience, his intention was to obtain a Canadian passport, which he thought would cause him fewer troubles at the border. Since Canadian passports appear to be more valuable in the black market, Kumar paid US$1000, despite the fact that the photo did not much resemble him. To improve his chances, he obtained an ID card that matched the name of the legitimate owner of the passport. This time his journey included a stop in Hong Kong, after crossing several borders to prove the authenticity of his travel document (cf. Khosravi 2010). In Hong Kong he boarded a flight bound for his dream destination. Yet in Japan, Kumar was again denied entry. This time, he was sent to Hong Kong, where he was detained for investigation.

Other participants told of how they were stopped in Hong Kong en route to another destination. One Sri Lankan asylum seeker, for instance, said he travelled on a Singaporean passport via Hong Kong to Europe and was stopped by immigration officials when already seated on the plane, awaiting take-off. A fellow countryman, who had previously been recognized as a refugee in another Asian country, but wanted to bypass lengthy resettlement procedures and join his friends in Europe, was questioned in similar circumstances, leaving him with no option but to reapply for asylum.

Among the participants who, at the time of the interviews, had recently arrived in Hong Kong at the airport, Somalis made up the largest group. The pattern of arrival observed in their cases is very similar among all of them. Most commonly, this was their first experience overseas and their journey was organized by agents who promised to take them to a safe country in Europe or North America.

110 *Crossing borders into Hong Kong*

However, when they and their agents arrived in Hong Kong, the asylum seekers were left stranded in the airport transit area. 'Sit here while I go buy something to drink' is what they were generally told, before the agent embarked on another flight and disappeared. Left with no documentation other than a phone number of the UNHCR office in Hong Kong, these asylum seekers were generally taken into custody, to be later released on recognizance.[3]

Entry by land

If the journey of airborne travellers is certainly impacted by heightened securitization at the border, many participants said that they opted to enter Hong Kong by land, particularly those who had arrived more recently. This pathway included entry either by train or bus after journeys often via Guangzhou Airport as an alternative route to taking a direct flight to Hong Kong. Other than reflecting the growing number of foreigners from developing countries who transit in South China for business reasons, more importantly taking this route was said to minimize the possibility that travellers would be quickly returned to their country of origin. Indeed, for many travellers from countries in Africa and Asia, the visa for China was obtained fairly easily. In some cases, the visa also permitted one brief seven-day stay in Hong Kong, thus helping to circumvent the restrictive policies faced when travellers request Hong Kong visas only.

Moreover, in the case of the Bangladeshi participants, not only would flying to Guangzhou avoid the risk of being denied entry at the airport in Hong Kong, but due to their country's proximity to China, they could also take advantage of a commonly used strategy involving multiple crossings of the borders with China and other neighbouring countries before applying for an entry visa for Hong Kong. Developing a travel history was thought to lower the perceived risk of their overstaying in the eyes of the Hong Kong authorities after visa requirements were imposed on Bangladeshi nationals transiting in the city. In this regard, several participants stressed that in their constant search for better ways to adapt to and circumvent the ever-changing border control practices, they found that using Kunming as an alternative entry point into China would improve their chances of a successful border crossing. Border controls in Kunming appeared to be more relaxed than those in Guangzhou, as the city had a new airport and air traffic needed boosting to improve tourism numbers. In an effort to open up to the world and become a competitive second-tier city in Southwest China, Kunming has been rapidly developing its infrastructure and transportation links. The city now boasts one key regional airport, which is part of the central government's plan to increase fast-growing passenger volumes while releasing some of the pressure from the airports at Beijing, Shanghai and Guangzhou (*China Economic Review* 2003).

Gaining entry into China was vital for many of the participants in order to leave their country and the threats they faced there, while offering the best chance of securing onward travel to their desired destination. On the one hand, it is in this context that we can explain why Bangladeshis have been arriving in Hong Kong

Crossing borders into Hong Kong   111

in very small numbers in recent years. When a well-informed participant was asked about recent arrival trends, he stated that his co-nationals were now having problems obtaining visas for China, thus making arrival in Hong Kong more arduous. On the other, if visa requirements for China probably impacted on land routes at a time when visa requirements for Hong Kong made entry via air routes less viable, maintaining one's legal status in China was understood to lower migration costs. It gave travellers the time to plan their next move when their journeys involved multiple legs and required that long distances be covered and bureaucracy and border controls navigated in several countries. Legal stay in China also circumvented the risk of being harassed by police. Many participants reported that they had been forced to quickly find alternative ways to facilitate their migration, including unauthorized crossing into Hong Kong, after they had lost their legal status in China and became deportable. Conversely, when they could plan their options, several interviewees stated that they changed their itineraries after exhausting alternative possibilities. For example, a Bangladeshi participant said that his intention had never been to go to Hong Kong, but his stay in China was aimed at gaining legal entry into Korea. When his attempts failed and his visa was about to expire he decided that Hong Kong would make a viable alternative, as he was told by fellow countrymen in Shenzhen.

Importantly, while Africans tended to make use of Guangzhou as their main transit point, Shenzhen was the most popular city in which to stay before entering Hong Kong for most of the South Asian participants. Many Bangladeshi and Sri Lankan interviewees explained that they had stayed for days or months at some of the guest houses which over time have opened along the border to cater for the large number of travellers doing business in China or in transit on their way to Hong Kong. These places are important nodes where people meet and share information. As will be discussed later, in this city travellers and agents find the means to organize the last leg of their journey into Hong Kong when legal options are not available. Shenzhen is also a place where asylum seekers sometimes decide to set up their own business. For example, one interviewee, who had previously been abandoned in Macao by his agent, travelled to Shenzhen when a friend in Hong Kong told him he could seek asylum in the territory. In Shenzhen, however, this participant invested in the guest house business and consequently stayed in China for months, during which time he travelled to Hong Kong every now and then to renew his Chinese visa. When he realized that the Hong Kong authorities were becoming increasingly suspicious about his many crossings, he decided he could no longer ensure his own safety and with regret left his business to seek asylum.

Entry by sea

In this chapter, I posit that the form of entry into Hong Kong adopted by asylum seekers appears to have followed more composite and unauthorized routes in recent times than used to be the case when a permit to stay was granted to those who arrived without a visa. Subsequent to what looks like an attempt by the Hong

112 *Crossing borders into Hong Kong*

Kong Government to filter and exclude travellers deemed to pose a risk of over-staying and seeking asylum, some asylum seekers of certain nationalities were probably deterred from travelling to the territory. Many others, however, simply resorted to unauthorized methods of entry. Two important considerations are note-worthy here. On one side, visa policy in China seems to have generated bigger obstacles to entry into Hong Kong than have Hong Kong's own visa restrictions. If the rationale behind targeted visa regimes and measures aimed at deterring risky populations far beyond the national border of receiving states is supported by this finding, thereby indirectly revealing the value of (collaborative) restric-tive immigration management (cf. Weber and Pickering 2011), it is significant that, on the other side, a large number of the participants in this study had trans-ited or gained travel experience in China before arriving in Hong Kong. This seems to support Mathews's (2011) findings that China is now positioned as semi-peripheral in contemporary migration hierarchies, which elevate Hong Kong to core status. From this perspective, the harder it is to reach the core – in this case Hong Kong – the more its peripheral regions seem to join if not replace Hong Kong as regional nodal points for travellers from Africa and South Asia. The data presented by Içduygu and Toktas (2002) and Akcapar (2006, 2009) in relation to Turkey, and Yacobi (2010) in relation to Israel, in part reveal similar scenarios in the countries surrounding 'Fortress Europe'. As journeys become more frag-mented, these places on the periphery acquire new significance. Information is consumed and arrangements are made in the peripheral countries, affecting the agency and composition of, and the consequences facing, the people heading to the core. If Hong Kong can be viewed as an alternative and at times unexpected destination to hardly reachable developed countries, it is apparent that migration policy in the territory has shifted to align more closely with the policy of those developed states. In other words, as this global city advances its status at the gate-way to China's expanding manufacturing power (see Chapter 1), greater numbers of people are finding themselves drawn to it, leading the city to introduce more measures to deter those travellers deemed the least desirable.

The previous contention is supported by the increasing importance of the mega-lopolises of Guangzhou and Shenzhen in directing asylum flows to Hong Kong. I was told by several participants that they crossed into Hong Kong by land after transiting through China for varied periods of time. A number of Bangladeshi and South Asian participants, who did not have the necessary travel documents and/or a valid visa to legally cross the border, relied on smuggling networks found in Shenzhen. They explained that this route normally began with the traveller being picked up at their guest house to be delivered to one of the small speedboats that make the crossing at night. This is a dangerous ride that obviously increased their vulnerability. For example, a young Sri Lankan participant described being approached by some middlemen when he had already lost all hope of making it to a safe place after his agent abandoned him in Shenzhen. That same night, he found himself on a speedboat to Hong Kong. He recalled that it was pitch dark and cold, and the passengers were wet from the splashing seawater. As they neared the coast of Hong Kong, the police boat seemed to approach fast. Then they were suddenly thrown into the water and told to swim ashore. The water was up to their necks, and they were scared. Their belongings were lost. Somehow they reached the shore.

Importantly, the evidence obtained from this research indicates that, whether the participants' journeys to Hong Kong were organized while they were in China or somewhere else beforehand, the asylum seekers were generally not informed of the details of the journey they would take, and nor did they know the route or method of travel. Some interviewees said that they guessed they would cross the border irregularly because they had no visa, but others learnt of this only once they were on the boat. In addition, some participants explained that even once they had boarded the boat they had no idea there was a border to cross, nor did they know their whereabouts. As a brief example, one young African man recalled, not without a hint of irony in describing the disappointment he felt when he discovered the truth, that '[i]n my country there is no tall building and no clear roads. . . . When in Guangzhou I saw that very big city, with big buildings and lights. I really thought it was close to Europe' (African participant, 27).

Dealing with borders, people and documents

A number of studies on migration systems (Massey et al. 1993) have shown that network connections constitute a valuable form of social capital upon which people draw to reduce the social, economic and emotional costs of migration, as well as to minimize their risks (Massey et al. 1987; Boyd 1989). Other research has revealed conversely that social networks do not always channel migrants to the destination of their choice, especially when unauthorized border crossing strategies overrule the positive effect of networks and lead travellers to alternative destinations (Robinson and Segrott 2002; Collyer 2005). The following data demonstrate how family networks appear to facilitate migration when cash capital is not available to finance movement outright. However, the data also suggest that Hong Kong is not the intended destination of all the people who end up seeking asylum there. Most importantly, far from reducing costs, network ties can increase the monetary and psycho-social risks associated with migration, especially when little information is provided to travellers and third parties take control of the migratory journey.

The people who 'facilitate' migratory movements to Hong Kong form relationships with their clients that align with the category of bridged networks and relations that are structured by a power imbalance between the parties involved (cf. Atfield et al. 2007; Harpviken 2009). These networks between asylum seekers and third parties are not strong, yet the facilitators maintain a high degree of control over the migrant's decision making. Further, third parties are rarely as professional as the agents or smugglers whose successful business is dependent on their reputation. Koser (2009) argues that, in irregular people movements, the greater economic risk lies with the smugglers, as they are often paid upon arrival at the destination. However, this scenario of payment was rare among the people I met in Hong Kong, thus increasing the power of third parties, and in turn heightening

114   *Crossing borders into Hong Kong*

the risk faced by asylum seekers. Among the participants, third parties were often ordinary citizens and friends (Zhang 2008; van Liempt and Doomernick 2006), who only occasionally profited from the recruitment and irregular movement of people (Andrijasevic 2010). In this regard, reputation played only a minor role when short-lived profit considerations outweighed an interest in long-term business operations. If some interviewees reached their destination for a reasonable price, many others found themselves stuck, incapable of going home and unable to secure safety.

Third parties were often said to be friends and relatives who were knowledgeable of Hong Kong. They were also sub-agents, document facilitators and employment and travel agents. In most cases, these 'agents' were businessmen who independently resorted to using the services of other smugglers when unauthorized border crossing or passports were required. Besides those few individuals who purchased a plane ticket and obtained the travel documents by themselves, the great majority of my interviewees relied on third parties, even when a visa was not needed.

Meeting the agents

The migration of many of the Bangladeshi asylum seekers I met in this research clearly illustrates upon whom they relied to ensure their successful border crossing. As per their accounts, many of these participants arrived in Hong Kong in the company of co-nationals who either had been in Hong Kong before or had knowledge of Hong Kong's visa policies because of previous business dealings between Hong Kong and Bangladesh. When asked about the people who had helped them organize their journey, the participants most commonly replied by saying something along the following lines: 'My uncle helped me. He arranged a friend of his to bring me to Hong Kong' (Bangladeshi participant, 39), or 'In my neighbourhood some friends helped me and they brought me here' (Bangladeshi participant, 42). Others said: 'Some people who lived near my home said that this person had sent other people to many countries, so I met him' (Bangladeshi participant, 50), or 'I had my cousin's husband who was living in Hong Kong at that time and he had some friend in Bangladesh who was doing business between Bangladesh and Hong Kong. It was this person who helped me come here' (Bangladeshi participant, 45). In relation to these arrangements, the participants demonstrated very little understanding of how the journey was organized. The agent was indeed the only person with whom they had been in contact, and this person arranged and obtained the necessary documents. According to the participants' stories, agents appeared in particular to be persons who had turned to facilitating people's migration when they sensed that they could make a quick fortune by acting as middlemen or taking friends with them on their next trip. The participants who were bound for Hong Kong said that they had paid significant amounts of money to make the journey, normally between HK$12,000 and HK$40,000, while a return ticket from Dhaka to Hong Kong would normally cost less than HK$5000. One participant, grinning rather happily when recalling the 'cheap' price he was able to negotiate, said that he paid 'only HK$9000 for the whole journey', adding that this was because the travel was organized by a friend who 'did not overcharge me' (Bangladeshi participant, 55).

In addition to relying on friends and relatives, many interviewees visited travel agencies or met agents who were linked to them. According to their accounts, these agencies recruited labour for overseas placement and varied in size and organizational structure. However, what emerged clearly from the interviews is that the participants who resorted to using these services were vulnerable to fraud. Not only were they forced to pay exorbitant fees for journeys that sometimes included being tossed from agent to agent, but they also fell prey to unscrupulous people who wasted a great deal of their client's money and arranged travel to places either different from that agreed upon or where the conditions of stay were not as initially described to the travellers. Most striking was the case of a group of Bangladeshis who had been taken to Hong Kong by plane and then brought to the Tsim Sha Tsui ferry pier, opposite Hong Kong Island. Here they were told they were looking at Italy, Taiwan or Japan, depending on the destination they had been promised. They were told that if they swam from the pier, no one would stop them. I was told of one occasion in which seven people jumped into the water and began swimming in broad daylight under the eyes of astonished tourists who, fearing a mass suicide attempt, called the police.

According to many participants, third parties most commonly deceived them by promising destinations that were simply out of their reach. For example, one participant was told that he would be taken to Brunei. He recalled meeting a man at his shop in his home country and talking amicably with him over a period of several days, before this man suddenly suggested that he travel with him to take up a three-year job in an ironing factory. Considering the rising violence in his neighbourhood, and tempted by this opportunity, the participant sold his shop and his land and took a loan to pay the HK$80,000 needed to process the visa, in Hong Kong. The pair stayed together for 12 days in Hong Kong, till the man suddenly gave him US$300 and disappeared. Similarly, his Hong Kong roommate had been told he would travel to South Korea with another six people, but after a few days in Hong Kong, their agent vanished, together with the HK$40,000 they each paid to travel to South Korea. In both circumstances, the participants did not know what their agents were doing during the time they waited to leave Hong Kong. They were repeatedly reminded by their agent that they would soon travel to their final destination, only to be left to fend for themselves. In yet another case, a Bangladeshi participant travelled to Hong Kong having been promised Italy as his final destination. He agreed that he would pay HK$110,000, half while in Bangladesh and half upon arrival. His family sold properties, and money was raised from friends in Korea and Italy to help him cover the cost. In Hong Kong, however, he was asked by his agent to produce the second half of the money together with his passport, which the agent said he would take to the Italian consulate to apply for the participant's visa. Believing the money would constitute proof that he would not overstay, the participant did as told, but the agent disappeared. When I asked him whether the agency had a regular office and whether he had been able to

116   *Crossing borders into Hong Kong*

contact the agent again, the participant said: 'Yes, he had an office in the city, but when I asked my friends in Bangladesh to go there and find him the office was closed already' (Bangladeshi participant, 62).

Many of the participants faced such problems in Hong Kong. When they found that they had been cheated, they were unable to retrieve their money. They were powerless before agents who either changed the location of their travel agency, most likely to continue their scam elsewhere, or simply refused to return their money. In many circumstances, agents artfully played with their clients' trust by inducing them to sign false contracts or make arrangements only by verbal agreement. A group of asylum seekers who had been promised that they would be taken to Singapore, for example, were brought to Hong Kong and abandoned in some squatter housing in the New Territories. Here, they called their relatives and asked them to complain to the agency. However, the agency refused to help, and when they approached the police, they were informed that without a legal invoice of the payment there was nothing the police could do. Further questions were put to some of the more well-informed participants in order to better understand the nature of the recruitment process in their countries. I was told that the following occurs in South Asia: 'Agents control more agents who control other agents who may or may not be affiliated to licensed agencies. . . . Also, there are agents who give money to other people for each person they bring to them who wants to go overseas' (Pakistani participant, 34). The picture provided by such accounts is one of extensively ramified small groups, at times created ad hoc, at the end of which, however, there is rarely a criminal syndicate controlling the entire operation. The agencies that organized the interviewees' migration appeared to be amorphously structured in ways similar to that described by Zhang (2008) in relation to Chinese smuggling, whereby facilitators are loosely connected and often choose this line of business to diversify their income (Içduygu and Toktas 2002). This structure relies for its success upon the inexperience or naivety of the asylum seekers.

These findings are significant for a number of reasons. First, they confirm that Hong Kong has become a destination within global routes of asylum migration. While this does not seem so much due to the specific objectives set out by asylum seekers themselves, it is apparent that third parties have encouraged travel to Hong Kong. In this view, the data presented previously are similar to the findings of previous research such as that by Gilbert and Koser (2006) on asylum seekers in the UK, in revealing that not only do third parties control the timing, routes, entry methods and destinations of migration, at times causing asylum seekers to be 'spatially dissociated' from their friends and relatives overseas (Koser 1997), but also that the generally low level of education among asylum seekers influences their attitudes towards information seeking. This leaves third parties a considerable degree of control over the consequences of migration, as will be further discussed subsequently. Second, it is plausible that while a number of travellers were taken to places they did not know, where they were forced to live under conditions of stay different from those they had been promised – often resulting in a great deal of suffering – increasing awareness among the Hong Kong public of the involvement of smugglers, and of asylum seekers being deceived with false promises of jobs in Hong Kong and elsewhere, has raised public concerns about the real intent of new arrivals claiming asylum in the territory (see Patel 2008).

The results of this study suggest that sharp distinctions between categories of migrants are becoming increasingly blurred. While the specific motivation of the participants for travelling to Hong Kong is examined in the following section, it has been identified here that asylum seekers whose movement is facilitated and even initiated by third parties often find themselves abandoned along the way or unable to continue their journey. Far from indicating abuse of the system by asylum seekers, this seems to reflect the vulnerability of people who are denied vital information by their agents, within circumstances that expose them to greater insecurity while encouraging generalist claims about asylum abuse.

The migration of the Sri Lankan and other participants illustrates this point. While a few participants explained that their movement was facilitated by reliable and professional smugglers, who provided the exact service agreed upon departure, many others said that agents were people who sold them dreams of a better life that did not eventuate. In this case, many Sri Lankan interviewees recounted unfortunate stories of scams they and their friends faced. Indeed, such accounts of deception were an endless topic of discussion that many interviewees gladly shared, perhaps in an effort to minimize their own traumatic experiences and, ironically, to laugh at the bitter result.

In one such story, a young and inexperienced Tamil man was said to have paid a considerable amount to go to Hong Kong. Once in the territory, the agent took him to the UNHCR and told him that he could apply for a visa there. The young man walked in and in very poor English asked for an application form. In the field for 'reasons for going to Hong Kong', he wrote in his language 'to seek a good job'. When he had completed the form, he was given a UNHCR certificate. Thinking he had obtained a visa, he returned to the agent and was informed that a job could be arranged if he paid a little extra. The young man thought that the agent had indeed been reliable and so agreed to pay US$500 to get a cleaning job at a nearby park. One morning, he was brought to meet his boss, an old Chinese man who claimed to be the company's director. He was given a badge with his name printed on it and told that his job was to water the plants and clean. He was then shown the McDonald's where he would have lunch and the storage room where the next day he would find his uniform. However, on the following day when he returned to the park he found no one waiting for him. For a week, he diligently continued to carry out his duties, until one staff member asked him what he was doing. When he tried to call the phone number printed on the business card he had been given earlier, he found that it was a sex chat line.

Similarly, many participants arrived in Hong Kong with the assistance of agents who took advantage of their vulnerability. Apparently, when the area in Sri Lanka controlled by the Liberation Tigers of Tamil Eelam was subjected to embargo, communication with the outside became difficult, and not knowing what to expect other than the good stories they had heard from agents, prospective Tamil migrants tended to believe that they could achieve the prosperous future they had been told about. It is generally said that asylum seekers are often thankful to the agents for the chance to flee their country when the need arises, despite border controls and stringent visa regimes (Gilbert and Koser 2006; van Liempt and Doomernick 2006). Nonetheless, it seems that by leaving their clients in Hong Kong without the necessary knowledge of asylum, agents put prospective asylum seekers in great danger. The claim of the young man described previously was quickly rejected by the UNHCR because he had no understanding of what the UN agency was about. By writing in the registration form that he had travelled to Hong Kong to work, he irremediably jeopardized his chances of presenting a credible case later, which considering his personal circumstances would have probably won him international protection.

Likewise, I was told the story of a Sri Lankan man who was promised work in Italy but was later abandoned in Hong Kong. In this case, the man was recognized as a refugee in the HKSAR, but because of the excessive time he had to wait before resettlement, while he worried about his family, he decided to return home. His circumstances in Hong Kong thus compelled him to make a drastic decision. It is difficult not to wonder what might have happened to him if, instead of being abandoned in a place where asylum could be sought, he had been taken to a country where asylum could be obtained, in terms of rights and family reunion. Some asylum seekers and recognized refugees have chosen to make the perilous journey home from Hong Kong, while others opt to remain in the city despite the hardship they endure. The heartbreaking story of a Somali asylum seeker named Awil, who died at the age of 52 in Hong Kong in July 2011, confirms how bleak the future can look for some asylum seekers in Hong Kong. Caught up in a system he never fully understood, Awil died after five long months in a coma into which he slipped after he allegedly lost his appetite and the will to live (Vision First 2011).

The circumstances surrounding the migration of many African participants follow similar patterns. As noted previously, Somalis were normally abandoned in Hong Kong by co-national agents who lived overseas and promised them travel to Western destinations. Other Africans, instead, more commonly resorted to seeking assistance from friends and relatives to obtain the necessary travel documents. In ways similar to the experiences of some of the Bangladeshi participants, the journey was frequently organized by people who suggested the destination or tout court made arrangements without consulting the traveller. These people were generally said to be members of the military, government employees or traders who had the knowledge and acquaintances to facilitate the migration of their friends, often via the acquisition of passports that specified a nationality or identity different from that of its holder.

Travel documents, fabricated identities and evading visa regimes

Travel documents are central to any type of border crossing, whether for leisure or temporary or permanent migration (Torpey 2000). In refugee movements, possessing travel documents may mean all the difference between people who are able to travel and those whose movement is impeded. Nation-states have put in place systems that are highly unequal in granting access to foreign territory, imposing

Crossing borders into Hong Kong 119

restrictions on the basis of nationality (Neumayer 2006) which primarily affect those countries that produce the higher numbers of asylum seekers (Betts 2010). The brief discussion that follows of the documents used by asylum seekers to enter Hong Kong is helpful for it contributes to understanding of the types of people who travel to the territory and the dynamics that underlie their transit at the border, therefore revealing the consequences of restrictive border controls and the extent to which choice of destination is possible.

Within the limits of the data presented here, it is apparent that the visa regimes of both Hong Kong and China have facilitated the arrival in the territory of people who would otherwise have found it extremely difficult to travel regularly to safe and relatively wealthy destinations. In addition, routes to South China appear to be frequented in particular by travellers bound for Western countries from Africa and South Asia because, as the participants explained, 'to Chinese all Africans look alike' (African participant, 07), making it simpler to transit using dodgy and unlawfully obtained travel documents. The story of Kumar, who legally crossed several borders in Asia by travelling on someone else's passport, is already known. Two more examples from my field notes further illustrate the arguments made in this section.

> Michael is an asylum seeker from an ex-Soviet country who found himself stuck in Hong Kong on the way to Samoa, one of the few countries that would have accepted him visa-free. After travelling across China, he arrived in Hong Kong on a seven-day visa, where he tried to buy a flight ticket for his destination. However, the only air route included a transit in either Australia or New Zealand, and both governments refused to grant him a transit visa because, as he was coming from an unstable, war-torn country, they feared he would claim asylum (Ip 2011). Michael remembered that while New Zealand refused to allow him to apply for a visa, Australia allowed him to apply but rejected his application. He then begged them to grant him a visa, saying that it was not his intention to stay in Australia, and were they more comfortable handcuffing and escorting him to the next plane he would have gladly accepted. Five years later, he expressed his frustration to me, because all of his attempts to build his future had failed miserably in Hong Kong. He said that he felt that he was not seen as a person, as a normal human being, but rather as simply a passport. He did not try to sneak in, circumventing rules or taking advantage of them. Yet, precisely because of his honesty, he was forced to become a refugee when faced with the oppressive and unequal political system that governs international visa regimes.

Overwhelmed by the border control policies of various states, Michael ended up staying in Hong Kong. In contrast, Abdul, an African traveller seeking refuge overseas, took advantage of these policies to enable his travel:

> After obtaining an Ethiopian passport Abdul travelled to Guangzhou where, on two subsequent attempts, he tried to board a flight to Europe. The first time he had a one-way ticket to Ethiopia via Amsterdam, but he was denied

120   *Crossing borders into Hong Kong*

boarding when the airline personnel at check-in determined that he would likely claim asylum in transit. Undeterred, Abdul reclaimed his money for the flight and bought a second ticket, this time via Paris; but again he was refused boarding for similar reasons. He then moved to Hong Kong, in the hope of travelling to Europe from there. Abdul visited several travel agencies, but the answer he was given was always the same: flights to Ethiopia made a transit stop in either Bangkok or India, and this was not what he was looking for. Still determined to reach his destination, Abdul returned to China. Here, he met an agent, who for US$1300 obtained an original passport from a small African country bearing Abdul's photo, personal data and an exit stamp in an otherwise spotless travel document, shipped to him from Africa within a few weeks of the request being made. Apparently, he later travelled to Singapore, once again with Europe as his final destination.

From such stories, it is clear that travel can either be facilitated or hindered depending on the nationality stated in the passport that is used to cross the border. Passports and visas function to signify the possible threat to society that may arise if the traveller is allowed entry, in accordance with state foreign politics (Salter 2004). As they are intended, however, passports do not indicate a traveller's intention concerning his or her movement. It is evident that customs officials can only guess at what a traveller will do based on previous experience, de facto labelling people as a risk solely because they belong to national groups that tend to have higher numbers of people perceived as 'troublemakers', whether criminals or asylum seekers (Neumayer 2006). Through this process people come to be depersonalized and represented merely by their passports, as Michael perceptively argued after experiencing this himself. However, in addition to preventing people from attempting to secure a better life overseas, it is clear that identities, nationalities and dates of birth can also be altered to serve the desired purpose. In the performance of border crossing (Khosravi 2010), travellers may wear suits or behave as the immigration authorities' 'gaze' desires, according to the passport they are holding, or they may act differently from what would be expected of the owner of that passport. As one participant told me, 'You know Africans! If you close one door, they will immediately open 10 more' (African participant, 18). While Western travellers tend to be confident about their reasons for travelling, as their passport will only rarely be refused an entry stamp, travellers from developing countries may need to either present 'show money' to customs officials or alter their identity, by assuming a role or acquiring a document that is not theirs.

Passports can be purchased on black markets around the globe, but, more importantly, several participants pointed out that it was relatively easy in their country to obtain valid travel documents, both for their own or other countries, either by presenting fake information or acquiring other documents with which it is possible to legally request the passport in a country other than the applicant's. Sadiq (2009) notes that irregular migrants in countries like India, Pakistan and Malaysia can easily acquire citizenship of these countries if they can prove to the authorities that they belong to that society, for example, by showing a membership card to a political party, a driver's licence or a birth certificate obtained with the complicity of neighbours, city councillors or registry officials. Sadiq explains that this happens because in developing countries membership is often unconfirmed, with citizens unrecognized or unverified by agents of the state for many years into adult life. The present study confirms the findings of Sadiq's research. Many Bangladeshi participants noted that as they were born in their home, they received documents proving their identity only after they requested them, at times specifically to apply for a passport. When asked their age, many participants were not sure, as they said age is remembered by heart in their home village. In addition, many had had their date of birth altered in their passport because they believed that it would be easier to travel if they were perceived as older. Some of their travel documents were handwritten, and occasionally names were misspelled, if not deliberately changed. Afghan asylum seekers reported similar dynamics in their country, adding that valid Pakistani and Iranian passports could be easily acquired.

In a similar vein, the Somali participants said that people in their country could buy birth certificates in neighbouring countries and later become regular citizens when registration officers visited their villages, which they did every three months to register residents who had turned 18. In this way, several interviewees from Africa were travelling on passports that were either not their own or in which the nationality indicated was not their real one. For example, some Nigerians were posing as citizens of other countries. Other Africans said that passports from a few small and richer African countries were particularly popular among people in countries that did not enjoy favourable treatment by the visa regimes in overseas destinations of the Global North. Some of these passports allowed transit in Paris visa free, yet the participants who obtained such passports failed in their attempt. Abdul first obtained an Ethiopian passport by presenting a birth certificate unlawfully obtained by posing as the brother of an Ethiopian man who accepted money to declare that Abdul was his relative. While an Ethiopian passport was still not good enough to travel unhindered to Europe, it was sufficient to travel around Asia. To obviate this impediment, he subsequently bought another African passport from the authorities, who only required a photo and money to take care of the formalities.

Clearly, this raises more than one question concerning the efficiency of the present global visa regime, which appears to press people into looking for alternative means of entry to find a better life. Furthermore, alternative methods require personal financial resources, the possession of which may allow arrival in different locations depending on the amount of money that can be invested in migration (Koser 1997). In this regard, it is apparent that for those who cannot afford to travel to or are impeded from reaching their desired destination, Hong Kong and China are viable alternative locations where asylum seekers may find temporary refuge and enjoy better living standards at an affordable price. It is in fact the relatively lenient visa regime for certain nationalities, and the economic development that distinguishes South China and Hong Kong, which appears to have prompted large numbers of people to transit at their borders, whether voluntarily

122   *Crossing borders into Hong Kong*

or unintentionally. When departure from home countries is a necessity and the number of destinations is limited by either the costs associated with unauthorized migration or possession of the wrong passport, other places may serve the purpose. In this regard, the role of agents, friends and relatives is significant in directing people to Hong Kong as the city has gradually become known for its liberal border controls and, as will be discussed subsequently, its asylum policies, or lack thereof.

Explaining asylum seeking in Hong Kong

Richmond (1988, 1993) argues that a clear distinction between voluntary and involuntary migrants is largely misleading because asylum seekers make decisions regarding flight, at the very least to consider whether or not to move and to whom to entrust their migration (Van Hear 1998). On this subject, several commentators have attempted to address the reasons why asylum seekers apply for asylum in specific countries (Böcker and Havinga 1998; Barsky 2000; Thielemann 2003). In particular, Harpviken (2009) and Papadopoulou-Kourkouta (2008) assert that information acquired at origin or in transit and individual perceptions of different places and oneself (Goodman 1981; Barsky 2000) influence decisions about destinations and asylum. In this section, I try to unravel the decision making undertaken by asylum seekers in relation to Hong Kong – specifically, to identify the level of information available about Hong Kong on which the participants based their decisions, the mechanisms by which such information was conveyed and the expectations that consequently arose regarding destinations. In order to examine why and to what extent the people who travelled to Hong Kong chose it over other countries, the questions put to the interviewees were aimed at identifying their knowledge about the territory, their socioeconomic background and the living conditions they left behind in their home country. Moreover, the questions sought to uncover the involvement of household or family members in the participants' decision making and their long-term expectations related to migration. At first glance, the results clearly evince that two broad categories of asylum seekers arrive in Hong Kong: those who possess absolutely no knowledge of the city; and those who do have some knowledge, however inaccurate, superficial or misleading.

Hong Kong overseas: What and how it is known

In examining how knowledge is sought by prospective asylum seekers and what information is available regarding Hong Kong, the participants who were forced to remain in the territory due to circumstances beyond their control while in transit have been omitted from the following analysis. Their knowledge of Hong Kong is deemed of little relevance to understanding the agency of travellers in actively selecting Hong Kong as their final destination. For example, in the case of participants who were prevented from continuing their journey by immigration officials at the airport, the only reason they gave for remaining in Hong Kong was that they did not want to be returned to their country of origin. A handful had the UNHCR emergency telephone number to be used precisely in the event that some problem occurred in transit. The others learnt either from immigration officials or fellow detainees that they could seek protection in the territory while in custody.

In all other cases, a clear trend was noticeable. Of course, there are significant exceptions to the following, but in general terms, while the participants who arrived in earlier years appeared less aware of their travel arrangements and destination, usually having little or no knowledge of Hong Kong, more recent arrivals seemed to have a greater awareness of their circumstances and, at times, specific reasons for travelling to the territory. Second, the findings presented subsequently do not appear to differ markedly from the results of similar research conducted in Europe, especially in terms of asylum seekers' perceptions of the human rights policies, welfare support provisions and economic prosperity in destination countries (Block et al. 2011; Zimmermann 2009b; Robinson and Segrott 2002). Nonetheless, specific to the context of Hong Kong it emerged that the perception of less intrusive police enforcement in the city influenced the decision making of both would-be migrants and the agents who organized their journey. To illustrate the discussion that follows, Figure 3.2 groups the kinds of information that were found to have a greater influence on the decision to go to Hong Kong.

Exemplary of the people who tend to have little or no knowledge of their destination, a number of participants from Africa and Sri Lanka, who arrived between 2004 and 2006 when entry into Hong Kong was easier, explained that their only knowledge of Hong Kong was that entry into the territory was visa free. Furthermore, some of these participants did not intend to stay in Hong Kong, as they had been told China would be their destination. Upon landing in the city, however, their plans changed. One participant noted that he was supposed to travel to the UNHCR office in China but changed his plans: 'I was sitting on the plane next to a person from Ghana who said . . . I had better stay in Hong Kong because it was safer' (African participant, 17). Another participant similarly stated that his initial plan was to travel to China, as advised by the travel agency that booked his ticket. Yet once he landed in Hong Kong, instead of continuing the journey as planned, he realized he had travelled already long and far enough to what appeared to him a relatively safe city; rather than moving on to a place he did not know, he chose

Figure 3.2 Facilitators of migration to Hong Kong

124 *Crossing borders into Hong Kong*

to remain in Hong Kong. In this case, the decision to stay was consequential also on learning that there was a UNHCR office in the city, which made continuing the journey to China to seek asylum a pointless endeavour.

Likewise, the participants who had been deceived and abandoned in the territory generally had no understanding of Hong Kong prior to their arrival. As Paul, a Somali participant, explained:

> Hong Kong is not a destination for asylum seekers because no one knows about Hong Kong, that here is a developed country and it is peaceful. And even if it was so, no one thinks that they can get a life in Hong Kong. When you go out from my country you want to go to a place where you can legally stay, you can work and have a life. (African participant, 70)

Among the participants who said that they acquired some information before commencing their travels, it appears that they only had a very limited understanding of the city, giving them at best an approximation of what to expect. The great variety of experiences narrated can be summarized and explained by the following findings.

First, the importance of the economic link between China and Africa in establishing networks now used for refugee flight has become evident in recent years. Whether participants were prompted to travel to Hong Kong or China by their agents and acquaintances, many interviewees from African countries assumed that the increased number of Chinese people in Africa was related to the parallel economic growth of China, as testified, for example, by the grandeur displayed at the 2008 Beijing Olympics. On this point, Bodomo (2010) argues that Guangzhou is home to an estimated 100,000 Africans who make a living mostly as tourists and overstayers by trading cheap Chinese-manufactured garments and electronics with their country (Yang 2012; Haugen 2012). Indeed, African traders in Guangzhou play a significant role in establishing links that go beyond purely economic interests. It is plausible that, on the one hand, the greater the number of Africans who go to Hong Kong and China for business-related trips, the more Africans at home will be introduced to this unknown region through either the stories they hear from their co-nationals or the cheap imported goods that appear in the local markets. On the other hand, the more China and Hong Kong become known as developed destinations in which people appear to be making good profits, the more prospective travellers will be inclined to travel to these two destinations. As an example, a young man from a West African country, who had recently arrived in the territory at the time of our interview, described his knowledge of Hong Kong as follows:

> I knew Hong Kong was in China, but nothing more than that. I knew that many women in my country go to China to buy goods and later sell them at home. . . . I also knew that many of my co-nationals are in China, and so the officer who helped me arrange my visa said that I could go there and meet some of them. I could explain my problems and see whether they could do something for me. (African participant, 04)

Crossing borders into Hong Kong 125

Travel to Hong Kong was also influenced by previous travel experiences in the former British colony, which also shaped decisions regarding asylum. For instance, analogous to the migration trajectories of other African participants, one interviewee explained how he had gone to Hong Kong on a business trip to buy mobile phones before returning to the territory a second time to seek asylum. He said that what he knew about Hong Kong was strictly related to business. When he finished his studies at school, he looked for opportunities for work. He soon realized that many people appeared to make huge profits by trading mobile phones, and he wanted to do the same. This participant then began making frequent visits to a particular shop to ingratiate himself with the owner and learn about his business. After some time he learnt that the owner used to make short trips to Hong Kong. He borrowed money and travelled to Hong Kong on a seven-day visa to get started in the same business. He bought two boxes of phones, which he carried home. He sold the phones at a price four times higher than that he had paid for them. This participant explained that he had intended to continue this business, but for some reason, he received death threats from his neighbours, forcing him to seek shelter abroad. In these circumstances, Hong Kong appeared to be the obvious destination to stay temporarily and consider his options for the future, while still having the opportunity to continue his business. During his previous stay, he had learnt that many Africans who resided in the territory were relatively untroubled by the police.

Second, while information about the economic development, business opportunities, tenuous law enforcement and the presence of co-nationals in Hong Kong has spread quickly throughout Africa, expanding or opening new routes into China, business relations between China/Hong Kong and developing countries that enabled this information to flow are certainly not limited to the African continent. As has already been revealed, many of the agents and friends who facilitated the migration of Bangladeshi and Sri Lankan participants were businessmen who travel to Hong Kong to trade mobile phones and other items. These people were the participants' major source of information. The South Asian participants who had some knowledge of Hong Kong had usually been informed that there were a sizeable number of their co-nationals in the territory who could help them if the need arose. In addition, and probably most importantly, they were told that they could stay in Hong Kong, whether legally or not, and manage to have a reasonable life, occasionally finding work to sustain a living. While jobs were rarely arranged, some participants knew that earning basic salaries would not be too difficult. Furthermore, reports of the 'humane' treatment of overstayers by police in Hong Kong were largely shared for the benefit of travellers. It is clear that the more accessible and less troubled that living in a developed country is, the more attractive that destination will become for people in flight situations. In this context, legal status becomes less relevant per se when the opportunity to remain in the territory is ensured regardless, and the means to make a livelihood are de facto granted by relatively lenient law enforcement (see Chapter 5). In the minds of several participants and most likely their agents, legal status, asylum and stay were largely conceived as synonymous. In practice, their meaning overlapped,

126   *Crossing borders into Hong Kong*

revealing the objective of 'working and having a life', as Somali participant Paul noted.

The following conversation with a long-time asylum seeker illustrates the kind of knowledge that is typically deemed relevant when making the decision about a destination and how this knowledge is shared:

Did you go to Hong Kong by yourself?
Yes I travelled by myself.
Did anyone help you arrange the flight ticket and the papers you needed?
Actually, one person suggested how to do it, what to do, how to talk to Immigration. He only suggested me.
How did you know this person?
That person used to go to Hong Kong to buy things like watches and mobile phones to sell in Bangladesh, so he had experience about going there. He told me that if I wanted to go somewhere, Hong Kong was a good place. It was safe and I could live there. . . . At that time I didn't have enough idea about visas, about the stay, how many days I was allowed – I only knew what that person in my country told me. He said that I could go to Hong Kong and if my visa expired I could go to China, just that. . . . Actually at that time I didn't have many choices. If I wanted to go to other countries it was expensive, but going to Hong Kong is cheaper because you only need the air ticket. This person told me how to do it. He said it was good and I could stay. He also said that if I overstayed, police would not send me back, and they will not beat you. Police was good, and even if you overstay and they catch you, they will let you go. He said this, so I came.
How did you think you would sustain your living?
Before, I didn't know. I didn't know much about Hong Kong. My parents gave me some money. I had maybe US$500. That person said I could use this money for how long I needed to find a place to stay. After that he said I could find some other way to stay, maybe meeting some friends or other persons; anything could be arranged. I just needed to try.
Did you think you could find some work?
Yes, at that time I thought about it. One friend was staying here so I thought I could stay and find something to do, just to support myself. I thought people don't die of starvation [in a developed country]. (Bangladeshi participant, 60)

Third, beyond possessing the knowledge that Hong Kong was a place where people could stay for a relatively long period of time, the Bangladeshi participants also appeared to be exceptionally well informed about the asylum policies in the territory. In particular, they knew that it would be relatively easy to access government assistance in terms of food, accommodation and medical services. While most of these participants said that they were told of these opportunities by friends in Hong Kong, their families in their home village or agents, one participant also mentioned that he found this information in a national newspaper in his home country. He said that he read that the Hong Kong Government was helping many Bangladeshis in difficulty by providing them with free services. He later enquired about this at a travel agency, and when he confirmed the news he decided to go to Hong Kong. However, on this point, it is necessary to add that very few participants knew what the ISS was, how services could be accessed or how such service provision related to asylum. Additionally, no one was well informed regarding the extent of assistance provided to asylum applicants. Many of them indeed lamented that what they experienced in Hong Kong did not correspond to the expectations they had developed in their country based on the information obtained prior to their departure. This point thus confutes the rationale supporting the current welfare system for asylum seekers in Hong Kong. Official policy states that assistance be provided in-kind and to a very minimal degree, with the aim of preventing destitution but avoiding the 'magnet effect' of encouraging people to travel to Hong Kong in search of such services (see Chapter 2). When information is conveyed by unreliable or uninformed third parties, deterrent methods lose their function and simply become means to punish those who utilize such services.

Finally, an important point to highlight here concerns the knowledge about Hong Kong as a former British colony. A number of participants said that they either had learnt in school or had been told by friends and agents that Hong Kong is a place that is strongly influenced by the UK, and as such where it is possible to settle and receive 'humanitarian help'. As a former colony, the territory was thought of as governed by the rule of law, where the medium of communication was English. As one interviewee further clarified: 'In Africa there are no human rights. Even China is a communist country where there are no human rights. But someone told me that Hong Kong was a former colony of England. Hong Kong had an administration structure like England, so I said OK' (African participant, 65).

In this regard, African asylum seekers appeared to be more knowledgeable about asylum and human rights than their South Asian counterparts. For some, Hong Kong was seen as the perfect alternative location to more difficult-to-reach Western destinations. For others, although travel to the former did not exclude efforts to reach the latter, Hong Kong was a place where they could make a living and acquire legal documents. Some participants had been informed that they would receive a Hong Kong ID card upon arrival and would later either be resettled in Canada or after seven years become Hong Kong permanent residents. Obviously, such information was at best misleading, as the only ID the participants were entitled to receive as overstayers was the 'recognizance paper', which attested to their illegal status and consequently excluded them from the seven-year residency rule. Resettlement, instead, was dependent on the outcome of refugee screening determination procedures.

Searching for a destination overseas: What is expected of Hong Kong

The pre-migration information and the many promises made to participants by agents and other third parties, whether with the intent of profiting from their migration or benevolently helping them to travel to a safe destination, certainly contributed to building up travellers' expectations, and inducing them to head to Hong Kong. Such information concerned the liberal political culture of the former colony, the rule of law, the flourishing business opportunities that have attracted their co-nationals and the possibility of staying relatively safely, far from the problems at home. Likewise, the promises that prompted the decision to migrate often described long-term stay in a 'good' place and certainties related to asylum and resettlement, government assistance and economic gain.

In reality, according to the accounts of many participants from both Africa and South Asia, the information they possessed about Hong Kong was not always as influential on their decision making process as might be assumed. This is not to say that the migration of these asylum seekers was largely without aim. However, it is possible to identify in the migratory trajectories of these people a sort of simplistic vision of their movement based on the assumption that any destination would do as long as it were known to be developed and therefore seen to offer the chance of a better life. This supports the findings of research conducted by Robinson and Segrott (2002), from which it clearly emerged that asylum seekers long for safe and prosperous places, with little distinction made between one and another. In other words, all Western countries are perceived as desirable destinations because they are imagined to be safe and wealthy, regardless of the preferences for certain countries that may at times exist (Barsky 2000).

Whatever reasons the participants had for fleeing their countries of origin, it is evident that the socioeconomic conditions in the destination country were important factors in raising their expectations and, consequently, in shaping their migration decisions. The participants held an impression of life in developed countries as far better than life at home. For those bound for Hong Kong, the former colony was understood to be a developed country and therefore in the same category as Western states. In this regard, while marginal in influencing the participants' motivation to travel, the information they gathered before departure seems important in relation to confirming that Hong Kong has become one of a few destinations where it is possible to achieve security and a better standard of living, yet can also be relatively easily reached and costs relatively little to travel there.

As one participant explained, for many travellers who flee either or both political persecution and economic hardship, the hardest part of their migration is managing to arrive in a rich country. What directs them towards one destination or another is not necessarily related to the specific information they have about the destination, but rather the assumption that life in that country cannot be but superior. One participant described how, when he was in his home country, facing the need to leave, he made plans to go to Italy. As he recounted:

> I decided to go to Africa and then by sea to Italy. It is dangerous. But dangerous will do, because you will enjoy your life afterwards. Many people die while they try, but life is worse at home. We know about the journey to Italy. We know about the ferries. I knew all. Still, I had to go. . . . Hong Kong nowadays is a well-known destination too. . . . In my country there are people who are announcing they can send you to Hong Kong. And those people who want

Crossing borders into Hong Kong 129

to go don't ask them if they are able to employ them. Only enter into Hong Kong is OK. Like me, I was thinking that only getting into Europe was OK. It would solve half of my problems. People in South Asia are like this. They will enter Hong Kong if they can. And once there, they believe they will find the way. (Pakistani participant, 76a)

This type of scenario was portrayed by many participants, who travelled with the intention of improving their life either by permanently migrating overseas, and eventually bringing their family to join them in the host country, or by returning home at a later stage if circumstances allowed them to achieve that better life. In this regard, a significant difference emerged. While the South Asian and Bangladeshi participants in particular tended to see their migration as fairly temporary, at least at first limited in duration to the achievement of their initial objectives, the African and Tamil Sri Lankan participants appeared to see their movement as more permanent, even in the event that they maintained stable economic and political links with their home country. When the participants were questioned about how long they had intended to stay overseas when they first decided to leave their country, and whether or how that decision changed in exile, the Africans said that while no initial time frame was determined, they had had only a vague idea of returning. The majority of African participants said that what impacted their decision was that they had had no hope in their country, as corruption, violence and abuse were too widespread to conduct a normal life. When a young Somali participant was asked about whether he had family in his country, he surprisingly replied, 'Yes, I have two sisters, they are still alive' (African participant, 27). Many other participants commented that the violence in their countries had reached such a level that death was a daily occurrence. Many interviewees had either witnessed or personally experienced life-threatening events, leaving psychological scars that contributed to their desire to seek a better life overseas. One Pakistani asylum seeker, for example, recalled that life in his country was marked by constant reports of killings, bomb explosions and gun confrontations, out of which he lost friends. Similarly, the Bangladeshi participants narrated personal stories of people not being protected by the authorities, as police are either bribed to frame a rival or rarely intervene in a timely manner, often only taking action days after the criminal offence has occurred.

Of course, such difficult experiences and conditions meant that the participants tended to believe that a radically different situation could be found elsewhere. Lack of protection and unemployment at home indeed shaped the predisposition to move to any place where it was believed that human rights, education, work opportunities, government assistance and asylum would be ensured for everyone. Perhaps it is in this light that we can best understand the excessively demanding attitude of certain asylum seekers about which NGO workers in Hong Kong often lamented when dealing with their clients (see Chapter 4). When asylum seekers see the collision of their dreams of freedom, equality and opportunities with the border that their host society erects to confine and exclude them (see Chapter 2), they are often unable to accept the stark reality. Thus, for example, the necessity of queuing for services to which they think they are entitled is seen as a 'problem'. Such circumstances would appear to them appropriate within 'sub-standard' realities, to be expected in their countries of origin, but not in developed states. Such circumstances contradict the participants' preconceptions of 'developed' countries, thus becoming a source of frustration.

The fact that many of the South Asian participants initially thought of their migration as temporary can perhaps best be understood in light of the political situation in their countries, where radical changes in government following an election are not uncommon, and of the cultural bonds between members of extended families. Ullah (2010) argues that for Bangladeshis the decision to leave is often up to the head of the family, whether the father, brother or uncle, who then makes arrangements to find the money to cover the journey. The participants in this study described similar circumstances. To finance their travel, ancestral land was sold together with small businesses, shops, tractors, livestock and other property. Money was sometimes also sourced from moneylenders. Similar practices were observed among the Somali and Sri Lankan participants, who often mortgaged their house or traded it with the agent. The generally low level of education and working experience prior to departure among the participants probably impacted on this process of obtaining financial resources. The South Asian and Somali participants, together with a large number of the African asylum seekers interviewed, confirmed that prior to their departure they were either unemployed or were only occasionally working, often on family land or in small businesses. The African participants, however, generally possessed greater financial resources, and the decision to leave was normally made solely by the asylum seeker. As I was told, 'the situation in Africa is not stable, and due to political and economic problems we need to seek our way out to take care of our future' (African participant, 83e). The participants reported that high unemployment, corruption and violence affected their lives to the extent that migration was the only practical alternative: 'I told my family that I wanted to go. They said it was fine, because they know how difficult it is' (African participant, 83e).

The asylum seekers' socio-demographic background and the method used to finance their migration appear to have greatly impacted their expectations of economic gain and subsequent decisions regarding voluntary return to their country of origin (Ullah 2010). Few of the interviewees believed that they would return home any time soon, despite the fact that their initial plans might only have included a short stay overseas. This was due partly to the unchanging political and personal situations at home, and partly to the fact that the costs related to migration had not been recovered, making it unviable for them to return home as they would be empty handed. If migration is often a sort of investment (Samers 2010), it is understandable that a number of the participants felt compelled to remain in Hong Kong, despite their wish to return home, when their expectations regarding work opportunities in Hong Kong were crushed by the reality of low salaries that did not suffice to repay the money they had borrowed to fund their travel, often at exorbitant interest rates. At the same time, even the participants who had not borrowed money to finance their journey believed that returning home without savings would signify their failure, as people at home believed that whoever goes overseas becomes rich. Others found that life in Hong Kong, despite its problems, was still better than life in their country of origin and wished to stay longer. In particular, the lower the migrant's economic and social status at home, the more life in Hong Kong appeared to be an improvement, even when remittances could rarely be sent home. If family in the country of origin was missed at times, the peaceful and increasingly familiar surroundings in Hong Kong helped to alleviate this loss.

In connection to this, I was surprised when those participants who had sons and brothers of an age to migrate commented that they were considering ways to assist their relatives to leave their home country. Despite the difficulties faced in Hong Kong, the participants all believed that life overseas was better and necessary. They realized, however, that unauthorized travel would bring few advantages, especially in Hong Kong. A Bangladeshi interviewee, for example, said that he was planning to send his brother to Australia to attain an education with the money he had earned from illegally running a business in Hong Kong. Similarly, an African father of two was hoping to enable his sons to study in a developed country with the money he thought he would receive from the Hong Kong ImmD to compensate for his unlawful detention. Yet another participant explained that because of his problems in his home country, his son was facing discrimination, and regardless of whether money had to be spent, it was better for him to travel overseas than to another part of the country, where family networks were nonexistent and living costs very high.

In this regard, it appears that accessing the asylum system was not the sole method used by the participants to ensure their safety. Rather, it may be possible to claim the opposite, as many participants had never even heard of asylum before leaving their home country. For South Asians in particular, migration for study and labour migration were the only forms of travel of which they were aware. It is understandable that when their circumstances worsened at home, a few participants sought working opportunities overseas. Some of them travelled to the Middle East, while others attempted to enter Europe or other countries where they became acquainted with the asylum system. After some returned home and faced the same problems they had previously, they chose to travel to Hong Kong. In doing so, their thinking was that in Hong Kong they would find similar circumstances in terms of screening mechanisms, support and work opportunities to those found in other Western destinations. However, this expectation was largely not realized, not only because the laws prevented them from working, but also because the long period of time they had to wait for their claim to be decided forced them into a state of duress which affected their livelihoods (see Chapters 4 and 5).

In conclusion, the participants justified their migration to Hong Kong primarily by citing their need to find a safe place where they could rebuild their life and enjoy a peaceful existence, as can any other person in a developed country. At the same time, they wanted to improve their status, whether through temporary or permanent migration. If some participants, especially those who were aware of the UNHCR and its purpose, relied on the hope that they would be helped to build their future if they gained asylum, others stated that supporting themselves through work was an important goal. Achieving an education and economic gain to support their family, being independent and joining their relatives were also

132　*Crossing borders into Hong Kong*

common expectations. However, while they were important for the interviewees, these aims were not dependent upon the information they possessed about Hong Kong prior to departure. Conversely, expectations more often appeared based on the lack of opportunities and other problems at home rather than any precise knowledge of the conditions in Hong Kong. What seemed to have driven the participants to Hong Kong was the belief that they would manage their life in the territory, as the partial or inaccurate information they did possess seemed to broadly confirm that they would achieve their objectives.

From this perspective, socioeconomic betterment and safety concerns largely conflated, as the vast majority of the interviewees saw them as inextricably intertwined. Nonetheless, dreams and expectations of attaining a normal life through migration collided in Hong Kong with public attitudes and inflexible policy, which represented asylum seekers' desires and economic engagement as suspicious or even criminal. Quoting from my field notes, a final example, provided subsequently, powerfully reiterates the arguments made previously:

> One college-educated participant affirmed that he felt useless in Hong Kong. He said that he had two arms, two legs, two eyes, and was in all respects similar to a local resident, but was forbidden from making any meaningful contact with the host society. He was frustrated because in his home country people like him have no significant opportunities to utilize their talent. On the contrary, they are persecuted by those who feel threatened by younger and brighter rivals. Travelling overseas became his dream, as the land of opportunities awaited him. In Hong Kong, however, he found a different reality. Life in the territory was still better than life at home though, because he was assisted by the government, he found some work to cover his expenses, he made friends, had a girlfriend, and life went on without too much trouble. On the downside, his stay was approaching its end. New CAT screening procedures introduced in December 2009 put a number of asylum seekers through a very quick process, ending with their almost certain repatriation. He told me that he was afraid that his number would soon be called and he would be rejected after a few interviews, because the government was now taking a tough stance on dealing with CAT cases. He believed that this was one of the reasons why the attractiveness of Hong Kong as a destination had diminished in the eyes of his co-nationals. Indeed, if one cannot at a minimum live safely in a destination country, with some prospect of improvement, it is difficult to justify spending a substantial quantity of money on travel, which strains limited family financial resources.

Conclusion

The purpose of this chapter has been to explore the vulnerability of asylum seekers in relation to the reasons why Hong Kong has become a preferred destination in which to seek refuge for people whose voices often go unheeded in debates about asylum seeking. In so doing, the chapter has revealed two major points that

Crossing borders into Hong Kong 133

consistently emerged from this investigation. First, many of the stories presented previously may understandably raise concerns about possible asylum abuse, in light of both the methods of entry adopted, which clearly reflect increased unauthorized border crossing, and the expectations generated by third parties for their own personal gain. It is clear, however, that asylum seekers' perceptions of safety rarely coincide with the assumptions that structure asylum systems and dominate the public debate. Second, by analyzing the methods of border crossing used, the increasing illegality that surrounds them and the processes by which destinations are chosen, this chapter has highlighted Hong Kong's global reach over peripheral societies and its likely impact on populations distant by culture, economic attainment and geography (Mathews 2011). Asylum seekers wish to travel from troubled areas of the periphery to the prosperous core. Hong Kong has emerged as a core destination in all respects similar to liberal and safe Western countries that have high standards of living. Indeed, as the borders of the core and well-known states of Europe, North America and Australia become increasingly secured, asylum seekers are driven to other economically booming countries that were previously at their periphery. As the status of these destinations rises, and they become better known overseas, expectations of easier entry and a better future to be attained there also rise, causing new destinations to become less welcoming places for particular categories of traveller. In the case of Hong Kong, this may explain why the majority of the most recent arrivals had transited in China for varied lengths of time, although China and Hong Kong were not always their intended destinations.

This analysis further confirms that expectations relating to economic and sociopolitical betterment affect routes of refugee mobility (Zimmermann 2009a, 2009b). The narratives explored previously demonstrate that safety and security are strictly related to endogenous conditions in countries of origin and destination. With rising chaos, corruption, economic deprivation and violence in origin countries, there is a concomitant decrease in levels of safety and security (Schmeidl 1997, 2001). It makes sense that people will seek to escape socio-politically unstable and dangerous conditions in troubled countries by travelling to places that are expected to be politically stable, socially responsible and economically developed (Robinson and Segrott 2002). To this end, co-national communities and international trading activities between destination and origin countries inform and support the journeys of prospective migrants. Additionally, while the findings presented in this chapter may at times support the rationale for government policy aimed at deterring arrivals, the illegalization of certain categories of border crosser does not appear to act as a deterrent as it does the traveller's perception of the level of law enforcement against unauthorized migrants in countries of destination. In other words, the harder it is for migrants to stay in a country, the less attractive that country will be. Nonetheless, the deterrent effect of border control measures is largely dependent on the quality of information travellers possess and the means such policy relies on to disseminate its message. It is apparent that chance plays a far greater part in shaping migration flows, as information on government efforts to secure their borders often does not reach external audiences. The reasons why this obvious

134 *Crossing borders into Hong Kong*

incongruity materializes in Hong Kong and elsewhere (cf. De Genova 2002; Calavita 2005) form the core of my inquiry in the following chapters.

Another notable finding is that deterrent and risk-reducing border control measures raise the cost of migration and the level of harm to which certain travellers are exposed (Weber and Pickering 2011). Lured by the evident profitability of border crossing activities, a considerable number of unprofessional agents have turned to assisting asylum seekers to travel to Hong Kong. If this enables their clients to flee potentially life-threatening situations, the minimal structural organization of such networks has serious implications for both the number and composition of people going to Hong Kong and for their well-being upon arrival. While at the macro-level third parties seem to operate as a business (Salt and Stein 1997), with migrants, their families, smugglers and even the receiving society sharing the profits (see Chapters 4 and 5), at the micro-level migration often occurs at the expense of asylum seekers. Travellers are in many cases either abandoned in countries they do not choose, finding themselves unable to move further and unwilling to return home due to a lack of money, or face a great deal of hardship upon arrival, particularly as important information about asylum is culpably withheld. In addition, they may journey perilous routes, draining family resources, in turn possibly impacting the migration opportunities available to other family members who may equally be in need of escape. The 'structural violence' of the border reverses the risk certain migrants are believed to pose to society by exaggerating their deviancy, thus amplifying the risk they must take to cross the border, which may not result in injury or death but will certainly lead to their social exclusion (cf. Weber and Pickering 2011).

It is in this context that the rationale underlying the current visa regime can be challenged. As it is structured, the system has serious consequences for asylum seekers and for the states that prevent their entry. If the intention of travellers is not discernible from their passport, visa or financial resources (Neumayer 2006; Salter 2004), it is concerning that while the poorest and perhaps the most honest people in developing countries are denied freedom of movement, the same freedom can easily be bought by others who have the networks and financial means to acquire a new identity which the richest countries consider better suited to their security and economic needs. If this is true for asylum seekers, the same is especially true for those whose journey may hide terrorist and other intentions. Contrary to the expectations of their governments, the countries that have the most stringent visa regimes seem to cause heightened insecurity at their borders. Moreover, while primarily affecting the most vulnerable asylum seekers, these visa regimes alter the direction of refugee flows by diverting them to alternative destinations where resources may be scarcer and their rights not always granted.

Notes

1 Since 11 December 2006, Bangladeshi nationals who want to enter Hong Kong for whatever reason have needed a visa. In the previous year, visa requirements were made stricter for nationals of Cote d'Ivoire, the Democratic Republic of the Congo, Ethiopia,

Sri Lanka and Somalia, while in 2006 the same policy was applied to nationals of Togo and the Republic of Congo. Since the beginning of 2007, even Ghanaians have required visas for entry to Hong Kong. Available at: www.immd.gov.hk/ehtml/press_releases.htm.

2 Available at: www.hkairport2030.com/en/masterplan/demand_hkia.html.

3 There was at the time of my fieldwork, and there currently is to my knowledge, a lack of available data concerning the nature and content of the agreements that supposedly exist between immigration authorities and the airline companies that transit Hong Kong in relation to the return to the country of departure of those individuals who are denied entry into Hong Kong. It is understood that Bangladeshi and other nationality arrivals are generally returned as soon as is feasible and a large number of travellers reportedly transit at the airport detention facilities waiting for their flight. However, immigration authorities may investigate the use of forged travel documents and human smuggling activities. As in the case of Somali arrivals, who are generally found without travel documentation, and rarely know their whereabouts, removal actions are often lengthy and indeed suspended when an application for asylum is made.

References

Akcapar, S. K. (2006) 'Conversion as a Migration Strategy in Transit Country: Iranian Shiites Becoming Christians in Turkey', *International Migration Review*, 40(4): 817–853.

Akcapar, S. K. (2009) 'Re-thinking Migrant's Networks and Social Capital: A Case Study of Iranians in Turkey', *International Migration*, 48(2): 161–196.

Andreas, P. (2000) *Border Games: Policing the U.S.-Mexico Divide*, Ithaca: Cornell University Press.

Andrijasevic, R. (2010) *Migration, Agency and Citizenship in Sex Trafficking*, Houndmills: Palgrave Macmillan.

Atfield, G., Brahmbhatt, K. and O'Toole, T. (2007) *Refugees' Experiences of Integration*, Birmingham: Refugee Council and University of Birmingham. Viewed 13 May 2009: www.refugeecouncil.org.uk/NR/rdonlyres/7FD44ADF-5270–4148–91BF-37790DBAA940/0/Integrationresearchreport.pdf

Barsky, R. F. (2000) *Arguing and Justifying: Assessing the Convention Refugees' Choice of Moment, Motive and Host Country*, Aldershot: Ashgate.

Betts, A. (2010) 'The Refugee Regime Complex', *Refugee Survey Quarterly*, 29(1): 12–37.

Bigo, D. (2002) 'Security and Immigration: Toward a Critique of the Governmentality of Unease', *Alternatives*, 27: 63–92.

Block, A., Sigona, N. and Zetter, R. (2011) 'Migration Routes and Strategies of Young Undocumented Migrants in England: A Qualitative Perspective', *Ethnic and Racial Studies*, 34(8): 1286–1302.

Böcker, A. and Havinga T. (1998) *Asylum Migration to the European Union: Patterns of Origin and Destination*, Luxembourg: Office for Official Publications of the European Communities.

Bodomo, A. B. (2010) 'The African Trading Community in Guangzhou: An Emerging Bridge for Africa-China Relations', *China Quarterly*, 203: 693–707.

Bodomo, A. B. (2011) 'The African Traveler and the Chinese Customs Official: Ethnic Minority Profiling at Border Check Points in Hong Kong and China', Presented at *Recognition and the Politics of Identity and Inclusion in the 21st Century: Managing Diversity in Plural Societies*, Hong Kong, 28 April.

Boyd, M. (1989) 'Family and Personal Networks in Migration', *International Migration Review*, 23(3): 638–670.

136 *Crossing borders into Hong Kong*

Calavita, K. (2005) *Immigrants at the Margins: Law, Race and Exclusion in Southern Europe*, Cambridge: Cambridge University Press.

China Economic Review (2003) 'Up, Up, Up and Away', 1 January. Viewed 1 June 2013: www.chinaeconomicreview.com/node/30367

Collyer, M. (2005) 'When Do Social Networks Fail to Explain Migration? Accounting for the Movement of Algerian Asylum-Seekers to the UK', *Journal of Ethnic and Migration Studies*, 31(4): 699–718.

Dauvergne, C. (2008) *Making People Illegal: What Globalization Means for Migration and Law*, Cambridge: Cambridge University Press.

De Genova, N. P. (2002) 'Migrant "Illegality" and Deportability in Everyday Life', *Annual Review of Anthropology*, 31: 419–447.

Gerard, A. (2014) *The Securitization of Migration and Refugee Women*, Abingdon: Routledge.

Gilbert, A. and Koser, K. (2006) 'Coming to the UK: What Do Asylum-Seekers Know about the UK before Arrival?', *Journal of Ethnic and Migration Studies*, 32(7): 1209–1225.

Goodman, J. L. (1981) 'Information, Uncertainty, and the Microeconomic Model of Migration Decision Making', in G. F. De Jong and R. W. Gardner (Eds.) *Migration Decision Making: Multidisciplinary Approaches to Microlevel Studies in Developed and Developing Countries*, New York: Pergamon Press: 130–148.

Guild, E. (2009) *Security and Migration in the 21st Century*, Cambridge: Polity Press.

Harpviken, K. B. (2009) *Social Networks and Migration in Wartime Afghanistan*, Houndmills: Palgrave Macmillan.

Haugen, H. Ø. (2012) 'Nigerians in China: A Second State of Immobility', *International Migration*, 50(2): 65–80.

Huysmans, J. (2000) 'The European Union and the Securitization of Migration', *Journal of Common Market Studies*, 38(5): 751–777.

Içduygu, A. and Toktas, S. (2002) 'How Do Smuggling and Trafficking Operate via Irregular Border Crossing in the Middle East?', *International Migration*, 40(6): 25–52.

Immigration Department (ImmD) (2013) *Immigration Department Review 2012*, Hong Kong: Author. Viewed 25 June 2013: www.immd.gov.hk/en/press/press-releases/2013 0208.html

Ip, C. (2011) 'Stateless and Stuck on the Way to Samoa', *South China Morning Post*, 19 June. Viewed 19 June 2011: www.scmp.com/article/971009/stateless-and-stuck-way-samoa

Khosravi, S. (2010) *'Illegal Traveller': An Auto-Ethnography of Borders*, Houndmills: Palgrave Macmillan.

Koser, K. (1997) 'Social Networks and the Asylum Cycle: The Case of Iranians in the Netherlands', *International Migration Review*, 31(3): 591–611.

Koser, K. (2000) 'Asylum Policies, Trafficking and Vulnerability', *International Migration*, special issue 1: 91–111.

Koser, K. (2009) 'The Economics of Smuggling People', *Refugee Transition*, 23: 10–13.

Koser, K. and Pinkerton, C. (2002) *The Social Networks of Asylum Seekers and the Dissemination of Information about Countries of Asylum*, London: Home Office. Viewed 1 March 2009: www.homeoffice.gov.uk/rds/pdfs2/socialnetwork.pdf

Massey, D., Alarcon, R., Durand, J. and Gonzalez, H. (1987) *Return to Aztlan: The Social Process of Transnational Migration from Western Mexico*, Berkeley: University of California Press.

Massey, D. S., Arango, J., Hugo, G., Kouaouci, A., Pellegrino, A. and Taylor, J. E. (1993) 'Theories of International Migration: A Review and Appraisal', *Population and Development Review*, 19(3): 431–466.

Crossing borders into Hong Kong 137

Mathews, G. (2011) *Ghetto at the Center of the World: Chungking Mansions, Hong Kong*, Chicago: The University of Chicago Press.

Mountz, A. (2010) *Seeking Asylum: Human Smuggling and Bureaucracy at the Border*, Minneapolis: University of Minnesota Press.

Neumayer, E. (2006) 'Unequal Access to Foreign Spaces: How States Use Visa Restrictions to Regulate Mobility in a Globalized World', *Transactions of the Institute of British Geographers*, 31(1): 72–84.

Oelgemöller, C. (2011) ' "Transit" and "Suspension": Migration Management or the Metamorphosis of Asylum Seekers into Illegal Immigrants', *Journal of Ethnic and Migration Studies*, 37(3): 407–424.

Papadopoulou-Kourkouta, A. (2008) Transit Migration: The Missing Link between Emigration and Settlement, Houndmills: Palgrave Macmillan.

Patel, N. (2008) 'Asylum Seekers Conned', The Standard, 21 January. Viewed 21 January 2008: www.thestandard.com.hk/archive_news_detail.asp?pp_cat=12&art_id=60414& sid=17205503&con_type=1&archive_d_str=20080121

Pickering, S. and Weber, L. (2006) (Eds.) Borders, Mobility and Technologies of Control, Dordrecht: Springer.

Richmond, A. H. (1988) 'Sociological Theory of International Migration: The Case of Refugees', *Current Sociology*, 36(7): 7–26.

Richmond, A. H. (1993) 'Reactive Migration: Sociological Perspectives on Refugee Movements', *Journal of Refugee Studies*, 6(1): 7–24.

Robinson, V. and Segrott, J. (2002) *Understanding the Decision-Making of Asylum Seekers*, Research Study No. 243, London: Home Office. Viewed 23 March 2009: www.homeoffice.gov.uk/rds/pdfs2/hors243.pdf

Sadiq, K. (2009) *Paper Citizens: How Illegal Immigrants Acquire Citizenship in Developing Countries*, Oxford: Oxford University Press.

Salt, J. and Stein, J. (1997) 'Migration as a Business: The Case of Trafficking', *International Migration*, 35(4): 467–494.

Salter, M. B. (2004) 'Passports, Mobility, and Security: How Smart Can the Border Be?', *International Studies Perspectives*, 5: 71–91.

Samers, M. (2010) *Migration*, London: Routledge.

Schmeidl, S. (1997) 'Exploring the Causes of Forced Migration: A Pooled Time-Series Analysis, 1971–1990', *Social Science Quarterly*, 78(2): 284–308.

Schmeidl, S. (2001) 'Conflict and Forced Migration: A Quantitative Review, 1964–1995', in A. R. Zolberg and P. M. Benda (Eds.) *Global Migrants Global Refugees: Problems and Solutions*, New York: Berghahn Books: 62–94.

Smith, D. and Timberlake, M. (2002) 'Hierarchies of Dominance among World Cities: A Network Approach', in S. Sassen (Ed.) *Global Networks, Linked Cities*, New York: Routledge: 117–141.

Thielemann, E. R. (2003) *Why EU Policy Harmonisation Undermines Refugee Burden-Sharing*, National Europe Centre Paper No. 101, Canberra: Australian National University.

Torpey, J. (2000) *The Invention of the Passport: Surveillance, Citizenship and the State*, Cambridge: Cambridge University Press.

Ullah, A. A. (2010) *Rationalizing Migration Decisions: Labour Migrants in East and South-East Asia*, Aldershot: Ashgate.

Van Hear, N. (1998) *New Diasporas: The Mass Exodus, Dispersal and Regrouping of Migrant Communities*, London: UCL Press.

van Liempt, I. and Doomernick, J. (2006) 'Migrant's Agency in the Smuggling Process: The Perspectives of Smuggled Migrants in the Netherlands', *International Migration*, 44(4): 165–189.

138　*Crossing borders into Hong Kong*

van Munster, R. (2009) *Securitizing Immigration: The Politics of Risk in the EU*, New York: Palgrave Macmillan.

Vision First (2011) *In Memory of Awil*, 24 July. Viewed 24 July 2011: http://visionfirstnow.org/2011/07/24/in-memory-of-awil/

Webber, F. (2004) 'The War on Migration', in P. Hillyard, C. Pantazis, S. Tombs and D. Gordon (Eds.) *Beyond Criminology: Taking Harm Seriously*, London: Pluto Press: 133–155.

Weber, L. and Gelsthorpe, L. (2000) *Deciding to Detain: How Decisions to Detain Asylum Seekers are Made at Ports of Entry*, Cambridge: Institute of Criminology.

Weber, L. and Pickering, S. (2011) *Globalization and Borders: Death and the Global Frontier*, Houndmills: Palgrave Macmillan.

Yacobi, H. (2010) 'Let Me Go to the City: African Asylum Seekers, Racialization and the Politics of Space in Israel', *Journal of Refugee Studies*, 24(1): 47–68.

Yang, Y. (2012) 'African Traders in Guangzhou: Routes, Reasons, Profits, Dreams' in G. Mathews, G. L. Ribeiro and C. Alba Vega (Eds.) *Globalization from Below: The World's Other Economy*, Abingdon: Routledge: 154–170.

Zhang, S. X. (2008) *Chinese Human Smuggling Organizations: Families, Social Networks, and Cultural Imperatives*, Stanford: Stanford University Press.

Zimmermann, S. (2009a) 'Irregular Secondary Movements to Europe: Seeking Asylum Beyond Refuge', *Journal of Refugee Studies*, 22(1): 74–96.

Zimmermann, S. (2009b) 'Why Seek Asylum? The Role of Integration and Financial Support', *International Migration*, 48(1): 199–231.

4 Establishing life at the destination

This and the next chapter form the corpus of my scrutiny of asylum seeker agency and how this agency is perceived and labelled as deviant by many commentators. The outcomes of the livelihood strategies adopted by the asylum seekers in Hong Kong, for both asylum seekers themselves and the wider community, are also analyzed. In regard to these outcomes, recently a concerned citizen argued in a local Hong Kong newspaper that asylum seekers in the city are forced into an intolerable situation which compels them to devise 'negative coping mechanisms', for which they are unfairly criticized, thus impacting both their social inclusion and sense of self-worth (Wisniewski Otero 2013). Here, I further my arguments presented in previous chapters on the vulnerability constraining asylum seeker agency to advance the idea that not only do government policy and societal attitudes pressure asylum seekers into undertaking morally deviant, rule-breaking behaviour, but also that some of their so-called negative coping mechanisms may indeed not be negative for the broader Hong Kong society.

It is clearly demonstrated in this chapter and the following that asylum seekers are confined within specific spaces, due to their lack of capital and their social exclusion, wherein they must rely on networks, through which they develop certain types of interpersonal relations, to cope with their circumstances and maintain a livelihood. In short, they attempt to realize their dreams and expectations of a better and safer life by using networks to learn of and access resources and by adopting the strategies they learn are required to achieve certain goals (cf. Matsueda 1988). Additionally, their goals are reshaped by the context in which they live, generating a process that has significant implications for the host community. More specifically, I argue that the interplay of structure and agency in Hong Kong effectively transforms asylum seekers into instruments that ease the local social inequalities caused by processes of economic restructuring involving particular strata of the local (legal) population. The legal exclusion of certain categories of traveller may indeed lead to their 'deviant' behaviour, and this situation is tolerated for the benefits their so-called deviancy provides to local people whose social status and survival strategies are affected by scant social welfare and the polarizing consequences of neoliberal capitalism. The illegalization of asylum seekers thus emerges as a critical factor within processes of global city formation, as asylum seekers are poorly supported and denied legitimate means of achieving

140 *Establishing life at the destination*

material survival, and their circumstances, values and aspirations are severely disrupted (cf. Zhang 2010). Drawing upon the narratives of my participants, this chapter shows how asylum seekers often lament that the physical and psychological obstacles they encounter in Hong Kong exacerbate their frustration and alienation. The impacts of the discrepancy between reality and the asylum seekers' expectations of achievement are revealed in this context, helping to explain asylum seekers' disposition to behave in certain ways (Agnew 1992).

Importantly, the matrix of risk inferred by border control regimes which represent migration as a security concern is further analyzed here in relation to the understanding built in the previous chapters that the shifting of the location of border control activities to sites and spaces other than the physical external border underscores a sense of crisis about illegal immigration. This crisis lends momentum to calls for more stringent controls and raises levels of distrust and suspicion towards migrant populations that are not deferential and compliant with state regulation (see Chapters 2 and 3). In this context, the burden of proof has increased for people seeking international protection, while policing, screening and surveillance mechanisms have been boosted to distinguish between unwanted arrivals and those who are in 'genuine' need (Ticktin 2011). In this chapter, it is posited that service providers, albeit unintentionally, reproduce securitization mechanisms via their efforts to serve and advance the rights of asylum seekers. Consequently, the asylum seeker community becomes fractured (see Chapter 2), and their agency is differently affected. From the data gathered in this research, the degree of psychosocial exclusion of asylum seekers in Hong Kong paradoxically appears to be inversely related to their propensity to engage in what is deemed deviant behaviour.

Dealing with people and survival

This study has found that asylum seekers must often redefine their identities and personal goals, while striving to reach their objectives given the available resources, the needs and expectations that surface at different stages of their exile and the changing means adopted to meet them. This is not to say that asylum seekers always have a clear idea of their goals and how to achieve them. Upon arrival at their destination in particular, their decisions can at times appear rather circumstantial. Nevertheless, the asylum seeker narratives herein show that their actions are aimed at making sense of particular circumstances by adjusting their survival strategies, which is seen to demonstrate their deviancy and thus the bogusness of their claim in the eyes of the public and authorities. Yet such deviancy can be plausibly explained otherwise. More specifically, individual livelihoods and decision making occur within social contexts of co-national, co-ethnic and other social relations, which occasionally enable resources and strategies to be channelled for the individual's benefit. Therefore, irrespective of the validity of their claim for asylum, it is reasonable to expect that asylum seeker agency will be contingent on social networks which, on the one hand, do not always produce positive social capital (van Meeteren et al. 2009; Korac 2009) and, on the other, result in capital that, while enabling survival, is labelled as either suspicious or as breaking established societal rules.

In this regard, as outlined in Chapter 3, most of the people who participated in this research had either no information regarding Hong Kong prior to arrival or held perceptions of the former colony that were unrealistic. In addition, while certainly expecting to be able to enjoy a better and safer life at their destination, the great majority of the interviewees had made no plans about how to accomplish this goal. Several participants had an almost blind trust that either upon arrival or shortly afterwards they would gain unconditional access to resources and opportunities available to local legal residents. Apart from the rare occasion when an asylum seeker had been promised a job, most appeared more concerned with gaining access to opportunities than with working out how they would make use of them. The social relations that new arrivals established at their destination therefore became essential to their adjustment to the new environment. In other words, the opportunities that shaped asylum seekers' perceptions of their destination became available, evolved or changed depending on the conditions found upon arrival and the social networks formed or accessed in Hong Kong.

Here, it is argued that different networks relay or enable different resources, assets and strategies. This is evident in the quality of information provided to the asylum seekers in this research and the degree of risk they consequently took to ensure their survival. In addition, while social relations with fellow asylum seekers were significant early in their stay, for providing information and the means to develop survival strategies, the longer an asylum seeker remained in Hong Kong, the less tangible and intangible support appeared to be available within the refugee community. Indeed, time spent in the destination and the degree of support available seem to be inversely related. While new arrivals were focused on day-to-day survival, long-time asylum seekers adapted their survival strategies to increase the likelihood that they would achieve their long-term goals in relation to their livelihood, although this was not always possible. In the following sections, I explore the asylum seekers' marginalization and how their goals were altered by the need to ensure basic and legal survival. Then, in the last section, and the following chapter, I describe how this condition seems to benefit the wider community.

Making connections upon arrival

A number of places in Hong Kong were particularly important in terms of enabling relationship building and the exchange of information with co-national and co-ethnic asylum seekers and other populations. These places were Chungking Mansions, the immigration detention facilities, and some small northern towns in the New Territories.

Mathews (2011: 1) argues that Chungking Mansions is 'the haunt of South Asian merchants, African entrepreneurs, Indian temporary workers, African and South Asian asylum seekers, and penurious travelers from across the globe'. He also claims that this dilapidated building in the heart of Hong Kong is probably

142 *Establishing life at the destination*

better known in developing countries than in the territory itself. Following his travels to India, Mathews recalled that he would be asked about Chungking Mansions when telling locals he was from Hong Kong. Many of my participants said that they had arrived in Hong Kong from either their country of origin or China with a small note in their hand containing the phone number of a local contact and the words 'Chungking Mansions'. As per the participants' accounts, and as had been explained to them, the benefit of staying in this place was that it would increase their chances of meeting their fellow countrymen and other asylum seekers who could help them adjust to their new life in Hong Kong.

Cheap accommodation in the New Territories was also frequently rented by the participants. Here the asylum seekers were left on their own or in the care of flat or guest house owners, who demanded money, soon exhausting all of a traveller's limited savings. This tended to increase their vulnerability and reliance on social networks. Yet it was in these sites that asylum seekers also acquired the knowledge they needed to inform their decision making. The information obtained upon arrival most commonly concerned pressing needs, such as securing accommodation, food and asylum. For some participants, obtaining information in Hong Kong also meant realizing that they had ended up in a place quite different from what they had expected. For example, one participant recalled crossing the border by boat and being taken to a park, where the agent left him, saying that he would find a hotel for the two of them: 'I waited and waited. It was cold. . . . The next morning the police came and arrested me, I asked why . . . I was a refugee and I came from a country at war. I said, "I'm in America, why do you catch me?" The police said this was not America' (African participant, 30) and took him away.

In such circumstances, co-national and co-ethnic networks effectively became critical service providers when asylum seekers' initial cash reserves were quickly exhausted or deportation had to be avoided. Nonetheless, while a number of the interviewees found sympathetic asylum seekers and other individuals who could assist them by providing a meal, temporary accommodation or information about the asylum system, for some the learning process was negatively impacted by a lack of access to networks or interaction with networks that did not offer appropriate support. Time spent on making sense of their new life could be either shortened or lengthened depending on whether meaningful and reliable information was provided, prior to, upon or after their arrival. This condition of precariousness plays right into the hands of those who are convinced that asylum seekers are deviant characters, as new arrivals are forced to struggle for their basic survival. The participants' knowledge about their circumstances at times led to a quick UNHCR rejection of an asylum claim as a result of meeting other asylum seekers who recommended story fabrication to increase the odds of success, while at other times it resulted in criminal conviction. For example, a couple of participants served a prison sentence for robbing a 7-Eleven only days after arriving in Hong Kong. This was a reckless gesture that one of them explained in the following terms: 'We suddenly saw money and we got crazy, because we were hungry, had no money, and nobody helped. We didn't have any idea of doing this. In my country I was working in an executive job' (Sri Lankan participant, 21).

Chance played a significant role in shaping the participants' networks. Several Bangladeshis explained that they first learnt how to manage their new life in Hong Kong when they found a large Bangladeshi community in Ping Che, in the New Territories – a relatively inexpensive and isolated rural area close to the border with Shenzhen. 'Ping Che is a sort of Bangladesh city', I was told. 'We don't know each other, but maybe our relatives in the village at home know or hear of others who have someone in Hong Kong, and they mostly stay here' (Bangladeshi participant, 36). In this case, co-national networks functioned to facilitate the inclusion of new arrivals into the Hong Kong way of life, which for the majority meant working to secure food and shelter.

For example, a South Asian participant explained how he had met someone in Chungking Mansions who brought him to the New Territories. Here he was asked to pay rent, but since he did not have enough money, he was made to work in a recycling yard. About four weeks later, he was arrested. He recalled: 'At that time I was like a baby, I didn't understand about the police, illegal work – many police came to our place. I had to jump a fence trying to escape. More than 10 people were arrested' (Bangladeshi participant, 68). Similarly, another participant revealed that after he was forced to leave the rented room in which his agent had placed him, he wandered the streets. For seven days he could not afford to eat. Homeless and hungry, he considered returning home. Then he met a fellow countryman who offered him accommodation and food in exchange for helping out at his home. Afraid of going out because he was overstaying his visa, months went by during which he did not leave the premises, until one day he decided to take his chances and leave. A few days later, he was arrested. Three years later, he said that he had made the right decision. He explained that he met many people in detention and was then able to apply for asylum.

Two important conclusions can be drawn in consideration of the previous discussion. First, the sorts of networks established with co-nationals impacted on accommodation arrangements and place of residence, which in turn influenced livelihood strategies. Second, for a minority of the participants, everyday tactics of survival increasingly turned towards securing alternative resources not readily available within co-national and co-ethnic refugee groups, when initial pressing needs had been met and the participants' focus could then shift towards achieving long-term solutions to protracted insecurity.

In relation to the first point, it is noteworthy that shared accommodation was the general housing model for the great majority of the participants, especially the South Asians. They normally grouped in a number of areas according to ethnicity and nationality. In addition, depending on which area they lived in, they engaged in a range of income-generating activities, if they could secure any at all. While this subject forms the focus of the next chapter, it is important to highlight here that the interviewees responded to their poverty and lack of consistent, comprehensive support by devising strategies either in relation to the opportunities available in or near their place of residence, or by changing their place of residence in order to find ways to complement or increase their meagre income. In this regard, labour-intensive work in recycling, construction and car dealing

144   *Establishing life at the destination*

was abundant in the New Territories, while retail and other trading activities were mostly carried out in Kowloon. Thus, the participants either moved to a place where co-nationals, friends and relatives were residing, subsequently living the way of life of the people in that location, or they moved to take advantage of the different opportunities available to them, which they learnt about over time. In other words, while many followed the people they fortuitously met upon arrival, who offered them accommodation and/or work, others weighed up the range of information obtained from a number of people. One South Asian participant, for instance, described how in Chungking Mansions he met a man who offered him a job in a scrapyard for monthly wages, but after meeting a friend, he decided to go with him to another place, where he eventually landed work in a different business. He said: 'If I hadn't found my friend's number . . . I would have gone with that man' (Bangladeshi participant, 60).

Opportunities to earn an income were related to a variety of services or activities, including the services provided by charities and churches. Given the transportation costs in particular, the farther participants lived from the city centre, the less they appeared to benefit from the assistance offered by service providers in Hong Kong. In addition, as is suggested in the following section, while the majority of the participants in the New Territories responded to the pressure to come up with a money-making strategy by effectively excluding themselves from other social contexts, often remaining trapped in a cycle of activity between home, work and boredom, some participants in Kowloon became dependent on service providers. In some cases, this negatively affected their perceptions of each other (see Chapter 2 and later in this chapter). Yet the financial resources that were occasionally obtained from service providers enabled different forms of refugee agency, particularly because, as some asylum seekers became relatively less constrained by time and money, opportunities for socializing increased, which expanded the range of livelihood strategies they might adopt. It will be demonstrated later that opportunities for long-term improvement were presented to the participants who were less constrained by financial insecurity, and who could therefore form meaningful bridged relations with people extraneous to their community who had access to the resources needed to achieve their main objective: to obtain legal status. With the passage of time, asylum seekers in Hong Kong learn that security, and arguably a mentally healthier life, can be achieved only by those who have the legal right to reside and work in the city.

Companionship as a long-term survival strategy

In line with Agnew's (1992) work on the classification of strains and the structural factors that mark people's failure to achieve positively valued goals, from my interviews with asylum seekers it was clear that many participants suffered from the realization that their reality did not conform to their expectations. Furthermore, most grasped the injustice of being prevented from attaining what they believed was their right – to conduct a decent and safe life while seeking asylum. The survival strategies outlined subsequently must be understood in light of the significant indigence and psychophysical frustration imposed upon asylum seekers in spite of their desire to abide by the rules. For example, although it is a practice often frowned upon by those commentators who are concerned with the genuineness of claimants, the vast majority of male participants had one or more girlfriends in Hong Kong, most commonly Filipina or Indonesian nationals working as domestic helpers, but also local Chinese or Western women.

Companions are important for asylum seekers, not only for their emotional well-being, but also because they extend financial support to their partners (Ip 2011). As I was often told when I asked how they managed to pay rent if the ISS provided only HK$1000 a month, the interviewees responded along the lines of: 'I manage as anyone else. I have a girlfriend' (Bangladeshi participant, 37). Girlfriends were said to help with the room security deposit, utilities and the telephone and Internet connection. In some cases, companions also widened their partners' networks by introducing informal opportunities, such as tutoring, domestic work or occasional indoor construction work. On this point, despite many South Asian participants explaining that couples living together outside marriage is forbidden in their religion, many engaged in such behaviour, which meant that their cultural values were irremediably altered. As an old Pakistani man affirmed, these relationships were 'a big problem' as many asylum seekers were turning their back on family commitments when they found Hong Kong's lifestyle allowed them greater freedom than they had ever experienced. In his opinion, these girlfriends were spoiling 'the boy, as he gets mobile phones, money, house. . . . They enjoy this life. They are totally earning. They are exploited at work, but they enjoy the weekends with their girlfriends' (Pakistani participant, 37). This view is consistent with that of other participants who argued that some asylum seekers were losing their focus in Hong Kong, or according to some non-refugee participants, were 'exploiting the system', causing troubles for women who were said to be lured into relationships by the promise that 'they are businessmen with connections here and there and that they will be going to Canada' (Refugee worker, 02). In such circumstances, many women were said to become pregnant, which jeopardized their job and caused a number of them to shelter from deportation by claiming asylum. Nonetheless, some male and female interviewees confirmed that, while their initial intention was to stay in Hong Kong temporarily, they later reviewed their thinking in consideration of the hard time they would have readjusting to their home country's values were they to return home. In addition, a number of male participants stated that romantic relationships in Hong Kong negatively affected their pride, confidence and self-worth. Thus, they were reluctant to return home: 'We are men, but we rely on girlfriends. We are shy to ask because of our condition, but we cannot do otherwise. Sometimes we think we are not men anymore. In our culture boys take care of girls. Here, we are falling down' (Bangladeshi participant, 44).

It also emerged that while South Asian men were mainly involved in relationships with Indonesian domestic helpers, the girlfriends of African interviewees were mostly Filipinas or local Chinese. Moreover, new arrivals were more likely to have partners who worked as domestic helpers, as they were said to be easier to meet and more likely to help with survival needs; yet some longer-term asylum seekers were more likely to partner with a local Chinese or Western woman. As many participants openly admitted, this greater interest in local women among the longer-term asylum seekers was based on the fact that marriage often came to be the only avenue to obtaining legal status. This point is well illustrated by one interviewee, who complained that his fellow African asylum seekers were treating their ex-girlfriends unfairly. He noted that many long-time African asylum seekers terminated their relationships with their old girlfriends – often domestic helpers – to pursue more (legally and financially) promising relationships. This participant said that his wife, who was employed as a domestic helper, was unable to help him change his legal status, but he was grateful that she was there when he was in need of shelter and food. Despite his appreciation, he nonetheless bitterly agreed that often the only way male asylum seekers could regularize their status was to marry a local or Western woman.

The participants all tended to agree with the view that 'marriage without love is not good'. However, as one interviewee stressed rather vehemently: 'Maybe they don't have 100 per cent love, but you are looking for a way out. Everyone has the right to live. Here, you don't have that right, and people get married' (African participant, 18). He later continued by pointing to marriage as the only available means to secure a future: 'People spend time here and get old. You will die soon if you don't fight for your life. I know some people who have been here for five to six years and nothing changed. How come?' In this regard, it is important to note that those participants who did get married in Hong Kong were a small minority. In addition, many participants convincingly argued that if the prevalent view was that asylum seekers must get married to obtain 'papers', those who actually did so did not always find happiness.

The literature on 'marriage migration' tends to emphasize the difficulties that migrants travelling for the purpose of joining their foreign spouse encounter in finding work, when language and skills barriers hinder entry into the labour market (Newendorp 2008). At the same time, as Smyth and Kum (2010) argue, refugees often undergo a process of deprofessionalization and loss of occupational status in the host society. Problems may also arise in terms of culture and language affinity within the newly formed household (Piper 2003; Kim 2010). In Hong Kong, a common perception among the participants was that Chinese women were rather 'bossy' and money oriented, and when asylum seekers were not able to provide for themselves they felt they were pushed into unequal power relations in which they were not able to exert the control over their life that they sought to regain through migration. In other words, while some of the participants did share relationship stories that had a happy ending, others described marriage as akin to 'falling from the frying pan into the fire'. For example, one interviewee recalled a friend's bitter experience: 'Every morning he wakes up at 6 a.m. because his wife tells him to go out and look for work. He packs his bag, leaves home, and goes to sleep on the staircases at the stadium. I told him, "Man, what are you doing here?" and he said, "These Chinese people – they will kill us all". . . . You see? You don't have peace of mind' (African participant, 06).

Establishing life at the destination 147

This comment is even more significant when considered in light of the profound cultural shock many African and South Asian men experience when they arrive in Hong Kong and see women treated as equal to men (Mathews 2011). In this regard, some participants revealed that their fellow compatriots were looking forward to a time when they could express their anger at their wife without harming their chances of obtaining legal status. Further, one South Asian interviewee observed that, despite the fact that he had a religious wedding with an Indonesian former domestic helper, he did not intend to make the arrangement legal because he wanted to keep the door open for both of them to take advantage of future opportunities to receive legal status through marriage, after which they would seek a divorce to return to each other.

Stories of husbands who left their wives after obtaining legal status were repeated throughout the asylum seeker narratives. In one case, the South Asian interviewee cited previously recalled hearing two women on a bus talking rather excitedly in Cantonese and hearing one of them say 'black men are no good'. Intrigued by what he was hearing, the participant asked the woman to explain her thoughts. After repeatedly urging the woman to reply, she finally revealed that she had married an African man years before. She had believed him when he told her that he would work hard and take care of her. However, in order to keep his promise her husband needed to open a business, and she provided him with her savings to do so. This proved to be a mistake, as she never heard from him again. When this and similar stories were recounted by the Bangladeshi participants, they expressed the view that because African men had proved themselves to be unreliable to their partners, South Asian men had a better chance of winning a Chinese woman's trust. As they argued, trust had to be nurtured over time, and in their opinion, they were better suited to this task than the Africans, to whom Chinese women nevertheless seemed to be more attracted.

The previous discussion certainly gives the impression that some opportunistic travellers take advantage of their fellow asylum seekers and local and migrant women in seeking to advance their socioeconomic and legal status. Nonetheless, while this might seem to support the view that these people should be kept out, as they are 'fooling local girls',[1] it also highlights the link between the circumstances facing asylum seeker arrivals examined in the previous chapters and the strategies that this environment encourages them to adopt at the micro-level. Furthermore, I did not analyze the establishment of co-national bonds and relations with persons of the opposite sex as strategies for coping with the despair, loss and hopelessness that refugees certainly experience (Korac 2009). The scope of this research did not include in-depth examination of the interplay of practical and existential needs. Instead, the discussion is focused on highlighting the consequences of the condition of chronic deprivation (Zhang 2010; Agnew 1992), which impacts the asylum seeker experience by ascribing importance to certain goals that asylum seekers then pursue via the few channels available to them.

Although government policy is not intended to encourage the exit strategies adopted by the more resilient asylum seekers who seek to escape their precarious circumstances, it should be said that, at the time of the interviews, only limited

148 *Establishing life at the destination*

numbers of asylum seekers successfully obtained legal status through marriage because of the excessive length of the visa procedures required. While such visas are processed within a few weeks under normal circumstances, some asylum seekers revealed that they had been waiting for well over a year. Because of their deprofessionalization, the majority of those who obtained such a visa were either precariously employed in menial, labour-intensive service jobs or self-employed in transnational trading activities, in the sectors in which the majority of asylum seekers were working. In relation to this, I argue that legal status is used as a source of state control. As Landolt and Goldring (2010) demonstrate at length, once migrants' status is regularized their employability is limited by diminishing the choices available to them in the labour market. The skills and networks acquired during the period of irregular immigration status are frequently relied upon even after a visa is granted. Therefore, the participants who shifted status continued to work in the low-wage sectors that are useful to Hong Kong's economy (see Chapter 5). Further, such state control can be seen as a form of risk management (Weber and Pickering 2011), according to which the limited number of people who 'make it' is tolerated because of the exclusion of the majority, which is justified by their purported deviant character in scheming to access alternative ways to live and work in the host society. As I was told by an asylum seeker who had placed his trust in refugee screening processes: 'If you get married without even waiting for the UNHCR it is like even you don't believe in your case' (African participant, 02). At the same time, marriages were put under considerable financial and emotional strain while applicants awaited the results of their visa application. Some couples divorced as a result, preventing asylum seekers from shifting their status. However, this resulted in a few Hong Kong citizens – their wives – having to face the harmful consequences of losing their money and of divorce.

Balancing between agency and dependency

This section presents the argument that border politics and policies aimed at marginalizing the asylum seeker experience have generated a context that severely impacts the services that local civil society groups provide to asylum seekers. At the same time, these services appear to influence official, public and asylum seekers' own representations of asylum seeking. On the one hand, the following discussion describes how some asylum seekers are required to alter their behaviour to fit the norms that society expects of them, in order to access the limited resources offered by civil society groups. On the other, it reveals that certain asylum seekers adjust their agency according to widespread perceptions of appropriate behaviour expected of refugees, which normally favour vulnerability, and thereby render desirable a human condition which in normal circumstances is undesirable (Ticktin 2011; Fassin 2012). Historically, humanitarian intervention has been forged around notions of refugee poverty, trauma and needs that place refugees in a condition of dependency on aid organizations (Malkki 1995; Harrell-Bond 2002). This modus operandi, however, affects refugee livelihoods, as those who do not seem to fit certain categories of vulnerability are excluded. In this way, asylum seekers appear to be disciplined within specific categories that represent their value in the host society.

To illustrate, a limited number of religious and charitable organizations were providing for the needs of asylum seekers in Hong Kong during the time of this research. As outlined earlier, co-nationals and other asylum seekers constituted the primary source of information through which the interviewees learnt of the existence of support and asylum opportunities. Basic information was also provided by the UNHCR, the ISS and charities. Yet some participants argued that they had no knowledge of these services. Moreover, many felt that they were left to fend for themselves, although life would have been easier had more information been circulated. For example, one resentful West African participant explained:

> Most of the people are here [in the New Territories], but many know nothing. There are people who don't know how to apply for food, for house. . . . Maybe it happens that in detention you don't see other blacks that can tell you anything. Indians and Pakistanis maybe don't speak your language. And Immigration will not tell you what to do. (African participant, 07)

Indeed, if the flow of positive social capital varied among co-nationals depending on the networks they formed, knowledge about charities was acquired via the same means at different stages of stay. While variation in the individual inclination and curiosity of asylum seekers to seek out information cannot be overlooked as a factor here, the lack of information about support services must also be related to the way charities approached refugee work, which rarely involved any proactive distribution of information to the larger refugee population. Studies on 'inhumane' humanitarian assistance (Harrell-Bond 2002; Fassin 2012) and the impact of refugee work on staff and volunteers who provide charity services (Hollands 2001) have emphasized the negative (involuntary) consequences of an industry of humanitarian organizations that has flourished around the provision of assistance to refugees. According to Harrell-Bond, rather than helping the populations of their concern, this macro-setting of aid imposed upon refugees from above has perpetuated the unique status of the refugee as victim, thus diminishing the dignity and rights of the people purportedly being served. While this strips refugees of their agency, refugee workers are also affected, as disappointment and prejudices may surface when images of needy refugees collide with the reality of people who do not always act like victims (Hollands 2001). Further, in a context in which asylum seekers are increasingly suspected of lying about their traumatic experiences of persecution, their vulnerability acquires new meaning. As if it were a vestment, asylum seekers are required to wear their vulnerability in order to validate their genuineness (Fassin and d'Halluin 2007) and arguably justify the efforts of refugee workers in providing them with services.

In Hong Kong, the way in which charities and some churches operated was found to influence the types of services they offered and the perception their beneficiaries had of them. First, only one such charity had an outreach programme,

150 *Establishing life at the destination*

intended to expand its range to access people who were prevented by monetary constraints from travelling long distances. Charities relied extensively on drop-in centres where they would meet their client population, but asylum seekers' access to these centres was dependent on their capacity to retrieve information about and reach these sites. The beneficiaries of these services were consequently mainly connected through the same networks, living in or close to the city centre. In addition, religious institutions with significant numbers of asylum seekers among their attendees were many and of different belief and cultural systems, but substantial resources were only made available to asylum seekers in Christian congregations. Muslim and other non-Christian asylum seekers were consequently placed at the margins of such efforts.

Second, as one participant cogently argued, the high turnover of refugee workers and a lack of accountability towards asylum seekers placed stress upon relations between worker and asylum seeker. While asylum seekers normally need time to learn to trust service providers, especially in the context of unbalanced power relations (UNHCR 1995), the 'lifespan' of workers in certain organizations is often shortened by their pursuit of career moves to further their professionalization in the ever competitive global labour market. In addition, refugee work increasingly resembles other forms of humanitarian work, such that aid is generally dispensed from above. Fassin (2012) argues that humanitarian assistance is directed from the above and implies compassion based on unequal power relations whereby the benefactor provides for the weaker and more vulnerable. In this regard, while workers help asylum seekers in need, asylum seekers must assume the role of needy, vulnerable people to qualify for such assistance (Hollands 2001). In particular, just as Harrell-Bond (2002: 57) recalled a Mozambican refugee in Malawi crying out to refugee workers, 'Remember, you have a job because we are here', so in Hong Kong a number of interviewees similarly stressed that they had the right to demand the services due to them. One African participant recounted quite animatedly how he argued with ISS staff whenever he was asked in the shelter to abide by their rigid rules, of which he disapproved. He said: 'That home was our home. It was our money that they used to pay for its rent. . . . ISS was given that contract [by the government] because of us' (African participant, 09). While this comment could be taken as an example of disrespect for the work of others, it is understandable in view of the visible expansion of the ISS refugee programme in the past few years, with dozens of recent social work graduates employed to distribute government-funded aid. In similar terms, another participant referred to a charity group as a business set-up when he complained about an unjustified increase in office staff in light of the scant services offered.

Based on extensive observation, informal discussions with refugee workers and interviews with the people who supposedly benefited from their work, it emerged that the practice of working with asylum seekers in Hong Kong was largely shaped by a lack of awareness about global migration and refugee issues. This shortcoming sometimes affected workers' commitment and gave rise to prejudice. In particular, refugee workers' understanding of the political world of refugees was mainly informed by macro-settings and legal definitions. Thus, a number of

Establishing life at the destination 151

them grappled with the definition of a 'genuine' asylum seeker, impacting their perception of the type of person who is deserving of help. As these charities had limited resources, such knowledge was necessary to ensure that their services were going to the 'right' people. However, their efforts in identifying and categorizing asylum seekers according to their own perceptions of deservedness fostered consensus around the supposed propensity of certain asylum seekers to use asylum for reasons unrelated to persecution (see Chapter 2).

Partly reflecting the labelling process that occurs in the wider society, the empathy with which genuine refugees were regarded was paralleled by equal detachment, if not overt hostility, towards those perceived as seeking asylum for economic gain. As one refugee worker explained, their organization wanted to serve the most vulnerable and deserving, who in their view were people whose life was made difficult by the excessive length of screening procedures, which was seen to be caused, at least in part, by the submission of asylum applications by economic migrants. Remarkably, the so-called non-genuine refugees were believed to belong predominantly to particular nationalities and to behave in certain ways, such as having a companion and working illegally. While some refugee workers tacitly condoned such behaviour, it appears that these asylum seekers' moral stance before the worker was clearly undermined. For example, particular South Asian nationalities, which form the highest proportion of asylum seekers in Hong Kong, appeared to be positioned largely at the margins of charity efforts. From a conversation with a refugee worker arose the perception that because the asylum claims of South Asians were thought to be less believable, they were being fast-tracked through refugee screenings. One senior refugee worker questioned the validity of Sri Lankan and Indonesian former domestic helpers seeking asylum upon completion of their work contracts. She commented: 'It is rather ironic to claim torture when you have been allowed to go home every year, and you can still do that, or when you can freely contact your consulate and get involved in its activities, and yet say that your government is torturing you' (Refugee worker, 02).

Such views implied state-centric and geographically based notions of persecution that do not take into account the unwillingness or inability of state actors to protect their citizens. More importantly, although the Hong Kong courts have stressed the importance of deciding claims according to the highest standards of fairness – a pronouncement that was championed by all refugee advocates in Hong Kong – this does not seem to occur in practice. Conversely, Somali asylum seekers were being accepted as genuine refugees more quickly than other groups. Not only do they originate from a country where the conflict is well recognized, but they also spend a lot of time frequenting the drop-in centres. Further, their vulnerability was evidenced by their tendency to respect the laws that prohibit them from working, making their survival appear all the more tenuous and their situation more desperate without charity aid.

It is clear that charities can choose their target population. It is also true that some people do seek to abuse the asylum system. However, the moral worthiness of the protection needs of certain refugee groups appeared to be diminished on

152 *Establishing life at the destination*

the basis of arbitrary representations of refugee vulnerability, which also reproduced inequality and trauma, contrary to each charity's stated mission (cf. Ticktin 2011). On the one hand, I was told that accepting one Pakistani or Indonesian asylum seeker would invite more of them, and in consideration of their numbers in Hong Kong, precious resources would then be quickly spent. On the other, service providers placed a remarkable amount of faith in the UNHCR's often dubious screening procedures to determine the genuineness of their client population. For example, one African asylum seeker was denied assistance from a church group after receiving rental aid for a number of years because the UNHCR closed his case. He was told that he was not a 'genuine' asylum seeker and so resources had to be diverted towards more deserving people. Surprisingly, he was later recognized as worthy of international protection by the UNHCR – years after his first application. In addition, one refugee worker, while stating that he did not believe in clear-cut distinctions between genuine and fake asylum seekers, revealed that this distinction was often employed for fundraising purposes. Donors tend not to have expert knowledge on refugees and so had formed the idea that Hong Kong was plagued by economic migrants posing as asylum seekers. In this regard, Musarò (2011) perceptively argues that NGOs' financial strategies often have long-term ethical impacts, in that they reinforce stereotypes based on the asylum seeker as a victim.

That assistance appeared to flow towards people who better fit moral categories of deservedness seemed to affect the way asylum seekers responded to the role expected of them. On one side, a number of the participants said that they would not seek help from these aid organizations because they believed that they would not receive any sympathy. Their friends had tried, and this was enough for them to learn 'how things go'. On the other side, some participants seemed to develop identities accordingly, for example, by leading a sort of 'double life'. Evidence was found of people who by night were loud, cheerful, 'enjoying' life and drinking with their girlfriends, while by day they were quiet and devout. In other cases, some asylum seekers who received help from charities revealed that they tended to hide the details of the help they obtained from other asylum seekers so as not to invoke envy. A few interviewees, for instance, claimed that their compatriots would argue about why some of them had received particular assistance while others had not, wondering what tactics had been used to persuade refugee workers and whether they could be replicated.

While asylum seekers who sought to use such tactics certainly appeared to be a small minority, the effect of prevailing views nonetheless clearly impacted their agency. Not only did some become prone to using 'little tricks' to appear more deserving, but others also applied the distinction that they learnt about genuine and bogus refugees to their fellow asylum seekers, based in unwarranted suspicion. According to some interviewees, the way in which asylum seekers were living their life in Hong Kong was partly a result of the problems they faced in their home country. In other words, the private life of asylum seekers was seen as grounds for unofficially 'reading' the basis of their claim, as if, for example, a person who was working illegally or had a girlfriend was more likely to be a camouflaged economic migrant than a genuine refugee simply trying to cope with his circumstances because, in the words of one African refugee, 'if you were persecuted you can't be so happy' (African participant, 27). While this may be a reasonable assessment at times, it is important to note that the nature of persecution and its impacts can vary a great deal in reality (Zolberg et al. 1989), and the negotiation of trauma can differ depending on individual psychological processes and predispositions (Herlihy and Turner 2009). Nevertheless, those participants who believed in a connection between the nature of one's private life and the genuineness of one's claim were those less likely to be involved in any income-generating activity for fear of being associated with one of 'them' – the 'bad' or fake asylum seekers. It is no coincidence that these asylum seekers were also the participants who shared an acute sense of loss of agency and a resultant feeling of being trapped in a meaningless routine of sleeping, eating, walking around and visiting charities. Fearing to engage with anything that they believed might cause trouble with the UNHCR, they relied heavily on the services of charities, churches and other charity-minded individuals to supplement the ISS assistance they received, remarkably excluding themselves from the wider refugee community. In doing so, their actions and persona mirrored the idealized needy, pitiful and voiceless refugee victim that refugee workers expected them to be.

The narrative of one Somali participant provides a powerful example of this scenario. This asylum seeker argued that his strategy of survival included attending counselling at one charity, not because he felt he needed it but because he believed that it would improve his chances of becoming a recognized refugee if he were diagnosed with depression. He explained: 'The only reason why I do therapy is because . . . I want the counsellor to write a letter to the UNHCR. . . . I hope that I can talk to him and he understands the problem. I don't see much use in it [counselling], but I hope the UNHCR will give me status' (African participant, 23).

Beyond the previous considerations, those charity organizations and the few religious institutions that provided material support were also important in that they gave asylum seekers the opportunity to establish social networks with other asylum seekers, compatriots and members of the local community. Two points are significant here. First, several scholars have stressed that religion can offer the social, spiritual and psychological capital needed to cope with the hardship associated with migration (Hagan 2008; Akcapar 2006). At times, it redefines identities and notions of spirituality. However, as substantial resources were made available to asylum seekers only in Christian churches, one of the most significant effects of this disparity in assistance between Christians and people of other faiths (or indeed with no faith) was a marked inequality in the circumstances of asylum seekers. While those who had access to churches, especially churches that provided financial support, were normally found to have greater opportunities in terms of money, time and access to bridged networks, many Muslim interviewees, whether Somalis or other South Asians, faced tougher circumstances. In this regard, while Somalis relied on charity groups based in the city centre for help, Bangladeshis living in rural areas were the most marginalized of the populations

154   *Establishing life at the destination*

under study. In contrast to the other nationality groups, they had virtually no access to alternative forms of income other than illegal work, support from girlfriends or the scant assistance shared within their community of asylum seekers.

Second, while some asylum seekers relied on charities for their survival, a number of others made use of charities to exert greater control over their life. In this sense, one important resource available at the drop-in centres was the Internet. Some participants said that they relied on the Internet to remain informed about the latest news in their country, maintain or re-establish relations with family members and friends overseas, solicit remittances, encourage awareness of human rights or access business opportunities (cf. Siddiquee and Kagan 2006; Muhtaseb and Frey 2008). Furthermore, some relied on the limited services available to them to meet their most urgent needs and therefore be able to focus on long-term solutions to their predicament. For example, while some participants residing in the New Territories argued that because they were excluded from such networks their opportunities to pursue relationships with local women were reduced by time and financial constraints, others not living in the New Territories developed successful relationships and business strategies. In relation to the latter, some participants revealed that they used the Internet to search for overseas business partners. For example, a few individuals said that they managed to act as middlemen between buyers in China and suppliers in their country of origin, and vice versa. They were trading stones and raw minerals, which were said to be in high demand among Chinese manufacturers, in exchange for finished products which Africans were now able to afford. One such interviewee explained that after he had concluded his first business negotiation he started searching for more business opportunities and was then able to lead a comfortable life in Hong Kong.

Refugee life and community profit

A number of findings emerge from the previous discussion. Stringent border control policies, and their impact on refugee work, homogenize and categorize the asylum seeker experience into clustered classes of asylum seekers. Depending on their response to their adverse circumstances, asylum seekers either appear to be disciplined into poverty, accepting their condition and adopting survival strategies to which they often become bound, or they revolt against their status and strive to achieve goals that they see as unjustly denied to them. In the former case, asylum seekers' self-worth is affected as they become more reliant on the help of others to meet their daily needs, incurring the risk that even the kindest supporter may tire of helping them, or they may realize that earning wages in the informal economy is one of the very few viable solutions to their problems. In the latter scenario, asylum seeker choice is impacted by the realization that their lack of resources to negotiate and cope with the stress of their environment makes it all but essential to seek a shift in their status – a difficulty that feeds anger and resentment, which may then lead to behaviours that foster negative public perceptions of asylum seekers. Regardless, in all cases, resource-seeking strategies are developed, mainly involving income-generating activities. Again borrowing from

Agnew (1992) and his typology of how individuals cope with structural strains, if social and informational support and high self-esteem tend to function to reduce the likelihood that an individual will respond to stress by adopting delinquent behaviours, it is suspicious that by reducing both support and self-esteem, the outcome of border control policies appears to diverge considerably from the state's aims. Rather than preventing migrants from abusing the asylum system, asylum seekers are effectively placed in a position where they are driven to further their self-esteem and survival by engaging in the informal economy or, if unable to do so, leaving the city (see Chapter 2).

Indeed, several refugee participants observed that work was regarded by many asylum seekers as a boost not only to personal finances but also to one's sense of achievement and life balance, just as previous research has shown that being able to work promotes mental well-being (Valtonen 2004; Fozdar and Torezani 2008). While certainly being physically strenuous and often emotionally draining due to the exploitative conditions encountered, working in Hong Kong entailed normality and participation in society for the participants. 'When you go to work in the morning, you work all day; you get tired. Then you go home, you cook dinner, and at 10 p.m. you can go to sleep, nicely. . . . If you only eat and sleep, you think too much, and you don't know what is going on with your [asylum] case. That is the problem' (African participant, 24), I was told.

Trapped between punitive policies on the one hand and harsh living conditions on the other, asylum seekers are effectively forced into socio-legal and economic spaces where their goals are necessarily redefined, and social, human and economic capital can be earned solely by engaging with certain strata of the local community that can provide the necessary resources to support their survival. In the remainder of this chapter, and in the next chapter, I analyze which and how local residents benefit from asylum seekers' purported deviant survival strategies.

Rental, consumer and commercial markets

Grabska (2006: 302) notes that refugees in Cairo, both with and without legal status, 'contribute by bringing financial and human capital into the country, as active consumers and a cheap yet productive source of labour'. An analysis is offered here of how the people who seek asylum in Hong Kong impact the city's rental and consumer economy. As outlined previously, asylum seekers are normally accommodated in self-arranged rooms for which the ISS provides them with monthly rental assistance worth HK$1000. The vast majority of the participants stressed that they had to overcome a number of challenges in order to secure accommodation in the rental market. Remittances from overseas were injected into the local economy to pay for security deposits and rent in the first months following arrival, generally when ISS services were still not known of or an application for assistance had been lodged but not yet evaluated. In particular, South Asian participants depended on their overseas contacts far more than did the other interviewees, often relying on relatives and friends in Saudi Arabia, Bahrain, Italy and Korea to send cash remittances.

156　*Establishing life at the destination*

The majority of the people who had no access to foreign hard currency relied mostly on family members in their country of origin. Informal networks between countries of origin and Hong Kong allowed the interviewees to receive money at a small price. One participant explained: 'There are some people from Bangladesh who travel often. My father gave money to one of these people at their home in Bangladesh. Then I met this person here and he gave me the money' (Bangladeshi participant, 42). A West African participant who had only recently arrived in the territory said that he travelled with little cash, but before departing, he had instructed his wife on how she could send money to him in case of emergency. Another interviewee similarly concluded: 'My family sends money. They helped me with the room and sometimes they help with the bills and clothes. They send it through Western Union. No one here can survive with [the] ISS only' (African participant, 01).

Partners in Hong Kong helped with covering accommodation expenses. While this topic was examined earlier in this chapter, it is important to note that a large amount of money earned by domestic helpers, intended to be sent home, is instead being reintroduced into the local economy to help their boyfriends. The amount of rent paid by asylum seekers ranged from HK$1000 to HK$2200, of which HK$300–400 was said to be regularly contributed by girlfriends out of their meagre minimum salary of HK$3740 per month[2] – an arrangement that greatly limited the quantities of money they could send home to their own families. If in the broader economic context this contribution appears minimal, it is important to stress that at the micro-level, apart from families in countries of origin receiving less remitted cash, a large number of landlords in Hong Kong appeared to profit from renting out rooms to asylum seekers.

I normally met interviewees in their homes to conduct extensive observation of the spaces and the kinds of rental markets that asylum seekers generally accessed. Many participants lived in housing provided by landlords who owned several rooms specifically built to accommodate asylum seekers. As one participant described: 'Some people are very clever. My landlord is running a business by renting small rooms. Before, she had only a few rooms for mainland Chinese. But after people from my country started to arrive and [the] ISS paid for rent, she started to make more rooms' (Bangladeshi participant, 48). When I interviewed her, this landlady later confirmed that mainlanders were indeed 'troubles' as they would not pay rent on time and would sometimes disappear, either because they had been caught by the authorities if they were living in Hong Kong illegally or they had upgraded to better accommodation. Conversely, she made a stable income out of asylum seekers and frequently offered to take them to the ISS to submit the required papers, occasionally complaining to the agency on their behalf that asylum seekers should be provided with more assistance for rent.

Some landlords were found to have more than 10 and sometimes 20 rooms rented to asylum seekers. Seeing an opportunity for an easy profit, one employer I met who owned a recycling yard showed me a strip of land on which he was planning to build 10 wooden rooms, with separate entrances, for the bargain price of HK$1000 each. Well known to the public is the case of 'the compound under a tree' – an illegal structure made of iron sheeting, timber and tarpaulin in a remote

Establishing life at the destination   157

area in the New Territories in which a dozen asylum seekers resided (Carney 2013; Vision First 2013). In this regard, the fact that in-kind assistance offered a rental allowance of HK$1000, to be paid into the landlord's bank account, has undoubtedly influenced the rental market at the lower rungs of the social ladder. Whether housing consisted of small, newly built rooms partitioned out of single flats or old, barely safe shacks and cabins, several landlords earned a stable income from regular ISS deposits into their bank accounts for properties that probably would otherwise have been vacant or would not have existed at all. An old local man, for instance, said that he was earning a monthly income of HK$10,000 driving a minibus. His income, however, almost doubled when he rented four rooms adjacent to his house in a desolated area in the New Territories to six asylum seekers for a total of HK$7200 a month. Similarly, a retired old farmer rented for HK$6000 annually a large cabin previously used as a tool shed to a group of Bangladeshis who transformed it into a mosque. In another case, an old retired labour worker rented out his ancestral home when all of his children left home.

The literature on urban refugees generally indicates that refugees are subsets of other foreign-born migrants and local poor, with whom they compete for cheaper housing and low-skilled employment opportunities (Jacobsen 2002). If this is true to some extent of asylum seekers in Hong Kong, it appears nonetheless that rather than being competitors only – for example, by sharing the same housing needs with the lowest strata of the local poor – they provide the means by which a portion of the Chinese and migrant underprivileged resident population can negotiate both increasing social polarization and 'professionalization' (Zhao et al. 2004; Lee et al. 2007). While it is often the case that younger, better-educated generations find their family's living arrangements unacceptable or inconvenient, others may need to raise or supplement their income via alternative strategies to escape the poverty trap (Lee et al. 2007) or pursue greater comfort elsewhere. As has been said earlier in Chapter 1, Hong Kong is a 'bureaucratic-capitalist state . . . backed by a weak legislature in which major policies are jointly decided by the SAR's senior officials and its business elite' (Chan 1998: 280). Consequently, welfare expenditure is minimal in Hong Kong as the government adheres to the principles of maintaining a balanced budget, fiscal reserves and low taxation. This policy lowers the sense of security among the resident classes at the bottom of society (Wong et al. 2010). In addition, as Chan (1998: 282) explains: 'The government always makes it plain that the ultimate objective of social security is simply to bring the income of needy individuals and families up to a level where basic and special needs can be met: that is, only providing a safety-net.' This safety-net is temporary and inaccessible in most of cases (Chan 2011). Seen in these terms, the rationale behind Hong Kong's welfare system seems remarkably similar to that underpinning the asylum seeker in-kind support system. Welfare policies in Hong Kong foster an ideology of 'self-reliance' as a personal and necessary virtue, conversely attaching great stigma to those who rely on state welfare (Chan 1998, 2011). In short, in a society in which the rich become richer and low-income households struggle to make ends meet, a number of local people living far from the bright lights of the financial quarters of this global city manage to complement or replace unstable low wages and insufficient welfare by profiting from asylum seekers in this marginal rental market.

158 *Establishing life at the destination*

Importantly, low-income residents similarly benefit from the presence of asylum seekers in other sectors of the economy. For example, one successful survival strategy adopted by many participants was to sell the food they received through the ISS. A significant number of interviewees explained that they felt compelled to sell either the whole or part of the bag of food items, despite these provisions being insufficient for the allocated 10-day period. Ethnic grocery shops and small restaurants targeting low-income earners were buying asylum seekers' food supplies for a few dollars which asylum seekers would then use to buy credit on their mobile phones and cheaper and more culturally appropriate foodstuffs. As one participant rather emotionally revealed: 'I tell you the truth, if I get food, sometimes I sell it to charge HK$20 on my phone or pay for transportation. Now I'm waiting for my food. Saturday I will collect it and I will sell some of it to pay my bills' (African participant, 13).

Although asylum seekers may thus appear to be making a profit, for which they are often criticized, in reality the participants were probably benefiting the least from this trade. Indeed, some participants said that they tried to eat less in order to sell some of their food. In contrast, ISS-contracted ethnic shops earned a stable income by providing supplies to asylum seekers. At the same time, food items sold by asylum seekers, generally for half the invoiced price on the day of collection, were purchased by the same or other grocery shops, which would resell these items at about 20 per cent less than the market price. As explained by a South Asian participant, in grocery shops contracted by the ISS, 'a pack of chili powder is [listed at] HK$12. I can sell it for HK$6 to another shop and they resell it for HK$10' (Sri Lankan participant, 84g).

ISS-contracted and other owners of shops frequented by asylum seekers were most often of ethnic background, either Hong Kong permanent residents or former asylum seekers who had acquired legal status. In general, their businesses faced high levels of competition in a segment of the economy in which profits are achieved by reducing either labour costs or the price of items. I was told by one such owner, who had four shops in different areas of Hong Kong, that he had tried to win a contract with the ISS. This opportunity would have helped him support his business. He told me: 'You see? We have been talking for 15 minutes now. How many customers have you seen coming in?'(African resident, 10). He revealed that because he failed to win an ISS contract he would have to downsize and close at least one of his shops. Yet it appeared that his entire business operation was precariously hanging on the verge of collapse. As he explained, and as will be further investigated in the next chapter, a lack of viable opportunities in Hong Kong was obstructing his economic advancement in other sectors.

Reading the asylum seeker contribution: Concluding remarks

If the influx into the local economy of cash brought from or meant for overseas countries has benefited some of the underprivileged households that have established social and commercial relations with asylum seekers, this study shows that these low-income residents are also sharing the benefits of the government's in-kind assistance to asylum seekers. In this light, the implications of the points made previously for the perceptions and expectations of asylum seekers in Hong Kong shall be further examined. This is important because many participants expressed the desire to make a contribution to the host society. Many wanted to be involved and to engage with the local community. However, the opportunities they were looking for and through which they would have effectively achieved their goals, and thereby have contributed to society, were only available to people holding a legal permit to work.

Several interviewees blamed the Hong Kong Government for their skills being wasted in the city. Many shared the view expressed by one participant that 'they [the government] must use us!' (African participant, 13). At stake here was people's youth and ability to work hard to make their dreams come true. One African participant angrily recalled the time he helped his landlord clean the backyard, when he felt that there was much more he could do in Hong Kong, but was trapped by laws and regulations that tied him to the informal economy:

> My landlord came to move some stuff some time ago; after a few minutes he sat down and said, 'Let me rest for 30 minutes'. I said, 'You are wasting my time', and then I asked what he wanted to move and where to put them. He stood there all the time, looking at me and said, 'You really have power'. He was shocked. Another Chinese I helped out before, after he saw me working, said, 'You really can work'. These people can't do tough work! (African participant, 07)

The 'power' this participant repeatedly mentioned during our conversations referred not only to physical strength, but also to his ambition and drive to succeed, shared by other asylum seekers, who only wanted a fair chance to do their best. If the majority of participants believed that 'this is my time to make money, build myself, but I'm here as a useless person' (Bangladeshi participant, 45), at times losing morale, they also showed great resolve in striving to achieve security and a better life.

As stated earlier, lack of legal status was closely tied to the realization that there were no opportunities to improve one's life. One participant articulated his thoughts as follows: 'This situation has already broken our life. Our future is compromised. The Hong Kong Government shatters our future.' He continued: 'I want a better life. I want some permanent status, a normal life, the same as the life that local Chinese have here' (Bangladeshi participant, 45). Throughout the narratives of several participants emerged the shift in their thinking over time, as they sought to make sense of their future, when the lack of financial resources, knowledge and institutional opportunities appeared to hinder any step forward. As we saw in previous chapters, this was a cause of distress, disorientation and uncertainty about the meaning of life and future choices, prompting people to shift continuously between the wish to return home, the desire to move on and the determination to 'stay put' in Hong Kong and somehow weather or fight the difficulties as best they could.

160 *Establishing life at the destination*

This sense of precariousness led the participants to hold onto the life they were leading, in many cases only managing their survival on a day-by-day basis. While they felt that their skills and 'power' were not being properly used by the host society, the local community did benefit from their presence. In other words, asylum seeker expectations about making a contribution to society did not align with the reality that 'they must use us'. Rather, they were turned into instruments enabling the redistribution of resources, which eased local social inequalities within a context of increased social polarization in part caused by government social welfare policies aimed at advancing a 'productivist orientation' (Wong et al. 2010). From this perspective, the legal marginalization of asylum seekers, which the participants often blamed on the government's unwillingness to help them, may not be the unintended consequence of unclear asylum policies or of deterrent methods to stop new arrivals, as advocacy groups and government officials claim. Rather, official policies and practices around asylum seekers point to the emergence of categories that seem to define clear social and political levels of inclusion and exclusion, with the effect of forcing asylum seekers to pursue impoverished livelihoods in specific sectors of society (Calavita 2003, 2005; Dal Lago 2009), despite their aspirations. Precisely because they are denied full legal and economic rights, asylum seekers are restricted in their actions to taking up housing in specific areas under certain conditions, while interacting primarily with particular social strata of the local population. In this regard, Hong Kong's way of life may indeed benefit from the arrival of asylum seekers, in that they create opportunities for a number of low-income Hong Kong residents who lack access to comprehensive welfare, thus supporting Hong Kong's ideology of self-reliance.

In this light, and in view of the discussion in the previous chapters, it can be concluded that, while the majority of asylum seekers are demonized as abusive illegal migrants and penalized for working illegally, those few who abide by the rules are perceived and helped as the genuine refugees, in turn furthering the legal exclusion of the former. The lack of agency and constant need of care among the so-called genuine refugees, however, raises public fears about the impact on Hong Kong were the floodgates to be opened, specifically on the official policy of minimal spending on welfare (Wong et al. 2010; Goodstadt 2013). Therefore, whether they are depicted as a burden or as abusive, deviant characters, asylum seekers typify a new form of socio-legal stratification, at the bottom of which they function as the key means of inducing redistributive benefits and labour flexibility, while at the same time embodying an easy target for public resentment (Cohen 2006). A self-fulfilling cycle is thus fashioned (Squire 2009), arguably assisting the government to administer and articulate social order through immigration control (Bosworth and Guild 2008; Law and Lee 2006).

Notes

1 See, for example, online comments posted in the *South China Morning Post* to Carney (2013).
2 Labour Department, *Practical Guide for Employment of Foreign Domestic Helpers.* Available at www.labour.gov.hk/eng/public/wcp/FDHguide.pdf.

References

Agnew, R. (1992) 'Foundation for a General Strain Theory of Crime and Delinquency', *Criminology*, 30(1): 47–87.

Akcapar, S. K. (2006) 'Conversion as a Migration Strategy in Transit Country: Iranian Shiites Becoming Christians in Turkey', *International Migration Review*, 40(4): 817–853.

Bosworth, M. and Guild, M. (2008) 'Governing through Migration Control', *British Journal of Criminology*, 48(6): 703–719.

Calavita, K. (2003) 'A "Reserve Army of Delinquents": The Criminalization and Economic Punishment of Immigrants in Spain', *Punishment & Society*, 5(4): 399–413.

Calavita, K. (2005) *Immigrants at the Margins: Law, Race and Exclusion in Southern Europe*, Cambridge: Cambridge University Press.

Carney, J. (2013) 'Bangladeshi Refugees' "Unliveable Conditions" Appals Activists', *South China Morning Post*, 19 May. Viewed 19 May 2013: www.scmp.com/news/hong-kong/article/1240911/refugees-shabby-compound-appals-activists

Chan, C-K. (1998) 'Welfare Policies and the Construction of Welfare Relations in a Residual Welfare State: The Case of Hong Kong', *Social Policy & Administration*, 32(3): 278–291.

Chan, C. K. (2011) 'Hong Kong: Workfare in the World's Freest Economy', *International Journal of Social Welfare*, 20: 22–32.

Cohen, R. (2006) *Migration and Its Enemies: Global Capital, Migrant Labour and the Nation-State*, Aldershot: Ashgate.

Dal Lago, A. (2009) *Non-persone: L'esclusione dei Migranti in Una Società Globale*, Milano: Feltrinelli.

Fassin, D. (2012) *Humanitarian Reason: A Moral History of the Present*, Berkeley: University of California Press.

Fassin, D. and d'Halluin, E. (2007) 'Critical Evidence: The Politics of Trauma in French Asylum Policies', *Ethos*, 35(3): 300–329.

Fozdar, F. and Torezani, S. (2008) 'Discrimination and Well-Being: Perceptions of Refugees in Western Australia', *International Migration Review*, 42(1): 30–63.

Goodstadt, L. F. (2013) *Poverty in the Midst of Affluence: How Hong Kong Mismanaged Its Prosperity*, Hong Kong: Hong Kong University Press.

Grabska, K. (2006) 'Marginalization in Urban Spaces of the Global South: Urban Refugees in Cairo', *Journal of Refugee Studies*, 19(3): 287–307.

Hagan, J. M. (2008) *Migration Miracle: Faith, Hope and Meaning on the Undocumented Journey*, Harvard: Harvard University Press.

Harrell-Bond, B. (2002) 'Can Humanitarian Work with Refugees be Humane?', *Human Rights Quarterly*, 24(1): 51–85.

Herlihy, J. and Turner, S. W. (2009) 'The Psychology of Seeking Protection', *International Journal of Refugee Law*, 21(2): 171–192.

Hollands, M. (2001) 'Upon Closer Acquaintance: The Impact of Direct Contact with Refugees on Dutch Hosts, *Journal of Refugee Studies*, 14(3): 295–314.

Ip, C. (2011) 'The Shanty Towns of Hong Kong', *South China Morning Post*, 22 May. Viewed 22 May 2011: www.scmp.com/article/968425/shanty-towns-hong-kong

Jacobsen, K. (2002) 'Livelihoods in Conflict: The Pursuit of Livelihoods by Refugees and the Impact on the Human Security of Host Communities', *International Migration*, 40(5): 95–121.

Kim, M. (2010) 'Gender and International Marriage Migration', *Sociology Compass*, 4(9): 718–731.

162 Establishing life at the destination

Korac, M. (2009) *Remaking Home: Reconstructing Life, Place and Identity in Rome and Amsterdam*, New York: Berghahn Books.

Landolt, P. and Goldring, L. (2010) *The Long Term Impacts of Non-Citizenship on Work: Precarious Legal Status and the Institutional Production of a Migrant Working Poor*. Viewed 15 August 2012: www.yorku.ca/raps1/events/pdf/Landolt_Goldring.pdf

Law, K. Y. and Lee, K. M. (2006) 'Citizenship, Economy and Social Exclusion of Mainland Chinese Immigrations to Hong Kong', *Journal of Contemporary Asia*, 36(2): 217–242.

Lee, K. M., Wong, H. and Law, K. Y. (2007) 'Social Polarisation and Poverty in the Global City: The Case of Hong Kong', *China Report*, 43(1): 1–30.

Malkki, L. H. (1995) 'Refugees and Exile: From "Refugee Studies" to the National Order of Things', *Annual Review of Anthropology*, 24: 495–523.

Mathews, G. (2011) *Ghetto at the Center of the World: Chungking Mansions, Hong Kong*, Chicago: The University of Chicago Press.

Matsueda, R. L. (1988) 'The Current State of Differential Association Theory', *Crime & Delinquency*, 34(3): 277–306.

Muhtaseb, A. and Frey L. R. (2008) 'Arab Americans' Motives for Using the Internet as a Functional Media Alternative and Their Perceptions of U.S. Public Opinion', *Journal of Computer-Mediated Communication*, 13(3): 618–657.

Musarò, P. (2011) 'Living in Emergency: Humanitarian Images and the Inequality of Lives', *New Cultural Frontiers*, 2: 13–43.

Newendorp, N. D. (2008) *Uneasy Reunions: Immigration, Citizenship and Family Life in Post-1997 Hong Kong*, Stanford: Stanford University Press.

Piper, N. (2003) 'Wife or Worker? Worker or Wife? Marriage and Cross-Border Migration in Contemporary Japan', *International Journal of Population Geography*, 9(6): 457–469.

Siddiquee, A. and Kagan, C. (2006) 'The Internet, Empowerment, and Identity: An Exploration of Participation by Refugee Women in a Community Internet Project (CIP) in the United Kingdom (UK)', *Journal of Community & Applied Social Psychology*, 16(3): 189–206.

Smyth, G. and Kum, H. (2010) 'When They Don't Use It They Will Lose It: Professionals, Deprofessionalization and Reprofessionalization: The Case of Refugee Teachers in Scotland', *Journal of Refugee Studies*, 23(4): 503–522.

Squire, V. (2009) *The Exclusionary Politics of Asylum*, Houndmills: Palgrave Macmillan.

Ticktin, M. (2011) *Casualties of Care: Immigration and the Politics of Humanitarianism in France*, Berkley: University of California Press.

United Nations High Commissioner for Refugees (UNHCR) (1995) *Interviewing Applicants for Refugee Status (RLD 4)*. Viewed 12 May 2008: www.unhcr.org/publ/PUBL/3ae6bd670.pdf

Valtonen, K. (2004) 'From the Margin to Mainstream: Conceptualizing Refugee Settlement Processes', *Journal of Refugee Studies*, 17(1): 70–96.

van Meeteren, M, Engbersen, G. and van San, M. (2009) 'Striving for a Better Position: Aspirations and the Role of Cultural, Economic, and Social Capital for Irregular Migrants in Belgium', *International Migration Review*, 43(4): 881–907.

Vision First (2013) *The Compound under a Tree*, 9 May. Viewed 9 May 2013: http://vision firstnow.org/2013/05/09/the-compound-under-a-tree/

Weber, L. and Pickering, S. (2011) *Globalization and Borders: Death and the Global Frontier*, Houndmills: Palgrave Macmillan.

Wisniewski Otero, V. (2013) 'Do Not Misrepresent Refugees', *South China Morning Post*, 10 June. Viewed 10 June 2013: www.scmp.com/comment/letters/article/1257372/do-not-misrepresent-refugees

Wong, T. K-Y., Wan, P-S. and Law K. W-K. (2010) 'The Public's Changing Perceptions of the Condition of Social Welfare in Hong Kong: Lessons for Social Development', *Social Policy & Administration*, 44(5): 620–640.

Zhang, J. (2010) 'Marriage and Suicide among Chinese Rural Young Women', *Social Focus*, 89(1): 311–326.

Zhao, X., Zhang, L. and Sit, T. O. K. (2004) 'Income Inequalities under Economic Restructuring in Hong Kong', *Asian Survey*, 44(3): 442–473.

Zolberg, A. R., Suhrke, A. and Aguayo, S. (1989) *Escape from Violence: Conflict and the Refugee Crisis in the Developing World*, Oxford: Oxford University Press.

5 Asylum seeker engagement with the informal economy

This chapter advances understanding of asylum seekers' engagement with income-generating activities in Hong Kong and their socioeconomic contribution to that society to propose a framework within which two major findings strongly emerge. On the one hand, if the sectors in which some low-income residents generate income are shaped by the diminished opportunities resulting from public policy that overtly supports economic neoliberalism (Law and Lee 2006; Chan 2011; Goodstadt 2013), such conditions are equally impacted by the asylum seekers who are resident in Hong Kong. On the other hand, asylum seekers' income-generating strategies are necessarily related to the characteristics of the local ethnic community in which they are embedded and the market opportunities that are intertwined with co-ethnic demand (cf. Aldrich and Waldinger 1990). In other words, asylum seekers seem to exploit specific local and transnational opportunities in the pursuit of their livelihoods, while at the same time becoming instrumental in enabling local entrepreneurs to generate profit.

In addition to the previous argument, this chapter contends that, while asylum seekers effectively save or generate jobs for certain local residents, they do not take jobs from local workers. Rather, they provide labour supply in specific sectors and jobs affected by a chronic or occasional shortage of labour because citizens and other legal residents are either prevented from engaging in or are possibly unwilling to engage in such labour-intensive, often dangerous jobs. Conversely, in responding to their marginalization, asylum seekers form networks with specific strata of the local population engaged in risk-taking entrepreneurialism in low-value-added, often small-scale economies and localities. Further, by informally providing these entrepreneurs with flexible and cheap labour, while also furnishing reliable networks that create and connect trading opportunities both within and far beyond the geographical boundaries of Hong Kong, asylum seekers create economic opportunities for themselves and these local entrepreneurs. Yet it is through the institutional and political framework that the engagement of asylum seekers in the informal economy is effectively regulated. Local selective border control and global economic forces combine to rank individuals by their presumed abilities and legal status, de facto offering those residents who rank slightly above asylum seekers in the social ladder the means to pursue profit-making activities by exploiting the labour and social capital of asylum seekers.

Engagement with the informal economy   165

In what follows, I first analyze the involvement of asylum seekers in the informal economy in view of the fieldwork I conducted in the outer areas of the city, in a few selected sectors in which illegal work – defined as the employment of foreigners who do not have the legal right to work – was available (see Map 1.2). This analysis brings into light both licit and illicit activities: the former being the production and distribution of goods and services that are legal, although carried out in violation of the public regulatory framework in terms of conditions of work, wages and employment (Castells and Portes 1989); whereas the latter is defined as the distribution of goods which, for their very nature, occurs 'underground', even where salaries and conditions of work are in line with public norms or better than in other sectors (Sassen 1991).

Second, the economic experiences of asylum seekers are examined vis-à-vis the networks they establish within co-national and co-ethnic transnational communities. Drawing on the participation of the people involved in trading activities across Hong Kong, and more specifically in the core business-oriented districts of the Kowloon peninsula, at the two edges of the city's hierarchy of wealth distribution – Tsim Sha Tsui and Sham Shui Po – the international dimension of this global city is brought to the fore by identifying the niche markets in which asylum seekers work. Yet this analysis is limited to only some of the activities in which asylum seekers engage. The recycling trade and the garment, mobile phone and car parts trade with the economically developing countries from which asylum seekers originate are examined for the considerable number of male asylum seekers involved in them, and because they clearly illustrate the complex processes that affect refugees' job opportunities and the strategies they adopt.

The micro-economy of recycling waste

While answering questions about their experience of working in the city, many participants showed me their work sites and the tasks they performed. I was then introduced to their colleagues and employers, and extensive time was spent on observing the activities, patterns of engagement and places where asylum seekers generate income. I was told that a very high number of asylum seekers are employed as labourers in the many yards that recycle fabrics, plastics and electrical and electronic waste, or e-waste. In rather desolate locations in the northern regions of Hong Kong, surrounded by dust, dirt and overgrown grass, and tall metal walls with cameras at the front gate to protect privacy, several of these worksites recycle the waste produced by rising urban consumerism. The disposal of waste, including e-waste, is an emerging and increasingly significant industry worldwide (Grossman 2006), an examination of which reveals the impact on contemporary society of both the technological innovations that drive globalization (Castells 2000) and the new high-end lifestyles and consumption behaviours said to contribute to gentrification and conversely to increased demand for low-wage workers (Sassen 2001). In Hong Kong, the recycling of garments, plastics and electrical and electronic equipment provides employment for low-wage workers in low-status jobs. Additionally, the management of the disposal of such materials

166 *Engagement with the informal economy*

has created opportunities for segments of society to procure stable income in a mainly survival-oriented economy, running on marginal profits and involving several levels of production relations.

Contrary to what is generally believed, superfluous waste materials no longer needed in developed countries are not always dumped in developing countries. At the same time, waste often has some form of value (Lepawsky and McNabb 2009). As Yang (2008) observes in the case of China, various types of waste in Hong Kong are regarded as a resource. In particular, e-waste contains valuable materials such as gold and copper which can be reused or resold for processing in other sectors. In Hong Kong, everything that can be recycled is generally collected from the streets, sold to small workshops in urban areas and then transported to larger yards in the New Territories. Usable items are either dismantled or repaired before being sold for reuse in China and developing countries. For example, several yards I visited collect air conditioners, refrigerators, photocopy machines, computers and TV sets. Incoming e-waste generally originates in the city; however, in many cases containers of e-waste are imported from countries such as Japan.

In general, scrapyards specialize in either dismantling machines or fixing reusable items. Other yards deal in cars and car parts, cutting and selling spare parts or fixing them when purchased second-hand in local or Japanese markets for export to developing countries. While yards specialize in one or another service, it is clear that the site owners nonetheless tend to diversify their work in response to arising business opportunities and the availability of the items normally recycled. In addition, work is mainly seasonal, with disposal of electronics occurring most often in the months between March and November.

This rudimentary but highly stratified system of informal collection and disposal of waste involves the employment of asylum seekers as cheap labourers and street collectors.

Labouring in the scrapyards

The interviewees said that the tasks assigned to them included loading and unloading containers and cargos from trucks and dismantling or fixing the items handled by the yards. As the participants pointed out, this was 'hard work', 'very difficult' and 'dangerous'. It generally involved the use of heavy hammers and chainsaws to break apart electronic appliances and metals, from morning until dusk in dirty conditions and fear of police arrest. Gloves were normally available, but they were not useful when dealing with thick TV screens and piercing metals 'sharp as knives that easily cut you' (Pakistani participant, 34). As an example, during my site visits I regularly met one African interviewee, and on two occasions over a five-month period he had his fingers badly injured, requiring six stitches each time. Another South Asian participant was first interviewed when he was taking a break from work because a finger on his right hand had been cut 'to the bone' (Pakistani participant, 83d) while handling a sharp iron sheet. While emergency medical care is free and accessible to recognizance paper holders, no

Salaries were said to be exploitative. Some asylum seekers worked on a monthly basis for long hours at minimal salary. In most cases, other forms of payment included wages ranging from HK$50 to HK$300 per day or salaries paid by the piece. In the latter case, some participants explained that for dismantling a large refrigerator they would receive HK$7, while HK$5 was paid for other appliances. One Pakistani interviewee said that he tried to work as much as he could from Monday to Saturday to earn between HK$2500–3000 monthly, while he devoted Sundays to his girlfriend. The longer and faster he worked, the more he could earn. However, the faster people worked, the more tired and careless they would become, which reportedly increased the likelihood of injuries. Some asylum seekers were paid per task performed. For instance, a group of Pakistanis revealed that they had been tasked with building the office unit of a new yard, for which they would be paid a fixed amount of money regardless of the time or number of people needed to complete the task. Again, the faster they worked the sooner they would complete their task, making themselves available for other work.

Despite payments being agreed with site owners, the participants revealed that at times they worked for weeks, or even months, and received no wages. Some were arrested before they could be remunerated for their work; others who were new and knew nothing about the city were too scared to leave the yards, so they endured hard work for no wages, contrary to what they had been promised. Some other interviewees recounted that payment of their wages was constantly delayed. For example, one African participant explained that he vehemently protested to his employer on more than one occasion, threatening to go to the police, and that he spent long hours in front of the main gate until he was finally paid the money he was owed. As he said, the site owner did not pay him on time not only because this was standard practice among some employers, but also because he had no money as 'business was slow' (African participant, 07) in the winter months.

Conditions of work were reportedly exploitative regardless of whether the sites were managed by Chinese or non-Chinese residents. Some asylum seekers, however, stated that the conditions were worse in the yards where production was organized by non-Chinese entrepreneurs. In particular, I was often told that 'Pakistanis are no good. . . . Sometimes they give you work, but they don't pay' (Sri Lankan participant, 84g). While this view was generally shared by the ethnic groups under study, and even by Pakistani interviewees who had direct experience of working in this sector with different employers, the employers of African origin were also normally disliked because they were considered greedy. On this point, it is noteworthy that distinctions based on people's legal status often overruled more traditional distinctions based on social status, education or other achievements. As one Pakistani asylum seeker claimed when describing the attitude of his co-national Hong Kong residents towards their employees, 'It depends on the [legal] status that people have here. In Hong Kong even if you come from a very low caste, it doesn't matter. But if you don't have a Hong Kong ID card, then you are exploited' (Pakistani participant, 76a).

168 *Engagement with the informal economy*

Kloosterman et al. (1999) identify that the rate of participation in entrepreneurship among lawfully resident immigrant populations is influenced by their socioeconomic and ethno-social characteristics and the specific opportunity structure prevalent in that society. Lacking in most cases the means to finance larger enterprises or to engage in mainstream society, or higher educational qualifications and local language skills, residents of immigrant background start up their own businesses often on the margins of the sectors in which they can comfortably operate (Newendorp 2010). Further, discriminatory attitudes towards culturally different immigrant populations force ethnic minority residents into elementary employment, poverty or unemployment (Ashencaen Crabtree and Wong 2012), thus increasing the likelihood that they will seek to establish their own business. However, as seen in Chapter 1, the lower the barrier of entry into the more accessible economic activities, the higher will be the level of competition in that sector (Kloosterman et al. 1999; Panayiotopoulos 2010). Therefore, business owners engage in undercutting and evade regulatory systems to ensure their business's survival (Jordan and Travers 1998). In this view, if co-national and co-ethnic irregular migrants are highly sought after as low-wage workers, these employees do not necessarily gain from working within their local community. Because of their monopolistic position as lawfully present residents, employers often exploit their co-ethnic and co-national newcomers who have irregular immigration status (McKay et al. 2011).

From my interviews with employers working in this line of business, it became apparent that several employers of non-Chinese background, including former asylum seekers who had acquired legal status through marriage, worked in the recycling business because of what they perceived were their poor prospects for social mobility in Hong Kong. For instance, a Pakistani employer who established his business by selling luxury second-hand cars to developing countries explained that he had worked for years in the construction sector before he managed to earn enough capital to start his own company. When he decided to set up his own business, opening a recycling yard dealing with markets in his native country was the easiest way to earn an income and thereby attempt to advance his social status, as he believed that his career options were limited to employment in low-wage menial work or self-employment in such niche and ethnic markets. Similarly, another employer revealed: 'I tried to get a job in a factory, office, but it is difficult for the fact that I'm not Chinese. . . . Also, if you want to work, probably you are not paid much to support your family. And then, by looking around I realized that there are certain areas that are still not developed' (African resident, 03). In such areas, demand was not being met and a stable income could thus be made by investing relatively smaller amounts than are required in other sectors. For this participant, limited as he was by a lack of education and language skills, his career choice was also influenced by the relatively little capital needed to start such a business. As he said, in addition to money for goods and rent, 'the rest is all about hard work' – which asylum seekers could provide.

The asylum seeker participants expressed mixed feelings of understanding and resentfulness towards their employers. They knew that employers could

Engagement with the informal economy   169

not afford to pay higher salaries, and at times they were clearly grateful for the help they received, but they also resented their employers for taking advantage of them while making a stable profit. On the other hand, employers stated that because work was irregular and largely seasonal, they could not afford to formally employ workers. While most did not confirm that they were hiring asylum seekers – rather, they claimed they were helping friends and compatriots to get by in 'difficult Hong Kong' – they often stressed that wages for local residents were higher. Thus, employing locals would decrease the number of workers they could employ, thereby reducing production output and profit margins, which were already stretched by the low value of the product and the many levels of production relations involved.

As an African site owner eloquently explained concerning this line of business, he and other entrepreneurs like him relied on asylum seekers because 'asylum seekers are like scavengers. They get jobs that the residents cannot do, like in these workshops. . . . These are the kinds of jobs that don't need documentation. You know what I mean? It is not done on a permanent basis. It is flexible work. So I would prefer the government kept a blind eye on what they do' (African resident, 06). Another employer commented that in this type of work, 'It is all about providing a good service to customers. If you want to work, you need to adapt to the market and develop some means to beat the competitors. . . . [For] locals, you would have to pay them what you may not be able to pay, because if you pay them you cannot keep up' (Pakistani resident, 02). In practice, as labour costs and competition were high but profit margins low, 'many of these companies pay workers HK$150 or HK$200 for 12 hours of work. Do you think that local people can do that job? Impossible. You need to pay them at least HK$800. But if you spend HK$800 for one worker, you can't open these kinds of companies' (Bangladeshi participant, 79d), a Bangladeshi asylum seeker explained. This same man also claimed that he would eventually open a similar business, after acquiring legal status, because this was the job he was familiar with, and e-waste and asylum seekers were a reliable source of income, albeit limited and involving a degree of risk of discovery by the authorities.

Importantly, a significant majority of the refugee interviewees were working from about 3 or 4 up to 20 days a month. Their employers and jobs varied depending on the business opportunities available. As outlined in the previous chapter, friends and relatives were the primary source of information to assist in securing a job in this sector, but a number of participants revealed that another tactic used was to wait on the streets to be approached by prospective employers. As Ullah (2010) describes in the case of Bangladeshi migrants in Sham Shui Po, even in outer areas asylum seekers have certain places where the hiring process is facilitated. Nonetheless, as they were fearful of venturing near the yards and being questioned by the authorities, the norm for many participants was the following: 'Most of the times we just sit at home. If they need us, they will call us' (Bangladeshi participant, 36).

The flexible recruitment of asylum seekers as cheap labour, always available to perform casual work, can be said to positively affect this sector of the economy.

170   *Engagement with the informal economy*

Several scholars have examined the benefit of having a large army of people with irregular status waiting to supplement the insufficient and/or expensive local workforce while providing the operational means for small enterprises to survive (Borretti 2010; Calavita 2003). In Hong Kong, it can be said that recycling activities would hardly remain viable for the local resident population engaged in such work were not asylum seekers acting as the instruments of cheap labour casualization. Moreover, as they patiently 'wait at home', asylum seekers rarely find work in the sectors in which the local resident population seeks employment. As the employers interviewed explained, one of the reasons why they needed to employ asylum seekers was that they are physically strong, in addition to their willingness to work long hours for low wages. Africans and South Asians were seen as better able than Chinese to handle bulky electrical equipment and heavy car parts without any mechanical assistance.

Collecting waste on the streets

Another form of income generation devised by asylum seekers was to collect garment, plastic and electronic waste on the streets to sell to small recycling workshops, who would later resell the waste to recycling yards. I was told that numbers of asylum seekers venture around their neighbourhood for this purpose. They overcame their shame at collecting rubbish off the streets, to generate a small income from the valuable items they find in or near garbage bins, because 'Chinese people throw away many things and if I go around two to three days a week, I can find something useful' (Bangladeshi participant, 45). Items were then weighed, and a few dollars could be made from a successful day. These asylum seekers often operated alone but, mindful of the needs of their compatriots and roommates, would often share the workload so that everyone could have a chance to find useful materials to sell. However, during conversations with a group of Bangladeshi participants and later on with other asylum seekers, I was informed that this practice of informal waste collection had been recently jeopardized by heightened policing following the 2009 amendment of the Immigration Ordinance, which made illegal work a crime (see Chapter 2).

While many participants argued that police checks were often taking place in or near the recycling yards, with the consequence that asylum seekers caught working were sentenced to very long prison terms, they affirmed that they were surprised and outraged that collecting garbage on the streets would now amount to illegal work. Until the change in legislation, this had been considered a safe means to make some money for those who did not want to risk jail sentences by working in the yards. 'I collect garbage, but now even this is a problem with the police. They have stopped me three times already, asking what I was doing with those metals and where I was taking them. This is not work. People throw away a lot of things and I just collect to sell them. But now police said I can't do it' (Bangladeshi participant, 48), I was told by a visibly angry but resigned asylum seeker.

The discussion presented in this chapter reveals the policing of asylum seekers in Hong Kong to be a racialized, gendered practice, dependent on the variables of

Engagement with the informal economy   171

time and space, or the temporal and geographical context. Mathews (2011) argues that policing in the HKSAR operates largely in response to complaints, demonstrating at times a permissible attitude towards unregulated businesses or activities that raise no or few complaints. Based on his fieldwork, but also doubtless generalizable to the territory as a whole, Mathews (2011: 165) identified that by and large the police 'operate under the principle of laissez-faire neoliberalism: as long as the Hong Kong public is not harmed, let business go on unimpeded, since business is the foremost priority of Hong Kong'. Under this scenario, whereas asylum seekers working as labourers in the scrapyards were rarely taking jobs from locals, informal garbage collection is an activity that local elderly Chinese residents often perform as a means to support their living expenses in the absence of comprehensive government welfare (Chan 1998). Consequently, asylum seekers undertaking this work may be viewed as competing for resources with the local poor. While competition between asylum seekers and Hong Kong locals for housing and food is minimal, and the asylum seeker 'market' is actually beneficial to specific strata of the local population (see Chapter 4), asylum seeker engagement with work opportunities implies that certain local residents may be 'harmed'. Thus, increased policing of practices such as carton collection may reflect the intention to dissuade strangers from engaging in activities that could affect the livelihoods of local residents. This occurred at a time when, following the criminalization of illegal work, policing became more focused on controlling this population as their numbers were rising and, as will be argued later, global economic conditions and urban structures appeared to be widening social polarization and income disparities. Street collectors consequently found themselves in a very difficult position. Unwilling to work in the yards but prevented from collecting waste, they felt compelled to seek a viable form of income generation by returning to those yards they had previously left for fear of police arrest. The escape routes in these yards, and the practice of asylum seekers guarding the premises by being on the lookout, lowered the risk of apprehension, while effectively taking them off the streets.

Underground economy and formal work performed illegally

This section examines the involvement of asylum seekers in economic activities which are either illegal or legal and performed according to the law, but for which asylum seekers falsify their identity to gain access to formal labour opportunities. On the one hand, the evidence shows that asylum seekers were working in the production and distribution of goods and services that are illicit and therefore normally prosecuted under the law, for example, as labourers in factories and scrapyards or as touts on the streets. On the other, some asylum seekers had falsely obtained documents, such as counterfeit ID cards, to perform work in the formal labour market. While this analysis does not intend to cast ethical judgements on the types of activities undertaken or the moral integrity of the people involved, and nor does it seek to jeopardize in any way the security of the asylum seekers involved, these activities are briefly analyzed for they further illustrate the

172   *Engagement with the informal economy*

kinds of structural opportunities exploited by asylum seekers. At the same time, this analysis advances the argument that asylum seekers fill labour demand while enabling workplace flexibility. However, the sweatshop conditions that surface in other global cities do not always emerge as significant in the Hong Kong context (Sassen 1998).

The informal economy is heterogeneous in terms of the variety of activities performed and the relations of production that underlie its formation. According to Castells and Portes (1989: 13), the informal economy affects various elements of the work process. It may refer to the status of labour, which may be undeclared, underpaid or employed 'under circumstances that society's norms would not otherwise allow', such as in the absence of a legal permit or with a counterfeit permit. It may denote the conditions of work, which are often characterized by tasks that are dangerous and safety measures that are insufficiently implemented. It may refer to the way enterprises are managed, such as when taxes are evaded and unrecorded payments are made under the table. Or the informal economy may include economic activities that by their nature are defined as criminal by the laws of the country in which they take place.

In contrast to licit activities occurring in violation of the public regulatory framework, which could otherwise take place formally in broad daylight were the local structural economic conditions more favourable, due to the hazards they are believed to pose for society some economic activities cannot occur 'above ground'. This may be so even when conditions of work, employment and salaries are in line with public norms. Sassen (1991) defines such activities as shaping the 'underground economy'. In Hong Kong, as I observed in the many months spent in the field, such activities mainly take the form of the distribution of drugs and the production and transfer of goods whose existence defies health and hygiene safety requirements or copyright laws.

Producing and trading illegally

Although I could not visit the sites at which underground activities were said to be occurring because of the secrecy that surrounded those activities, a few participants narrated their direct experiences with working in such yards. For example, one Sri Lankan participant who fled his country in 2005 explained that in his first year in Hong Kong, when ISS services were not available and he knew little about asylum or other forms of support, his fellow asylum seekers suggested that he approach a scrapyard managed by local Chinese to find work. The yard was dealing in Chinese-manufactured electronic items assembled in Hong Kong to be shipped overseas in violation of copyright laws. As he and other participants who performed similar work affirmed, employment took the form of day labour, but wages were relatively higher than in recycling. An African participant mentioned that he normally earned HK$300 for a few hours packaging goods that violated copyright laws. Similarly, another interviewee claimed to have worked for a short time in an underground factory where high-end desktop computers were illegally assembled by asylum seekers for HK$500 a day.

Engagement with the informal economy 173

Although first-hand observation could not be carried out to sustain such claims, I was told that the tasks performed consisted of unloading containers of meat originating from China and marking it with a different country of origin stamp. The containers were then reloaded with the altered goods and transported to the port for export. Similarly, Chinese-manufactured flat-screen TV sets were said to be labelled as expensive foreign brands, packed into cartons that resembled those of these manufacturers and prepared for shipping. In the previous cases, employers were generally local Chinese, which is understandable in view of the substantial capital that at times had to be invested into such businesses. In one case, an asylum seeker revealed that one of his occasional employers produced over 200 computers daily, or roughly one container per day, amounting to a total value of several million Hong Kong dollars.

In these businesses, the final products were not usually intended for sale in Hong Kong but were shipped to various destinations around the world. A recent report by the *New York Times* on unauthorized makers of Nike shoes confirms that fake Chinese-manufactured goods are normally shipped through Hong Kong (Schmidle 2010). This is no surprise for the shipping industry is a critical sector of the Hong Kong economy (Loughlin and Pannell 2010), especially given Hong Kong's role as an entrepôt economy facilitating the re-export of goods from China to the rest of the world. As argued by Feenstra and Hanson (2004), intermediaries in Hong Kong take advantage of the territory's proximity to China and its location as a hub for international shipping to make considerable income by sorting, packaging and marketing Chinese goods. Of course, some of these goods may be processed irrespective of the intellectual property and safety norms legally protected in Hong Kong and elsewhere, and for this reason, their profitability may increase.

In particular, when goods are shipped to countries in which copyright laws are rarely enforced, if they exist at all, and items produced by the rightful brand makers are affordable only for a minority of the local population, cheaper alternatives may appear in the market to meet the growing demand for products advertised globally. The significance of copy watches and the mobile phones trade for small businesses and asylum seekers alike in Hong Kong will be explored in more detail subsequently. However, it is worth noting here that some interviewees argued that they could make a stable profit only when either or both laws protecting the intellectual property of the goods they dealt with were violated and taxes were evaded in countries of destination by declaring less than the actual shipment value. At times, this was achieved by hiding valuables in the back of containers or bribing customs officials and police at destination countries. In relation to this, a South Asian asylum seeker, who knew several resident co-national entrepreneurs, explained that some of the scrapyard owners were smuggling cars into South Asia with the help of customs and registry officials in countries in that region. The following extract from one of our many conversations illustrates this point, while also suggesting a strict link between social and economic conditions in some of the developing countries that produce the highest numbers of asylum seeker arrivals in Hong Kong and the exploitation asylum seekers were subjected

174 *Engagement with the informal economy*

to by residents who took advantage of the growing inequality in earning capacity in origin and destination countries:

> When they buy spare parts, they can sell them in my country for very expensive price. . . . There is a good margin of profit. If they buy cars, they may pay something to police and securities. . . . Then they need to pay for the number plate. Maybe there are about four or five different cars in different cities of the country travelling with the same number plate. . . . They do this because they can save money from the official registration. . . . You know, there is a lot of corruption, mafia and police officers, politicians, landlords – these people can buy, and whatever they do they can do it without fear. The poor cannot get justice. If you want justice, you have to buy it. (Pakistani participant, 34)

As demand for certain products increases worldwide, so does the number of people in Hong Kong who develop transnational links to service these emerging markets. McEwan et al. (2005) argue that ethnic businesses shape and are shaped by transnational opportunities arising under conditions of globalization. In such a view, transnational networks can be said to reduce costs and thus support the development of migrant communities as migrant entrepreneurs seek to establish their position in a host country (Massey et al. 1987; Sassen 1998). Indeed, trading with overseas markets is often the best career option for local residents of immigrant background, as they are knowledgeable of their native country and can rely on the social capital of asylum seekers, who develop social capital either in the country of origin or in Hong Kong by approaching co-national tourist traders. Partly confirming the prevalence of this phenomenon, when a Sri Lankan participant who had been in Hong Kong for over five years was asked whether he had thought of starting some sort of business there, given his entrepreneurial background, he explained that trading with countries in which his language was spoken was not only ideal but also often the only viable path for foreigners, as little chance of success was available to self-employed ethnic minorities who did not rely on co-national networks. As he put it: 'Doing business [in Hong Kong] would mean from here to India or from here to Sri Lanka. But I can't go to Sri Lanka, and I don't have any friends in India' (Sri Lankan participant, 16). Similarly, one African employer argued that he was handling e-waste while providing shipping services to growing numbers of African customers who were buying cars for re-export to expanding African markets. He said that buying second-hand cars in Hong Kong and spare parts to move the steering wheel from right- to left-hand drive was cheaper than buying second-hand cars in Europe or North America. A 40-foot-long container could be shipped to West Africa for approximately HK$6000, plus a little extra that he would pay to his friends to ensure customs at the destination would not bother checking the contents or would take a good part of the shipment as informal customs duty. His business relied significantly on bonded interpersonal connections, to avoid the risk that shipments would be considerably lightened before delivery were he to do business with strangers.

Interestingly, some participants argued that small, economically low-scale ethnic enterprises could operate in Hong Kong rather undisturbed for reasons including the complicity of local authorities. The degree of policing of such businesses appeared to be related to Hong Kong's role as a global logistics centre and a destination for tourists from developed and developing countries alike. As one very resourceful South Asian participant who worked in this sector argued, trading in goods that breach copyright laws is largely tolerated due to the business it generates for Hong Kong, in terms of both employment and tourism. In the case of the latter, his opinion was that '[t]he authorities know all the shops and the faces of the people on the streets that sell these things. They know, but they don't care. Why? . . . Because Hong Kong is a tourist place and a business city; a lot of people come from Australia, Europe and other countries to buy fake bags and copy watches. If they don't come here, they will go somewhere else' (Bangladeshi participant, 79d).

The edge that such activities gives Hong Kong, enabling it to remain competitive in an increasingly crowded but vital shipping market (Byron 2010; Loughlin and Pannell 2010) while fostering its global position as a one-stop shopping destination (McDonogh and Wong 2005), arguably renders this officially shunned but active market of goods produced and traded informally invaluable to the city. As the previous participant explained, if a few people are arrested and shops and yards closed at times, nothing would really change; business would continue undisrupted to meet the growing demand.

Fabricated identities

An interesting consequence of the significant flow of goods through Hong Kong for re-export relates to labour demand in the occupations in which such materials are handled and shipped. In the more visible companies in particular, over which government controls tend to be tighter and regulatory norms governing labour followed more scrupulously, a number of asylum seekers were said to be employed using other persons' identity documents or fake IDs. In these cases, it appears that wages were in line with those paid to other local employees with regular immigration status, and this was certainly a reason for this type of work being particularly attractive to asylum seekers despite it being 'tough' and 'dangerous'.

Some asylum seekers were working for small companies, probably subcontractors at docks and on ships. When the genuine identity documents of compatriots were used, these people received a few thousand dollars monthly from the asylum seekers who were using their ID, while the worker would pay taxes. As one South Asian interviewee revealed, he worked 'loading and unloading containers' before the rightful owner of his ID card returned to his native country. He said, '[I]t was like he was working legally, but actually I was working in his place' (Pakistani participant, 85h). Furthermore, this participant explained that after he quit his job he occasionally returned to his previous employer for a few days of relatively well-paid work whenever the company was short of labour in busier times.

176 *Engagement with the informal economy*

Labour shortage in the just-in-time economy

Three findings strongly emerge from the previous discussion. First, at a time of heightened labour casualization and subcontracting there seems to be demand for unskilled menial workers in Hong Kong which does not necessarily involve marginal processes of production in exploitative conditions of work. While work in the underground economy was most likely to be exploitative, hard and dangerous, wages were normally higher than those in recycling, and at times, local Chinese were also employed. In the formal labour market, asylum seekers were paid regular wages, although locals tended to consider such wages too low given the conditions of work (Lee 2013). In this regard, further research could endeavour to analyze whether and how asylum seekers impact wages in the formal labour market in Hong Kong. In light of the probable low numbers of asylum seekers in the formal labour market, what seems more striking, however, is that work was available at regular salaries in occupations in which the local resident population either was reluctant to work or could not entirely fulfil market demand. One African participant, for example, explained that on one occasion, when he and his friends were playing football next to a construction site, they were approached by the site manager who offered them work. He would pay them HK$16,000 a month until project completion, but when the asylum seekers said that they had no legal permit to work in Hong Kong, the prospective employer left, disappointed. Some participants said that, other than unloading containers at docks, South Asian asylum seekers were also filling vacancies in road construction, laying down pipes or operating heavy machinery. In this case, South Asians had the advantage of blending in more easily than Africans, who would raise suspicion were they seen engaging in open-air work due to the small number of legal African residents in the territory. 'It is easier to ask a black person for his Hong Kong ID card than bothering asking Indians and Pakistanis' (African participant, 09), I was often told.

Second, it is clear that asylum seekers filled unskilled positions and provided extra help when needed to complete tasks that were at times well paid with respect to the profit that employers presumably made (Hutchins 1999). To illustrate this point further, it was found that asylum seekers are often employed as 'professional queuers' when new electronic gadgets are released, for which they are paid substantially. On the occasion of the launch in Hong Kong of a new iPhone (Cheung 2011), some asylum seekers were paid HK$300 to line up at the Apple store overnight and HK$1000 if they succeeded in purchasing the new phone. This move was apparently driven by the fact that in China this model was sold a few weeks later, which guaranteed a significant margin of profit for those who could deliver the product across the border ahead of its official release. In practice, while some of the conditions of work for asylum seekers could be viewed as exploitative, relatively higher wages were said to positively offset the difficulties experienced in the 3D jobs.

Third, exploitative conditions of work were noticeable in work activities that normally take place within the ethnic migrant community, in which legal status or

Engagement with the informal economy 177

lack thereof marked the extent of such exploitation. However, if asylum seekers enjoyed relatively better treatment when performing illegal work for local Chinese residents, based on the data in this research the difference in treatment does not seem to be based entirely on ethnicity, as much as it is related to the sector of employment and the margins of profit available in that sector. Those residents who achieved higher revenues paid their workers more and tended to offer better working conditions than business owners engaged in low-end activities structured around very low-added-value production. In both cases, asylum seekers served a precise role as casual workers, from which legal Hong Kong residents benefited. To some extent, these trends are more obvious when gender and international trade are inserted into the picture.

Women in the informal labour market

While the engagement of women in income-generating activities was not the focus of this research, during the fieldwork it became clear that female asylum seekers play a considerable role in the informal economy. As only a few women were interviewed, this section only offers partial conclusions on this topic, pointing to areas where further research is needed.

The majority of the female asylum seekers I encountered had worked as maids in Hong Kong, mainly employed by dual-income families to look after their homes, children or the elderly. Foreign domestic helpers are strictly forbidden from working for more than one employer at a time and from changing sector of employment when given a domestic work visa. Yet earlier research has shown that domestic workers may perform illegal work when their formal employer assigns them tasks to be carried out outside the normally accepted definition of 'household chores' (Constable 1997). For example, maids may choose or be forced to work as waitresses in bars and restaurants, as clerks in shops or in small factories owned by their regular employer. Mathews (2011) found domestic helpers who were supposedly only allowed to work in their employer's home servicing guest houses and other businesses. Constable (1997) argues that foreign domestic helpers working illegally while also regularly employed provide an important source of cheap labour, which can be exploited by their resident employers. If domestic helpers are generally paid the minimum salary of HK$3740 per month, or reportedly sometimes less (Lee and Petersen 2006), employers may also save considerable money in salaries by having their maids carry out the work for which other people should be employed at higher wages.

This research found that while employers sometimes exploit their foreign maids who are regularly employed under the strict immigration rules set by the scheme that governs their employment (Ozeki 1995), domestic helpers can also benefit from conditions of informalization and casualization of labour. What emerged most clearly during the fieldwork is that a number of women had voluntarily stepped into illegality, giving up their regular employment to access economic opportunities otherwise legally unattainable for foreign domestic helpers. As the women participants explained, whether they had left their job because they terminated their contract or could not find another employer after being dismissed, a number of domestic helpers were resorting to seeking asylum with the ImmD in order to prolong their stay in the territory. While no doubt is cast here on the genuineness of their claims, it is argued that, in the context of Hong Kong, in some cases the decision to engage in irregular work was dependent on the convenience of working by the hour rather than full-time. For example, some interviewees explained that they could earn between HK$20 and (more commonly) HK$40 per hour in domestic work. If six to eight hours of work per day could be secured, with different families, instead of the regular salary of just over HK$3000 paid for day-long work, sometimes in conditions of abuse (Constable 1997; Mok 2008), one's monthly income could be raised substantially.

On this subject, a Sri Lankan asylum seeker explained that she was often asked by families to cook for them in their homes, equating to a commitment of a couple of hours per day for HK$40 on average. Another interviewee stressed that many employers either did not need a full-time maid or did not want to be bound to one. While some residents employed maids only when they needed them for a few hours a week, paid in cash, others regularly employed domestic helpers, ostensibly on a full-time basis, but requested that they find some additional work to complement their wage salary. In fact, under these arrangements employers would pay them less than the minimum monthly wage because they worked fewer hours at home. One interviewee said that she retained her legal status in this way. She was paid HK$2000 by the employer who sponsored her visa for full-time work, but her employer then told her to work only three hours per day three times a week, so that the rest of the time she needed to work for other families, who only occasionally wanted help with household chores or childcare. In another case, a male participant said that he helped a few former domestic helpers obtain irregular work through the Internet. 'Especially at Christmas there are many people who answered to my posts because they wanted extra help for cleaning, shopping, day-care and things like that; it is only part-time' (Sri Liankan participant, 84g), I was told.

As the women participants explained, some believed that their life would become 'easier' this way compared to working full-time. The extent to which conditions of work can become abusive and exploitative when workers become invisible, hidden behind domestic walls, has been widely reported in Hong Kong and elsewhere (Anggraeni 2006). Some of my interviewees experienced such forms of abuse. One Sri Lankan domestic helper, for instance, said that she worked for six to seven months for a family who paid her only HK$2000 per month to work long hours with little time for rest. In a moment of profound desperation, she escaped the premises while both of her employers were out. She then met a co-national on the streets who helped her find full-time work in a nursing home for a salary of HK$4500, using someone else's Hong Kong ID card, where her hours of work were from 7 a.m. to 7 p.m. However, she was arrested a few weeks later and was never paid.

In domestic service, it appears that both employers and workers involved in casual work arrangements benefited from a sort of win-win situation. However,

Engagement with the informal economy 179

the asylum seekers faced significant risk, in addition to being subjected to economic market forces to a greater extent than were regular workers. In particular, it was said that with the provision of ISS support for asylum seekers, worth about HK$2000 in accommodation and food, more money could be saved, spent on boyfriends or remitted home. One Indonesian interviewee explained that after she found a South Asian asylum seeker boyfriend she quit her job to be re-employed part-time by her same boss. While the former maid explained that she was earning more overall, and having more and better quality time for herself, without holding on to her legal status, the employer was paying her less money for the same number of hours of work. Nevertheless, practical advantages were evident when multiple part-time opportunities could be secured and when asylum screening procedures involved long periods of waiting – something which the ImmD appeared firmly committed to eradicating by prioritizing the screening of such claims.[1]

In view of the increasing feminization of migration (Li et al. 1998; Sassen 1998) and the equally evident surge of women in the labour force in Hong Kong (Lee et al. 2007; Tai 2013), this aspect of asylum certainly requires further study to enable better understanding of all facets of migrant women's engagement with the informal economy. It appears that in the context analyzed here, within those sectors in which women are more prevalent, the connection between asylum and illegal work is as striking for women as it is for men. However, while many male participants stressed that it was hard to find work when not in possession of legal status, or that working illegally was problematic for fear of arrest, female participation in informal labour markets seemed less risky as a result of the strong demand for cheap, flexible labour in the sectors in which women tend to work, and the presence of many of their compatriots regularly employed in Hong Kong, sometimes with permanent residency status. Their situation was also helped by the months of skills and language training that they often had to undertake in order to be deployed in Hong Kong. As one Bangladeshi boyfriend affirmed: 'Many Indonesian girls now are torture claimants, and they can work in restaurants. They can speak Chinese, so they can work, do cleaning, washing, or maybe in the house. They can work easily' (Bangladeshi participant, 51).

This finding suggests that the demand for casual labour is high in low-end occupations, especially when flexible employment arrangements are valued in service, low-profit and rigidly regulated markets, and local domestic helpers are not easily recruitable (Chiu and Lui 2009). If employers appeared to benefit from these scenarios, so did their workers in terms of conditions of work and salary. A Pakistani man, speaking of his co-national male asylum seekers, whose remarks could equally be applied to women asylum seekers, explained: 'Mostly boys do not prefer to work regularly [paid monthly]. When they work regularly, they work every day for maybe HK$3000–4000 [per month]. But when they work sometimes, they can earn up to HK$300–400 per day. It is more money comparatively' (Pakistani participant, 34). Furthermore, working fewer hours could provide them with the time needed to build relationships with fellow asylum seekers, partners and others. Conversely, employers could easily hire and dismiss them according

180   *Engagement with the informal economy*

to their needs, saving on fixed costs, which although low are not always in line with the employers' needs.

Trading in a service economy

As argued in the previous chapters, Hong Kong is being visited by increasing numbers of traders from Africa and South Asia looking for cheap goods to export to their home countries (Mathews 2011). During the fieldwork, asylum seekers were found to be managing cheap guest houses for these tourist traders as well as travellers. Some asylum seekers were working in the kitchen or serving at the tables of small ethnic restaurants which mainly cater for the previously mentioned groups. Others were standing on the streets and approaching people they believed to be tourists to sell them copy watches and other Chinese-manufactured goods. Some were offering tourists tailor-made suits, shirts and fine fabrics from nearby, often ethnic-owned shops. Many other asylum seekers worked as middlemen in the mobile phone or garment trade, or in the re-export of second-hand cars and car parts. In the words of one interviewee, these asylum seekers 'created jobs for themselves' (Pakistani participant, 76a), and by doing so performed crucial liaison functions between local and overseas markets.

Compelled to trade: Following co-ethnic and tourist demand

Many participants stated that they had developed services that could be useful both for their co-national traders, so that they would make the most out of the short stay permitted by their visas, and for tourists from developed economies seeking low-cost but classy souvenirs. Asylum seekers would earn commissions for bringing customers they identified on the streets to shop dealers where they could bargain on the price of copy watches and other goods. This was usually a good line of business, often quite profitable for those involved. In several instances, I was told that people who had started working as touts on the streets made substantial profits and, after they mastered the mechanisms of trade in this sector, could afford to move to other, at times more profitable lines of business. For example, one Bangladeshi participant recalled how he was able to sideline this main activity and start a different business using the money he had made from selling copy watches. He revealed that he had opened a business, which 'is illegal because I'm illegal, but I'm doing it using someone else's name, under which the company is registered' (Bangladeshi participant, 79d). He was buying foodstuffs in his country to sell in Hong Kong. In our conversation, this bright participant often reminded me that he had achieved a 'position' now. As he observed, '[B]efore, I was living a life where I needed help, but now I make [my] money', hiring local residents while also paying income tax. This participant explained that, concomitant with his main business activity, he also used to buy copy watches and mobile phones and sell them in his home country, in order to diversify and expand his income-generating opportunities. He recalled that while economic exploitation and social marginalization were faced by people who sought

Engagement with the informal economy   181

asylum in Hong Kong, a number of participants managed to take advantage of their condition as illegal migrants to become relatively wealthy entrepreneurs, admired as middle class in their country of origin and by fellow asylum seekers who desired to attain a similar level of prosperity. In other words, as I observed, and as was evident from his story and that of his business partners, while many asylum seekers became trapped in low-status, low-paid, dangerous jobs in conditions of exploitation, other self-employed asylum seekers attained superior work conditions, often with the goal of legalizing their stay in Hong Kong. Schuster (2005) and other commentators argue that the informalization of certain economic activities does not necessarily constitute a mobility trap (Maroukis et al. 2011), as migrants often shift between statuses, with improvements emerging primarily for those who tailor their strategies to the particular opportunities that present themselves. The stories of some of the asylum seekers in my research certainly support this claim. However, rather than shifting status, what emerges as significant is the asylum seekers' capacity to shift lifestyles as a result of successful business endeavours. Additionally, transnational co-national and co-ethnic networks played an important role in facilitating such a result. In contrast to networks developed with co-national legal residents in Hong Kong, which were often found to augment the costs of migration by increasing refugee vulnerability, transnational networks established with tourist traders and trusted business partners in the country of origin appeared to generate positive outcomes.

Previous research has identified that migrants exploit social capital and the ethnic networks in which they are embedded to generate opportunities for themselves (Panayiotopoulos 2010). Campbell (2006) reveals how Somali refugees in Kenya have created numerous large-scale and smaller commercial businesses relying on transnational ethnic linkages to informally deliver a wide variety of items, which even the local retailers buy to resell at lower prices. Others argue that, beyond generating specific work opportunities, ethnic networks form expectations of economic advancement which can become incorporated into 'culture' (Eve 2010), or accepted values among those intending to make a living and eventually climb the social ladder, thereby following in the steps of their fellow asylum seekers. This has been identified by Mathews (2011) in Hong Kong, suggesting that exploitation is often accepted as a temporary condition to be tolerated in the pursuit of goals that will align migrants' status with that of their employers, thus allowing migrants to eventually replace their employers, in turn exploiting those following in their footsteps.

From this perspective, it is evident that while a large number of asylum seekers were working in Hong Kong in contravention of immigration regulations, the kinds of economic activities in which they became involved did not seem to overlap with the economic activities of the local resident population. On the contrary, several participants and their friends were able to generate income by entering niche markets which seemed of little interest to the local population. The ethnic networks on which asylum seekers relied enabled them to develop specific opportunities which only they could develop or access. In other words, as immigrant entrepreneurship generally revolves around specific economic activities

182 *Engagement with the informal economy*

(Kloosterman et al. 1999), niche markets appear more often in economic segments that are heavily dependent on ethnic ties and demand (Wright et al. 2010). In addition, these activities are self-perpetuating as a result of constant (ethnic) demand and more asylum seekers wishing to enter these sectors – providing that they possess the funds to start a business. If asylum seekers were uniquely positioned to operate within certain economic contexts, the sectors of the economy in which they worked differentially impacted on their chances of upward mobility (Maroukis et al. 2011), with some asylum seekers becoming labourers and others self-employed entrepreneurs.

Such agency was nonetheless constrained by a political and institutional framework which specified the socioeconomic boundaries outside of which they would not be permitted to work. As one West African participant attentively noted in relation to his trading activity, this was a business that he and other asylum seekers like him developed out of necessity due to their status: 'Most of the asylum seekers do business like me. . . . They get money from Africa and buy goods that they later ship to Africa. We can only do this because we are not allowed to work. So we buy something and sell it to our country' (African participant, 01).

Many participants persuasively argued that because they created jobs for themselves, these activities were either seen as not amounting to work or were tolerated for their positive social impact. For example, in relation to asylum seekers pushing trolleys for tourists and tourist traders, one participant claimed that they gained a fictitious right to work by performing jobs about which no or few public complaints arose. As he said: 'If they don't have it [the right to work] officially, they gained it unofficially, because you see police walking near them, but they are not catching them. . . . Why? They know that Hong Kong ID holders will not complain against handymen. They need their help. That's why they are allowed to work. . . . They fetch their own jobs [that] Hong Kong ID holders find not acceptable' (Pakistani participant, 76a).

In this participant's opinion, if not legally allowed to work, asylum seekers performing the tasks needed for local businesses to prosper had gained a sort of unofficial, unspoken, but manifestly evident right to work. This view was reiterated by another interviewee, who argued that 'many people work and few are caught. Maybe one shop is caught, three people are caught, and then they [the police] stop. No need to go on arresting others. After three to four months they again catch some other people; just to scare them so they don't do it openly' (Bangladeshi participant, 58).

It should be said that, in reality, while arresting individuals who are working illegally may be an easy thing to do, successfully prosecuting them for the crime of working illegally can be rather difficult in Hong Kong. A Sri Lankan participant with whom I met numerous times over several months was arrested for allegedly working in a scrapyard, separating plastics from paper. When the yard was busted by police and immigration officials, several workers rushed to the backdoor and left the compound to hide in a nearby garden. Here, the participant was found, questioned and brought back to the scrapyard by police officers, who later took photos of him within the perimeter of the premises under investigation.

The court before which he subsequently appeared held that the evidence gathered by investigators was insufficient to proceed with the prosecution. In other cases, immigration officers had to spend several hours over a number of days videotaping asylum seekers on the streets before compiling enough evidence to arrest them. Similarly reducing the chances of conviction, Mathews (2011) argues that undercover cops can be easily identified when they approach ethnic restaurants in Chungking Mansions. If the police are seen, any asylum seekers working illegally as waiters or shopkeepers can simply pretend to be customers helping their retailer friends.

Escalating global economic transaction flows at the lower end of small-scale economies

Asylum seekers developed services for co-national traders that included arranging their accommodation and escorting them to shops where prices could be bargained. One West African participant, for instance, argued that after five years in the city, he had learnt much that could be useful to his customers and had established a good reputation for himself and honest relationships with his clients. He noted: 'The first time I helped someone he said that he would give my phone number to other people. I said it would be my pleasure. So from that time the people that come here call me and I help them with whatever they need to do' (African participant, 09). Of course, as he continued this work, the more his customers grew familiar with Hong Kong, and the less they needed his services. Nonetheless, with the growing awareness in Africa of Hong Kong as an inexpensive place to buy goods for export has come rising numbers of African small traders entering the city, and with them more opportunities for asylum seekers to generate income while linking Hong Kong to markets in their country of origin.

In reality, a number of traders were increasingly turning to mainland China to cut out intermediaries and buy cheaper products. Research on African communities in Guangzhou has highlighted the booming business and personal relations between Africans and Chinese across the border (Bodomo 2010; Yang 2012). The previous participant viewed this change in the following terms: 'The market here [in Hong Kong] is still better than in China. It is not better in terms of prices, but in terms of quality. If traders come to Hong Kong they want to spend more money for better quality' (African participant, 09). In a similar fashion, other participants revealed that 'in China you can pay less, but you may have difficulties to sell the goods at home. . . . Also, if you go to China by yourself to place the order, they can do anything they want with it, and once you go back you can't sell' (African participant, 18).

Several stories were recounted of traders who ventured into mainland China seeking to reduce costs and avoid intermediaries by directly contracting with the manufacturer. Many of these traders fell prey to scams devised by local Chinese factories looking to increase their profits. For example, on one occasion, when I was expecting a participant for an interview, he arrived late because he had to take a customer to the train station. The customer had just arrived from Africa and was

184   *Engagement with the informal economy*

heading to China to check on the delivery of goods he had purchased on his prior trip. As was explained, several manufacturers in China tried to take advantage of the fact that their customers were often on short-term visas and so would delay their shipments to force them either to return to their country empty-handed or to overstay, thus increasing their vulnerability while reducing the likelihood that they would complain if the merchandise did not match the agreed volume, quality or cost.

In this regard, several participants commented that their mediation helped customers track their business transaction from start to finish. In addition, in many cases the asylum seeker's reliable reputation and honest relations built over time with their customers resulted in traders entrusting considerable amounts of money to them, to buy and ship the merchandise on their behalf. Thus, asylum seekers acted as informal but reliable trading agencies, sorting orders and shipping the materials requested overseas. They operated within the Hong Kong entrepôt economy but connected destinations that are difficult to access for local Chinese who lack similar human capital. In this way, asylum seekers exploited the specific structural conditions in Hong Kong to obtain or facilitate work in niche markets that are heavily dependent on ethnic ties and demand, which benefited the local economy. One interviewee explained that every week he would have at least one customer sending him US$20,000 to buy clothes that he would later ship to Africa in a container the cost of which he would share with another asylum seeker involved in similar trading. Considering the benefits for Hong Kong, he commented that if the majority of the asylum seekers he knew provided these services, receiving similar amounts of cash per week, the share of business generated for Hong Kong would be substantial. Indeed, while this trade was probably marginal to the final computation of national GDP, it was primarily affecting certain categories of wholesalers, particularly small enterprises which would have had difficulty continuing their line of work had they not developed effective connections with developing markets overseas. As one shop owner explained, 'Africa [*sic*] people are troublesome, but buy very many' (Chinese resident, 01), adding that had it not been for their regular purchases she would have moved her business across the border, where opportunities were rising. Similarly, the owner of a small grocery store said that he engaged in the garment trade to supplement his meagre income, 'because if these Africans buying cars have some space in the container, they may want some clothes to fit in, and I'm close by' (Pakistani resident, 04).

Although it may be difficult to support without hard evidence, particularly as I did not identify any research that analyzes the economic advantage to Hong Kong retailers of business transactions with developing countries, based on my fieldwork and observations carried out previously, it is clear that the business activity in some neighbourhoods has been transformed in order to service increasing numbers of African and South Asian traders visiting Hong Kong. In Sham Shui Po, in particular, I found local garment wholesalers whose clientele, in the span of only a few years, became almost exclusively African. Along the streets of this old, impoverished district lay large, dark green jute bags full of clothing

Engagement with the informal economy   185

stacked at the entrances and empty corners of shops, their sides imprinted with the delivery address, often in Lagos, Accra or Lome. Similarly, in the New Territories, growing numbers of scrapyards were serving rising overseas demand, thus changing the landscape of Hong Kong's rural areas. Although scrapyards have always existed, their non-Chinese character is a relatively new phenomenon. It is no coincidence that one long-time Pakistani resident of a small town in the New Territories opened a multicultural food store at the same time that the South Asian and African population in that area was growing.

This finding is consistent with the literature which highlights the role of immigrant communities in transforming local urban spaces, acknowledging their agency and everyday lived experiences as a driving force for change from below (Kloosterman et al. 1999; McEwan et al. 2005; Benton-Short et al. 2005). Nonetheless, surging demand for cheaper products in booming markets in economically emerging countries has clearly influenced the rapid reshaping of district activities and small Chinese businesses which now target ethnic markets. It is contended here that asylum seekers have channelled increasing demand from their countries of origin, establishing reliable linkages between shops in Hong Kong that normally specialize in low-value-added products, which require relatively modest capital spending, and overseas markets, where low-budget traders cannot afford more expensive goods.

If speaking of transnationalism in this context is perhaps inappropriate (Portes et al. 2002; Portes 2001), as asylum seekers are geographically immobile, the asylum seekers in this research engaged in extensive mediation between parties, performing meticulous liaison functions between local and overseas markets while adapting their lifestyle to better serve their customers at each end of the transaction. For example, when I visited a few places where asylum seekers were engaged in the car and car parts trade, I saw groups of Africans who, at a certain hour in the afternoon, would stand on the roadside in proximity to car dealers, waiting for the imminent arrival of new shipments of second-hand cars, in some cases collected in numbers and types according to demand. These people would normally buy the cars that either they had been asked to provide or which they knew would sell well in their home country, anticipating demand when they had the financial resources to do so. Additionally, one interviewee explained that other than mediating between buyers and sellers he would also buy cars for himself, as he was planning to operate them as taxis in his native country, where he expected this business would boom in view of rising average wealth. At the time of our interview, he had purchased six cars in recent months and, following the next shipment of three cars, when conditions there allowed it, he was planning to return home in approximately six months' time, if all went well.

Notably, certain economic activities undertaken by asylum seekers did create or expand market spaces in which their agency, embedded within specific social and economic structures, not only allowed them to generate income, but also remarkably to benefit local ethnic and Chinese retailers who responded to increased demand for affordable consumer goods in emerging markets. This was made possible in part because asylum seekers involved in trading were subjected

186 *Engagement with the informal economy*

to less policing than were people working illegally in sectors in which their presence was perhaps more visible and thus appeared to openly challenge the government's authority. For instance, one interviewee revealed that he had tried to find work, but he was so concerned about being caught working illegally that he gave up. He then started trading because according to him this could not be called 'work', as it was not performed for regular wages in a specific workplace. Indeed, while the participants providing escort and trading services rarely experienced problems with the police, others were afraid of being caught after many of their friends working in scrapyards had been sentenced to 15 months' imprisonment.[2]

Policing the most vulnerable

Although official statistics to support this argument are not available, my data indicate that the introduction of new legislation on illegal work must be understood in relation to, on the one hand, the suspension of the CAT screening interviews for a large part of 2009 (see Chapter 2), during which time the number of CAT applications skyrocketed to about 300 new cases per month,[3] and on the other, the context of the global economic crisis that hit in 2009, impacting on consumption behaviours worldwide and in Hong Kong.[4] It was noted previously that asylum seekers are involved in markets characterized by economies of low scale and unstable and uncertain labour demand. While many of the places in which asylum seekers worked illegally in Hong Kong were raided by the authorities following the implementation of the new amendment at the end of 2009, police and immigration raids were said to be conducted mainly in the winter months. Both employers and asylum seekers, however, argued that 'business is slow in winter', and employers lamented that, specifically in late 2009, they could hardly afford to keep their recycling companies open because of the lack of second-hand materials available. On this point, it is plausible to claim that in times of economic downturn, the more affluent citizens tend to alter their consumption patterns to avoid excessive spending on superfluous items such as refrigerators, air conditioners and cars.

In 2009, with the looming economic crisis and the simultaneous rise in the number of people seeking asylum in the territory, many asylum seekers found themselves with fewer opportunities to work in the recycling trade. When asked whether this was a result of heightened policing, which meant they feared being caught, or the result of a lack of work opportunities, a number of participants replied along the following lines: 'Before, we had chances, because the government was not so strict. But now it is very difficult because they said that if they catch us, we will spend 15 months in jail. So we are scared to work' (Bangladeshi participant, 60). However, others noted, 'It is because of both. Last year there was more work [than in 2010]' (Bangladeshi participant, 67), and 'People are more scared, but they still work. When containers come, we can work. But if they don't come, we can't work' (Sri Lankan participant, 80c). The participants also observed that, as a consequence of changing conditions in what is probably the largest sector that employs asylum seekers, a significant number of their friends

Engagement with the informal economy 187

'went back home, and some others have applied to go home' (Bangladeshi participant, 67). One Bangladeshi participant explained the dilemma concerning his future as follows:

> If you ask me now, I have to say that I still don't know. I don't know what I will do. I just hang on; because if I want to stay for long time, I still don't have future here, as the government is strict now. My friends have nothing at home and they don't want to go back, but they are forced to go back. So I'm also thinking. Immigration calls people for interview and after a few of them they send them to Bangladesh. Soon this may happen to me too. (Bangladeshi participant, 60)

Despite a few participants being unsure about their next move, from 14 November 2009, when the amended Immigration Ordinance came into effect, until the end of 2010, 1536 torture claimants withdrew their claims with the ImmD and voluntarily requested to return home, especially in the months immediately after the implementation of the amendment.[5] Concomitantly, new CAT applications went down by 44.9 per cent in 2010 (ImmD 2011).

If this mechanism of immigration control seemed to cause a decrease in the number of torture applications, and probably arrivals, another result was a reduction in the size of the asylum seeker population, both through voluntary repatriation prompted by fear of long-term imprisonment and quicker CAT screening procedures introduced in December 2009 (see Chapter 2). At the same time, while these new measures eventually led to a decline in the number of asylum seekers, police controls over the territory came to be implemented more often during certain periods of the year – most notably in the winter months, which were said to be the least favourable for securing employment, as 'police go around and check' (African participant, 07), and the least productive, when asylum seekers were less likely to be employed. It may be argued, therefore, that especially at the end of 2009, while production output decreased for companies whose sources of supply declined, asylum seekers, who had grown in number until the implementation of the amendment and are generally compelled to provide for such labour markets, could have turned into a real social problem had they become economically idle, therefore raising the need to reduce their number. In addition, the most evident consequence of increased control over asylum seekers, whether it was deliberate or circumstantial, was to worsen the precarious conditions of this vulnerable population, while further consigning it to the mercy of liberal market forces that ruthlessly regulate specific traits of Hong Kong's extensive informal economy.

Although debated among refugees, some interviewees argued that wages decreased in 2010. One participant commented on the tough conditions of work in scrapyards by saying: 'We work [at night] from 7 p.m. to 7 a.m. It is 12-hour work and one hour for eating. And now we are even paid less. Last year this business was better, but many businesses closed some months [after illegal work was criminalized] and now they pay less' (Sri Lankan participant, 80c). In short, as work opportunities decreased, so did the profit to be made by local employers in extremely fluid markets characterized by high levels of uncertainty. Pressure to downgrade wages therefore increased, at a time when government policies seemed to respond to economic conditions which made growing numbers of illegal workers redundant. Heightened insecurity and fear of apprehensions by police increased among asylum seekers as a result, furthering the exploitability of asylum seekers whose wages were pushed further down by employers who told them that they faced higher risks of arrest, although police raids were occurring in the months when their business did not require as much labour. While asylum seeker traders and middlemen have probably suffered the least from the legislation criminalizing illegal work, dependent as they are on stable demand from developing overseas markets, those employed as day labourers suffered the most, and this was likely not an unintentional consequence of government policy.

Conclusion

Hong Kong is a leading business centre that operates as an advanced services and export-oriented hub. The city connects with solid and expanding business and trade networks in China and emerging overseas markets, in which production is low but interest in new affordable technologies and fashionable items is being amplified by globalization. In this view, the specialization of Hong Kong as a service economy appears to generate distinct consequences for local labour and social structures. This chapter confirms that at the lower echelons of society, in communities defined by markedly uneven earning capacities, a marginalized type of worker emerges. However, rather than solely producing a vast, illegal, low-income and exploitable population, the socioeconomic conditions in Hong Kong produce a fairly segmented reality, as some asylum seekers are able to take advantage of opportunities that allow them to evade the informal economy mobility trap (Maroukis et al. 2011). However, only occasionally do these asylum seekers shift their legal and socioeconomic status, in which case they most likely engage in activities through which they can find employment and which they have already mastered in their time spent in Hong Kong (Landolt and Goldring 2010).

Asylum seekers rely heavily on social capital. Social ties established with co-national tourist traders in Hong Kong have transformed this capital into positive economic outcomes, although trading activities were based on ties that can produce a range of outcomes depending on the strength of the bond formed between those involved. At the same time, social networks established with trusted friends and relatives in home countries were generally advantageous for entrepreneurial asylum seekers. Conversely, bridged social relationships with co-national and co-ethnic legal residents in Hong Kong tended to negatively affect the vulnerability of asylum seekers, even while such ties enabled their survival. Precisely because of this population's illegal status, lawfully resident ethnic employers were largely found to exploit their fellow countrymen when they provided labour (cf. Grzymala-Kazlowska 2005). Further, because of their socioeconomic and political vulnerability asylum seekers were impeded from breaking free of these ties, de facto forging their dependency on ethnic employer demand

Engagement with the informal economy 189

(McKay et al. 2011) when other resources were either unavailable or were rendered inaccessible by government policy. Indeed, this chapter has highlighted the correlation between legal status and income generation and the differential impact of policing priorities and practices in effectively shaping refugee agency.

As observed by some participants, traditional caste divisions in home countries tended to be overruled by the new socioeconomic hierarchies established in Hong Kong, based on one's legal status in the host society. Redefinitions of migrant social characteristics and consequent perceptions of status appear related to the neoliberal socioeconomic transformations occurring in the global city, which have led to a decline in the value of some workers as a result of the downgrading of the value of the tasks performed at the lower end of the occupational structure. As Sassen (2001) explains, this process increases the likelihood of exploitation for some members of society. Border control supports this exploitation (De Genova 2002, 2011; Calavita 2003). In Hong Kong, asylum seekers' illegal status, their concomitant lack of comprehensive support and, arguably, their being differentially policed effectively regulate their economic engagement in society. The Hong Kong asylum system appears aimed more at governing and controlling this vast illegal population than providing it with protection. It defines spaces of legality and illegality, often forcing asylum seekers to ensure their survival through illegal means while attempting to shift between predetermined categories to improve their status and security (Schuster 2005).

While negotiating these conditions, asylum seekers must transform themselves either into flexible, cheap workers, physically prepared to endure long hours of arduous work, or self-employed entrepreneurs in niche markets that serve the vast number of tourists and tourist traders from developed and emerging economies. In both circumstances, they come to be inserted into processes of global city formation. Their agency, albeit limited, indirectly empowers the capabilities and economic independence of certain economically active strata of the legally resident population who are impacted by an accentuated paucity of alternative labour markets and welfare support (Chan 1998; Goodstadt 2013). Asylum seekers thus serve the cost-reduction needs of underprivileged locals who possess or need to develop the entrepreneurial drive to initiate transnational economic activities, despite the generally low profits available and the dependence of their business on specific social networks. In this sense, asylum seekers expand the city's global economic transaction flows via the creation of reliable networks between Hong Kong's small-scale economies and growing overseas markets.

In conclusion, asylum seekers are embedded within urban socioeconomic structures in which their presence is both a product of and beneficial to the service economy. It is said that Hong Kong's economic miracle is owing to its 'numerous small local firms that are deeply involved in the international economy' (Cheng and Gereffi 1994: 201). While this statement may not entirely apply in today's economic reality, considerable segments of Hong Kong's society do make an income from small-scale, low-end, informal businesses, which remain feasible because asylum seekers are able to provide flexibility and networks in an age of increased competition, risk and pressure to reduce costs.

190 *Engagement with the informal economy*

Notes

1 This point was made by civil society representatives in a public forum organized for refugees in Hong Kong on 15 September 2010.
2 In *HKSAR v Usman Butt*, HCMA70/2010, 27 October 2010, the Court of Appeal upheld a decision made in 1988 to adopt a standard sentence of 15 months' imprisonment after plea for persons unlawfully remaining in the territory and caught working.
3 *HKSAR v Usman Butt*, HCMA70/2010.
4 See, for example www.e-to-china.com/financial_crisis/Industry_Influence/2009/0707/56736.html.
5 *HKSAR v Usman Butt*, HCMA70/2010.

References

Aldrich, H. E. and Waldinger, R. (1990) 'Ethnicity and Entrepreneurship', *Annual Review of Sociology*, 16: 111–135.

Anggraeni, D. (2006) *Dreamseekers: Indonesian Women as Domestic Helpers in Asia*, Jakarta: International Labour Organization.

Ashencaen Crabtree, S. and Wong, H. (2012) '"Ah Cha"! The Racial Discrimination of Pakistani Minority Communities in Hong Kong: An Analysis of Multiple, Intersecting Oppressions', *British Journal of Social Work*, 43(5): 945–963.

Benton-Short, L., Price, M. D. and Friedman, S. (2005) 'Globalization from Below: The Ranking of Global Immigrant Cities', *International Journal of Urban and Regional Research*, 29(4): 945–959.

Bodomo, A. B. (2010) 'The African Trading Community in Guangzhou: An Emerging Bridge for Africa-China Relations', *China Quarterly*, 203: 693–707.

Borretti, B. (2010) 'Da Castel Volturno a Rosarno. Il Lavoro Vivo degli Immigrati tra Stragi, Pogrom, Rivolte e Razzismo di Stato', in P. Basso (Ed.) *Razzismo di Stato: Stati Uniti, Europa, Italia*, Milano: FrancoAngeli: 493–524.

Byron, H. (2010) 'Changing Tides', *A Plus*, 11(6): 14–18. Viewed 1 March 2012: http://app1.hkicpa.org.hk/APLUS/1011/14–18-shipping.pdf

Calavita, K. (2003) 'A "Reserve Army of Delinquents": The Criminalization and Economic Punishment of Immigrants in Spain', *Punishment & Society*, 5(4): 399–413.

Campbell, E. H. (2006) 'Urban Refugees in Nairobi: Problems of Protection, Mechanisms of Survival, and Possibilities for Integration', *Journal of Refugee Studies*, 19(3): 396–413.

Castells, M. (2000) *The Rise of the Network Society: The Information Age*, Oxford: Blackwell.

Castells, M. and Portes, A. (1989) 'World Underneath: The Origins, Dynamics, and Effects of the Informal Economy' in A. Portes, M. Castells and L. A. Benton (Eds.) *The Informal Economy: Studies in Advanced and Less Developed Countries*, Baltimore: The John Hopkins University Press.

Chan, C-K. (1998) 'Welfare Policies and the Construction of Welfare Relations in a Residual Welfare State: The Case of Hong Kong', *Social Policy & Administration*, 32(3): 278–291.

Chan, C. K. (2011) 'Hong Kong: Workfare in the World's Freest Economy', *International Journal of Social Welfare*, 20: 22–32.

Cheng, L-L. and Gereffi, G. (1994) 'The Informal Economy in East Asia Development', *International Journal of Urban and Regional Research*, 18(2): 194–219.

Engagement with the informal economy 191

Cheung, S. (2011) 'Professional Queuers Disrupt Line for New iPhone', *South China Morning Post*, 9 November. Viewed 9 November 2011: www.scmp.com/article/984307/professional-queuers-disrupt-line-new-iphone

Chiu, S. and Lui, T-L. (2009) *Hong Kong: Becoming a Chinese Global City*, Abingdon: Routledge.

Constable, N. (1997) *Maid to Order in Hong Kong: Stories of Filipina Workers*, Ithaca: Cornell University Press.

De Genova, N. (2011) 'Alien Powers: Deportable Labour and the Spectacle of Security', in V. Squire (Ed.) *The Contested Politics of Mobility: Borderzones and Irregularity*, Abingdon: Routledge: 91–115.

De Genova, N. P. (2002) 'Migrant "Illegality" and Deportability in Everyday Life', *Annual Review of Anthropology*, 31: 419–447.

Eve, M. (2010) 'Integrating via Networks: Foreigners and Others', *Ethnic and Racial Studies*, 33(7): 1231–1248.

Feenstra, R. C. and Hanson, G. H. (2004) 'Intermediaries in Entrepôt Trade: Hong Kong Re-Exports of Chinese Goods', *Journal of Economics & Management Strategy*, 13(1): 3–35.

Goodstadt, L. F. (2013) *Poverty in the Midst of Affluence: How Hong Kong Mismanaged Its Prosperity*, Hong Kong: Hong Kong University Press.

Grossman, E. (2006) *High Tech Trash: Digital Devices, Hidden Toxics, and Human Health*, Washington, DC: Island Press.

Grzymala-Kazlowska, A. (2005) 'From Ethnic Cooperation to In-Group Competition: Undocumented Polish Workers in Brussels', *Journal of Ethnic and Migration Studies*, 31(4): 675–697.

Hutchins, D. (1999) *Just in Time*, Aldershot: Glower.

Immigration Department (ImmD) (2011) *Immigration Department Year-End Briefing 2010*, 13 January. Viewed 20 January 2011: www.immd.gov.hk/en/press/press-releases/20110113.html

Jordan, B. and Travers, A. (1998) 'The Informal Economy: A Case Study of Unrestrained Competition', *Social Policy & Administration*, 32(3): 292–306.

Kloosterman, R., van der Leun, J. and Rath, J. (1999) 'Mixed Embeddedness: (In)formal Economic Activities and Immigrant Businesses in the Netherlands', *International Journal of Urban and Regional Research*, 23(2): 252–266.

Landolt, P. and Goldring, L. (2010) *The Long Term Impacts of Non-Citizenship on Work: Precarious Legal Status and the Institutional Production of a Migrant Working Poor*. Viewed 15 August 2013: www.yorku.ca/raps1/events/pdf/Landolt_Goldring.pdf

Law, K. Y. and Lee, K. M. (2006) 'Citizenship, Economy and Social Exclusion of Mainland Chinese Immigrations to Hong Kong', *Journal of Contemporary Asia*, 36(2): 217–242.

Lee, K. M., Wong, H. and Law, K. Y. (2007) 'Social Polarisation and Poverty in the Global City: The Case of Hong Kong', *China Report*, 43(1): 1–30.

Lee, P. W. Y. and Petersen, C. J. (2006) *Forced Labour and Debt Bondage in Hong Kong: A Study of Indonesian and Filipina Migrant Domestic Workers*, Occasional Paper, 16, Hong Kong: The University of Hong Kong.

Lee, S. (2013) 'Hong Kong April Port Volume Fell 12% as Strike Diverted Traffic', *Bloomberg*, 16 May. Viewed 16 May 2013: www.bloomberg.com/news/2013–05–16/hong-kong-april-port-volume-fell-12-as-strike-diverted-traffic.html

Lepawsky, J. and McNabb C. (2009) 'Mapping International Flows of Electronic Waste', *The Canadian Geographer*, 54(2): 177–195.

192 *Engagement with the informal economy*

Li, F. L. N., Findlay, A. M. and Jones, H. (1998) 'A Cultural Economy Perspective on Service Sector Migration in the Global City: The Case of Hong Kong', *International Migration*, 36(2): 131–155.

Loughlin, P. H. and Pannell, C. W. (2010) 'The Port of Hong Kong: Past Successes, New Realities and Emerging Challenges', *FOCUS on Geography*, 53(2): 50–58.

Maroukis, T., Iglicka, K. and Gmaj, K. (2011) 'Irregular Migration and Informal Economy in Southern and Central-Eastern Europe: Breaking the Vicious Cycle?', *International Migration*, 49(5): 129–156.

Massey, D., Alarcon, R., Durand, J. and Gonzalez, H. (1987) *Return to Aztlan: The Social Process of Transnational Migration from Western Mexico*, Berkeley: University of California Press.

Mathews, G. (2011) *Ghetto at the Center of the World: Chungking Mansions, Hong Kong*, Chicago: The University of Chicago Press.

McDonogh, G. and Wong, C. (2005) *Global Hong Kong*, New York: Routledge.

McEwan, C., Pollard, J. and Henry, N. (2005) 'The "Global" in the City Economy: Multicultural Economic Development in Birmingham', *International Journal of Urban and Regional Research*, 29(4): 916–933.

McKay, S., Markova, E. and Paraskevopoulou, A. (2011) *Undocumented Workers' Transitions: Legal Status, Migration, and Work in Europe*, Abingdon: Routledge.

Mok, R. (2008) 'Foreign Domestic Helpers in Hong Kong: Towards Equality of Rights', *Queensland Law Student Review*, 1(2). Viewed 12 May 2012: www.law.uq.edu.au/articles/qlsr/Mok-FDH-in-HKG.pdf

Newendorp, N. (2010) ' "Economically Speaking, I am the Breadwinner": Chinese Immigrant Narratives of Work and Family in Hong Kong', *International Migration*, 48(6): 72–101.

Ozeki, E. (1995) 'At Arm's Length: The Filipina Domestic Helper-Chinese Employer Relationship in Hong Kong', *International Journal of Japanese Sociology*, 4(1): 37–55.

Panayiotopoulos, P. (2010) *Ethnicity, Migration and Enterprise*, Houndmills: Palgrave MacMillan.

Portes, A. (2001) 'Introduction: The Debate and Significance of Immigrant Transnationalism', *Global Networks*, 1(3): 181–193.

Portes, A., Guarnizo, L. E. and Haller, W. (2002) 'Transnational Entrepreneurs: An Alternative Form of Immigrant Economic Adaptation', *American Sociological Review*, 67(2): 278–298.

Sassen, S. (1991) 'The Informal Economy', in J. H. Mollenkopf and M. Castells (Eds.) *Dual City: Restructuring New York*, New York: Russell Sage Foundation: 79–102.

Sassen, S. (1998) *Globalization and Its Discontents: Essays on the New Mobility of People and Money*, New York: New Press.

Sassen, S. (2001) *The Global City: New York, London, Tokyo*, second edition, Princeton: Princeton University Press.

Schmidle, N. (2010) 'Inside the Knockoff-Tennis-Shoe Factory', *New York Times*, 19 August. Viewed 19 August 2010: www.nytimes.com/2010/08/22/magazine/22fake-t.html?pagewanted=all

Schuster, L. (2005) 'The Continuing Mobility of Migrants in Italy: Shifting between Places and Statuses', *Journal of Ethnic and Migration Studies*, 31(4): 757–774.

Tai, P. F. (2013) 'Gender Matters in Social Polarisation: Comparing Singapore, Hong Kong and Taipei', *Urban Studies*, 50(6): 1148–1164.

Ullah, A. A. (2010) *Rationalizing Migration Decisions: Labour Migrants in East and South-East Asia*, Aldershot: Ashgate.

Wright, R., Ellis, M. and Parks, V. (2010) 'Immigrant Niches and the Intrametropolitan Spatial Division of Labour', *Journal of Ethnic and Migration Studies*, 36(7): 1033–1059.

Yang, W. (2008) 'Regulating Electrical and Electronic Wastes in China', *Review of European Community & International Environmental Law*, 17(3): 335–344.

Yang, Y. (2012) 'African Traders in Guangzhou: Routes, Reasons, Profits, Dreams' in G. Mathews, G. L. Ribeiro and C. Alba Vega (Eds.) *Globalization from Below: The World's Other Economy*, Abingdon: Routledge: 154–170.

6 (Un)wanted people in the global city

This book has drawn from a wide range of disciplines to produce a detailed analysis of asylum seeking in Hong Kong. Framed around the idea of unfolding the narratives of the people who seek protection in the former British colony, my research has sought to provide a reliable and well-documented account of the agency of asylum seekers and the circumstances surrounding and shaping this agency. No doubt certain issues have remained unanswered or only partially explained. Nonetheless, the key arguments that have been posed depict a condition of contemporary asylum seekers that is inclusive and explanatory of their vulnerability and the complex relations that surface in ever more globally connected places. This condition, in turn, raises a number of questions about the current structure of asylum and the emergence of discourses aimed at categorizing and homogenizing the needs of certain urban populations. Against this backdrop, this chapter is intended to summarize the main findings and claims detailed in the previous pages to shed light on the experience of asylum seekers, as both individuals and objects of policy. The aim is also to offer conclusive arguments about the significance of this research and the dynamics underlying the mobility and control of unwanted people in this global city.

Asylum seeking and the global city

Departing from a personal desire to develop a critical understanding beyond popular conjectures of the reasons why asylum seekers arrive in Hong Kong and what they do upon arrival, the research underpinning this book has focused on the complex interplay between global economics, the state and individual agents, operating at different levels, which has an impact on the experiences of certain groups engaged in economic activities seen to be characteristic of the contemporary form of capitalism and post-industrial city development. The goal of this research was to identify the nature of and reasons for asylum seekers' purported deviancy, in the specific context of Hong Kong, where misconceptions regarding asylum abound. In the pursuit of this endeavour, I made use of a livelihood framework to analyze urban refugee experiences. Within this schema, I outlined the specific vulnerability of the people who seek asylum in the territory, the assets and strategies they utilize to overcome the structural barriers constraining their agency and the outcomes of structural and agency factors for them and the host society in general. Taking Hong Kong as a case study, I focused on the 'vagabonds' (Bauman 1998) in the polarized flow of border crossers who most often land in Western countries and the HKSAR. In so doing, several important links have been revealed between the processes that produce and reproduce mobility and the urban-based social inequalities that in part define the global city. One such link relates to considering asylum seekers as important gears in the delicate mechanisms that drive current patterns of economic restructuring. Asylum seekers are said to be both the cause and the outcome of processes of globalization (Castles 2003), and it is from this perspective that they have been analyzed. In this view, the findings of this research suggest that shedding light on the experiences of asylum seekers is not solely revealing of the role they play within their specific urban environment, but that this understanding can also advance the current body of knowledge on the global city – and in light of this, I develop the arguments presented subsequently.

I believe this book contributes meaningful perspectives to further explore the social outcomes of neoliberal economic restructuring. It does so not by directly examining social polarization through variables and comparison of data at the different levels of the occupational and income structure. Rather, it offers an alternative perspective to that provided by the use in a large proportion of the research on social polarization of official statistics and secondary data as main sources of information (cf. Tai 2006, 2010; Chiu and Lui 2004; Lee et al. 2007). The irregular migrants engaged in informal market activities seldom appear in such data, despite claims that they are a product of economic restructuring and constitute one important contributor to rising inequality (Samers 2002). It can be assumed that polarization and labour market dynamics are in part shaped by the activities of such migrants; yet money generated via the informal economy is generally unrecorded by officialdom. In this scenario, this research has examined the livelihoods of the people with irregular immigration status in Hong Kong, who are the most likely to become involved in income-generating activities at the lower end of the local occupational and income structure. The aim of this study was to look beneath and beyond the threshold of statistical data to bring to the fore the non-persons hidden in the shade of the high-rise towers from where much of the mainstream global economy is regulated. In so doing, it has offered a clear picture of the subsistence living conditions of and employment opportunities available to these people. Based on an ethnographic approach, it has highlighted the important role played by the asylum seekers generally marginalized in society and has argued that, rather than representing an isolated and minor exception in the context of Hong Kong, asylum seekers are embedded participants within this city's socioeconomic transformation. This makes research on them and their experiences all the more significant for unfolding the power, hierarchies and forces that constitute and remodel the 'materiality' of the global city (Acuto 2011: 2964). In this view, the global city has been examined as this paradigm offers a fascinating framework for understanding much recent global mobility and the conditions in which migrants often end up when their agency is manipulated into providing specific economic outcomes. Moreover, this paradigm suggests that the new urban economic structure entails strong social discrimination in upwardly mobile Hong Kong, which appears to have become so interdependent with the acquisition of global city status that this status increasingly seems to be achievable only at the expense of classes of people viewed not only as different, but also as a real and growing social problem.

In light of the previous discussion, a number of conclusions may be drawn. First, this research identifies a piece of the puzzle initiated by numbers of scholars who have recently focused on the specific urban dynamics that define the contemporary condition of inequality in global cities. Tai (2010) argues that certain criteria must be set for comparative analyses of what constitutes polarization and whether this is a replicable phenomenon in global cities. This research has instead taken what Tai calls a narrative approach to the study of polarization to describe asylum seeker experiences, which are heuristically valuable; that is, they present an example to view and explain general dynamics, which are intertwined with the emergence of splintered, 'dualizing' metropolises. While evidence for polarization may not yet be clearly established in the literature, it is the process of widening inequality that is at the core of analysis. Acuto (2011) cites Graham and Marvin's (2001) research on the spatial effects of globalization in the urban environment. Other scholars have focused on the specific dynamics that are beneficial to and that evince global city status, revealing how subcontracting (Wills et al. 2009), sex work (Chin 2013) and government management of the poor are the outcomes and drivers of economic prosperity in global and globalizing cities (Müller 2013; Beckett and Hebert 2008). My research adds to this effort a marginal yet significant snapshot of the situations in which various actors experience and affect the new urban economy, thereby informing understanding of the multiple processes that combine to form the global city and Hong Kong's positioning in the world system.

In relation to this latter point, as Hong Kong becomes a city of growing importance in an increasingly important region for the global economy, this research boosts understanding of geographical contexts other than those that dominate the literature, such as the North American and European regions (Short and Kim 1999). Although the significance of this critique for global city research may be somewhat reduced as many studies on Asian cities have recently been undertaken (Baum 1999; Tai 2006, 2010, 2013), not least of which includes Chiu and Lui's (2009) detailed research on Hong Kong, my unique contribution is the analysis of asylum seeker involvement in processes of global city formation, relevant in the case of Hong Kong. Important in my view is that a link can be identified between Hong Kong acquiring global status and its attractiveness to asylum seekers, and vice versa. While the process by which this occurs is discussed in the following section, noteworthy is that, as posited in the previous chapter, Hong Kong's economic competitiveness within the emerging markets of the Global South is in part fostered by those people to whom the Hong Kong Government denies many basic rights, as asylum seekers find themselves inserted into specific socioeconomic spaces in which they provide the best outcomes for local entrepreneurs. On this account, social polarization appears to be the product of regional and endogenous influences in combination with global forces initiated by capitalistic relations of production.

The findings presented in this book offer (only) a hint that polarization and growing social inequalities are underway in Hong Kong. They are nonetheless revealing of government authorities fostering conditions conducive to unbalanced, unequal and bipolar societies. The impact of finance and producer services on broader social and economic structures in Asian cities has often been examined in relation to the role that the state exercises through infrastructure planning and economic, social and immigration policy to foster economic development and transform cities into hubs within the new global capitalist order (Baum 1999; Hill and Kim 2000). In relation to this, welfare structures have been argued to mediate global economic forces to result in specific labour market patterns (Hamnett 1994, 1996; Burgers and Musterd 2002). Social policy can also fashion dramatic changes that intensify poverty and polarization. Chan (2011) details the extremely humiliating welfare scheme that Hong Kong authorities implemented in the years that saw an expansion of neoliberal influences, which drove the poor into an increasingly competitive labour market without protection of wages and working hours. These changes have minimized the government's social responsibilities while positioning social policy at the service of the labour market (Wacquant 2009). In a similar fashion, immigration policy is identified as another domain where policies and practices are helping to reconfigure Hong Kong and its role in the wider economy. It is important to remember that in Hong Kong, a renowned global city within the global economy map, there exists a group of individuals who are persistently and legally bound to making a living at the bottom of society. While local poor are made to struggle in an 'open workhouse' (Chan 2011: 29), the Hong Kong Government's promotion of an entrepreneurial environment has effectively furnished these strata of the local population with the workforce and clients they need to sustain growth and facilitate transnational connectedness.

The new urban economy and the politics and policies of asylum are thus closely connected. Here lies the significance of this research. This book has advanced the notion that, rather than endorsing the idea of asylum seekers and other migrants as recipients of the social, political and economic consequences of globalization, these individuals can and do use their reasoning to overcome what they perceive as barriers. Rational calculations, emotions, beliefs and moral sensibilities intersect with structural factors to shape the choices available to migrants, which in turn impact on them and the city more broadly (Wessel 2000). In advancing this argument, detailed findings of the multifaceted relations that lie at the heart of new urban and social hierarchies have been produced, which suggest the human implications of global economic and political processes. Critically, this migrant agency is part of the complex and multi-level agency that in the introductory chapter of this book was said to shape certain cities and lead them to acquire a prominent position in the management and control of the global economy (Acuto and Steele 2013). It is understood that explanations of the role global cities perform in reshaping the new global 'geography of centrality' are primarily and most

198 *(Un)wanted people in the global city*

importantly economic (Parnreiter 2013). However, these roles are by no means the result of abstract constructs. Rather, they are also rooted in the social and legal dynamics that have been explored in this book and which the remainder of this chapter considers.

Asylum seeking and networks

Human mobility is a major process through which the new global political economy is constituted and global cities are formed (Sassen 1998, 2001). Doug Saunders (2010) elegantly portrays the social changes occurring worldwide with massive shifts of populations out of rural, marginalized and often impoverished lives into larger, networked cities, in an endless search for better opportunities to advance them and their children in the global race for acceptability, connectedness and centrality. On this view, Sassen (1998) argues that the city becomes the focus point for regional and international movements of underprivileged people who later become the marginal assets in new urban geographies of power. Within this scenario, a livelihoods perspective on refugee experiences is in my understanding silent about the reasons for this mobility towards specific localities (cf. Buscher 2011). In contrast, the global city paradigm has unquestionably increased our understanding of controversial yet crucial economic, social and cultural dynamics that simultaneously result from and escalate globalization. Yet it has also been claimed that this kind of structuralist approach does not adequately explain the role of both the state and individual agents in initiating and enabling different forms of migration and the links connecting specific places of origin with destinations (Samers 2010; Arango 2000). It is this knowledge, or the lack thereof, that can result in perceptions of asylum abuse, affecting the vulnerability and agency of asylum seekers.

As stated previously, this book suggests that global economic factors and localized and micro-factors interact to affect migration flows towards Hong Kong. Nonetheless, the patterns of movement of the people originating from certain developing countries arriving in Hong Kong increasingly mirror the general trend observed in other geographies and migratory contexts, especially in relation to the growing diversification of migrants' destinations, the commercialization of the migration process and the changing nature of the social networks of asylum seeking (Collyer 2005). The aim of this section is to review the arguments leading to such conclusions and to reveal the reasons why, and under what consequences, Hong Kong has become a new destination in the geopolitical map of safe places with high standards of living. Two levels of analysis are pursued to this end: the first focuses on the macro-factors that help explain the impact of the global city on peripheral developing markets for constructing Hong Kong as a desirable destination, and the second emphasizes how the experiences of asylum seekers at the micro-level shape transnational networks.

In relation to the former, the case of Hong Kong seems to empirically confirm the arguments contained in world-systems theory concerning migration at a macro-level. Scholars advancing this model posit that, within a global capitalist system, production and consumption are linked through a newly emerging international division of labour based on relations of inequality and dependency between core developed places and underdeveloped countries of the semi-periphery and periphery (Wallerstein 1979; Cohen 1987; Sassen 1988). On this account, people from poorer countries migrate to wealthier places following the transnational linkages created by foreign investment, trade and the unprecedented flow of goods, services and information along complex networks now connecting geographies previously little exposed to world influences. In this context, the global city emerges as both the driver and the result of increased interconnectedness and patterned human mobility (Sassen 1998). My empirical fieldwork in Hong Kong revealed that the expansion of China's economic and industrial power into the countries of Africa and South Asia, as well as the elevation of Hong Kong to the status of a stable economy at the gateway to China's thriving manufacturing sector (Meyer 2000; Feenstra and Hanson 2004), has played a significant role in forming transnational linkages between newly emerging markets and this global city. New consumption patterns made possible by the distribution of cheap Chinese-manufactured products in countries whose average citizen could previously hardly afford such products generate demand that Hong Kong firms fulfil by handling, marketing and shipping Chinese products. In this context, the mediation provided by asylum seekers in procuring market shares for the Hong Kong economy and the business of tourist traders flocking into the city in pursuit of life-changing opportunities in burgeoning and accessible China converge to create and expand the networks along which asylum seekers move.

If transnational linkages are critical for the development of Hong Kong as a desired destination, the previous context is pitched at a level that hardly explains how such ties are formed and the ways in which asylum seeker decision making around destinations is affected. The people who sought asylum in Hong Kong, in fact, generally had very limited and often inaccurate knowledge about the HKSAR prior to their arrival. In addition, several participants stated that they were bound for a different destination and only accidentally ended up in Hong Kong. In this regard, state regulations and increasingly restrictive border controls (Weber and Pickering 2011) emerge as factors which explain the surge of global cities and the evident dissociation between actual and intended destinations for many asylum seekers. Indeed, increasing difficulties entering some of the countries of the Global North have contributed to the creation in Hong Kong of ties that facilitate the flow of people, capital and goods. Research into the experiences of people seeking asylum in the HKSAR brings to the fore the changing map of destinations for migrants affected by increased border controls worldwide. As Haugen (2012: 66) notes in relation to Nigerians travelling to China, some migrants in developing countries are undeterred in undertaking ever more risky journeys to reach their preferred destination. Others, however, simply 'head for countries that are more open to migration and/or less capable of enforcing immigration regulations'. Additionally, the legal barriers met along the way by refugees often result in transforming those countries that initially were only transit destinations into final destinations (Khosravi 2010; Içduygu and Toktas 2002).

200 *(Un)wanted people in the global city*

This book has demonstrated that the HKSAR is far more accessible to desperate people in the developing world than are the borders at the militarized frontier now dividing Europe, North America and Australia from the poorer and troubled countries (Weber and Pickering 2011). It shows that with migrant journeys ever more interspersed as a result of the increasing difficulties faced in journeying from origin to planned destination countries, certain places shift from being semi-peripheral transit destinations to more permanent arrival cities. At the same time, local immigration policies in Hong Kong aimed at attracting tourists and foreign capital to benefit the city's service economy contribute towards the growing numbers of people seeking asylum in the territory when flight is urgent and/or other destinations become unreachable.

It is plausible that the decision making of each individual who comes to know about or travel to Hong Kong complements global economic trends and different state immigration rules that close some borders while forcing others open. The macro-forces that channel migration flows are themselves shaped by the decisions and actions that asylum seekers undertake at the micro-level, often in the context of structural conditions that diminish their choices. The experiences of the asylum seekers revealed in this study suggest that these people form new, and build upon existing, local and transnational networks in order to migrate and pursue their livelihoods in Hong Kong. It is clear that the social networks that they establish or access on a daily basis to meet their and their business partners' goals in part create the conditions that facilitate migration to Hong Kong. In this regard, a number of conclusions can be drawn that explain the circumstances that impact on the formation of networks and the rise of Hong Kong as a final destination.

First, empirical data suggest that choice of destination is increasingly surrendered by migrants to the people who are in charge of organizing their journey. As the legal barriers protecting the developed world from undesirable populations cast numbers of people in directions previously relatively unexplored, migrants resort to various forms of unlawful border crossing in order to gain access to places that respond to increasing arrivals by enforcing more restrictive border controls. In the case of Hong Kong, if entry is relatively easy, legal border crossing is not an option available to everyone. Restrictions apply for a number of nationalities, leading undeterred travellers to contact third parties and acquaintances to obtain information and/or evade the legal barriers to entry. In this sense, the case of Hong Kong confirms that an extensive commercialization of the irregular migration process is occurring (Kaizen and Nonneman 2007; Içduygu and Toktas 2002). Indeed, very few of the participants did not employ third parties to organize their journey. Consequently, the itineraries of the asylum seekers were affected by this choice, as the organizers of their journeys drew on their previous experience to channel their friends and clients to the destination about which they had some knowledge.

Second, the growing importance of third parties has clearly changed the nature of the social networks of asylum seekers (Koser and Pinkerton 2002). This research confirms that bonded networks structured around specific foci generally established among co-national and family members to convey information,

(Un)wanted people in the global city 201

food, shelter and financial and emotional support (Boyd 1989; Massey et al. 1987) become less important in conditions of heightened legal barriers to the free movement of impoverished people. Collyer (2005) argues that restrictive migration policy in different European countries has caused a distortion of the normal flows of asylum migration, with Algerians, for instance, arriving in the UK despite having no significant co-national community in London, whereas they do often have extensive family networks in France. According to Massey et al. (1993), social networks are ties that bind migrants, previous migrants and non-migrants in origin and destination countries. They mediate structural factors by facilitating and supporting migration, even when the initial forces driving migration have long changed the environment at the two extremes of the flow (Hugo 1981; Sassen 1998). In this regard, when social networks expand, new resources are made available, and eventually a broader base of people in the country of origin is able to move along the path established by their friends and family members.

In Hong Kong, only a few asylum seekers interviewed for this study had friends and relatives in the territory before they arrived. The majority based their decision making about the destination on the information they obtained from third parties. In so doing, they sought access to resources extraneous to their network, which would not otherwise have been available (Koser 1997; Andrijasevic 2010). Third parties, however, may have little interest in providing accurate information or even the services for which they are paid, with the obvious consequence that migrants frequently end up in places they do not expect and which they know little about. It is to the undue trust placed by asylum seekers in newly established bridged relations with third parties that hasty departures and often tragic consequences can be ascribed. Contrary to the claims of Koser (1997) and others, in the case of Hong Kong the spatial dissociation between the choice of destination and the location of relatives and friends overseas is not entirely the result of asylum seekers basing their decisions on the advice of family members overseas and resourced third parties. Rather, it is an unintended consequence of their often naive trust of uncaring and uninformed third parties. In this sense, the desired final destination of the asylum seeker frequently does not correspond to the country in which they seek asylum. Instead, their desired destination may well be the country in which friends and relatives reside but which is never reached for reasons beyond the asylum seekers' control.

Third, due to the relatively new mobility of certain nationalities and the spatial dissociation between chosen and final destinations, family ties in Hong Kong are rare and thus do not often play a part in reducing the costs of migration of asylum seekers. On the other hand, family ties with members in the country of origin acquire new meaning in terms of helping asylum seekers cope with their difficult circumstances. A few participants were assisted by their family members, who sent them cash capital and/or helped them to form reliable partnerships to enable informal trading opportunities. Having no family members in Hong Kong, asylum seekers also formed new networks at the destination. In this context, it becomes especially important to develop bridged relations to gain access to resources normally accessed through bonded networks in the country of refuge (Collyer 2005).

Local low-end businesses and the Internet, in particular, provide opportunities for asylum seekers to forge new connections which help them improve their livelihood and status. This was found to be true even in the rare event that asylum seekers did have family members in Hong Kong. Indeed, the most common type of family relations observed in Hong Kong involved situations of neglect or exploitation of migrant workers by their relatives, rather than those fitting the cost-reducing network migration model (Massey et al. 1993). For example, one participant's relatives in Hong Kong told him to go to Hong Kong when he needed to leave his country. However, rather than sponsoring his visa, they organized for him to cross the border irregularly and then to be employed in their shop, 12 hours a day for HK$1500 per month.

In this regard, this research found that the normal interpersonal relations within co-national groups, especially between the people who have control over resources and those seeking access to them, are profoundly affected by the government policies on asylum seekers. The lack of legal status of the latter constitutes a barrier that forces asylum seekers into a state of grave and persistent need. This may discourage co-national residents from taking responsibility for a group which is thus regarded as a long-term burden (Collyer 2005) for the communities who sit at the bottom of Hong Kong's hierarchy of income distribution (Ashencaen Crabtree and Wong 2012). In addition, the low opinion of asylum seekers held by the broader Hong Kong population impedes strong bonds between asylum seekers and their co-national legal residents, as the latter are afraid that their social standing may be negatively affected should they associate with the former (Crawford and Tsui 2009). This condition of legal marginalization and social isolation leads asylum seekers to look elsewhere for the social capital they need for their survival. The functions previously associated with bonded relations in the country of destination then come to be fulfilled by bridged social capital, in terms of the extent and reliability of tangible and emotional support.

Fourth, when networks are established between asylum seekers and local co-national groups, these are generally of an economic nature and are often exploitative. These networks include ethnic entrepreneurs and former asylum seekers who have become entrepreneurs and employ vulnerable new arrivals. This exploitative relation can be explained by the fact that local ethnic minorities have limited opportunities available to them to make a decent living without resorting to employing cheap labour (Panayiotopoulos 2010). As new asylum seekers lack the necessary capital to provide for themselves, they must rely on these new associations with their co-nationals; however, these connections can only provide them with a limited set of resources, often involving informal economic activities. Previous research has similarly shown that in the case of Polish irregular migrants in Belgium local resident co-national groups were mainly engaged in competitive market activities and thus generally resorted to employing cheap, newly arrived migrant labour to improve their profitability. As a result, irregular migrants were often given inaccurate or partial information, paid lower salaries and had to pay inflated prices for housing and goods (Grzymala-Kazlowska 2005). Likewise, in Hong Kong the legal resident ethnic minorities largely make a living by pursuing

(Un)wanted people in the global city 203

short-lived strategies of survival in very competitive informal economies which leave little room for concerns beyond purely economic ones (Mathews 2011). While their efforts mirror Hong Kong's well-established ideology of self-reliance (Chan 1998), asylum seekers provide a useful means of ensuring the survival of the fittest.

To conclude this section, it can be argued that, in a region where more asylum seekers might be looking for refuge in the years to come, a dynamic assemblage of forces at different levels contributes to the establishment of networks underlying the expansion of Hong Kong's economic competitiveness. On the one hand, global economic factors establish the transnational networks that foster increasing mobility. On the other, restrictive migration control measures affecting both the external and internal borders in Hong Kong and elsewhere have altered the nature of asylum seekers' social networks by changing the geographies of arrival and increasing the burden that asylum seekers reportedly impose on the host society. As a result, new opportunities have presented themselves for the global city to further its economic prosperity, as new transnational ties are formed at the micro-level, facilitating certain trading activities and enabling impoverished local residents to benefit from exploitable yet connected (or connectable) asylum seekers.

Asylum seeking and the policing of foreigners

In pursuing a level of analysis that links asylum seeking to the global city, it is noteworthy to recall that global cities are defined as sites of a remarkable convergence between a great concentration of corporate power and large numbers of 'others' (Sassen 2001). As explained previously, the intensity and magnitude of such change in Hong Kong and cities worldwide has been at the centre of academic debate. In the case of this research, significant evidence is revealed suggesting the existence of a bipolar labour market and deep-seated inequalities when the experiences of asylum seekers are examined. Hong Kong has become a destination on a new geopolitical map of safe places with high standards of living, and as such it has attracted increasing numbers of asylum seekers who have resorted to pursuing livelihoods on the margins.

A number of important conclusions are therefore made here concerning why Hong Kong receives what is generally called 'unwanted' immigration. If transnational networks and global economic and policy factors can explain why these travellers end up in Hong Kong, there seems to be a gap between the government's firm stance on not granting asylum and the numbers of people who slip through the tight mesh of border controls and apply for asylum in the territory and work in low-income jobs. To address this issue, this research takes as its basis much of the literature that explores mobility in relation to the political economy and the criminalization of migrants in the Global North. In so doing, the key point is that apparent distortions in the operation of the local labour market are heavily intertwined with local politics and policies, which produce an effective new legal regime specifically aimed at migrant populations. In this sense, while high-skilled migrant workers have been made the target of a global talent headhunt, with Hong

204   *(Un)wanted people in the global city*

Kong devoting resources and people to attracting investments and elite recruits, a number of other schemes have been implemented to temporarily import low-paid domestic and labour workers. A similar process has apparently occurred, albeit informally, for asylum seekers.

It is certainly hard to demonstrate here that the government has deliberately designed a mechanism of migration control to make use of asylum seekers as a temporary, flexible, knowledgeable and inexpensive workforce. However, it is possible to claim that the interplay of global factors and largely locally contained historical, political and policy developments has had a clear impact on the experiences of asylum seekers in creating legal liminal spaces of exclusion in which asylum seekers are inevitably left to fend for themselves, in ways that happen to satisfy the interests of Hong Kong. The result of this process, synthesized by the formation of the dual asylum mechanism, in fact seems to reveal surprisingly similar situations of organized vulnerability and exploitation to those observed in other regional contexts (De Genova 2002; Calavita 2005; Basso 2010; Cohen 2006), although this is perhaps the first study to highlight this condition in a global city, with its own particular implications.

Two main arguments are made here. On the one hand, the findings of this research show that, instead of constraining the authority of the Hong Kong Government, the legal process – that is, the state's obligations in regard to the legal texts and conventions to which the city is a signatory – possibly strengthens its sovereignty over foreigners in the territory. On the other, the meaning of 'unwanted' immigration can be questioned in view of the contradiction between official rhetorical discourses around asylum abuse and the reality of the marginalization and economic contribution of asylum seekers in Hong Kong.

Following the phenomenon by which increasing numbers of unwanted immigrants are entering wealthy destinations despite the impressive surge of restrictions imposed to keep them out (Cornelius et al. 1994; Cornelius 2005), scholarly debates have focused on examining the extent to which the arrival of unwanted or unskilled migrants can be controlled by receiving states (Joppke 1998). Sassen (1996) addresses this issue by arguing that migration is largely embedded in the conditions within the destination society. As she explains, the state's control over its borders is shaped by a series of constraints which are structural and based in international agreements and conventions, as well as the increase in the number and type of social and political actors engaged in migration. Freeman (1994) speaks in terms of 'embedded liberalism' to explain intrinsically expansionary policies that follow 'client politics' inclined towards increasing immigration. Rather than politics, Joppke (1998) argues that it is the 'legal process' that prevents the state from selectively excluding migrants based on certain categories as the liberal courts system is immune to political demands when applying national or international law.

The conflicting relationship between the political and legal processes described by Joppke is particularly evident in the case of asylum policies and politics in Hong Kong. As discussed at various points throughout this book, some judicial review cases have been won by asylum seekers in Hong Kong. In this view, it appears that the sovereignty of the government is limited by decisions that extend the rights of asylum seekers. In particular, some courts were critical of the government's policies on detention and support provision (Daly 2009). The findings of the fieldwork presented in the preceding chapters, however, paint a slightly different picture. First, it is questionable that the courts in Hong Kong are not influenced by the political process. It was noted in Chapter 2 that in the case of *MA v Director of Immigration* the court made explicit reference to political arguments to dismiss the review challenge brought forward by a group of recognized refugees who demanded the right to work. The court made it clear that the situation of the claimants was regarded as an unanticipated but necessary outcome of structural conditions that had to be considered when determining legal outcomes. Second, it has been demonstrated that the consequences of the judicial reviews, which ended with a victory for some refugee applicants, only partially limited the sovereignty of the government over the admission and control of asylum seekers. Rather, it can be said that the state's power was strengthened while the asylum seekers who apparently benefited suffered from increasing marginalization.

In response to previous court decisions (see Chapter 2), one of which found that a group of Pakistani asylum seekers was not breaking the law by working in street markets, and another that CAT screening procedures had failed to meet appropriate standards of fairness, thus requiring changes that were more favourable to asylum seekers,[1] the Hong Kong Government enacted the Immigration (Amendment) Ordinance in 2009, which specified that unlawful employment was a criminal offence for illegal immigrants and persons pending removal. In addition, it introduced a purportedly 'fairer' but certainly quicker CAT screening mechanism to clear the backlog of applications – with the result that between December 2009 and April 2013 only two torture victims were identified (Vision First 2013). Conversely, court decisions against unlawful detention have only partially eased the appalling conditions of asylum in Hong Kong, as the very limited support and other measures supposedly intended to help the disadvantaged have instead resulted in severely containing asylum seekers within a space of limited opportunities which many of the participants described as an 'open-air prison'.

These conclusions are in line with the assertion made by several commentators that the political process can be very inventive in circumventing the norms inscribed in national and international human rights regimes (Joppke 1998; Hyndman and Mountz 2008). In effect, the claim that certain processes adopted by liberal states are expansionary in terms of migration intake can be questioned in light of the Hong Kong experience set forth in these pages. In Hong Kong, the government responded to any perceived or actual increase in the number of asylum seekers and/or legal developments in their favour by tightening the mesh of border controls, de facto pressing asylum seekers into processes of homogenization that foster their deportability and exclusion. On this account, not only is it debatable that the state has limited power over the people who cross its borders, but it also seems clear that through the illegalization of unauthorized immigrants and their activities the state reveals its strengths rather than its weaknesses (Yamamoto 2007; Arnold 2011; Calavita 2003). This understanding of the border

206 *(Un)wanted people in the global city*

is based on the evidence collected by many scholars in other geographical settings who have noted that public and official discourses of migration tend to increasingly lump together terrorists, refugees and economic migrants as posing a collective risk (Bigo 2002; Bosworth and Guild 2008). As a result, new mechanisms of border control are implemented to prevent undesirable migrants from landing at a time when the physical border has been transformed to better mirror the new logic of surveillance and control intended to order, categorize and mark the immigrant body as a potential threat (Weber 2006). In Hong Kong, new border control mechanisms do not seem to deter unwanted arrivals. Instead, this research has demonstrated that these mechanisms elevate the legal status of the individual to become a potent marker of inclusion and exclusion. Asylum seekers are routinely constructed as bogus claimants and denied legal status. Moreover, their categorization as 'illegals' reinforces public stereotypical images of the system being abused, resulting in a clear demarcation of socio-political boundaries which intensify state controls over asylum seeker agency and identity.

Drawing on Yamamoto's (2007) analysis of legality and state power, it is argued that, rather than being a symbol of migration out of control, asylum seekers have been turned into instruments that reaffirm state power. Their experiences are heavily shaped by the conditions they find in the place of asylum because of the state's capacity to make them illegal and effectively force an entire group of people to endure a life of deprivation, as if they were an underclass. This process of racial differentiation and criminalization has been extensively observed in the US and Europe (Basso 2010; Calavita 2005; De Genova 2002), and as demonstrated by the findings presented here is equally evident in Hong Kong. However, what this research has found which partly differentiates the HKSAR from other geographical contexts is that in Hong Kong it is the asylum system that routinely performs the function of excluding undesirable border crossers. Rather than protecting vulnerable individuals who seek refuge, Hong Kong's approach to international protection creates social outcasts who are mistrusted as abusers of the system. On the one hand, through the extremely low recognition rates and the numerous barriers that impede prompt and equal access to the system, as well as the limited support provided to refugees, asylum seekers in the territory are effectively cast as economic migrants who seek to challenge the territory's rule of law. Borrowing from Calavita (2003), it can be said that asylum seekers thus become a 'reserve army of delinquent' others, who consequently engage in informal economic activities. On the other, it is striking that while many parties have argued that the dual UNHCR and CAT screening mechanisms promote abuses (Ip 2010), the government has only recently shown an intention to change the system, after judgements such as those in *Ubamaka v Secretary for Security* and *C v Director of Immigration* determined that the screening process is defective (Lo 2013). As such, the exercise of restrictive control measures over this population is closely associated with persistent stereotyped representations of abusive asylum seekers. In addition, the more people surface from illegality and access the current asylum system, the more the state increases its control over this class of dispossessed individuals. Indeed, the present asylum system is characterized by its migration control function rather than by its responsibility towards human rights protection.

Contrary to what tends to happen in other contexts where asylum seekers may choose not to claim asylum for fear of being returned to their country of origin, de facto becoming illegal migrants (Castles 2007; Bohmer and Shuman 2008), several interviewees argued that, although generally afraid of dealing with the authorities, they nonetheless sought or hoped to be arrested in order to enjoy the limited benefits afforded to asylum seekers who lodge an application. Hong Kong's implicit accepted obligations towards *non-refoulement* (Loper 2010) and its practice of releasing asylum seekers into the community certainly impact on asylum seekers' decision making. As a result, I was told of people running out of shops at the sight of police on the streets to stand before them and demand to be arrested to apply for the CAT, and of people who walked into police stations for the same reason; however, I was also told of others who were torn between fear of repatriation and the need to make themselves known to the authorities. Moreover, the prolonged periods of waiting on claims, sometimes lasting years, and the requirement that asylum seekers regularly visit Immigration and service provider offices to update their contact details, combined to produce a sort of win-win situation for asylum seekers and the government. The former can stay in Hong Kong, albeit temporarily, while the latter can maintain a clear idea of the numbers of easily traceable illegal migrants in the territory.

In practice, while asylum seekers are constructed as bogus claimants, raising public concerns over their reasons for seeking asylum, and thus legitimating the use of blanket policies to deny them the rights enjoyed by local residents, illegal migrants become visible to the government, making it easier to manage them in case of economic downturn or excessive arrivals. Furthermore, as the distinction generally drawn between asylum seekers and illegal economic migrants becomes increasingly blurred, new arrivals engaging in income-generating activities to cope with exclusionary politics raise further suspicions about their reasons for seeking asylum. In so doing, they involuntarily contribute towards justifying and entrenching their own criminalization, such that a self-fulfilling cycle is created (Squire 2009). In this view, the formation of this 'asylum–migration nexus' (Castles 2007) embodies the power of the government to illegalize and render 'bogus' a certain group of people while shifting the issue of asylum to the realm of symbolic politics. The exclusion of asylum seekers further reaffirms state sovereignty as this appeases public concerns about the economy and local identity. It was noted in previous chapters how the Hong Kong people quickly adopted prejudices when they became aware of the risks that mainland Chinese migrants would pose for the quick transition of the city to a wealthy service-based economy. Some of those prejudices are still strong today (Newendorp 2008; Ku 2001) and are frequently used to describe the ethnic minorities and newcomers of non-Chinese background (Ashencaen Crabtree and Wong 2012). Yet, while they face such discrimination, asylum seekers continue to work at the lower end of the occupational structure. Indeed, their inclusion in these markets is controlled and

208 *(Un)wanted people in the global city*

articulated to a large degree by the asylum system, which purportedly aims to ensure durable solutions, while in reality offering no permanent protection.

It is from this perspective that asylum seekers arriving in Hong Kong can be seen as not entirely 'unwanted'. On the one hand, governments may strengthen their grip over the legal resident population by constructing the image of an ideal citizen in opposition to those who are selectively excluded as negative examples (Bosworth and Guild 2008). On the other, several scholars argue that it is not so much that government policies are failing to keep people out (Yamamoto 2007), but rather that governments adopt sophisticated techniques of control that allow them to deprioritize external border controls by strictly regulating illegal residents within their borders (Calavita 2003; Chiswick 2001). In relation to the political economy, this process bears significant advantages for the host society. The preceding chapters revealed that asylum seekers emerge in the Hong Kong labour market as convenient, networked and inexpensive workers who provide flexibility, which is arguably one of the most powerful 'antidote[s] to economic rigidities' (Calavita 2003: 409) and certainly a dominant trend in the Hong Kong labour market (Zhao et al. 2004).

To return to the global city, it is apparent that the socially marginalized and low-income asylum seekers in Hong Kong constitute a large body of 'others' living on the margins of this city. As Sassen (2001) notes, the underprivileged engaging in the low-grade and service sectors gather in urban spaces, possibly raising levels of social polarization and income inequality. However, rather than pursuing livelihoods according to their social and economic skills, these people become institutionally confined to endure a life of deprivation regardless of their educational background or motivations for travelling to Hong Kong.

While these findings on the impact of urban policies on the legal and social status of asylum seekers in Hong Kong cannot be easily generalized to other global cities, it does appear that economic deregulation and neoliberal policies weaken social equality and the rule of law – which paradoxically constitutes a salient identity discourse in Hong Kong that differentiates Hong Kong people from the mainland Chinese (Mathews et al. 2008; Newendorp 2011). Nonetheless, the authority of the government seems to be strengthened by the denial of the political and economic rights of people who, while being 'illegals', are welcome only when reduced to a temporary, submissive and readily controlled group (Arnold 2011). In this regard, the responsibility of the Hong Kong Government for the creation of an economically active social underclass is as prominent as that of global economic restructuring.

Casualization of labour and the refugee benefit

The main and perhaps most obvious finding of this research is that, to a large extent, cheap, contingent and informal labour in Hong Kong is provided by asylum seekers. This book reveals that many asylum seekers are involved in several sectors of the economy, mostly providing services and goods in what certainly appears to be a post-Fordist model of production that fosters the 'just-in-time'

(Un)wanted people in the global city   209

economy (Hutchins 1999). Asylum seekers are engaged in economic processes that are largely driven by demand. They are casually employed to provide labour and skills specifically for the period needed for an order to be fulfilled and become unemployed again once orders discontinue. In many cases, these services cannot be defined as low-grade, labour-intensive work typical of sweatshop economic conditions. Rather, considerable profits are possible in a relatively short amount of time when asylum seekers act as intermediaries, although the services they provide tend to be occasional and subject to a high degree of monetary and other risks. In this sense, casualization is certainly evident when the focus is on the form of income earned, which very often involves unstable commissions for procuring goods and business or wages paid by the day or for piecework. While asylum seekers must constantly negotiate this harsh reality, labour casualization raises production output, as asylum seekers are pressed to work faster and better to improve their chances of being called for work again. Their being exploited by their employers, while at the same time themselves exploiting labour market conditions in Hong Kong, is particularly observable in two broad sectors: recycling and trading.

The former sector is constituted by a range of relations of production that originate in the consumption patterns of wealthy societies of the Global North. As was observed during the fieldwork, and as Grossman (2006) explains in her work on high-tech trash, electronics and garments are mass-produced consumer products the recycling of which raises complex challenges, whether at the end of their life or sooner as new products are produced ever more quickly to appeal to the tastes of wealthy urban residents. In Hong Kong, the disposal of such materials has created opportunities for some people to generate an income when these items are reprocessed or reused as valued First World products in China and other developing countries. In this sector, asylum seekers work as casual garbage collectors, labourers, sometimes supervisors of other workers and often intermediaries guiding buyers through the maze of scrapyards and second-hand dealers. At times, they are the buyers themselves, betting the little profit they have made from labouring on their capacity to read their home market and supply trusted partners with the items they sell. Transnational trading, however, does not only involve recycled goods. To a significant extent, it comprises the new and often copied and extremely cheap Chinese-manufactured electronics and clothes that Hong Kong businesses market to the developing world. Here, asylum seekers furnish their networks with their knowledge of the local trade opportunities emerging in Hong Kong.

Importantly, in both sectors asylum seekers do not compete for jobs with the local resident population. This is because locals either do not possess the skills to make stable connections between low-end transnational consumer markets and services that often require the development of considerable trust, or they find unacceptable the kind of labour-intensive and poorly paid, untenured jobs that asylum seekers are willing to perform. Due to the low-value-added production output in recycling and certain forms of trading, processing services require very cheap, physically strong and flexible workers, the likes of whom are largely

210 *(Un)wanted people in the global city*

unavailable in the local labour market. Indeed, the only local residents met during the field visits to these businesses were the site owners, who were often of immigrant background and chose to conduct such a business to escape low-paid jobs and employment discrimination in the unskilled, mainstream market. Yet I was told that some local residents worked daytime shifts in some recycling yards while asylum seekers provided night-time and cheaper labour to complement the daytime production. In these businesses, however, production output was larger and profits were said to be high enough to hire regular workers, albeit in unsafe working conditions.

In light of these factors, the goal of this section is to discuss in a broader context the range of economic activities in which asylum seekers are engaged in Hong Kong, specifically to consider two apparently contradictory observations that can be made about economic informalization and labour casualization in this city. On the one hand, it is plausible to assert that the sectors in which asylum seekers work are affected by their agency but are not at all dependent on their presence. On the other hand, it appears that these economic activities would not have flourished to the extent that they have if not for the contribution provided by asylum seekers in terms of both labour and networks.

Several previous studies discuss the origin of the informal economy in global cities and the supposed capacity of such agglomerations of power and marginality to generate demand for low-wage workers. Sassen (2001) argues that at the lower end of the occupational structure, the city generates countless opportunities in the expanding services sector that require ever cheaper workers to raise profits in increasingly segmented labour markets. At the same time, the growing presence of a large pool of low-income migrants in global cities, who fill vacancies in low-grade service jobs, contributes to shape the structure of the market by increasing demand for cheaper services that cater for the limited earnings of this cohort, thus generating demand for more low-income migrants (Sassen 1998, 2001). Some critics of this account, however, have questioned the assumption that immigration is demand driven and that the informalization and casualization of labour is the driver rather than the consequence of the arrival of immigrants from the periphery of world (Light 2004; Hamnett 1994). Light (2004), for example, calls the informal and ethnic economy a buffer, the emergence of which signifies the transition from a demand-driven migration, where immigrants find work in the formal sectors, to a supply-driven immigration, where jobs can only be found in the informal economy. In his opinion, when the formal labour market saturates due to the arrival of new immigrants resulting from the cumulative effects of network migration (Massey et al. 1993), wages and living conditions deteriorate while the spaces for extra-legal residency and informal work expand, increasing both poverty and anti-immigration sentiment.

From this study emerged a rather different picture. In Hong Kong, it is evident that asylum seekers have taken advantage of pre-existing conditions of informalization and casualization of labour at a time when the local resident population has needed ways to expand and provide new services to enable their businesses to thrive or remain viable. In this regard, it has been noted, for example, that in

(Un)wanted people in the global city   211

Sham Shui Po local Chinese retail businesses quickly shifted towards wholesale production when new opportunities arose for them to gain access to fast-growing demand in developing countries. Mathews (2011: 150) describes traders arriving in Hong Kong and China as the 'Marco Polos of developing-world globalization'. These traders have created significant and growing links of various kinds between the small-scale businesses of the core and the relatively new markets of the periphery. Thus, asylum seekers greatly benefit from the local economy as new opportunities become available for local family-run and often one-person enterprises that engage in cross-border trade, often informally, between China and Hong Kong and then Hong Kong and elsewhere.

Moreover, conditions of informalization do not seem to follow asylum seeker involvement in income-generating activities. On the one hand, asylum seekers do not saturate the labour market. Rather, they create new spaces within it in response to demand for new services that have no significant negative effect on wages, as production is regulated by foreign-driven demand rather than worker supply. In addition, the local workforce appears to be unqualified to work in spaces of transnationalism. On the other hand, the housing market does not seem to be affected in the manner described by Light (2004). Indeed, the presence of an underpaid workforce does not facilitate a low-cost housing market. Illegal dwellings tolerated by the authorities and traded illegally have existed for decades in Hong Kong (Smart 1989, 2001). In this sense, the insertion of asylum seekers into the rental market does not produce a new trend. Instead, it can be seen as an element of continuity in existing patterns of informalization (Quassoli 1999), whereby new classes take up the spaces left behind by those who are able to move up the social ladder or apply for public housing.

More importantly, while asylum seekers do not seem to have a significant impact on increasing levels of informalization, in the pursuit of their livelihoods they nonetheless contribute towards a greater focus on certain informal economic activities which better enable local enterprises and landlords to secure the means to negotiate the effects of economic restructuring. In practice, just as structural spatial contexts shape migrants' agency, migrants' behaviour and approach to prevailing norms and local conditions help shape the environments in which they live (Samers 2002; Smith and Guarnizo 1998). Asylum seekers cannot be seen as the causes of undesirable economic changes that tempt the local population to resort to employing cheap labour in breach of government regulatory frameworks. Rather, they actively influence the economic and policy context of the place in which they live by making the most of their limited skills (Kloosterman et al. 1999; Portes 1997, 2001; Portes et al. 2002), although the results of their agency (such as increased securitization, legal marginalization and emotional hardship) may not always be in their best interests (Samers 2010).

The previous section highlighted one of the main findings of this book – that well-established and isolated legal categories function to contain asylum seeker agency. The illegal status of asylum seekers and the many government policies aimed at controlling them have come to regulate their economic engagement with the host society. This research has demonstrated that asylum seekers, limited in

212 *(Un)wanted people in the global city*

their livelihoods by exclusionary measures that prevent their full integration, tend to create bridged social networks with specific strata of the economically active local resident population – namely, those most likely to be sitting at the bottom of the income hierarchy, though often seeking the means to improve their status. Thus, asylum seekers effectively function to ease the social inequalities caused by economic restructuring in a context of insufficient government welfare, thereby contributing towards the reduction in the impact of the 'low-income-poverty cycle' (Lee et al. 2007).

In terms of social polarization, this analysis suggests that there exists in Hong Kong a range of classes that thrive on the margins of the official economy. The presence of asylum seekers, the kinds of working opportunities available to them and the people with whom they engage as part of their survival strategies reflect the income and occupational insecurity of more or less extended strata of the working population. On the one hand, part of this local population may have actually 'professionalized', as local, small-scale family businesses seek to negotiate the increasingly segmented and unstable labour structure of the Hong Kong market by resorting to innovative strategies that exploit asylum seekers to establish flexible, short-run-based services and transnational networks. On the other hand, legal barriers to asylum seeker integration into the host society have undoubtedly contributed towards the formation of a local underclass of illegalized workers for whom it becomes very difficult to move up the socioeconomic hierarchy. These people can live, stay and work in the HKSAR, but their existence is limited and precarious (cf. Dal Lago 2009; Landolt and Goldring 2010).

In this sense, the data presented in this book can certainly expand our understanding of social polarization in the context of Hong Kong. The analysis of the services mediated by asylum seekers and the local policy framework regulating their engagement with the economy suggests significant implications for the prospects of social mobility and employment for numbers of low-income people in this city. While the asylum seekers are only temporary outcasts, they appear to be a permanent product of economic restructuring and one of its many contributors in Hong Kong.

The politics and future of asylum

As asylum seekers have become a major political issue across the Global North, the increase in their number and diversity has been generally negotiated by the majority of the traditional destination countries for asylum seeking through a tightening of access to the institution of asylum (Price 2009). This has involved a wide range of deterrent and pre-emptive measures implemented to secure the physical border while denying access to internal judicial scrutiny and welfare benefits (Castles and Loughna 2005; Hyndman and Mountz 2008; Gibney and Hansen 2005). These punitive policies have produced extensive negative consequences for the people subjected to them. Border policing has raised the costs and dangers associated with their migratory journeys, denying the right to seek asylum to those individuals who are the least resourced to engage in migration

(Un)wanted people in the global city 213

or who perish in their attempts to reach their destinations (Weber and Pickering 2011). Additionally, asylum seekers who cross the borders into countries of refuge have been turned into peripheral underclasses (Schuster 2011; Gerard 2014).

According to Gibney (2004), this outcome constitutes a paradox of the Western state. In Gibney's opinion, while the language of liberal democracies remains firmly anchored in the affirmation of civil liberties and the moral significance of securing a free and just society within and beyond the national border, greater importance is attached to protecting those borders which have come to represent the last bastion to stop the inflow of external threats (Pickering 2011). From the standpoint of refugee rights, this means that while the governments of the Global North speak in terms of legal responsibilities towards refugees, the measures they implement to manage their borders are intended to ensure that few asylum seekers ever reach their territory and that even fewer receive protection (Martin 1989; Hathaway 2008–09). For Gibney (2004), this dual, indeed conflicting, approach generates a growing gap between the ethics and the politics of asylum: between what is ethically ideal – more inclusive policies that better adhere to the precepts contained in the human rights instruments to which these states are signatory – and the current policies that are increasingly restrictive if not deaf to the claims of people who seek asylum.

On this view, it can be argued that asylum has become one process of globalization that mirrors Sassen's (1996) logic of the renationalization of politics at the same time that the denationalization of economic spaces is growing. Asylum, in the form it currently takes, has come to be negotiated as a narrow pathway between roadblocks increasingly erected by the governments of the Global North to close off that pathway, for it is becoming more problematic to sort those who deserve protection from those who do not. As Muus (1997) argues, it is apparent that between the respect of human rights and the management of migration flows (and the social issues they engender), Western states have shown a clear tendency towards enforcing the latter – thus raising numerous ethical and practical questions concerning what remains of the institution of asylum and why.

In Hong Kong, asylum is physically available but largely inaccessible for most of the people who seek it (cf. Khosravi 2010). The previous chapters have provided an account of the failure of the city's asylum system to provide durable solutions to asylum seekers. This is interpreted here as the result of two intertwined social and legal processes. First, the politically destabilizing evidence that asylum seekers are a social category determined by their motivations contrasts with the legal definitions enshrined in conventions that make little mention of the voluntary or involuntary nature of flight, on which the political debate in Hong Kong pertaining to asylum is focused (cf. Zimmermann 2009a). Second, as a result of the previous argument, Zimmermann (2009a) notes that governments of the Global North are ever more hesitant to keep the door open to travellers who may resort to flight under duress but who still make decisions about when to leave and where to go. In the eyes of the government and the public in Hong Kong, asylum seekers' motivations for and expectations of landing in the territory are more important than whether they meet the criteria for refugee status. Asylum seekers are turned into undeserving illegal economic migrants even before their claim is evaluated. This research has shown that it is the asylum system that impedes those who seek to access it from proving their genuineness. In addition, what emerges as particularly appalling for asylum seekers is that their lifestyle in Hong Kong has itself come to be seen as evidence that indirectly influences the determination of their claim. It has been found that having a girlfriend, working illegally or enjoying their life in an exciting, thriving global city routinely raises suspicion over asylum seekers' real motivation for seeking asylum, as the people supposedly there to help them, and increasingly other members of the refugee community, believe that a person who has experienced trauma cannot be anything but fundamentally miserable and passive.

A staggering discovery made during the fieldwork was the widespread perception that dreaming of a better life is forbidden for asylum seekers in Hong Kong. Crock et al. (2006) associate the refugees seeking protection in Australia with people who are looking for a chance to rebuild their life. In what is an emerging body of literature that calls for recognition of the social experiences of asylum seeking, Zimmermann (2009a, 2009b) elegantly argues that refugees seek more than temporary refuge. Their journey is an ever-continuing quest for stability, whether to be achieved in the country of asylum, in other destinations or even in the country of origin were the conditions to improve to a level that offered the opportunities currently only found overseas. However, it would seem that seeking to improve one's circumstances and happiness is deemed indicative of a non-genuine asylum claim in Hong Kong.

This study has shown that the current asylum system in Hong Kong bears enormous responsibilities for it routinely punishes asylum seekers by forcing them to endure precarious and degrading living conditions. The dual and ineffective screening mechanisms, supposedly initiated to grant protection to those who flee persecution, help create the impression that those who make a claim for asylum are morally undeserving of protection until proved otherwise. The system distorts the agency of asylum seekers to portray them as solely responsible for their exclusion. Their dreams, their intention to build a better life in Hong Kong and the goals they want to achieve by working illegally and getting married, rather than being taken to represent a legitimate desire for normality, are seen to demonstrate an agency that is incongruous with the stereotyped images of refugees (Zetter 1991, 2007). It is in part because of this widely shared mistrust of asylum seekers that the institution of asylum is deeply weakened in Hong Kong.

On a similar note, it cannot but come to mind that the asylum seekers' views of their condition and their expectations of contributing to the society that were briefly examined in Chapters 2 and 4 are revealing of narratives of anxiety, suffering and frustration that were also found in a rare ethnographic study on the detention of foreign others in the UK conducted by Bosworth (2012). On this view, the Hong Kong system of releasing asylum seekers into society, which refugee advocates internationally claim to be a valid and preferable alternative to detention (Sampson et al. 2011), may be argued to strongly affect the dignity and mental health of the asylum seekers, in that my participants often complained of

(Un)wanted people in the global city 215

being subjected to 'mental torture' and pointed towards a process of dehumanization. As they often argued, they felt 'useless' and unfairly treated in Hong Kong. While they were not confined in detention facilities, the exclusionary measures to which my participants were subjected forced them into a 'state of immobility' (Haugen 2012), which resembled detention conditions. In reality, asylum seekers were found to be working and overall to be making the most of their limited spaces of inclusion. However, the opportunities to escape those spaces were extremely limited and often came at the cost of sacrificing one's integrity and dignity. It is no surprise that several participants described their experiences in Hong Kong as akin to living in a 'open-air prison', suggesting the effects of the restrictive and often humiliating procedures with which they were required to comply in order to claim asylum. Bosworth (2012) argues that the detainees in her study were relatively free within their detention facilities. Nonetheless, they were caught in a process of boredom, eating and sleeping, forced upon them for their lack of citizenship rights in the UK, which gave rise at times to national pride as a strategy to cope with the overarching homogenization of their persona which lessened their self-worth. What we see in Hong Kong is asylum seekers confined to certain spaces, forced to wait for their number to be called and subjected to rigid procedures of control that limit their agency and mobility, thereby equally impacting their identity and sense of worth. In such circumstances, asylum seekers perceive little difference between experiences in detention and their living in the host society – either way, they lack freedom. In the latter case, they can move in much larger spaces than detention facilities and meet many people. They can work and do business and at times advance their economic status (in those sectors that benefit Hong Kong). Nonetheless, many opportunities are simply out of their reach in a society where their status engenders serious risks and in which most of the locals are disapproving of their stay in the city.

It is clear that in Hong Kong asylum is not easily achievable, if not totally unobtainable. However, while in other countries legal and social barricades have been raised around the privilege of asylum, the current policies in Hong Kong effectively encourage irregular entries to seek asylum. As discussed previously, asylum procedures have become instruments of migration control. They allow the government authorities to compile detailed lists of the people illegally residing in the territory while providing them with very limited aid and virtually no durable protection. Ethical and practical issues thus emerge concerning the role of asylum in Hong Kong. More precisely, while other developed countries may envy Hong Kong's firm policy of not granting asylum, at the same time supporting its economy with the precious resources made available by asylum seekers, perhaps the main issue here is not whether the institution of asylum should be protected or strengthened. Rather, the more important question seems to be around whether there is still a need for asylum at all, and whether we should continue to sort migration flows into unrealistic categories that the majority of asylum seekers do not seem to understand.

From the point of view of sociological analysis, the asylum seeker emerges in the literature, and certainly in this study, as a being not particularly different from any other migrant. For example, in many areas of the Global South the political and economic reasons for engaging in refugee flight are strictly interwoven (Schmeidl 1997, 2001; Kane 1995). While asylum migration has become a critical mechanism to secure family survival (Van Hear 1998), labour migration is increasingly used as a form of asylum seeking. This research found that several of the male and female participants had previous experience working in the Middle East, where they certainly could not seek asylum but where refuge was found when circumstances at home became unbearable. It is in this light that the distinction between forced and economic migration can be seen to be blurred and reduced to a question of semantics (Haddad 2008).

This research has taken the stand of the asylum seekers and evaluated their expectations in relation to asylum. It identified that their major reason for engaging in migration was not to obtain the rather vague status of international protection. Rather, many travelled with the aim of seeking opportunities to conduct a normal life. As the asylum seekers themselves explained, this involved negotiating a way to gain work and seeking to attain an education, as they saw freedom as a fruit to be picked with their hands. From this perspective, leaving aside the ethical implications related to 'the West's fundamental political values' around asylum (Price 2009: 248), from a more practical standpoint it can be argued that protection may be accessed by engaging in overseas temporary work, out of which more opportunities may arise, geographically and socially, once sufficient cash capital is accumulated. One African asylum seeker, for instance, reminded me that many opportunities were there to be grasped, but that he lacked the money to reach them. Similar to the experiences of other asylum seekers who had applied for technical schools and university in Canada and Australia, this man had been accepted into a course in Canada but was unsure about how or whether he could get there. He explained:

> There is an education provider in my country that can help me apply for a visa to Canada. The school sent me a reminder asking if I [wanted to] take the seat or not. I have to go back to my country [to process the visa], but I need money. If I go back I can hide myself, maybe for a month, before I can go there. Now I have the number of this agent. This is a good opportunity for me, but I need money. (African participant, 07)

Some scholars have argued that asylum should be returned to its origins. Price (2009), for example, believes that the present crisis of asylum is a consequence of states adopting procedural rules that strike a balance between minimizing asylum fraud and maintaining an open door to those whose asylum claims are genuine. While it remains arguable whether wealthier states do indeed intend to keep the narrow gate of asylum open, it seems reasonable to assert that asylum policies should be more and better targeted. Price (2009) notes that asylum is currently animated by the larger humanitarian goals of protecting refugees from insecurity based on criteria not contained in the Refugee Convention. In his opinion, some of these cases could warrant extended protection through humanitarian aid in their countries of origin.

The findings of this research indicate that, rather than rethinking asylum in terms of human rights, it would be in the best interests of both asylum seekers and destination countries to simply furnish asylum seekers with the tools to secure their own protection. Moreover, human rights–centred perspectives such as that held by Price would make sense if, before embarking on their journey, asylum seekers understood the nature of asylum and how their experiences fit into the rigid criteria of the refugee and other conventions. In addition, it is possible that the adoption of humanitarian aid, development assistance and regional temporary protection as policy tools to complement targeted asylum policies in the Global North in the short run would not help asylum seekers to access the opportunities they seek: in essence, the skills and capital that are required to compete, in times of accentuated globalization, in an increasingly unequal international labour market. For the large majority of asylum seekers, persecution and exploitation are the result of socio-political conditions affecting those positioned at the bottom of the socioeconomic ladder. As my participants' experiences revealed, affluence is generally a protection against persecution. Expanding unskilled labour schemes in the cities in which labour demand is higher would thus provide a significant number of asylum seekers with the opportunities needed to escape persecution and poverty. In the context of Hong Kong in particular, both the asylum seekers and the host society would likely benefit greatly from such a policy change. On the one hand, granting economic rights to unskilled migrants from the countries that produce the higher numbers of asylum seekers, in specific sectors of the economy and for a limited period of time, would provide a legal workforce to those segments of the market that currently employ asylum seekers. In the event that these workers became 'regularized', employers could still hire them, as illegal Chinese migrants from the mainland would not be able to take up those positions requiring the specific human and social capital that other migrants possess. On the other hand, the participants suggested that they would accept their current working conditions in Hong Kong as long as they could work without fear of police arrest. In practice, regularized migrants would have access to what is essentially a working holiday visa for citizens of countries of the Global South. While an expedited and targeted asylum system would probably be needed to process applications in the most appalling cases, the asylum seekers could be given the opportunity to choose between either a significantly longer visa that grants them economic rights in certain sectors or having their asylum application quickly processed.

What emerged most powerfully from this study is the agency of asylum seekers, their capacity to adapt to different situations and emerge from different, often very difficult, experiences. They are not the voiceless, shapeless people who are often pitied and portrayed as incapable of surviving without 'our' help. Rather, they are capable and self-aware individuals who work to solve their own problems while making a significant contribution to the host society, and as such active agents should they be treated.

218 *(Un)wanted people in the global city*

Note

1 *FB v Director of Immigration*, HCAL51/2007, 5 December 2008.

References

Acuto, M. (2011) 'Finding the Global City: An Analytical Journey through the "Invisible College"', *Urban Studies*, 48(14): 2953–2973.

Acuto, M. and Steele, W. (2013) (Eds.) *Global City Challenges: Debating a Concept, Improving the Practice*, Houndmills: Palgrave Macmillan.

Andrijasevic, R. (2010) *Migration, Agency and Citizenship in Sex Trafficking*, Houndmills: Palgrave Macmillan.

Arango, J. (2000) 'Explaining Migration: A Critical View', *International Social Science Journal*, 52(165): 283–269.

Arnold, K. (2011) 'Economic Prerogative and Its Political Consequences: The Migrant Labor and Border Industrial Regimes', *Constellations*, 18(3): 455–473.

Ashencaen Crabtree, S. and Wong, H. (2012) '"Ah Cha"! The Racial Discrimination of Pakistani Minority Communities in Hong Kong: An Analysis of Multiple, Intersecting Oppressions', *British Journal of Social Work*, 43(5): 945–963.

Basso, P. (Ed.) (2010) *Razzismo di Stato: Stati Uniti, Europa, Italia*, Milano: FrancoAngeli.

Baum, S. (1999) 'Social Transformations in the Global City: Singapore', *Urban Studies*, 36(7): 1095–1117.

Bauman, Z. (1998) *Globalization: The Human Consequences*, Cambridge: Polity Press.

Beckett, K. and Hebert, S. (2008) 'Dealing with Disorder: Social Control in the Post-industrial City', *Theoretical Criminology*, 12(1): 5–30.

Bigo, D. (2002) 'Security and Immigration: Toward a Critique of the Governmentality of Unease', *Alternatives*, 27: 63–92.

Bohmer, C. and Shuman, A. (2008) *Rejecting Refugees: Political Asylum in the 21st Century*, Abingdon: Routledge.

Bosworth, M. (2012) 'Subjectivity and Identity in Detention: Punishment and Society in a Global Age', *Theoretical Criminology*, 16(2): 123–140.

Bosworth, M. and Guild, M. (2008) 'Governing through Migration Control', *British Journal of Criminology*, 48(6): 703–719.

Boyd, M. (1989) 'Family and Personal Networks in Migration', *International Migration Review*, 23(3): 638–670.

Burgers, J. and Musterd, S. (2002) 'Understanding Urban Inequality: A Model Based on Existing Theories and an Empirical Illustration', *International Journal of Urban and Regional Research*, 26(2): 403–413.

Buscher, D. (2011) 'New Approaches to Urban Refugee Livelihoods', *Refuge*, 28(2): 17–29.

Calavita, K. (2003) 'A "Reserve Army of Delinquents": The Criminalization and Economic Punishment of Immigrants in Spain', *Punishment & Society*, 5(4): 399–413.

Calavita, K. (2005) *Immigrants at the Margins: Law, Race and Exclusion in Southern Europe*, Cambridge: Cambridge University Press.

Castles, S. (2003) 'Towards a Sociology of Forced Migration and Social Transformation', *Sociology*, 37(1): 13–34.

Castles, S. (2007) 'The Migration-Asylum Nexus and Regional Approaches', in S. Kneebone and F. Rawlings-Sanaei (Eds.) *New Regionalism and Asylum Seekers*, New York: Berghahn Books: 25–42.

(Un)wanted people in the global city 219

Castles, S. and Loughna, S. (2005) 'Trends in Asylum Migration to Industrialized Countries, 1990–2001', in G. J. Borjas and J. Crisp (Eds.) *Poverty, International Migration and Asylum*, Houndmills: Palgrave Macmillan: 39–69.

Chan, C-K. (1998) 'Welfare Policies and the Construction of Welfare Relations in a Residual Welfare State: The Case of Hong Kong', *Social Policy & Administration*, 32(3): 278–291.

Chan, C. K. (2011) 'Hong Kong: Workfare in the World's Freest Economy', *International Journal of Social Welfare*, 20: 22–32.

Chin, C. B. N. (2013) *Cosmopolitan Sex Workers: Women and Migration in a Global City*, Oxford: Oxford University Press.

Chiswick, B. R. (2001) 'The Economics of Illegal Migration for the Host Economy', in M. A. B. Siddique (Ed.) *International Migration into the 21st Century: Essays in Honour of Reginald Appleyard*, Cheltenham: Edward Elgar: 74–85.

Chiu, S. and Lui, T-L. (2009) *Hong Kong: Becoming a Chinese Global City*, Abingdon: Routledge.

Chiu, S. W. K. and Lui, T-L. (2004) 'Testing the Global City-Social Polarization Thesis: Hong Kong since the 1990s', *Urban Studies*, 41(10): 1863–1888.

Cohen, R. (1987) *The New Helots: Migrants in the International Division of Labour*, Aldershot: Avebury.

Cohen, R. (2006) *Migration and Its Enemies: Global Capital, Migrant Labour and the Nation-State*, Aldershot: Ashgate.

Collyer, M. (2005) 'When Do Social Networks Fail to Explain Migration? Accounting for the Movement of Algerian Asylum-Seekers to the UK', *Journal of Ethnic and Migration Studies*, 31(4): 699–718.

Cornelius, W. A. (2005) 'Controlling "Unwanted" Immigration: Lessons from the United States, 1993–2004', *Journal of Ethnic and Migration Studies*, 31(4): 775–794.

Cornelius, W. A., Martin, P. L. and Hollifield, J. F. (1994) (Eds.) *Controlling Immigration: A Global Perspective*, Stanford: Stanford University Press.

Crawford, B. and Tsui, Y. (2009) 'Reopen Refugee Camps, Say S Asians', *South China Morning Post*, 8 March. Viewed 8 March 2009: www.scmp.com/article/672594/reopen-refugee-camps-say-s-asians

Crock, M., Saul, B. and Dastyari, A. (2006) *Future Seekers II: Refugees and Irregular Migration in Australia*, Sydney: The Federation Press.

Dal Lago, A. (2009) *Non-persone: L'esclusione dei Migranti in Una Società Globale*, Milano: Feltrinelli.

Daly, M. (2009) 'Refugee Law in Hong Kong: Building the Legal Infrastructure', *Hong Kong Lawyer*, 9: 14–30.

De Genova, N. P. (2002) 'Migrant "Illegality" and Deportability in Everyday Life', *Annual Review of Anthropology*, 31: 419–447.

Feenstra, R. C. and Hanson, G. H. (2004) 'Intermediaries in Entrepôt Trade: Hong Kong Re-Exports of Chinese Goods', *Journal of Economics & Management Strategy*, 13(1): 3–35.

Freeman, G. P. (1994) 'Can Liberal States Control Unwanted Migration?', *The ANNALS of the American Academy of Political and Social Science*, 534(1): 17–30.

Gerard, A. (2014) *The Securitization of Migration and Refugee Women*, Abingdon: Routledge.

Gibney, M. J. (2004) *The Ethics and Politics of Asylum: Liberal Democracy and the Response to Refugees*, Cambridge: Cambridge University Press.

Gibney, M. J. and Hansen, R. (2005) 'Asylum Policy in the West: Past Trends, Future Possibilities', in G. J. Borjas and J. Crisp (Eds.) *Poverty, International Migration and Asylum*, Houndmills: Palgrave Macmillan: 70–96.

220 *(Un)wanted people in the global city*

Graham, S. and Marvin, S. (2001), *Splintering Urbanism: Networked Infrastructures, Technological Mobilities and the Urban Condition*, Abingdon: Routledge.

Grossman, E. (2006) *High Tech Trash: Digital Devices, Hidden Toxics, and Human Health*, Washington, DC: Island Press.

Grzymala-Kazlowska, A. (2005) 'From Ethnic Cooperation to In-Group Competition: Undocumented Polish Workers in Brussels', *Journal of Ethnic and Migration Studies*, 31(4): 675–697.

Haddad, E. (2008) *The Refugee in International Society: Between Sovereigns*, Cambridge: Cambridge University Press.

Hamnett, C. (1994) 'Social Polarization in Global Cities: Theory and Evidence', *Urban Studies*, 31(3): 401–425.

Hamnett, C. (1996) 'Social Polarization, Economic Restructuring and Welfare State Regimes', *Urban Studies*, 33(8): 1407–1430.

Hathaway, J. (2008–09) 'The Human Rights Quagmire of Human Trafficking', *Virginia Journal of International Law*, 49(1): 1–59.

Haugen, H. Ø. (2012) 'Nigerians in China: A Second State of Immobility', *International Migration*, 50(2): 65–80.

Hill, R. C. and Kim, J. W. (2000) 'Global Cities and Developmental States: New York, Tokyo and Seoul', *Urban Studies*, 37(12): 2167–2195.

Hugo, G. (1981) 'Village-Community Ties, Village Norms, and Ethnic and Social Networks: A Review of Evidence from the Third World', in G. F. De Jong and R. W. Gardner (Eds.) *Migration Decision Making: Multidisciplinary Approaches to Microlevel Studies in Developed and Developing Countries*, New York: Pergamon Press: 186–224.

Hutchins, D. (1999) *Just in Time*, Aldershot: Glower.

Hyndman, J. and Mountz, A. (2008) 'Another Brick in the Wall? Neo-Refoulment and the Externalization of Asylum in Australia and Europe', *Government and Opposition*, 43(2): 249–269.

Içduygu, A. and Toktas, S. (2002) 'How Do Smuggling and Trafficking Operate via Irregular Border Crossing in the Middle East?', *International Migration*, 40(6): 25–52.

Ip, C. (2010) 'Twin Track on Refugees Leads Many into Limbo', *South China Morning Post*, 20 June. Viewed 20 June 2010: www.scmp.com/article/717623/twin-track-refugees-leads-many-limbo

Joppke, C. (1998) 'Why Liberal States Accept Unwanted Immigration', *World Politics*, 50(2): 266–293.

Kaizen, J. and Nonneman, W. (2007) 'Irregular Migration in Belgium and Organized Crime: An Overview', *International Migration*, 45(2): 121–146.

Kane, H. (1995) *The Hour of Departure: Forces that Create Refugees and Migrants*, Worldwatch Paper 125, Washington, DC: The Worldwatch Institute.

Khosravi, S. (2010) *'Illegal Traveller': An Auto-Ethnography of Borders*, Houndmills: Palgrave Macmillan.

Kloosterman, R., van der Leun, J. and Rath, J. (1999) 'Mixed Embeddeness: (In)formal Economic Activities and Immigrant Businesses in the Netherlands', *International Journal of Urban and Regional Research*, 23(2): 252–266.

Koser, K. (1997) 'Social Networks and the Asylum Cycle: The Case of Iranians in the Netherlands', *International Migration Review*, 31(3): 591–611.

Koser, K. and Pinkerton, C. (2002) *The Social Networks of Asylum Seekers and the Dissemination of Information about Countries of Asylum*, London: Home Office. Viewed 1 June 2009: www.homeoffice.gov.uk/rds/pdfs2/socialnetwork.pdf

(Un)wanted people in the global city 221

Ku, A. S. (2001) 'Hegemonic Construction, Negotiation and Displacement: The Struggle over Right of Abode in Hong Kong', *International Journal of Cultural Studies*, 4(3): 259–278.

Landolt, P. and Goldring, L. (2010) *The Long Term Impacts of Non-Citizenship on Work: Precarious Legal Status and the Institutional Production of a Migrant Working Poor*. Viewed 15 August 2012: www.yorku.ca/raps1/events/pdf/Landolt_Goldring.pdf

Lee, K. M., Wong, H. and Law, K. Y. (2007) 'Social Polarisation and Poverty in the Global City: The Case of Hong Kong', *China Report*, 43(1): 1–30.

Light, I. (2004) 'Immigration and Ethnic Economies in Giant Cities', *International Social Science Journal*, 56(181): 385–398.

Lo, W. (2013) 'Government Sets Aside HK$450m to Sponsor Torture Claimants', *South China Morning Post*, 3 July. Viewed 3 July 2013: www.scmp.com/news/hong-kong/article/1274121/government-sets-aside-hk450m-sponsor-torture-claimants

Loper, K. (2010) 'Human Rights, Non-refoulement and the Protection of Refugees in Hong Kong', *International Journal of Refugee Law*, 22(3): 404–439.

Martin, D. A. (1989) 'Effects of International Law on Migration Policy and Practice: The Use of Hypocrisy', *International Migration Review*, 23(3): 547–578.

Massey, D., Alarcon, R., Durand, J. and Gonzalez, H. (1987) *Return to Aztlan: The Social Process of Transnational Migration from Western Mexico*, Berkeley: University of California Press.

Massey, D. S., Arango, J., Hugo, G., Kouaouci, A., Pellegrino, A. and Taylor, J. E. (1993) 'Theories of International Migration: A Review and Appraisal', *Population and Development Review*, 19(3): 431–466.

Mathews, G. (2011) *Ghetto at the Center of the World: Chungking Mansions, Hong Kong*, Chicago: The University of Chicago Press.

Mathews, G., Ma, E. K-w. and Lui, T-l. (2008) *Hong Kong, China: Learning to Belong to a Nation*, Abingdon: Routledge.

Meyer, D. R. (2000) *Hong Kong as a Global Metropolis*, Cambridge: Cambridge University Press.

Müller, M. M. (2013) 'Penal Statecraft in the Latin American City: Assessing Mexico City's Punitive Urban Democracy', *Social & Legal Studies*, 22(4):441–463.

Muus, P. (1997) 'Shifting Borders: The Inclusion and Exclusion of Refugees and Asylum Seekers in the Netherlands', in P. Muus (Ed.) *Exclusion and Inclusion of Refugees in Contemporary Europe*, Utrecht: ERCOMER: 78–95.

Newendorp, N. (2011) 'Contesting "Law and Order": Immigrants' Encounters with "Rule of Law" in Postcolonial Hong Kong', *Polar*, 34(1): 95–111.

Newendorp, N. D. (2008) *Uneasy Reunions: Immigration, Citizenship and Family Life in Post-1997 Hong Kong*, Stanford: Stanford University Press.

Panayiotopoulos, P. (2010) *Ethnicity, Migration and Enterprise*, Houndmills: Palgrave MacMillan.

Parnreiter, C. (2013) 'The Global City Tradition', in M. Acuto and W. Steele (Eds.) *Global City Challenges: Debating a Concept, Improving the Practice*, Houndmills: Palgrave Macmillan: 15–32.

Pickering, S. (2011), *Women, Borders and Violence: Current Issues in Asylum, Forced Migration, and Trafficking*, New York: Springer.

Portes, A. (1997) *Globalization from Below: The Rise of Transnational Communities*, Princeton University. Viewed 23 September 2009: www.transcomm.ox.ac.uk/working%20papers/portes.pdf

Portes, A. (2001) 'Introduction: The Debate and Significance of Immigrant Transnationalism', *Global Networks*, 1(3): 181–193.

222 (Un)wanted people in the global city

Portes, A., Guarnizo, L. E. and Haller, W. (2002) 'Transnational Entrepreneurs: An Alternative Form of Immigrant Economic Adaptation', *American Sociological Review*, 67(2): 278–298.

Price, M. E. (2009) *Rethinking Asylum: History, Purpose, and Limits*, Cambridge: Cambridge University Press.

Quassoli, F. (1999) 'Migrants in the Italian Underground Economy', *International Journal of Urban and Regional Research*, 23(2): 212–231.

Samers, M. (2002) 'Immigration and the Global City Hypothesis: Towards an Alternative Research Agenda', *International Journal of Urban and Regional Research*, 26(2): 389–402.

Samers, M. (2010) *Migration*, London: Routledge.

Sampson, R., Mitchell, G. and Bowring, L. (2011) *There Are Alternatives: A Handbook for Preventing Unnecessary Immigration Detention*, Melbourne: The International Detention Coalition.

Sassen, S. (1988) *The Mobility of Labor and Capital: A Study in International Investment and Labor Flow*, Cambridge: Cambridge University Press.

Sassen, S. (1996) *Losing Control? Sovereignty in an Age of Globalization*, New York: Columbia University Press.

Sassen, S. (1998) *Globalization and Its Discontents: Essays on the New Mobility of People and Money*, New York: New Press.

Sassen, S. (2001) *The Global City: New York, London, Tokyo*, second edition, Princeton: Princeton University Press.

Saunders, D. (2010) *Arrival City: How the Largest Migration in History Is Reshaping Our World*, London: William Heinemann.

Schmeidl, S. (1997) 'Exploring the Causes of Forced Migration: A Pooled Time-Series Analysis, 1971–1990', *Social Science Quarterly*, 78(2): 284–308.

Schmeidl, S. (2001) 'Conflict and Forced Migration: A Quantitative Review, 1964–1995', in A. R. Zolberg and P. M. Benda (Eds.) *Global Migrants Global Refugees: Problems and Solutions*, New York: Berghahn Books: 62–94.

Schuster, L. (2011) 'Turning Refugees into "Illegal Migrants": Afghan Asylum Seekers in Europe', *Ethnic and Racial Studies*, 34(8): 1392–1407.

Short, J. R. and Kim, Y. H. (1999) *Globalization and the City*, Harlow: Longman.

Smart, A. (1989) 'Forgotten Obstacles, Neglected Forces: Explaining the Origin of Hong Kong Public Housing', *Environment and Planning D: Society and Space*, 7(2): 179–196.

Smart, A. (2001) 'Unruly Places: Urban Governance and the Persistence of Illegality in Hong Kong's Urban Squatter Areas', *American Anthropologist*, 103(1): 30–44.

Smith, M. P. and Guarnizo, L. E. (1998) (Eds.) *Transnationalism from Below*, New Brunswick: Transaction Publishers.

Squire, V. (2009) *The Exclusionary Politics of Asylum*, Houndmills: Palgrave Macmillan.

Tai, P. F. (2006) 'Social Polarisation: Comparing Singapore, Hong Kong and Taipei', *Urban Studies*, 43(10): 1737–1756.

Tai, P. F. (2010) 'Beyond "Social Polarization"? A Test for Asian World Cities in Developmental States', *International Journal of Urban and Regional Research*, 34(4): 743–761.

Tai, P. F. (2013) 'Gender Matters in Social Polarisation: Comparing Singapore, Hong Kong and Taipei', *Urban Studies*, 50(6):1148–1164.

Van Hear, N. (1998) *New Diasporas: The Mass Exodus, Dispersal and Regrouping of Migrant Communities*, London: UCL Press.

(Un)wanted people in the global city 223

Vision First (2013) Press release, 22 April. Viewed 23 April 2013: http://visionfirstnow.org/uploads/March-for-Protection-Press-Release-English.pdf

Wacquant, L. (2009) *Punishing the Poor: The Neoliberal Government of Social Insecurity*, Durham: Duke University Press.

Wallerstein, I. (1979) *The Capitalist World-Economy*, Cambridge: Cambridge University Press.

Weber, L. (2006) 'The Shifting Frontiers of Migration Control', in S. Pickering and L. Weber (Eds.) *Borders, Mobility and Technologies of Control*, Dordrecht: Springer: 21–44.

Weber, L. and Pickering, S. (2011) *Globalization and Borders: Death and the Global Frontier*, Houndmills: Palgrave Macmillan.

Wessel, T. (2000) 'Social Polarisation and Socioeconomic Segregation in a Welfare State: The Case of Oslo', *Urban Studies*, 37(11): 1947–1967.

Wills, J., Datta, K., Evans, Y., Herbert, J., May, J. and McIlwaine, C. (2009) *Global Cities at Work: New Migrant Divisions of Labour*, London: Pluto Press.

Yamamoto, R. (2007) 'Crossing Boundaries: Legality and the Power of the State in Unauthorized Migration', *Sociology Compass*, 1(1): 95–110.

Zetter, R. (1991) 'Labelling Refugees: Forming and Transforming a Bureaucratic Identity', *Journal of Refugee Studies*, 4(1): 39–62.

Zetter, R. (2007) 'More Labels, Fewer Refugees: Remaking the Refugee Label in an Era of Globalization', *Journal of Refugee Studies*: 20(2): 172–192.

Zhao, X., Zhang, L. and Sit, T. O. K. (2004) 'Income Inequalities under Economic Restructuring in Hong Kong', *Asian Survey*, 44(3): 442–473.

Zimmermann, S. (2009a) 'Irregular Secondary Movements to Europe: Seeking Asylum Beyond Refuge', *Journal of Refugee Studies*, 22(1): 74–96.

Zimmermann, S. (2009b) 'Why Seek Asylum? The Role of Integration and Financial Support', *International Migration*, 48(1): 199–231.

Index

Afghanistan refugees 121
Africa: economic link with China 124;
    former refugee interview 169; increase
    in refugees from 74–54; refugee
    interviews 66–7, 68, 70, 79, 80, 81, 85,
    86, 88, 89, 90, 91, 94, 96, 107, 108–9,
    113, 123, 127, 130, 146, 155, 158,
    159, 167, 168, 183, 216; refugees from
    105, 111, 112, 118, 119–20, 123, 127,
    129, 130, 131, 150, 152, 167; refugees
    in the labour force 178; refugees'
    view of women 147; traders living in
    Guangzhou 124; visa requirements in
    134n1; wives and girlfriends of refugees
    145–7; *see also* East Africa; North
    African refugee interviews; West Africa
agency 2; of asylum seekers, 4, 9–10, 12,
    38, 69, 78, 87, 148, 194
agents: deception by 115–18, 134; reliance
    on 114–18, 201; travel to Hong Kong
    suggested or arranged by 115–18
airport, as entry point 106–10
Asian financial crisis 41, 52, 186
asylum: politics, policies, and future of 7,
    197, 212–17; screening mechanisms for
    79–87; *see also* asylum abuse; asylum
    claims; immigration
asylum abuse 3, 81, 86, 133, 151–2;
    alleged by media and officials 75–7,
    84–5
asylum claims: length of time to process
    80–1; low approval rate for 79, 81,
    97n18
asylum-migration nexus 71–4
asylum seeker interviews 132; Africa
    66–7, 68, 70, 79, 80, 81, 85, 86, 88, 89,
    90, 91, 94, 96, 107, 108–9, 113, 123,
    127, 130, 146, 155, 158, 159, 167, 168,
    183, 216; Bangladesh 68, 83, 85, 86,
    89–90, 114–16, 126, 143, 145, 156, 159,

169, 170, 179, 180, 182, 186, 187; East
    Africa 67; North Africa 109; Pakistan
    78, 82, 93, 128–9, 166, 174, 179, 182;
    Somalia 12; Sri Lanka 68–9, 78, 81, 82,
    92, 93–4, 186, 187; South Asia 67, 78,
    82, 93, 147, 158, 166, 175; West Africa
    66–7, 69, 70, 77, 124, 149, 156, 182
asylum seeker origins: Afghanistan 121;
    Africa 105, 111, 112, 118, 119–20,
    123, 127, 129, 130, 131, 150, 152, 167;
    Bangladesh 1, 105, 106–7, 110–11, 112,
    115, 121, 126–7, 129, 130, 131, 153;
    China 2, 43, 44, 46, 48–50, 52–3, 65,
    75; Democratic Republic of the Congo
    105; East Africa 108; Eastern Europe
    119; Ethiopia 119–20, 121; Ghana 105;
    Guinea 105; India 120; Malaysia 120;
    Nigeria 121; Pakistan 75, 120, 129, 167,
    205; Sri Lanka 15, 111, 112, 114, 117,
    118, 123, 129, 130, 172, 178; Somalia
    10, 67, 105, 109, 118, 121, 129, 130,
    151, 153; South Asia 43, 44, 50–1, 112,
    127, 129, 130, 131, 151, 153, 155, 173,
    175; Sub-Saharan Africa 15; Togo 104;
    Uganda 105; Vietnam 53, 65, 71
asylum seekers: adaptive capacity of 10;
    agency of 4, 9–12, 38, 69, 78, 87, 148,
    160, 194; assistance for 42, 57, 59,
    83, 85, 87, 88–92; balancing between
    agency and dependency 148–54;
    communities of 15, 185; companionship
    as long-term survival strategy 144–8;
    confusion on meaning of asylum
    and content of conventions 84–6;
    counseling for 153; dealing with people
    and survival 140–8; decision to return
    home 118, 187; defined 12; depicted as
    bogus claimants 74–9; deportation of
    65–70, 187; depression among 118, 153;
    desire to escape from violence 12, 115,

129–30, 133; detention of 81–2, 85–6, 97n20, 109; difficulty caused by long wait for decision 80–1; discrimination against 50, 79, 196, 207, 210; as distinguished from irregular migrants 55; economic contributions of 4–5, 158–60, 164–5; education opportunities for 97n21; effect on labour market 211; employment opportunities for 143, 144; entry points of 104–5; expectations for 127–32, 141, 144, 216; family ties of 201–2; food issues of 91–3; as foreign 'other' 2, 64, 65, 208; genuine vs. non-genuine 151–4; girlfriends and wives of 145, 146; and the Hong Kong economy 196; housing issues of 17, 88–91, 97n22, 98n23; identities of 140; illegalization of 139; income-generating activities of 154–8; influenced by acquaintance with business travelers 125–6; influenced by economic link between China and Africa 124–5; influenced by Hong Kong asylum policies 126–7; involved in drug dealing 76; lack of information about refugee issues 150; language issues of 88; as liaisons 10; lifestyle changes of 92, 96; liminal existence of 10, 94–5; limited legal rights of 87; linked to illegal immigrants 53–4, 65, 70–71, 74, 87, 103, 160; low rate of successful claims by 79, 81, 97n18; making connections upon arrival 141–4; marginalization of 2, 50, 51, 66, 69, 70, 79, 81, 87, 91, 94, 95, 141, 160, 164, 180, 202, 204, 205, 211; means of financing migration 130; mental stress of 214–15; money issues of 93–4; network connections of 113–14, 139, 165, 198–203; objectification of 7; obstacles faced by 139–40; policing of 203–8; protection for 13; psychosocial exclusion of 140; questioning of other asylum seekers' claims by 77–9; reasons for leaving home 131–2; reasons for rejection of claims 82; refugee life and community profit 154–8; reluctance of to trust authorities 81–2; self-employed 41, 45, 55, 148, 168, 174, 181, 182, 189 (*see also* entrepreneurs); socioeconomic context of 4–5, 6–7, 27; stigmatization of 49–50; survival skills of 154–60; as underclass 206, 213–14; vulnerability of 5–9, 12, 14, 19, 27, 33, 37, 40, 47, 48, 51, 55, 64–5, 68–9, 71, 81, 90,

94–5, 103, 104, 112, 117, 132, 139, 142, 148–9, 151–2, 181, 184, 188, 194, 198, 204; *see also* immigration; immigration arrivals; migrants; refugees

Bangladesh: refugee interviews 68, 83, 85, 86, 89–90, 114–16, 126, 143, 145, 156, 159, 169, 170, 179, 180, 182, 186, 187; refugees from 105, 106–7, 110–11, 112, 115, 121, 126–7, 129, 130, 131, 153; repatriation of refugees from 135n3; visa requirements in 134n1
boat people (Vietnamese) 2, 65
border crossing: irregular 11; refugee routes and strategies 104–13; unauthorized 103; *see also* borders
borders: politics and policies of 6–7, 49, 118, 140, 164, 212; porous 6; as tools of exclusion 65–6; in Western countries 106; *see also* border crossing
bribes 173–4

C v Director of Immigration 71, 96n4, 96n6, 206
capital mobility 29, 38
capitalism 6, 28, 32, 33, 38, 139, 194
CH v Director of Immigration 96n3
charity groups 86, 153; target populations of 151–2
China: asylum seekers entering Hong Kong through 104; economic link with Africa 124–5; manufacturing in 46–7; non-ethnic illegal immigrants from 75; refugees/immigrants from 43, 44, 46, 48–50, 52–3, 65; as stopover for asylum seekers 110–11; trading in 183–4
Christians, receiving more support than Muslims 153
Chungking Mansions 141–2, 143
churches, as source of support 153
commercial and consumer trade 180–8; commercial market 158; consumer market 158; with country of origin 183; illegal 172–5; impact of asylum seekers on 158; niche markets 181–2; rental market 155–7; transnational 10, 174
Convention against Torture and other Cruel, Inhuman or Degrading Treatment or Punishment (CAT) 13
Convention Against Torture (CAT) applications 13, 14, 71, 83, 84–6, 132, 186; decrease in 75, 187; increase in 75
Convention Relating to the Status of Refugees 13, 53, 55, 74, 82–3, 216

Index 227

copyright laws 172–3
court cases: *C v Director of Immigration* 71, 96n4, 96n6, 206; *CH v Director of Immigration* 96n3; *D v Director of Social Welfare* 97n11; *FB v Director of Immigration* 96n1; *MA v Director of Immigration* 71, 96n5, 205; *Secretary for Security v SakthevelPrabakar* 96n1; *Ubamaka v. Secretary for Security* 206
customary immigration law (CIL) 71–2

D v Director of Social Welfare 97n11
Daly, Mark 71
deindustrialization 39, 49, 51
Democratic Republic of the Congo, refugees from 105; *see also* Africa
differential inclusion 4–5
discrimination 50, 79, 196, 207, 210
documentation *see* passports; travel documents; visas
domestic work 47, 145, 177–8

East Africa: refugee interviews 67; refugees from 108; *see also* Africa
Eastern European refugees 119
economic informalization 39, 44, 210
economic migrants 153
economic restructuring 4, 28, 33, 36–7, 48–49, 52, 54, 65, 139, 195, 208, 211, 212; governance in 38–47
economic rights 217
economy: formal vs. informal 43–7, 95; global 6, 20, 28–9, 31–32, 39, 195–7; informal 6, 8–9, 18, 20, 33–5, 39, 40, 55, 64, 94, 154–5, 159, 164–5, 172, 177, 179, 187, 188, 195, 202–3, 206, 208, 210; just-in-time 176–7, 208–9; urban 197; *see also* economic informalization; economic restructuring
education system 51
employment *see* labour market
entrepreneurs 43–6, 54, 55, 111, 141, 164, 167–9, 173–4, 181–2, 189, 196, 197, 202
entry points: by air 106–10; by land 110–11; by sea 111–13
Ethiopian refugees 119–20, 121; *see also* Africa
ethnic groups, distrust among 15–16
ethnography 14, 15, 79, 195
e-waste 165
exclusion: daily experience of 87–94; in food 91–3; in housing 88–91; in money 93–44; screening mechanisms of 79–87

exploitation 10–12, 18, 33, 35, 37, 43, 48, 76, 78, 95, 145, 155, 164, 167–8, 172–3, 176–8, 180–1, 184, 188–9, 204, 209, 212, 217; by co-nationals 202–3; by family 202; for labour 7–9, 27, 46

FB v Director of Immigration 96n1
ferry terminals 104
food issues 91–3
forced migration 9; *see also* migrants

Ghana: refugees from 105; visa requirements in 134–5n1; *see also* Africa; West Africa
global cities 5, 6, 28–32, 35, 37–40, 44, 46, 54, 108, 172, 195, 196–9, 203, 208, 210; asylum seekers in 194–8, 208; inequality in 196; as sites of exchange 44
global economy 6, 20, 28–9, 31–32, 39, 195–7
globalization 5, 10, 19, 28, 30, 34, 37, 38, 39, 42, 52, 54, 55, 165, 174, 188, 195–8, 211, 213, 217
global mobility 39, 195
Global North, social groupings in 8
Global South, business networks with Hong Kong 10
Guinea refugees 105; *see also* Africa; West Africa

HKSAR (Hong Kong Special Administrative Region) *see* Hong Kong
Hong Kong: cultural and geopolitical uniqueness of 47; as default destination 108, 113; as destination for asylum seekers 2, 115, 122–3, 133, 200; difficulty of obtaining asylum in 215; dual economy in 43–7, 64, 95; expat community in 30–1; expectations of asylum seekers 127–32; geographical location of 104; immigration and asylum 'problem' in 4, 47–54; as inhospitable toward asylum seekers 72–4; knowledge of by refugees 122–7; labour market in 32–6; legal environment in 70–74; opportunity structure in 28–38; perception of by asylum seekers 122–7; as post-industrial city 51; poverty in 36–8; service economy in 180–8, 200, 210; service sector in 31–3, 35, 36, 39–41, 52, 208; social transformation in 1, 28–30; as Special Administrative Region 9; as stopover for asylum

228 *Index*

seekers 109; transnational elites in 30; *see also* global cities
Hong Kong government: and income inequality 40–2, 49; policies favourable to business 40–1, 44, 49, 54; policies hostile to immigration 13, 50, 53, 55, 56n2, 74, 76, 94, 159, 196, 208; politics and policies of 203–8; and social polarization 39
Hong Kong Immigration Department *see* Immigration Department
Hong Kong International Airport 104–5; as entry point 106–10
Hong Kong police: asylum seekers wary of 85; perceived as less intrusive 123, 125, 126; policing of asylum seekers by 84, 170–1, 182–3, 186–8
housing issues 88–91, 97n22, 98n23
human resources 38
human rights 6, 71, 76, 123, 127, 129, 154, 205, 207, 213, 217
human smuggling 18, 112, 116, 135n3
humanitarian aid 148–50

identities: fabricated 118–22, 175; Hong Kong 50–1; national 9, 38, 69
illegal trade 172–5
immigrant communities 15, 185
immigration: control of 9, 104, 187; crime 6–7; detention facilities 141, 143; policies 7, 39, 52; *see also* asylum; immigration arrivals
immigration arrivals: by air 106–10; by land 110–11; means of transportation 104–5; per year 105; by sea 111–13; by swimming 115; entry points into Hong Kong 104–5
Immigration Department (ImmD) 30–1, 46, 72, 78, 82, 83, 93, 131, 178, 179, 187; unlawful detainment by 75
Immigration Ordinance 71, 77, 170
income inequality 35, 27, 40, 41, 50, 208
Indian refugees 120; *see also* South Asia
Indian Sikhs, in Hong Kong 51
International Covenant on Civil and Political Rights 13
International Social Services (ISS) 14, 67, 69; assistance as encouraging of marginalization 95; assistance provided by 83, 85, 87, 89; food provided by 91–2; housing assistance from 88–91; lack of financial assistance from 93; misconceptions about assistance 127

inward investment 38
irregular migrants 43, 55

labour: casualization of 39, 55, 170, 176, 208–12; policies regarding 39; *see also* labour market
labour market: function of asylum seekers in 204; government regulations related to 33; immigrant contributions to 195; informal 181, 210–11; professionalization of 34–6; shift in 32–3; and unregulated workers 35; women in 36; *see also* economic restructuring; labour; labour unions; unemployment; work
labour migration 215
labour unions 33, 40–1, 49, 52
language issues 88
The Late Mattia Pascal (Pirandello) 92
legal status 4, 7, 8, 10, 15, 19, 35, 53, 64, 66, 68, 70, 74, 79, 87, 88, 111, 125, 127, 144, 146–8, 155, 158, 159, 164, 167–9, 175, 179, 188–9, 202, 206, 211; as factor in state control 148; and labour opportunities 175–7
livelihood framework 12, 19, 27, 55, 194
Lo Wu entry point 104
Lok Ma Chau entry point 104

MA v Director of Immigration 71, 96n5, 205
Malaysia refugees 120; *see also* South Asia
marriage migration 146–8
micro-businesses 44
migrants: economic 153; irregular 43, 55; voluntary vs. involuntary 122; *see also* asylum seekers; immigrants; migration; refugees
migration: feminization of 179; forced 9; illegalization of 7, 10; labour 215; marriage 146–8
migration studies 9
money issues 93–4
Muslims, receiving less support than Christians 153

national security 6, 9
networks and networking 165; and asylum seeking 198–203; co-ethnic 181; co-national 202; social 86, 140–3, 188, 200–1; smuggling 18, 112–13, 116, 135n3; transnational 181, 199–200
New Territories 16, 67, 88, 92, 104, 116, 141–2, 149, 154, 157

Index   229

Nigerian refugees 121; *see also* Africa; West Africa
non-governmental organizations (NGOs) 1, 2; charitable 151–2
non-probability sampling technique 14
non-refoulement 13, 14, 71–2, 206
North African refugee interviews 109; *see also* Africa

opportunity structure 3, 4, 28, 45, 48, 168
overstayers 70; *see also* immigrants, illegal

Pakistan: refugee interviews 78, 82, 93, 128–9, 166, 174, 179, 182; refugees from 75, 120, 129, 167, 205; resident interview 184; *see also* South Asia
Pakistanis, in Hong Kong 51, 52, 184
Park, Robert E. 1
passports 107, 119–20, 121
phone charges 93
Pirandello, Luigi 92
polarization, social 6, 19, 28, 30, 32–5, 37–40, 44, 50, 56, 157, 160, 171, 195–7, 208, 212
populations, hidden 14
post-colonialism 38
poverty 51, 148; in Hong Kong 36–8, 43; in the US 42
privatization 39, 40, 41, 43

racial profiling, at immigration entry points 106, 107, 120; *see also* racism
racism, in treatment of asylum seekers 94–5; *see also* racial profiling
Refugee Convention 13, 53, 55, 74, 82–3, 216
refugees: access to resources by 11; attitudes toward 3; defined 12; engaging in business negotiations 154; ethical considerations relevant to 12–19; humanitarian aid for 148–50; 'illegal' 51–4; interpersonal connections of 11; legal status of 53; negative attitude toward 53–4; non-genuine 151, 152; protection of 3; psycho-social well-being of 68–9; rights of 213; screening procedures for 79–87; survival tactics of 143
religion, as source of support 153; *see also* asylum seekers; migrants
rental market, impact of asylum seekers on 155–7
research: ethical considerations 17–19; methodology 14–19

rights: of citizens 8; citizenship 215; economic 3, 67, 68, 87, 160, 208, 217; human 6, 71, 76, 123, 127, 129, 154, 205, 207, 213, 217; legal 71, 87, 160; of refugees 3, 4, 18, 52, 71, 84, 87, 90, 118, 134, 140, 149, 196, 205, 207, 213; social 3; work 4

Secretary for Security v Sakthevel Prabakar 96n1
self-employment 41, 45, 55, 148, 168, 174, 181, 182, 189
service economy 180–8, 200, 210
small businesses 5, 33, 39, 44, 45
smuggling networks 18, 112–13, 116, 135n3
social capital 9–12, 45, 113, 140–1, 149, 164, 174, 181, 188, 202, 217
social inequalities 6, 28, 32, 36, 37, 54, 139, 160, 195, 197, 212
social justice 40
social policies 39
Somalia: refugee interviews 124; refugees from 10, 67, 105, 109, 118, 121, 129, 130, 151, 153; repatriation of refugees from 135n3; visa requirements in 134–5n1; *see also* Africa; East Africa
South Asia: immigrants/refugees from 43, 44, 50–1, 112, 127, 129, 130, 131, 151, 153, 155, 173, 175; increase in refugees from 74–5; refugee interviews 67, 78, 82, 93, 147, 158, 166, 175; refugees in the labour force 178; refugees living in shared housing 143; refugees' view of women 147; wives girlfriends of refugees 145–7; *see also* Bangladesh; Pakistan; Sri Lanka
speed boats, as means of entry 104
Sri Lanka: refugee interviews 68–9, 78, 81, 82, 92, 93–4, 186, 187; refugees from 111, 112, 114, 117, 118, 123, 129, 130, 172, 178; visa requirements in 134-5n1; *see also* South Asia
subcontracting 33, 41, 43, 54, 175–6, 196
Supplementary Labour Scheme 47

Tamil people *see* Sri Lanka
terrorism and terrorists 3, 9, 134, 206
Thailand, as stopover for asylum seekers 109
Togo, refugees from 105; *see also* Africa; West Africa
torture claims *see* Convention against Torture and other Cruel, Inhuman or Degrading Treatment or Punishment (CAT)

230 *Index*

tourism industry 31, 38, 175
tourists, sale of copy goods to 175, 180
trade and trading *see* commercial and consumer trade
transportation allowance 87–8, 93
travel documents 118–22; forged or unlawfully obtained 104–5, 106, 120, 135n3, 171

Ubamaka v. Secretary for Security 206
Ugandan refugees 105; *see also* Africa
underground economy 171–7; *see also* economy, informal
unemployment 36, 37, 39, 43, 129, 130, 168
unified screening mechanism (USM) 13
United Nations High Commissioner for Refugees (UNHCR) 12, 13, 53, 56n8, 70–5, 78–86, 88, 93, 97n12, 110, 117–18, 123–4, 131, 148–50, 152–3, 206
University of Hong Kong 51
urban economy 197
urban transformation 185

Vietnam: boat people from 2, 65; refugees/immigrants from 53, 71
violence, desire to escape from 12, 115, 129–30, 133

visas 107, 111; employer-sponsored 178; requirements and policies 112, 134n1; visa regimes 114, 118–22
voluntary repatriation 118, 187

waste, micro-economy based on 47; *see also* waste collection; waste recycling
waste collection, as income generation 170–1
waste recycling 209; refugee participation in 165–70
West Africa, refugee interviews 66–7, 69, 70, 77, 124, 149, 156, 182; *see also* Africa
Western countries, border controls in 106
women: in the informal labour market 36, 177–80; as wives and girlfriends of refugees 145, 146
work: in illegal or underground activities 165, 171, 172–5, 182, 186; and the labour shortage 176–7; as professional queuers 176; performed using falsely obtained documents 171, 175, 178; as trade facilitators 183–6; women in the informal labour market 177–80; *see also* labour market; unemployment
workers: unregulated 35; *see also* labour market; work

PGMO 10/03/2018